Heaven and Hall: A Prodigal Life

STUART HALL

Heaven and Hall: A Prodigal Life

To Bob Paisley, the most successful manager in
football history. Avuncular, kind, down to earth;
a lover of the classic game, flair grafted onto pragmatism.
A man of simple taste, yet an epicure.

And to:
'Titters Tetters' Tetlow for transcribing
hieroglyphics into words.
Jean Tetlow, a very present help in trouble.
All the football clubs for their kindness,
and willingness to fill in gaps.
Ben Gunn of the BBC for his 'Black Spot'.
William Shakespeare for inspiration.
Percy Bysshe Shelley for iconoclasm.
King James I for wisdom.
Adam for the fig leaf!

Published by BBC Worldwide Limited,
Woodlands, 80 Wood Lane, London W12 0TT

First published 2000
© Stuart Hall 2000

The moral right of the author has been asserted.

ISBN 0 563 53811 2

Commissioning Editor: Ben Dunn
Project Editor: Charlotte Heathcote
Copy-editor: Hugh Morgan

Set in Utopia by BBC Worldwide
Printed and bound in Great Britain by Butler & Tanner Limited,
Frome, Somerset

STUART HALL

Stuart Hall was born on Christmas Day in Hyde, Cheshire: educated at Glossop Grammar School and U.M.I.S.T.

After National Service, Stuart joined the family business as Director of Catering. He was always keen on broadcasting, motor racing and sport. He played soccer with Crystal Palace, Derbyshire and Lancashire.

At school and college Stuart produced and directed many plays, he was chairman of the Debating Society, founder of the 'English Language Society' devoted to the preservation, through standard English, of the great British authors.

In 1959, Stuart joined the BBC as a general reporter on Radio Newsreel and as a sports journalist with *Sports Report*. Stuart is still broadcasting with *Sports Report*.

Between 1965 and 1990, Stuart presented the BBC's weeknight North West Tonight programme – with two million regular viewers. 'My fledglings included John Humphries, Nick Clarke and David Davies.'

From 1971–1982, he presented *It's a Knockout* and *Jeux Sans Frontieres* to a weekly audience of 15 million. The programme received an award for top rated show of 1977. In 1986, Stuart produced, with Prince Edward, and presented *The Royal Knockout*.

Stuart also presented many radio programmes including a two-hour entertainment and celebrity chat show on Fridays, and five hours of live music, guests, worldwide sport on Sunday afternoons. Both on Radio Two.

In the years 1990–1994, Stuart joined Granada Television and presented *Travellers Check,* a weekly half-hour travel programme that achieved a forty per cent share against *Eastenders*. 'This was the highest share in the ITV network.

He is married to Hazel. They have two children – Daniel and Francesca. He lives in penury in a shed in Wilmslow.

CONTENTS

PART ONE: HEAVEN AND HALL

89 Manchester City 2 – Queens Park Rangers 2
91 Blackburn Rovers 1 – Newcastle 0
92 A Man is Badly in Need of Advice When He Has Many Advisers
95 The Habit of Agreeing Seems Too Dangerous and Slippery
97 If Slighted, Slight the Slight, and Love the Slighter
SEASON 1996/97
99 Blackburn Rovers 0 – Tottenham Hotspur 2
100 Liverpool 0 – Sunderland 0
101 Bolton Wanderers 2 – Crystal Palace 2
102 Liverpool 4 – Nottingham Forest 2
103 Oldham Athletic 2 – Manchester City 1
104 Liverpool 1 – Burnley 0
105 Manchester City 1 – Crystal Palace 1
106 A Christmas Parable Set in Gaul (France), AD 42
SEASON 1995/96
108 Everton 2 – Southampton 0
109 Northwich Victoria 1 – Scunthorpe United 3
109 Manchester City 1 – Aston Villa 0
112 Manchester City 1 – Coventry City 1
113 Crewe Alexandra 2 – Peterborough United 1
114 Liverpool 2 – West Ham United 1
115 Strange Times at the Colosseum
116 Thirty-Nine Thousand at the Colosseum
SEASON 1994/95
117 Liverpool 3 – Aston Villa 1
118 Hyde United 1 – Darlington 3
119 Everton 0 – Tottenham Hotspur 0
120 Everton 4 – Ipswich Town 1
121 Tell it Not in Gath
121 Barnsley is Onomatopoeic
SEASON 1993/94
123 Leeds United 4 – Chelsea 1
124 Bolton Wanderers 3 – Gretna FC 2
125 Everton 0 – Queens Park Rangers 3
126 Manchester City 0 – Tottenham Hotspur 2
SEASON 1992/93
126 Everton 1 – Sheffield Wednesday 1
128 Oldham Athletic 5 – Nottingham Forest 3
129 Liverpool 2 – Wimbledon 3
131 Manchester City 2 – Nottingham Forest 2

131 Leeds United 3 – Sheffield United 1
132 Oldham Athletic 1 – Aston Villa 1
133 Manchester United 0 – Wimbledon 1
135 Liverpool 0 – Manchester City 1
SEASON 1991/92
135 Manchester United 2 – Sheffield United 0
136 Manchester United 1 – Sheffield Wednesday 1
137 Manchester City 1 – Tottenham Hotspur 0
138 Liverpool 1 – Coventry City 0
138 Oldham Athletic 1 – Arsenal 1
139 Oldham Athletic 2 – Nottingham Forest 1
SEASON 1990/91
140 Manchester United 2 – Coventry City 0
140 Everton 1 – Arsenal 1
141 Manchester United 2 – Sheffield United 0
142 Manchester City 2 – Tottenham Hotspur 1
143 Oldham Athletic 1 – Newcastle United 1
143 Manchester United 3 – Sunderland 0
144 Liverpool 1 – Wimbledon 1
144 Sheffield United 2 – Aston Villa 1
145 Leeds United 2 – Coventry City 0
146 Everton 0 – Nottingham Forest 0
147 Liverpool 2 – Tottenham Hotspur 0
148 Gods of the Shrine at Whose Sight All the Stars Hide Their Diminished Heads
SEASON 1989/90
150 Manchester City 1 – Queens Park Rangers 0
151 Manchester City 5 – Manchester United 1
153 Sheffield Wednesday 0 – Coventry City 1
153 Oldham Athletic 2 – Barnsley 0
154 Leeds United 1 – Wolverhampton Wanderers 0
155 Manchester United 2 – Southampton 1
156 Manchester City 3 – Crystal Palace 0
157 Everton 0 – Chelsea 1
157 Manchester City 0 – Nottingham Forest 3
158 Sheffield Wednesday 2 – Crystal Palace 2

PART TWO: A PRODIGAL LIFE

FOREWORD

Writers are categorised thus:
- If one can really write, one writes novels.
- If one can write a little, one writes biographies.
- If one aspires to writing, one writes a newspaper column.
- If one can't write at all, one becomes a television critic.
- If one should never, at any time, put pen to paper, one becomes a sports reporter.

Gentlemen, I am, come Saturdays, a football reporter. A somewhat different animal. The BBC permits flights of fancy, all colours of the rainbow in the prose and licence enough to hang *me* but keep *them* from the well of the courthouse.

I have been ostracised from Old Trafford. Cauterised by City. Lampooned by Liverpool. Bastinadoed at Blackpool. Spurned by Spurs. Shunned at Sheffield. Curmudgeoned at Carlisle. Bludgeoned at Burnley. Gurgitated at Goodison.

Bill Shankly was a great personal friend, and he told me once of his latest international signing. I awaited the usual jargon – he's got everything: catches pigeons, two great feet, the style of Matthews, speed of Seb Coe, the majesty of Dennis Law.

'He's got everything,' grunted Shanks. 'Bed bugs, lice, trench foot and clap.' Hooray for humour.

The reason is simple. I refuse to accept football as a matter of life and death. To me, most things in life have to be enjoyed. Latterly – and by that I mean in the decade that spans my 21st birthday and my 49th (well, what lady ever told the truth about her age anyway?) – latterly, there has been a decline in humour. But in that spread, legions of journalists spawning words like frogspawn, and to similar effect, have made our national game, the finest entertainment in the world, into intergalactic warfare. They, football management, and the poor deluded players, have driven laughter from their stage and replaced it with robotic football which stupefies the mind, induces severe boredom and stimulates the moronic, baying loonies into kicking hell out of anyone for any excuse. Oh, for the huge grin of Joe Mercer and the rough-hewn humour of Bill Shankly.

Tell me, dear reader, that you, too, miss the jokes. When footers used to be *fun*. That is why I shall always look for what is lost. Cherish Frank Worthington for ever. A Don Quixote, black-maned, romantic Romany who tilted his boots for loot and laughs.

Mind you, I have had my comeuppance often times. I remember describing Michael Robinson, the erstwhile Liverpool number nine, as a 'dyspeptic water buffalo grazing with a herd of gazelle'. Clumsy, awkward, a yard behind the play and a thousand yards from Dalglish's analytical, surgical football, he just did not fit. The following week he smote a hat trick at West Ham. My next Liverpool visit was awaited by all, if not by Hall.

Recently, at a Huddersfield Town soiree, a voice enquired, 'Do you remember describing a certain Steve Kindon as a "lumbering runaway wardrobe"?'

'Yes,' I perked.

'Well, he's 'ere and looking for yer.'

Many years ago, Don Revie, possibly the prickliest, most over-sensitive manager ever, rang the BBC – discreetly, mind you.

'About last Saturday. We listened to your broadcast and the lads didn't like it. Mick Jones isn't a heaving sweating Lincolnshire dray horse. Billy Bremner isn't fed on raw meat and iron filings, the Mafiosi Capo with a contract on his opposite number. Jack Charlton a giraffe on heat. And Jonnie Giles, the arch assassin with the Mona Lisa smile.'

'But my dear Don Corleone,' I said. 'When you've picked up the severed limbs of the opposition hacked off by Norman's left boot, isn't Giles the most feared in football, Jones the honest artisan, Bremner, though vastly talented, the ace hit man?'

'Pah', said Don Corleone, 'Elsie didn't like it either!'

Elsie is the wife. Elsie, the Queen Victoria of football. Her stentorian tones shrilled above the rest. Once at Wembley she stood up and bellowed, 'Show yourself, Hunter! Show yourself!' Norman was suitably taken aback, if not affronted, adjusted his codpiece, and played on.

What has all this football to do with industry, you entrepreneurs are demanding? Well, buried deep in us all is pride; it manifests in diverse ways. My wife is always 'doing' her face. I am for ever cleaning my motor cars. My son Danny is for ever at Lord Jim, an advanced boys' boutique flogging clothes that Grandad wore. My daughter Francesca, an actress, is constantly polishing her vowels – yes, vowels. But, we all support the local footie team.

When it wins, we rejoice – lose, and a globus descends with a micro disaster. A football team is, or should be, a barometer of goodwill within the community. From factory floor to office boardroom runs the *fils rouge* of pride. Take time out to study not the Stretford End at Old Trafford but the stands. A typical animal was an old pal, Frank. A staid company accountant, intractable, insular, introvert. Yet on Saturdays he would be on his feet, arms akimbo in rage, disgust, triumph – you name it, every emotion was manifest. Referees were the butt especially. None of them had parents. All should have a white stick, not a whistle. Bent as nine-bob notes, mentally deficient geriatrics. For 90 minutes, Frank vented his spleen, then retired into a nice, peaceful, law-abiding member of society. For Frank, that 90 minutes was the umbilical cord that united him with the lad on the shop floor. I am positive that United's European victory in 1968 boosted ego and profits. That City's distinct championship win of 1969 lifted the workforce morale. And where would the city of Liverpool be without the teams of Bill Shankly and Bob Paisley? That media vision of Merseyside is dereliction, vandalism, workshy, ale-swilling workers controlled by Marxists hellbent on self-destruction and total anarchy.

For nearly 20 years I have travelled Europe denying what Eurovision cameras have propagandised. Film crews from France and Germany have focused on the dreadful and ignored the good.

I have tried to explain that when hordes of drunken fans invade the pitch waving broken bottles, railway carriage doors, half-bricks, flick knives and flails, they are really only seeking to exchange gifts. And when they engage the foreign police in running warfare, they are simply testing EUC defence plans for the government.

But seriously, gentlemen, away from the headlines, can we win back the whimsy; let the old visage crease into a smile. Hand me mi bovver boots, cosh and Mohican wig. I have some friends to win over!

Liverpool football club has played a well-defined formative role through the years.

Shanks once allowed me to record the Kop in full voice. The *Real Kop* of the 1960s. When 'You'll Never Walk Alone' was the inspiration. Scarves akimbo, tonsils quivering, a united hymn from genuine fans determined that, despite Merseyside's slow descent into industrial decline and decay, aspiration still flowed with each tide. Armed with tape recorders and sweating technicians, I posted my team at the back of the Kop goal. I conducted the 'Kop choir' through a succession of chants and anthems. The hype was fever pitch. Steam rose from bodies packed tight. Furled up copies of the *Echo* doubling as urinals. How do 24,000 folk obey calls of nature trapped on the terraces?

The final anthem, 'You'll Never Walk Alone', sung as never before. The nape hairs bristle. Emotion overflows. Tears course down my cheeks. Through the public address, I thank the fans. The cheers resound, all bar one urchin perched on the retaining wall.

'Hey, mister,' he calls urgently. I hurry to him, thinking him overcome by this incredible occasion. I looked into his narrowing eyes and found truculence. 'Sod off, you short-arsed git,' he said, and shot off into the maelstrom.

Iconoclastic, divine, and so Liverpool. Collapse of short-arsed git.

When Shanks quit the club, he did so because he lost faith in Britain. He believed that our country was on the verge of bankruptcy. That the currency would, overnight, become worthless and devalued. He visualised mounds of notes being carted in wheelbarrows to buy a bunch of bananas. He even lost faith in pension funds, and promptly withdrew his. He was a huge man in every way. A sage in many ways, but, like all great men, he was flawed. Bob Paisley, his successor, quietly assumed greatness. The build of a farm labourer in Grey's 'Elegy'. Visage like a pickled walnut. The gait of a broken-kneed cab-horse. Kind, witty, avuncular, lover of the simple and honest, hater of pretension and pseud.

Who can forget the boardroom at Blackburn Rovers? A cavernous mahogany palace of Waterford glass and rounded, friendly, warm vowels. Hot real meat pies, apple crumble and cheesecake made by the plump, twinkling-eyed gals who serve it. And the boardroom at Burnden Park. I always put on my best suit to visit Bolton. Matching tie and pocket handkerchief. My routine is set. Arrive at 2 p.m. precisely. Meander to the room. Knock on the door of the tearoom. The door is opened by a slim lady of mature years. Hair permed in grand manner. Her chum is of more robust build – imagine the great Norman Evans and his hilarious 'Over the Garden Wall' sketch, and you will visualise the scene.

'Oh! Alice, look who it is.' I kiss both ladies on the cheek and stand back to be admired.

'Oh! Isn't he luvly?'

'Who got yer ready?'

I smile whimsically and reply, 'Me Mam.' The screenplay never varies; long may it, and the spirit that it moves it, live.

I revere nostalgia. The days of Joe Mercer and Big Mal at City. Matt Busby and United. Leeds United with the fabulous Bob Roberts, and Don Revie. When the Don gave the team its head, the play was inspiring. They won the championship with a nil–nil draw at Anfield. The reception from the Kop was so emotional that most of the players were reduced to tears. I remember, with joy, Eric Taylor of Sheffield Wednesday. Pert as a sparrow, deadly in administration. John Harris's Sheffield United with Joe Shaw the immaculate. So polished and suave he should have played in white tie and tails. Down the years, it has been my pleasure to bring you the delights of this wonderful football game. That polished writer Hunter Davies described my efforts as compositions.

I retained a few of those reports and essays with the intention of compiling a little tome for the future. I submit these to you, dear reader.

PART ONE: HEAVEN AND HALL

INTRODUCTION

I invented the phrase 'beautiful game'. I have been derided by many luminaries, or luminaries by assumption, as a romantic bumpkin. That I am somewhat overwhelmed by the exuberance of my own verbosity I admit. Lies, damned lies and statistics chill me to the marrow. I relish the eccentric, slavishly adore style, love the maverick. Littered under Mercury, aspected by Saturn, I was born bizarre.

To my invention, 'the beautiful game'. In a previous life I was Sir Edmund de Scrape, knight rampant in the service of Edward II. They were rumbustious times, knocking the Welsh and Scots about a bit, roistering in hostelries, toying with tartlets, quaffing malmsey by the flagon, and flaying the hide off dissenting peasantry.

Occasionally I slew the bad dragon mainly to impress the Denise van Outens of the day. The dragons were frightful beasts: green and yellow horny hide, huge yellow teeth, claws 12 inches long, sharp as butchers' knives, baleful bloody eyes, huge gaping mouth which issued fire and brimstone, inflicting pestilence and pain. Bit like Alex Ferguson – on a good day.

Summers then were hot. We had a climate in Cheshire then. Nowadays we have weather. To avoid listlessness we had tournaments. The knights fought with broadsword. Jousted on horseback on the palisades. Practised longbow to give the French as Harry subsequently said, 'A little touch of Harry in the night'. La nuit – not knight. We were not knights errant!

The peasants were spectators and bored with blood-letting. I asked them on 1 April 1315 to slay me a wild boar. It was slain on the estate of Sir Kenneth Baetes, the wild bore of Beswick. He was miffed and composed a diatribe. I invited him to my castle. We feasted well. I am renowned as a roaster of old bores. The boar's entrails were rotting in the sun. I espied the bladder. On impulse I seized it and, inspired by the peasants' ennui, blew it up using every ounce of my huge energy. I created the inflatable ball. I kicked it – Sir Ronald Atkinson caught it.

'Out, damned spot,' I cried, ''tis for kicking.' I disembowelled the fellow. 'Away, you scullion! You rampallion, you fustilarian – I'll tickle your catastrophe.' Thus I, Sir Edmund de Scrape, invented the 'beautiful game'.

It has here before been ascribed. Thus now in a later life can I help you, dear reader, imbibe the philosophy that drives me into surreal realms and paroxysms of joy when I behold my creation. I thus present my reportage. Forty years of a love affair that knows no end.

BE NOT A LION IN THY HOUSE, NOR FRANTICK AMONG THY SERVANTS

What is humour? asked Ibsen, and promptly penned another play on fratricide, matricide, incest, revenge and blood. Whatever happened to humour in football? I ask, and promptly extract the urine from another football match.

The game is so bloody serious – it's devoid of laughs. So serious, quasi-serious, that I am now driven forever to forswear the furrowed brow, spurn the analytical, and be the very antithesis of Andy Gray and the fellow-travelling pundits.

My headmaster (Gauleiter Lord) informed me one day (I was head boy): 'Everything matters, but nothing matters terribly.' He was anguished at my dilettante way of life, my maverick tilting at windmills, my incessant roistering, wenching, tavern-dwelling and falling off motorbikes. One winter's morning on a snow-covered road, I parted company from my BSA Gold Star to avoid a dustcart. I landed under the dustcart, which ran over me and parked on my crown jewels. The driver, in dead faint, enquired: 'What shall I do?'

'Reverse off my bollocks,' I intoned calmly. Ten tons on your todger is a real weight on your mind, I assure you.

My headmaster, informed of this incident, dryly observed: 'At least the sixth-form girls are safe for another month!' How droll! *Fortes fortuna juvat.* For the record: nubile nurses restored me to health, and, on my return to school, I became *Victor Ludorum* of athletics. I'd learnt to run fast to escape irate fathers protecting innocent daughters.

My idiosyncrasies have multiplied since those fledgling days in Glossop, made manifest in my reportage. I am grateful to a tolerant public who listen to the exuberance of my own verbosity. For instance, I remember one time at the School of Science 'twas Everton versus Southampton. 'Remember last season you described Everton's football as smooth and creamy as Sharon Stone's thighs?' (They beat West Ham six–nil.) We dissolved in fits. Another fan proffered a stick of KitKat which I promptly smoked. On Merseyside, they know how to laugh. As they traipsed over the Emerald Isle yonks ago with the potato famine, they know life as it is.

Later, in the boardroom, quaffing a '95 Chablis, the atmosphere was more sombre. Peter Johnson, the erstwhile chairman, sat on his shares. Bill Kenwright & Co. wanted to buy them – for multimillions. This is serious. Why did they bother? Two years from now there will be a European League. Manchester United, Chelsea, Arsenal, Rangers, Celtic, Real Madrid, Barcelona, Juventus, AC Milan, Inter Milan, Paris SG, Auxerre, Ajax, Feyenoord, Dinamo Kiev, Monaco, Porto and one other will be members. European League rules. TV money will follow. Non-members will feed on the scraps from the rich man's table.

What price a football club, then? Will the bubble burst? Will the fans pay exorbitant prices for an overhyped, overmarketed product? Will television be interested in a product divorced from Europe? Will there be a European Second Division? Transcending all through will be our sense of humour.

When the foreign Johnnies have looted the coffers and zoomed off to lucrative pastures – what's left? There's always the Theatre of Base Comedy, Moss Side, Manchester 14. Pure dross losing to Wycombe Wanderers yet crooning 'Blue Moon', waving giant bananas, parting with loadsamoney, dreaming of yesteryear. I loved Maine Road. I used to train with Bell, Lee, Summerbee and the arch-reprobate Bestie. The crack was great. Sojourns at Slack Alice's, peripatetic at the Phonograph, concomitant at the cabaret. A head like a stunned ox, a mouth like a hammer-thrower's jockstrap. Outré, louche, dégoûtant, a million miles from nendrolone.

'A quart of Bolly and the keys to your chastity belt, madame!' But the footie flowed, the spirit charged them. All was well with the world. Character was alive. Character is a habit long continued. Francis Lee was one. I saw his first game for Bolton, on the right wing. He was 15 years old. Scored, had his name taken. Years later he was Derby County's centre forward.

Frannie was playing against QPR. Four–nil up. He received the ball deep in QPR's half. Waved to me in the press box. Trapped the ball with his arse. Beat two defenders waggling his bunions and walloped a blinding goal. Quelle finesse. When the seagull follows the trawler, he expects smoked salmon and plovers' eggs. Heady days of individual blithe spirits. So as I watch today's unleavened bread, I delve into my literature lexicon to titillate your tastebuds and pray for the beautiful game. Exit – pursued by a bear!

VOILÀ LE COMMENCEMENT DE LA FIN
[Talleyrand, on Napoleon]
>For Alex Ferguson:
>*Remember the marvellous works he hath done,*
>*His wonders, and the judgement of his mouth.*
>For Martin Edwards:
>*Speak of me as I am, nothing extenuate,*
>*Nor set down aught in malice.*

MANCHESTER UNITED 1 – MANCHESTER CITY 0
Barclays Football League, Division One, 4 May 1991

A sea change is sweeping over the shrine; football as we know it will never be the same again. Manchester United are floating shares on the Stock Exchange at 385 pence per share. The club is valued at £20 million. Not long ago Michael Knighton juggled a ball and said he had bought United for £6 million. I wonder how Mr Knighton feels right now, pursuing the rainbow only to find the crock of gold has been appropriated by the bankers. For Michael, 'It is a kind of happiness to know exactly how far one ought to be unhappy'. For Martin, 'We are such stuff as dreams are made of, and our little life is ended with a sleep'. Martin will be mega-rich overnight. United will set a train in motion that will career through the football world, derailing smaller clubs in its path, destroying old myths, devaluing ancient loyalties, until it hits the buffers well into the next century. Greed will enter the game. The share price will mean as much as the last result. A new breed of supporter will enter the portals. Exit the Ford Popular, enter Mercedes Benz. United will become European, even global. Their merchandise sold in every country where English football can be seen and heard. Other clubs will follow suit. Arsenal, Chelsea, Spurs, Leeds, Aston Villa, Newcastle. It is a flood tide that will engulf the game. In time, only the strong will flourish and survive. What of Bury, Rochdale, Oldham and Stockport? The best players will gravitate to the richest clubs. A European league of wealth looms. Who will watch Rochdale versus Darlington if he or she can see Manchester United versus Real Madrid?

Alex Ferguson must feel like the Ancient Mariner navigating his ship alone; Archie Knox, his right-hand man, has decamped to Glasgow Rangers. Legend, though, says that the Ancient Mariner's ship was guided by angels and steered by 'The Pilot of the World'. Tomorrow and for ever, Alex will be Hercules, cleansing the Augean stables, grabbing the golden apples of Hesperides, slaying the Nemean lion. Win me silver, Alex; the glory may tarnish, but look at the share price! This is the future. For the present United have done it again on the pitch. A poor season in Division One; Arsenal will be champions, or maybe Liverpool. United languish sixth, 21 points behind the Arsenal; but typical United, when one hand is doing moderately, the other clutches trophies. They contest the final of the European Cup Winners Trophy in Rotterdam on 15 May.

Manchester City are fourth in the league – Peter Reid is their manager – their highest placing since 1978. Reid inherited the job when Howard Kendall left for Everton last November. City need success, the heady days of the Mercer–Allison axis a distant memory. A League Championship in 1968, FA Cup in 1969, European Cup Winners Cup and League Cup in 1970. Tony Book was the last manger to handle silver – the League Cup in 1976. So with all these ramifications and obfuscations, and 45,286 not caring a fig, the match kicked off. A fierce north-west wind blew skill awry. The pitch resembled a bear pit; incessant rain, nil sun, huge stands covering the greensward in shadow make the groundsman's job a nightmare.

As Joe Mercer used to say: 'We started badly and fell away.' Relentless din from the stands raised commitment to ridiculous heights, adrenalin coursed like the Irwell in flood. City deployed Pointon as last man in a Hill, Hendry, Redmond offside trap, reduced the match to stop–start, then compounded their negativity with dubious strong-arm roughhouse.

Bryan Robson mixed it; he loves a fracas, so strong in the tackle, committed to powerful surging runs, his left leg like a scythe on a bountiful golden wheat field. He is Captain Marvel. Neil Webb instigated crucial moves – Mike Phelan his lieutenant. Marvel marshalled them both. The goal came after 23 minutes. McClair centred, Margetson misjudged it on the wind, Redmond the centre back jumped for the ball, missed it through sheer lack of inches, Redmond is tiny by centre back proportions, Ryan Giggs snapped up the chance in off Colin Hendry.

First match, first goal for 17-year-old Ryan Giggs. Giggs is the first off the production line, the youth team on which United's future depends. Giggs has tremendous pace, an élan startling in one so young. He has that close control, all left foot, which distinguishes the artist from the artisan. He feints inside, dips the shoulder and hares down the left pursued by the fullback Hill. Giggs is raw but, as he builds his strength, improves his right-foot skills, assumes tactical awareness, he will be world class. The evidence, only 23 minutes old, is incontrovertible. The natural successor to George Best. Slightly built like a whippet, his looks are that of a dark Gypsy – a Romany, black hair, dark eyes, unsmiling visage, a mark of concentration, a matinée idol in embryo.

The Giggs goal sealed the match. Quinn missed a dolly chance, Mark Hughes hit a post. Peter Reid, now with flyaway pepper-and-salt hair, came on to show his charges how midfield should be run. He brought composure and sanity. City struck a post last minute. A goal would have been a travesty. United held sway.

Today, and I am not a soothsayer, I have glimpsed the future of English football. I am not entranced by it; money will rule sometimes unwisely. As a country boy, the term 'market forces' strikes a chill. It means the rich get richer, the poor get poorer. As the wind whistles round the wooden stands at Spotland, Rochdale, a thin crowd munching Holland's pies and imbibing polystyrene cups of instant coffee, how they must envy the rich at the shrine, canapés, confit of Aylesbury duck, caviar, Krug champagne. George Bernard Shaw said: 'Money is indeed the most important thing in the world. Every teacher or twaddler who denies it or suppresses it is an enemy of life. Money controls morality.'

Mr Ferguson will become Sir Alex, then Lord Alex of Govan if he oils the production line. If it stops, he will buy foreign mercenaries. Should United falter, he will be plain Mr Ferguson, subject, as usual, to market forces and a P45.

Manchester United: Gary Walsh, Denis Irwin, Clayton Blackmore, Steve Bruce, Mike Phelan, Gary Pallister, Bryan Robson, Neil Webb, Brian McClair, Mark Hughes, Ryan Giggs. Substitutes: Mal Donaghy, Mark Robins.

Manchester City: Martyn Margetson, Andy Hill, Neil Pointon, Adrian Heath, Colin Hendry, Steve Redmond, David White, Mark Brennan, Niall Quinn, Alan Harper, Mark Ward. Substitutes: Peter Reid, Wayne Clarke.

I wrote that essay on 4 May 1991. This morning, Manchester United shares hit a new peak (10 March 2000) of 402 pence. A minimum purchase of 50 shares in June 1991 cost £192.50. That stake is now worth £4,126. United are the first football club in the world to be valued at more than one billion pounds. That is twice as much as Barretts, the house-builders, or equal to Blue Chip, Courtaulds, House of Fraser, Sears and Body Shop combined.

United's take from home games is £1.6 million, equal to the annual income of all the clubs in the Third Division.

The meek shall inherit the Earth.

Mr Ferguson won the treble in 1999: the Premiership, the FA Cup, the European Cup – the Holy Grail. He is now Sir Alex Ferguson, OBE. Martin Edwards is as rich as Croesus.

Peter Reid was sacked from City by Peter Swales for finishing only fifth in the First Division. A brilliant player, a charismatic manager, he resurrected his career and Sunderland's moribund future. He is a major shareholder in Sunderland plc.

Peter Swales died.

THE MILLENNIUM REPORT

ARSENAL

The Arsenal. Venger, *veni, vidi, vici* (I came, I saw, I conquered). Shall Arsene be conquered by Manchester United or Liverpool? Age shall not wither them, nor the years condemn. Will ageing limbs in the back four, backstairs, creak and curvate?

Resolution: For Arsene a magic elixir for eternal youth. *Maxim:* The true way to render old age vigorous is to prolong the youth of the mind.

NEWCASTLE UNITED

Sir John 'Golden Bollocks' Hall and Bobby Robson. From slough and trough to the near pinnacle. They have the knowledge, but most men want knowledge not for itself but for the superiority that knowledge confers.

Will it ever be the championship, caviar, Krug champagne or flat sarsaparilla?

Resolution: A big, thick, crunching centre half. *Maxim:* It is the province of knowledge to speak. It is the privilege of wisdom to listen.

MANCHESTER UNITED

For a sellout to Michael Knighton for £6 million to a capitalisation of £1 billion. The shrine holding 64,000 supplicants for regular worship.

Martin Edwards, who once as a butcher's apprentice wielded his chopper, now wields the magic wand, the golden key to Ali Baba's cave of treasures.

Roy, a son of Cork, whose Irish charm melts the hearts of sympathetic referees, has trousered £55,000 a week.

Will the cave of treasures be emptied as Becks, Dwight, Andy, Jaap, Paul demand gold?

Is the shrine a 'South Sea Bubble' or the City's golden goose?

Resolution: To become the world's greatest club. *Maxim: Malheur ne vient jamais seul* (misfortunes never come singly). Or, as Eric would interpret: 'Gonads to you.'

WIMBLEDON

The Crazy Gang. No longer Flanaghan and Allen. Nervo and Knox. Monsewer Eddie Gray. Not the Victoria Palace and trouser-dropping farce, but the Palace of Crystal.

Robbie Earle is a pearl, long my favourite footballer. And black pearls abound in this fascinating blend of sublime and simple; they could drown in a sea of Nationwide.

Resolution: Let Egil smile (occasionally). *Maxim: Exitus acta probat* (the result justifies the deed).

CHELSEA

Aspetto del denaro da Londra. È arrivato? (I'm expecting dosh from London. Has it arrived yet?)

Pensioners' caps and jackets for the foreign legion being tailored as I speak. Le Boeuf with a sprig of Minto. Zola with a Carafino of Vialli. The Bridge a rest-home for the semi-retired artist. The flair is there, but where is the zest of prodigal youth? *Ou sont les Anglais?*

To win the championship would be akin to Chuck Heston pulling the Spice Girls.

Resolution: To put the Spice Girls in midfield. *Maxim: Caveat emptor* (let the buyer beware).

LIVERPOOL

Intent on gifting the championship to Manchester United. Shamefaced after Blackburn. Red-faced after Sheffield Wednesday. The Colosseum now safe for Christians. The lions have lost their teeth.

But I have consulted the mighty Caesar's soothsayer. 'Beware the ides of March.' 'Tis for the challengers not bravehearts in red. The legion is on the march. Caesar Houllier with the orb. Senators at his side. Virgil Parry reading the runes.

Resolution: Faint heart ne'er won fat tart. *Maxim: Ex nihilo nihil fit* (out of nowt, nowt comes). Keep cocking the fowling piece, Robbie. Tug the heartstring, Michael – not the hamstrings.

TOTTENHAM HOTSPUR

The Spurs stock gets a kick up the arse. Mr Sweetener opened his wallet. A moth flew out, the cockerel crowed. The scales dropped his eyes and became John Scaleish.

Eric Hall manipulated the transferish. Leeds miffed. Spurs chuffed (ish). Mr Graham chanced a smile. 'Twas like glimpsing Cilla Black's cleavage. You know it exists, but you do not want to see it again. Keep it stern, George – you are gorgeous.

Resolution: Nothing spoils a romance more than a sense of humour in defence. *Maxim:* Keep Sugar sweet.

EVERTON

Please. Am I going Barmby? Can the School of Science pull out the big one (and I am not talking about Bill Kenwright)?

Walter talks such a good game but – young Jeffers, young Barmby. There is potential, aspiration, expectation. Peter and Cliff made millions in hampers. From hampers to pampers. Can Bill get it Kenright? 'Great gadflies' – these moguls are magnificent, multifarious, mythomaniacs in hampers. Ferguson hampered them out!

Resolution: To restore the School of Science by degrees. Get the Three Degrees on the coaching staff. That would produce the big one. *Maxim: Dum spiro, spero* (while I breathe, I hope).

MANCHESTER CITY

The Theatre of Base Comedy. Sense of humour now wearing thin. Even thinner when Steve Boler, who bought himself half of Botswana as a back garden, mopped up a very swift rights issue. Steve's punt yielded riches rarer than a white rhino. Black Rhino Royle is on the horns of a dilemma. Share price talked up. A lush new stand put up. A team put down by daft transfers and potty wages.

City fans, a loyal bunch, grasp their crucifixes and busts of Kinkladze praying for miracles.

The chairman, who resembles Neville Chamberlain after returning from Munich, cogitates his cornflakes. Devoured by Wolves. Bastinadoed by Leeds, whither the faithful?

Resolution: Or whither the faithful! Transfer four Rhinos from Steve's national park. *Maxim: Facilis descensus Averno* (the descent to Hell is easy).

NOTTINGHAM FOREST

Lost in the wild forest of the Nationwide League, the wind blows strong. With it Forest's aspirations and ethics too. Will Robin Hood or the naughty sheriff come Hurtling Through The Thickets To Rescue Maid Marion?

David Platt is no Maid Marion. Rather Buttons or an Ugly Sister.

Gloom always tainted on high days. Now the brow is furrowed. If the Good Fairy waved the wand and wandering Stanley could return – what then?

Meanwhile, Clough Esquire walks on the waters of the Trent nightly. Walks on it – does not consume it (unless mixed with hops, barley and malt).

Resolution: Monaco moneybags unleash thy flow. *Maxim:* 'Rough winds do shake the darling buds of May, and summer's lease has all too short a date.'

COVENTRY CITY

Peter Pan. Wee Gordon. The Wunderkind. A smile, a song, a little dance. Now starring at the shrine, the Colosseum, the School of Science – major venues for the stars.

The gleam on McAllister's pate matches the gleam of ex-Ron's jewellery. But it is not the gleam of success.

A pity – if affability, bonhomie, straight-up honesty won honours, Coventry's boardroom would be festooned.

Resolution: 'Mischief, thou art afoot. Take thou what course thou wilt.'

Maxim: For Wee Gordon.

> He was not old, nor young, nor at the years
> which certain people call a certain age,
> Which yet the most uncertain age appears.

BRIGHTON AND HOVE ALBION

Perfidious Albion blasted by rude waves (from the sea) and ruder waves (from the fans).

Can it be that they graced Wembley? Should have won the Cup. Can it be that Des has turned a paler shade of grey? Can the mighty fall so low?

Goldstone – loadstone – any old stone. Uncover it and there is mad dissension. True Grit at Altrincham, Halifax, Southport, even Stalybridge.

Dwell on Accrington Stanley. (My mother still thinks it is a pseudonym for Stanley Matthews).

Resolution: Promote Des to president of mothers' union.

> Promote Des to Brown Owl.
> Promote Des to King Canute.
> Promote Des to Chancellor of the Exchequer.
> Promote Des to Prime Minister.
> Promote Des to Pope and pray.

Maxim: *Ave atque vale!* (Hail and farewell!)

Finally, Good Fairy Wishes:

To Manchester United: the European Cup again.

To the best team: the championship.

To Glenn Hoddle: a place among the greats. Best ever so Hamble.

To all managers, players, chairmen, fans: may your love affair with the beautiful game continue, but remember:

The moon returns, and in the spring
Birds warble, trees burst into leaf.
But love, once gone, goes for ever
And all that endures is the grief.

Happy new Millennium!

SEASON 1999/00: HE WOULD DROWN THE STAGE WITH TEARS, AND CLEAVE THE GENERAL EAR WITH HORRID SPEECH

BLACKBURN ROVERS 0 – PORT VALE 0
Nationwide Football League, Division One, 7 August 1999

Billed as the Princes versus the Paupers. Brian Kidd's team of gilded super-stars. Brian Horton's gallimaufry of nonentities and free transfers. Blackburn played as if gelded, not gilded. Vale like electricians with jump leads on their vitals. A large crowd tipped up at the mausoleum, a garden of Rosenburgs, and strangely, for East Lancastrians, they were highly vocal in fine humour. Rosenburg, for those of fitful memory, gave Blackburn a real tonking in the European Cup which led to the break-up of Dalglish's championship side. A thousand Vale fans arrived to sample a little high life. Role reversal arrived at half-time!

Rovers played a first half of arrogant, strolling football. They were show-boating. Jansen and Duff, though, were eager – parcels of dynamite. Carsley of convict hairdo was the hatchet man. Alas, Kevin Davies, the £7 million flop was as mobile as a brewer's drayhorse, as bubbly as last night's Babycham. The man is an enigma. He can play, as we saw at Chesterfield. It is as if he will not play. Pilkington was brave in Vale's goal.

Early in the second half Rougier of Vale missed two open goals. Rougier turned Blanchier in embarrassment. Suddenly we had a match. Rovers upped the tempo to allegro, but Horton's gutsy boys held firm. Nil–nil. Welcome to the bowels of football, Mr Kidd. Fashionable glitzy Old Trafford style is foreign to East Lancashire. I fear you must depart for pastures new – there will be no Rovers' Return with your team.

Blackburn Rovers: John Filan, Callum Davidson, Lee Carsley, Kevin Davies, Jason Wilcox, Damien Duff, Matt Jansen, Marlon Broomes, David Dunn, Craig Short, Simon Grayson. Substitutes: Jeff Kenna, Kevin Gallacher, Damien Johnson, Christian Dailly, Alan Kelly.

Port Vale: Kevin Pilkington, Michael Walsh, Dave Brammer, Anthony Gardner, Marcus Bent, Jeff Minton, Tony Naylor, Tony Rougier, Matt Carragher, Neil Briscoe, Simon Barker. Substitutes: Alex Smith, Carl Griffiths, Richard Eyre, Mark Snijders, Paul Musselwhite.

BRADFORD CITY 1 – SHEFFIELD WEDNESDAY 1
The FA Carling Premiership, 14 August 1999

Everyone should take the pilgrimage to Valley Parade, home of Bradford City. First, find it – it is easier to locate Wagga Wagga. Tucked away in a hollow – and Bradford's full of hollows – it is a mass of maroon and yellow. The people, the stands, the offices, the pavement, all – yes, maroon and yellow. Hysteria not seen since the roaring twenties. It is Bradford's first match in the Premiership. Managed by Paul Jewel, is he a diamond or a mere zircon? He is assertively

Scouse – subtitles are needed for radio interviews. On the right of the press box is a cute little stand yclept the Symphony Stand, redolent of those clapboard houses you see in Atlanta, Georgia. The England band belted out nonstop hymns from the nether regions of this Symphony Stand. I had parked my Hupmobile in Cleckheaton, a tram-ride away, scrambled to my seat in a deluge, pitied the pompom girls (in maroon and yellow) soaked to their pantihose, sympathised with the spectators as rain poured off the stand and soaked them. Euphoria dried them quick sticks. Bradford opened at the rampage, were denied two clear penalties, and were mortified when Wednesday scored on 30 minutes. A daft own goal off the head of Dreyer challenged by De Bilde. Thus unfolded a gritty, physical mauling; no-holds-barred Yorkshire derby.

Both sides short on pace and class, strong on perspiration. Carbone, on his birthday bubbling with ideas but, like Bo Peep searching for sheep, found them hiding.

'*Mille grazie,*' Benito. Then, at 91 minutes, Beagrie upended in the box by the Wednesday substitute Donnelly. Beagrie lay prone as if felled by a steam hammer. On the award of a penalty, Beagrie miraculously recovered health and smote the kick himself. One apiece, the final score.

Both sides will struggle this season. Bradford will run like hounds lashed by the whipper-in, Paul Jewel. His enunciation may sound Serbo-Croat but his tongue is sharp. Wednesday are in limbo. They have talented players like Jonk, Rudi, Hinchcliffe, De Bilde and Walker simply playing from memory bank. The zest, the will to impose on the opposition, has gone. Thome and Carbone will leave to ease Wednesday's massive debt. Which leaves Danny Wilson a wonderful wing half of yore, a charming gent of today, with a chasm to bridge. Both sides live on hope. There is no hope without fear, no fear without hope.

Bradford City: Gary Walsh, David Wetherall, Jamie Lawrence, Lee Mills, Gareth Whalley, Peter Beagrie, Dean Windass, Gunnar Halle, John Dreyer, Wayne Jacobs, Neil Redfearn. Substitutes: Andy Myers, Matthew Clarke, Andrew O'Brien, Darren Moore, Dean Saunders.

Sheffield Wednesday: Kevin Pressman, Peter Atherton, Andy Hinchcliffe, Wim Jonk, Emerson Thome, Des Walker, Benito Carbone, Petter Rudi, Niclas Alexandersson, Jon Newsome, Gilles De Bilde. Substitutes: Andy Booth, Simon Donnolly, Richard Cresswell, Lee Briscoe, Pavel Srnicek.

EVERTON 4 – SOUTHAMPTON 1

The FA Carling Premiership, 21 August 1999

The School of Science is delirious with joy. The Goodison gods presided on by *paterfamilias* Joe Mercer will nod and smile as poetic football flowed from Everton. A fan, from memory, asked: 'As smooth as Sharon Stone's thighs?'

'Not quite,' I replied, 'but a damned sight more glossy than Lily Savage's.'

Pembridge, Walter Smith's signing from Benfica, was inspiring. Fierce in the tackle, fluid with his running, all left foot – but who cares? He was the perfect foil for Collins and Hutchison rampant in midfield. Collins, who once gave Beckham a football lesson when he was with Monaco, was imperious. One touch, intelligent, beautiful to watch – I am a Collins disciple. Richard Gough, the centre of Everton's defence, was a tower – the Old Man of Skye. He thrust his head among the hard men of Southampton on the goal line and headed a bullet goal on 36 minutes. It opened Pandora's box. Two goals in two minutes after half-time undid Southampton. The first an own goal by Lundekvam pressurised by Campbell. The second a net-bursting blockbuster from Jeffers. Kevin Campbell is Autolycus: littered under Mercury, a snapper-up of unconsidered trifles. His contemptuous shot for four–nil embarrassed Southampton. Mark Hughes was direct, peripatetic but not the Sparky of yore. Kevin Davies was immobile. Pahars grabbed the consolation goal on 70 minutes. It is August, too early for soothsaying – but I read the half-time tealeaves: relegation for Southampton. A place in Europe for the School of Science.

Everton: Paul Gerrard, Richard Gough, David Unsworth, John Collins, Nick Barmby, Kevin Campbell, Don Hutchison, Mark Pembridge, David Weir, Richard Dunne, Francis Jeffers. Substitutes: Scot Gemmel, Danny Cadamarteri, Terry Phelan, Mitch Ward, Steve Simonsen.

Southampton: Paul Jones, Claus Lundekvam, Dean Richards, Mark Hughes, Kevin Davies, Stuart Ripley, Francis Benali, Marian Pahars, Scott Hiley, Hassan Kachloul, Tron Solvedt. Substitutes: Neil Moss, Marco Almeida, Matthew Oakley, Wayne Bridge, Shayne Bradley.

BOLTON WANDERERS 0 – MANCHESTER CITY 1

Nationwide Football League, Division One, 28 August 1999

Reebok, springbok, summertime shock schmok for the Trotters. Pig's ear for the Trotters. Their football was incisive, swift, delightful, charming. Their finishing as critical and polished as a Johnnie Prescott speech. City poached a goal and pinched the points. City endured a first half of embarrassment as Bolton's Danish pair, Frandzen and Jensen controlled midfield with out-landish flair.

'Can du tel dansk, Jie ilska die' (if you're Danish, I love you). Frandzen's blond thatch was ubiquitous. He is an intelligent, probing, teasing wing half of the old school – too classy for the Nationwide League. He will move on, and soon. Bolton could have, should have been four goals up by the interval. They were denied by Weaver in City's goal. Twenty years old. Six feet four inches. Athletic, finely tuned, honed by Alex Stepney into England material. He was stupendous. One save bordered on the impossible – diving to his right, he changed course in midair to make an astonishing block on his left. Goalkeeping of magnitude. I have only seen saves like that from the greatest: Frank Swift, Peter Schmeichel, Bert Trautmann, Dino Zoff and Gordan Banks. Great goalkeepers instil doubt in the minds of opposing strikers. They agonise, ponder, think twice before shooting.

'How do we beat this genius?' You can read the thought processes at 1,000 metres. Bob Taylor, Bolton's centre forward, was in a black hole of quandary. He has a problem – speed, or lack of. He played like an Italian armoured tank with seven speeds – one forward, six reverse. After 30 minutes of Bolton blitz, Mark Kennedy, City's £1.5 million purchase from Wimbledon, found himself loitering with no intent on the halfway line. He was as alone as Ruth amid the alien corn, his colleagues unavoidably absent chasing Bolton's shadows. With malice aforethought, he wilfully shimmied through the Bolton defence and unleashed a speculative left-foot shot that scythed into the net. One–nil. Bolton in meltdown. A crazy score line. City's ensemble burst into joyous song, 'Blue Moon' ascending into the azure-blue sky. Instantly, Joe Royle withdrew Cooke, a wide player, and dispatched Ian Bishop to bolster midfield.

Early in the second half, Jensen retired wounded. Bolton thus lost the muse, came off the pace and conceded. Richard Jobson, the cultured City centre half in his first game for 16 months, was mastermind and nursemaid in defence – an inspired Joe Royle signing. Joe is delighted, robbery without violence. Colin Todd is bemused.

'Joe,' he quipped. 'You would play upon me; you would seem to know my stops. You would pluck out the heart of my mystery. You would sound me from my lowest note to the top of my compass.' An old Lancashire idyll for 'You lucky bastard'.

Bolton Wanderers: Keith Branagan, Neil Cox, Mike Whitlow, Bob Taylor, Eidur Gudjohnson, Greg Strong, Per Frandzen, Andy Todd, Michael Johanson, Claus Jensen, Ricardo Gardner. Substitutes: Steve Banks, Jimmy Philips, Hasney Aljofree, Bo Hansen, Gudni Bergsson.

Manchester City: Nicky Weaver, Richard Edghill, Gerard Wiekens, Kevin Horlock, Paul Dickov, Shaun Goater, Terry Cooke, Jeff Whitley, Danny Tiatto, Richard Jobson, Mark Kennedy. Substitutes: Lee Crooks, Ian Bishop, Danny Allsop, Gareth Taylor, Richard McKinney.

MANCHESTER CITY 2 – CRYSTAL PALACE 1
Nationwide Football League, Division One, 11 September 1999

A good name is rather to be chosen than great riches, and loving favour rather than silver and gold. Great riches have never been bestowed at the Theatre of Base Comedy, nor silver or gold. The inmates love base metal and favour their team. It is in the blood, bred in the bone. Today nerves jangled, patience tested, resilience tried as Palace, flat broke, in administration, no hopes, fought like leopards. City were lethargic, casual, almost indifferent until Palace scored – Clinton Morrison, their red-booted number ten, gleefully slapping the ball past Weaver. Weaver was not amused. He is the future England keeper and knows it. Just before half-time, Richard Jobson, City's centre half, cantered up-field. Jobby is tall, pepper-and-salt hair, mainstay of Joe Royle's yesteryear. He is playing on borrowed time: age and injury taking their toll. A civilised, educated gentleman of some import. Then amid the flying boots, elbows, knees, heads and other appendages in the Palace box appeared Jobby. Thunderous header. One apiece.

Both sides threw on the subs: Bishop, Crooks, Taylor for City. Rizzo, Antunes, Svensson for Palace. Palace's subs made me laugh out load. They sound like a Chicago hit squad from the prohibition days. 'Just take your Gat – Rizzo, melt 'em down, waste 'em.' Rizzo was no assassin – he was a pet.

Gareth Taylor, City's sub, tore on to a rebound and lashed the winner. Thirty-two thousand rent the air with 'Blue Moon' – not in exultation but in relief. Palace, to their credit, fought with tenacity. Andy Linighan, who should be sorting out Liverpool's defence, was a stalwart. In goal was Fraser Digby. What a glorious name, redolent of vintage port, fine Stilton and crusty colonels on the North-West Frontier. On the Nationwide frontier, the jury is still out on City's prospects. The midfield lies too deep and lacks genuine pace. Their firepower is really a damp squib. Will they achieve the premiership pot of gold? The proverb says choose a good name rather than riches.

Manchester City: Nicky Weaver, Richard Edghill, Andy Morrison, Kevin Horlock, Paul Dickov, Shaun Goater, Terry Cooke, Jeff Whitley, Danny Tiatto, Richard Jobson, Mark Kennedy. Substitutes: Ian Bishop, Danny Allsopp, Lee Crooks, Gareth Taylor, Richard McKinney.

Crystal Palace: Fraser Digby, Jamie Smith, Dean Austin, David Woozley, Hayden Mullins, Fan Zhiyi, Lee Bradbury, Clinton Morrison, Andy Linighan, Stephen Thompson, Simon Rodger. Substitutes: Nicky Rizzo, Richard Harris, Matthew Greg, José Antunes, Matthias Svensson.

DERBY COUNTY 0 – BRADFORD CITY 1
The FA Carling Premiership, 25 September 1999

The pride has evaporated at Pride Park. When confidence is low, pride hides. Derby have a divine belief that their rightful place is among the cream – it is justice. But there is no such thing as justice; muscle is the reality. Bradford muscled like a Bradford northern rugby pack. Hustled, hassled, tackled non-stop; never mind the class, feel the bruises. They reduced an effete Derby team to abject apathy. Stimac and Wanchope have departed. Steel at the back, eccentricity at the front were sadly missed. Four thousand Bradford fans in yellow and maroon set up a constant cacophony. McCall and the troops relished it. The first half was a blur of falling bodies, expletives and total negation. Myers of Bradford was sent off for a misdemeanour. Fuertes of Derby followed a little later for misuse of an elbow. The enjoyment factor would have been enhanced if Fuertes had played with his elbows. For a South American he is poor. His control was fey, his movement like an armadillo, his vision as limited as Fidel Castro's. Maybe he should return to Boavista or preferably boa-constrictor. To think that Kinkladze, a pocket genius, languishes in the Ajax reserves. Jim Smith, that Yorkist Philosopher, will tear out his hair, if he had any. He played Dorigo and Borbokis, two fullbacks in midfield. The gap betwixt midfield was huge, a no man's land. It was as if we had planted bombs there, so reluctant were Derby to tread on it. Only Seth Johnson, with his Wormwood Scrubs hairdo, playing like an escapee from that institution, imposed at all. He really is a tearaway.

Sixty-one minutes a free kick in Derby's box. Wetherall and Mills compressed Carbonari, who promptly headed into his own goal. Came a rash of substitutions. Derby flung Carbonari upfront. But Wetherall, McCall and the fans scented victory. Life and limb were sacrificed. Walsh, in goal, looked like a trampolinist – he was magnificent. One–nil to Bradford. One in the eye for Jim Smith. Catching the eye, those vociferous Bradford fans, they are cockatoo. Worth the entrance fee to enjoy them. Do it now – it will not last long.

Derby County: Russel Hoult, Horacio Carbonari, Tony Dorigo, Seth Johnson, Dean Sturridge, Rory Delap, Spencer Prior, Steve Elliot, Esteban Fuertes, Vass Borbokis, Francesco Baiano. Substitutes: Richard Knight, Stefan Schnoor, Kevin Harper, Malcolm Christie, Adam Murray.

Bradford City: Gary Walsh, Andy Myers, Stuart McCall, David Wetherall, Robbie Blake, Lee Mills, Gary Whalley, Peter Beagrie, Andy O'Brien, Gunnar Halle, Dean Saunders. Substitutes: Ashley Westwood, Matt Clarke, Dean Windass, Wayne Jacobs, Bruno Rodriguez.

MANCHESTER CITY 2 – BLACKBURN ROVERS 0
Nationwide Football League, Division One, 23 October 1999

At 3 p.m. on a crystal autumn day, the distant Pennines shone gold in the sun. At 4.40 p.m. a squall swept in from Siberia. Thirty-three thousand at the Theatre of Base Comedy are ambivalent on weather: it is 'whether'. Their 'Blue Mooned' created a cascade of noise and inspired City. This was the big match. City to establish Premiership credibility, Brian Kidd fighting for his future. His massive squad of underachievers striving to live up to reputation. Blackburn could have been two up in the twinkling of an eye. They hit the bar and brought an incredible reflex save from Weaver. They surged forward, City's midfield slow in thought and deed. Then, 33 minutes, Mark Kennedy, a constant tease to Rovers, crossed low. Richard Edghill ghosted in far post for his first league goal. His celebration run finished in Gstaad, a province of nearby Oldham. It fired City. Their second half was dynamic. Razor in the tackle, fluent in movement, brimming with confidence. Horlock's penalty was saved by Filan. Kennedy tormented Blackburn to distraction. Four minutes from time Kennedy's floated corner, Jeff Whitley's brilliant header near post.

Astonishing the vicissitudes of football. Blackburn's stars were callow, whipped, even shamed. Brian Kidd's days are numbered. £30 million dissipated on Ward, McAteer, Jansen, Ostenstad, Gillespie, Carsley, Short, Frandzen and the rest. Quality like Flowers, Sutton, Sherwood, Gallacher sold along with Shearer, Le Saux, Batty, Hendry. Jack Walker spits iron filings and eats steel bars. Brian, prepare to receive your P45 and a million-pound payoff. Not bad for 12 months' failure.

City are a side of bit stars and cast-offs. Morrison and Jobson, unwanted centre backs of Huddersfield and Leeds. Morrison like a press gang swagger from the East End Docks. Horlock, Bishop and Dickov excess baggage elsewhere. But surely the biggest steal of all time, Nicky Weaver, the finest goalkeeper in Britain, £100,000 from Mansfield Town. City may be skint – but Premiership, here we come.

Manchester City: Nicky Weaver, Richard Edghill, Andy Morrison, Kevin Horlock, Ian Bishop, Paul Dickov, Shaun Goater, Jeff Whitley, Richard Jobson, Mark Kennedy, Danny Granville. Substitutes: Terry Cooke, Gareth Taylor, Lee Crooks, Danny Tiatto, Tommy Wright.

Blackburn Rovers: John Filan, Jeff Kenna, Callum Davidson, Lee Carsley, Jason Wilcox, Damien Duff, Matt Jansen, Per Frandzen, Christian Dailly, Craig Short. Substitutes: Alan Kelly, Egil Ostenstad, Martin Taylor, Simon Grayson, Jason McAteer.

LEEDS UNITED 2 – SHEFFIELD WEDNESDAY 0

The FA Carling Premiership, 16 October 1999

Clashing, thumping, martial music at the final whistle. Jubilation from 39,000 Leeds fans. Deep unrestrained joy dating back to 1931: even Revie and Elsie could not achieve it. But truly this was a pyrrhic victory, not of gold but of fool's gold. Sheffield Wednesday could have, should have been three goals up at half-time and their game by right. As I always say, 'There's no such thing as justice – muscle is the only reality'. De Bilde shot wide twice – it looked easier to score. Sonner was a bat's wing short of a goalpost – wrong side. Wednesday took the game to Leeds: desperation, inspiration, Danny Wilson creation? Walker was a lion at the back. Rudi, Sonner and Jonk dainty, assertive, progressive midfield. De Bilde casting off the shackles, exposing a glass-jawed Leeds defence. Nil–nil half-time. Mr O'Leary cracking the china, blistering the walls of the Leeds dressing-room. Leeds duly cracked on the pace. In full flight at Wednesday's throats. Wednesday came on the riposte, upped their game. They flowed like the Tiber in flood. Alexandersson blew the chance of the match. De Bilde followed suit. Came the turning point of the match. Connoisseurs and Pharisees await this moment like the apocalypse. This was Martyn's astonishing point-blank save from Booth's header. Pure instinct – the ball struck with such power. Booth, a Yorkshire lad, all raw-boned, knobbly-kneed and earthy, must have thought Martyn a divine intervention. Martyn smiled, rubbed his palms, patted Andy on his dome. All in a day's work for a first dan keeper. Wednesday were deflated. To mastermind a game and reap nothing is relegation fodder. In Wednesday's goal is Srnicek, a shot-stopper but second rate. Seventy minutes Huckerby the substitute piled in from the right, head down like a charging bison, shot obliquely, Srnicek spilt it, Alan Smith tapped in from three yards. Trust not yourself, but your defects do know. Seventy-seven minutes ping-pong Wednesday's box. Alan Smith. Tapped in a rebound off a post. Game won, Leeds off to Moscow in the highest spirits. Danny Wilson that honest, likeable warrior of Wigan, holds arms aloft and curses fate on high. But Danny, read, mark and learn. Alas, how prone are humankind to blame the powers of heaven. From us they say proceed the ills which they endure; yet more than fate herself inflicts, by their own crimes.

Leeds United: Nigel Martyn, Gary Kelly, Lucas Radebe, Jonathon Woodgate, Michael Bridges, Harry Kewell, Lee Bowyer, Stephen McPhail, Danny Mills, David Batty. Substitutes: Alf-Inge Haaland, David Hopkin, Darren Huckerby, Paul Robinson, Eirik Bakke.

Sheffield Wednesday: Pavel Srnicek, Peter Atherton, Andy Hinchcliffe, Wim Jonk, Emerson Thome, Des Walker, Andy Booth, Petter Rudi, Niclas Alexandersson, Gilles De Bilde, Danny Sonner. Substitutes: Kevin Pressman, Gerald Sibon, Richard Cresswell, Ian Nolan, Lee Briscoe.

LEEDS UNITED 1 – WEST HAM UNITED 0
The FA Carling Premiership, 30 October 1999

To damn with faint praise or 'twere these one whose fire fine genius kindles and flair flame inspires. Faint praise for the match which embered first half and kindled only in the second. The genius Ian Harte, the Leeds fullback, whose goal inspired and ignited the match. It came 12 minutes into the second half. Lomas, the West Ham captain, headed out weakly: Harte, on the edge of the box, half-volleyed sweetly – Hislop beaten at the near post. Harte smiled sweetly; the goal came from his right boot used for standing room only. Deadlock broken. Forty thousand fans alight. Biggest ovation until then reserved for Peter Ridsdale, the Leeds chairman, who announced at half-time that season tickets for 2000 would not rise.

But now, after the goal, Leeds pressing hard. West Ham defending deep, on the ropes, body language forlorn. Leeds at full chat. Kewell hunting down the left at speed, Bridges unveiling his subtle skills. Huckerby, caged on the subs' bench, unleashed as the secret weapon. At last, West Ham brought on Joe Cole, the white hope of English football. Harry Redknapp had turned puce on the touchline at the pusillanimous West Ham play: his arms flailing as Don Quixote. Cole instantly unsettled Leeds with tight control and bright vision. He is a slender reed, is Cole, but has two great feet and a Matthews-like body swerve. The rain poured down. Leeds lost the plot. Kitson missed two chances. Martyn brilliantly saved Lampard's free kick. Martyn anxious and busy. West Ham thwarted. The final whistle relief for Leeds. Leeds off to Moscow in high hopes. West Ham in the doldrums.

Leeds United: Nigel Martyn, Gary Kelly, Ian Harte, Lucas Radebe, Jonathan Woodgate, Michael Bridges, Harry Kewell, Lee Bowyer, Stephen McPhail, Alan Smith, David Batty. Substitutes: David Hopkin, Darren Huckerby, Paul Robinson, Danny Mills, Eirik Bakke.

West Ham United: Shaka Hislop, Neil Ruddock, Marc Keller, Paul Kitson, Steve Lomas, Paulo Wanchope, Marc-Vivien Foe, Rio Ferdinand, John Moncur, Frank Lampard, Javier Margas. Substitutes: Steve Potts, Michael Carrick, Craig Forrest, Joe Cole, Adam Newton.

STOKE CITY 1 – BRISTOL CITY 1

Nationwide Football League, Division Two, 14 November 1999

As I rolled through the russet and gold Cheshire plain, I dreamed of Tony Waddington's Stoke City of yore. Waddington the romantic dreamer, an entrepreneur, showman, roisterer, fond of his claret. A believer in style, preferably aged in a bottle. A galaxy of ageing stars in those days. Jimmy McIlroy, Stanley Matthews, Gordan Eastham, Jimmy Greenhoff, Gordon Banks, Alan Hudson. Wonderful, free-flowing, uninhibited football – a master class. It was played at the Victoria ground, a ramshackle wooden edifice: a throwback to the days when Josiah Wedgwood threw his first pottery amid the dark furnaces of this bleak land.

Suddenly the vast, icy carbuncle known as the Britannia Stadium earthed me. I hate modern stadia. Concrete, steel, soulless, lifeless testaments to money and Mammon. Like the Pompidou Centre in Paris and the Lloyds monstrosity in London. All pipes, tubes, girders like a human being inside out – intestines on show.

On this icy day, an Icelandic consortium assumed control of the club. Gunnar Thor Gislasou is the new chairman. He sat with the Icelandic ambassador, having bought a slice of *'Enski Boltinn'* – English football to you!

Gary Megson, the present manager, bared his arms at 3 p.m. Is it hello or goodbye? This is no Cold War – it is for real. So what is Iceland getting? Stoke were appallingly drab. A midfield of evaporation, a forward line of stultification, a back line of headless cockerels.

Bristol looked the better team, Paul Mortimer at ease with poise, the tiny Moldovan Tistmetanu aiding and abetting.

On 65 minutes Stoke scored – from a corner, their centre half Nicky Mohan headed in. The audience stiff with cold and boredom sang 'Delilah'. Why that old Tom Jones song mystifies me. But they sang and they meant it. The players rushed to embrace Gary 'Mystic' Megson on the touchline as if he were the saviour. The Icelanders were impassive. Disregard the emotion; Mystic Megson will be frozen out.

Five minutes from time Brian Tinnion, with a rasping volley equalized for Bristol.

If you have tears to spare, shed them now for Mystic Megson. With the temperature at zero they will freeze your coarsened cheeks. Stoke are about to enter the Ice Age. No coddin'.

Stoke City: Gavin Ward, Nicky Mohan, Chris Short, Graham Kavanagh, Peter Thorne, Kyle Lightbourne, James O'Connor, Clive Clarke, Matthew Bullock, Kevin Keen, Richard Dryden. Substitutes: Phil Robinson, David Oldfield, Paul Connor, Stuart Fraser, Ander Jacobsen.

Bristol City: Billy Mercer, Mickey Bell, Steve Jones, Paul Holland, Brian Tinnion, Paul Mortimer, Carl Hutchings, Peter Beadle, Scott Murray, Ivan Tistmetanu, Keith Millen. Substitutes: Greg Goodridge, Steve Torpey, Steve Philips, Aaron Brown, Alex Meecham.

MANCHESTER CITY 3 – SWINDON TOWN 0
Nationwide Football League, Division One, 18 December1999

In Homeric terms, Joe Royle is Hercules. He cleaned out the stables of Augeus, slew the Nemean lion – the golden apples of Hesperides await in next season's premiership. The other nine tasks await Hercules Royle when he gets there. Meanwhile the Odyssey at the Theatre of Base Comedy torments the inmates. An amazing pre-Christmas full house endured a laboured first half as City struggled for cohesion, pace, rhythm and style.

Jamie Pollock, a hand-me-down from yesteryear, eased the pain on the half-hour – a tap in after brilliant solo play from Kennedy down the left. Swindon, unfazed despite being bottom of the league, looked comfortable and had the temerity to hit a post. Hercules Royle invoked the wraths of the gods at half-time, flagons of nectar thrown against the portals.

The big stick worked. One minute into the second half, Robert Taylor, the expensive signing from Gillingham, scored his first goal for City. A simple pass from Goater, the shot bobbled in almost shamefacedly. Alas, I thought, our Robert Taylor is not the Robert Taylor I adored, erstwhile film star. He was suave, sleek, poised, fleet of foot. Our Robert Taylor is a run-away sideboard.

Tiatto, a little dynamo, came off the subs' bench to replace Kennedy and gave City like Harry the Fifth at Agincourt, 'a little touch of Harry in the night'. On the hour Shaun Goater pounced and snaffled a goal from nothing. Three–nil to City – match won. 'Blue Moon' rose like a Christmas carol from the throng. Swindon lost in a gallimaufry. Michael Carrick, a spindly 18-year-old on loan from West Ham, was a Swindon class act. He is a graceful player in the Hammers' mould. More will be heard of this lad. Swindon, though, are doomed.

City will enjoy Christmas.

Manchester City: Tommy Wright, Richard Edghill, Gerard Wiekens, Kevin Horlock, Shaun Goater, Robert Taylor, Ian Bishop, Jamie Pollock, Mark Kennedy, Richard Jobson, Danny Granville. Substitutes: Terry Cooke, Jeff Whitley, Richard McKinney, Lee Peacock, Danny Tiatto.

Swindon Town: Frank Talia, Mark Robinson, Gareth Davies, Alan Reeves, Andy Williams, Lee Collins, Michael Carrick, Scott Leitch, Ty Gooden, Charlie Griffin, Chris Hay. Substitutes: James Williams, Bobby Howe, Robin Hulbert, Steve Mildenhall, Sol Davis.

COWDENBEATH 2 – CLYDE 3
The Scottish Cup, Second Round, 8 January 2000

The gales rushed in from the grey, foaming Atlantic Ocean. Great black clouds angry with icy rain swept on Cowdenbeath as if Neptune himself had risen from the depths to rent his hurling bolts of thunder and lightning on the Highlands. To combat adversity is Cowdenbeath's destiny. They have to win this cup tie. The lads prepared to fight both the weather and the opposition – Clyde. Our dressing-room was a front-line trench. We were the Highland Light

Infantry, spirit coursing through the blood. The skirl of the pipes, the swing of the kilt, the war cries. What a bonnie side we are.

Scots wa ha'e wi' Wallace bled,
Scots wa ha'e we doon and ded.

A massive vocal audience, soaked to the skin, roared acclaim.

The pitch like a muddy no man's land of the Somme. Alas, Clyde scored first from the penalty.

'Never a penalty, referee – get a white stick.'

But Carrigan scored – just.

Half-time. Cowdenbeath nil, Clyde one. Our manager blasted, teacups flew. A wee dram administered to combat the Arctic blasts.

We began the second half charge with broadsword and claymore. Their goal under siege, Clyde wilted. Graeme Brown, our young hero, a transcendental Michael Owen, blasted two magnificent goals within five minutes deep in this second half.

We are wild, ecstatic – we'll beat Rangers in the final. Seventy minutes we reeled in shock – Clyde equalized. McLaughlin with a lucky header.

'Deus nobiscum,' cried the drenched faithful. A solitary Frenchman uttered, *'C'est magnifique, mais n'est pas la guerre.'*

The sides locked at two goals apiece. We marvelled at the muddied oafs – their strength, their skills, their spirit against all odds.

Then disaster. We lost focus. Carrigan, an honest yeoman of Clyde, stole in and scored their third goal. The time, 76 minutes.

Blow wind and cataract, the Atlantic gale matching the fierceness of the conflict. We hustled ourselves against Clyde. We marauded, we battered, ran like Highland wounded stags. We could not equalize. The referee, himself yclept 'Clyde', denied us. We should have read the portents, a referee called Clyde. The opposition Clyde. We needed Bonnie Parker and the Gattling gun to win.

We lost – but 600 of us will remember the day.

Cowdenbeath two, Clyde three, Stuart Hall for Radio One. Brigadoon.

Cowdenbeath: Stephen Hutchinson, David White, Shaun King, Scott Snedden, Keith McCulloch, Grant Carnie, Craig Winter, Mark Bradley, Murray McDowell, Graeme Brown, Willie Wilson. Substitutes: Willie Stewart, Craig McMillian, Paul Simpson.

Clyde: Gordon McIntyre, Darren Murray, Mark McLaughlin, Bryan Smith, Craig Cranmer, Jack Ross, Brian Carrigan, Andy McLay, Tom Woods, Pat Keogh, Allan Grant. Substitutes: Jamie Mitchell, Steve Convery, Martin McLauchlan.

WIGAN ATHLETIC 1 – MILLWALL 1

Nationwide Football League, Division Two, 15 January 2000

Wigan. I doubt whether the Queen Mother knows where it is, let alone paid a visit. It is in the Lancashire hinterland that once mined coal, dipped their bread in dripping, and bred huge strapping lads for Rugby League jousts. Eddie Waring country.

Now it is all tarted up *à la mode*. Blair's new Britannia. The mills that once wove cotton are now museum pieces. Wigan Pier, a hive of industry a century ago, is now a theme park. In tandem with new thinking is Dave Whelan, a florid son of the soil; short on words – short on temper. A Blackburn Rovers fullback who broke his leg and finished. With his compensation bought a market stall. The rest is history. Supermarkets bought and sold. And now J.J.B. Sports, a vast marketing exercise which keeps Dave in shape. He sells everything from designer golf clubs to infants track shoes. He owns Wigan Rugby and Wigan Athletic. His ambition, to see Wigan in the Premier League. Whelan can do it – he is a driver of men. In control, two ex-Manchester City managers, John Benson and John Bond. Benson – a dry-witted tactician with a heart complaint. Mr Bond a whimsical eccentric, fond of white suits and jewellery. A graduate of the West Ham Academy. 'Benson, Bond and Whelan' like a firm of country solicitors.

They were on their way to a record 29 games without defeat until Oldham were the more athletic. Whelan, sojourning in Barbados, choked on his lobster thermidor watching the game on TV. He has demanded a whipping of Millwall. A thousand fans have trekked from Millwall for the head to head. Hence the 1 p.m. kick-off.

The Bobbies of Wigan are teak-tough – any macho outbreak will be nipped in the bud or torn off the branch. Millwall fans beware.

At 1 p.m. the J.J.B. Stadium, brand spanking new, a glittering monument to market forces, was sparsely populated. A mere 6,000 in a 20,000 seater. Millwall out-shouted Wiganers. Both sides missed their shining lights: Neil Harris for Millwall, Liddell for Wigan. The match was an eye-opener for the itinerant, the non-committed, the neutered neutral. The movement of high quality from Wigan. Genuine skills from Barlow, an Everton reject, McLoughlin and De Zeeuw, a Dutchman purchased from Barnsley. A sweet, sophisticated little outfit. Millwall preferred route one – get the ball in the box – make 'em sweat – fire up the fans. Alas, 'twas Stuart Balmer, the Wigan captain, who succumbed to fire and brimstone. Sent off early for a spot of GBH. Wigan's 10 found Millwall's boisterous 11 a burden. Gilkes scored for Millwall. Roy Carroll, the Wigan keeper, coveted by many super-league clubs, illustrated why with some reflex saves and timely interventions. Half-time, nil–one. The referee, aptly yclept Mr Lynch, was the hanging judge – one red card, umpteen yellows. Friendless and roundly booed. Mr Benson, remember, the droll, witty Wigan manager with the pepper-and-salt hair, reshuffled the pack. Darren Sheridan, brother to John, and alike in their lovely, subtle, two-feet football, off the subs' bench. Upfront went De Zeeuw from centre half and it was all-out muck or nettles Lancashire hotpot. De Zeeuw equalised, scrambled head, body, legs, shoulders, whatever part the anatomy the ball was not informed. It lay in the Millwall net. One apiece. I was delighted with my first visit to the J.J.B. It is sumptuous, appointed like the Savoy Hotel. The natives are friendly with those broad, expansive, warm and welcoming Lancashire vowels. I was given a meat and potato pie of Cordon Bleu provenance; chunks of steak and succulent spud swimming in gravy. I ate it with a teaspoon. Social niceties count for nicht in Wigan. In the boardroom after the match I sat with Wigan and Millwall directors. Millwall's shares had been traded the day before in some demand; two million had been bought. The price had risen dramatically. Would the Stock Exchange tremble? Entrepreneurs rush for their wallets? No – rumour hath it that Chris Evans (a red-headed urchin from nearby Warrington) and Danny Baker (a very clever, audacious cherub from Londinium) would like to own the club. Topless football at the Den? Pole-dancing at half time? Real showbiz in footie. In reality the shares rose from three-quarters of a penny to – wait for it – one pence. Maybe Evans and Baker are wiser than the City's FT. In my match report I castigated the burghers of Wigan opining: 'There were 6,000 present today. Either tip up the numbers – or lose your several ventures.' I allude to Brutus (in a former life I was Brutus). Before the Battle of Philippi against Mark Antony, Brutus addressed Cassius, that arch-scoundrel, liar, coward and all-round scumbag, thus:

'There is a tide in the affairs of men,
Which, taken at the flood, leads on to fortune;
Omitted, all the voyage of their life
Is bound in shallows and in miseries.
On such a full sea are we now afloat,
And we must take the current when it serves
Or lose our ventures.'

They lost. Mark Antony won. Brutus fell on his sword. Dave Whelan will not lose. People of Wigan, take heed. Otherwise you will be impaled not on the sword but an Adidas boot. Watch this space.

Wigan Athletic: Roy Carroll, Scott Green, Kevin Sharp, Pat McGibbon, Stuart Balmer, Arjan De Zeeuw, Michael O'Neill, Alan McLoughlin, Stuart Barlow, Roberto Martinez, Jeff Peron. Substitutes: Derek Stillie, Gareth Griffiths, Andy Morris, David Lee, Darren Sheridan.

Millwall: Nigel Spink, David Livermore, Robbie Ryan, Ricky Newman, Stuart Nethercott, Scott Fitzgerald, Paul Moody, Michael Gilkes, Tim Cahill, Paul Ifill, Paul Shaw. Substitutes: Jamie Stewart, Richard Saddlier, Leke Odunsi, Byron Bubb, Phil Smith.

SHEFFIELD UNITED 1 – MANCHESTER CITY 0
Nationwide Football League, Division One, 22 January 2000
Bramall Lane is the Taj Mahal of Yorkshire, a noble edifice amid the bleakness of a Sheffield winter. Today it is gold-plated for the one Michael Brown, once an assertive abrasive midfielder with City. Rejected by Joe Royle, he came here for £400,000. Today he scored the winning goal on 40 minutes. Neat build-up by United. Brown cleverly shielded the ball, swivelled, punched a shot past a despairing, diving Weaver. City were torridly undone. The back four missing three key players were like blind mice as United simply ran at them with

purpose. Marcus Bent masterful in the air and on the ground. Notman, on loan from Manchester United, showed neat touches, bringing colleagues into play. The second half was a stormer, City throwing players forward in desperation. Tracey in United's goal was cool, excellent, brave. But despite their efforts City were exposed as pretenders. Taylor, the centre forward, I have previously described as a runaway sideboard. Today he was a static obstacle removed from the fray deep in the second half. There is a lack of pace in City – they want to play sweet football but teams like Sheffield United will close them down and expose them. Neil Warnock is off to China. Joe Royle methinks will break the china tonight.

Sheffield United: Simon Tracey, Paul Devlin, Rob Kozluk, Shaun Murphy, Wayne Quinn, Lee Sandford, Shaun Derry, Michael Brown, Bobby Ford, Marcus Bent, Alex Notman. Substitutes: Axel Smeets, Davy Gysbrechts, Bruno Riberio, Petr Katchauro, Curtis Woodhouse.

Manchester City: Nicky Weaver, Lee Crooks, Richard Edghill, Kevin Horlock, Ian Bishop, Shaun Goater, Richard Jobson, Mark Kennedy, Tony Grant, Danny Granville, Robert Taylor. Substitutes: Paul Dickov, Tommy Wright, Jeff Whitley, Danny Tiatto, Jamie Pollock.

STOKE CITY 2 – BURNLEY 2

Nationwide Football League, Division Two, 29 January 2000

Three thousand Burnley fans who had trekked down from the East Lancashire steppes on the Himalayan tundra found themselves at home in Stoke. A biting wind, squalls of icy rain blew in from the wasteland atop which is the Britannia Stadium. The fans trickled in hundred by hundred up to half-time, the reason – a lorry had overturned on the windblown, wretched, awful M6. The team, and the fans, were diverted past Manchester Airport and then through the Cheshire plain.

At the airport, they will have observed gleeful folk waving their giro cheques and boarding for sunshine. Stoke in winter a drab alternative. From my frozen eyrie in the Britannia stratosphere I could, with one eye, track the influx of fans and, with the other, track the match.

Gratified Burnley fans discovered that a goalless first half was blown asunder by the gale, livened only by the rival fans chanting. Stoke won this vocal exchange as they crooned the old Tom Jones hit 'Delilah'. Do not ask me why. The wind abated, the football improved, effort multiplied. Four goals in seventeen minutes set the blood coursing. Peter Thorne for Stoke, a tap in after deft work by O'Connor on the left. Stoke's second a ghastly miscue by Steve Davis, the Burnley centre half, his keeper advanced; Mr Davis had not chalked his head, the ball soared over and lodged in the net. Two–nil to Stoke. Seventy-four minutes Andy Payton, almost an OAP in footie terms, converted a hotly-disputed penalty. Eighty-three minutes Andy Payton again, a shimmy through Stoke's defence a hotshot borne on the wind. Two apiece. Seconds later Stoke awarded a penalty but brilliantly saved by Crighton.

The Admirable Crighton. The butler who saved the family from disaster, averting crisis. Fair result. Stoke are owned by Iceland, everything ends with -sson, or -ssen. Today they fielded a kipper, Frode Kippe. Does Froda mean 'cold' in Reykjavik? The Stoke mascot is a hippopotamus. The frozen tundra has weakened the spirit, snow blindness turned the brain. Like Lear on the blasted heath, I fear hubris. I am become 'a fond and foolish old man', I am not in perfect mind. I join the 15,000 on this biting winter's day – there's loyalty for you – I retrieve my snow cat from the wasteland, so barren even sheep will not graze, and set the autopilot for home. Will I encounter a friendly St Bernard with a barrel of cognac round its neck? Anything can happen in Stoke.

Stoke City: Gavin Ward, Brynjar Gunnarsson, Nicky Mohan, Graham Kavanagh, Peter Thorne, Kyle Lightbourne, Mikael Hansson, James O'Connor, Clive Clarke, Anders Jacobsen, Frode Kippe. Substitutes: Sigursteinn Gislason, Carl Muggleton, Paul Connor, Ben Petty, Kevin Keen.

Burnley: Paul Crighton, Dean West, Mitchel Thomas, Gordon Armstrong, John Mullin, Steve Davis, Paul Cook, Lenny Johnrose, Andy Cooke, Andy Payton, Graham Branch. Substitutes: Glen Little, Micky Mellon, Paul Smith, Peter Swan, Ronnie Jepson.

DERBY COUNTY 3 – SHEFFIELD WEDNESDAY 3
The FA Carling Premiership, 5 February 2000

Déjà vu at Pride Park. Wednesday play the opposition off the park in a pulsating first half. Fail to score, fail to win. It happened at Leeds weeks ago – same scenario at Derby today.

Wednesday three – one up with two minutes to play. Craig Burley, the Derby captain, blasts a goal; three–two: a face-saver, we thought. But 30 seconds later a wild flurry on Wednesday's goal line, Malcolm Christie, £50,000-worth from Nuneaton, bundles in the equalizer, in off a distraught Nolan the Wednesday fullback. Danny Wilson is stunned. Jim Smith incredulous. The audience in torment, disbelieving. Many of the Derby audience had fled the scene before the final whistle muttering foul imprecations, having lost the faith. They will count rams in their sleep – they missed the most thrilling climax of their lives.

Wednesday had a superb first half, their fast, concise football rippling through a fragile Derby defence at will. De Bilde glanced a header wide. Alexandersson and Quinn spurned chances. Wednesday on merit should be three up. Jonk was imperious; at last we saw Dutch total football. They compressed Derby in their own half. It was exotic. A slaughter, Derby humiliated. What a Jekyll and Hyde team are Wednesday. How can they be bottom of the league with so much dross above them? At last, justice. Twenty-two minutes a short corner to Hinchcliffe; a beautiful swinging cross, De Bilde's swift header. One–nil at half-time.

Seventy-one minutes Sibon crashed a volley of enormous power, a screamer, a goal of the season. Sibon, *c'est si bon*. Then two defining moments in the match: Wednesday withdrew three artists with injury; Jonk,

Alexandersson and De Bilde. Sonner, Scott and Donnelly the replacements. Their rhythm and confidence eroded. Derby apace were in quandary. The fans deafening Smith demanding Kinkladze into the fray. Why he, Sturridge and Prior were substitutes puzzles me. Enter thus, on the hour, Kinkladze. He is a genius. Ball control world-class. He mesmerised Wednesday. Shall we tackle or stand off? His speed is viper-quick. His first touch a swift chip to Strupar (Super Strupar). Strupar's header – Derby in the match. Strupar fan club, 100 strong ex-Belgium were in paroxysms of delight – 'Brussels sprouting'. Kinkladze wove a magical tapestry. Christie and Sturridge lusted themselves on the Wednesday barricade. Eighty-eight minutes Donnelly broke free of the pack as Derby thrust forward. Whites of the eyes with Donnelly and Poom, the Derby keeper. Donnelly's nerve held, a cool shot past Poom's despairing dive. Three–one game set and match. Derby fans left in droves and missed that heroic finish. Kinkladze had destroyed Wednesday. A world-class player lifting his colleagues' spirit. Alas, would it transpire that these two illustrious teams, beloved of all neutral fans, steeped in classical history, will play this fixture in the Nationwide next season? What of Kinkladze then? A real live Derby Ram paraded (for Kinkladze). The accompanying song, 'There'll Never Be Another Ewe'.

Derby County: Mart Poom, Stefan Schnoor, Tony Dorigo, Seth Johnson, Rory Delap, Malcolm Christie, Jacob Laursen, Steve Elliot, Stefano Eranio, Craig Burley, Branko Strupar. Substitutes: Dean Sturridge, Deon Burton, Spencer Prior, Andy Oakes, Georgie Kinkladze.

Sheffield Wednesday: Peter Atherton, Andy Hinchcliffe, Wim Jonk, Des Walker, Gerald Sibon, Niclas Alexandersson, Ian Nolan, Steven Haslam, Gilles De Bilde, Alan Quinn, Pavel Srnicek. Substitutes: Kevin Pressman, Danny Sonner, Richard Cresswell, Philip Scott, Simon Donnelly.

MANCHESTER CITY 2 – NORWICH CITY 1
Nationwide Football League, Division One, 12 February 2000

A biting, chilling day at the Theatre of Base Comedy. The Globe Theatre of football. The audience 33,000 to observe the play: *The Winter's Tale*, a tragedy for Norwich City; *Much Ado About Nothing*, a farce for City's faithful followers.

'How now, good City?' They opened like a pack of hounds on the fox a good league faster than Norwich. Kennedy hares down the left, skins his full-back Sutch, high cross to Goater's shaven pate, the ball dispatched into the Norwich net. One–nil and the game is but two minutes gone. Goater littered under Saturn applying a moral medicine to a mortifying mischief. Norwich ripe for devouring.

Fifteen minutes a Norwich corner on the right, Manchester's defence dwells, Iwan Roberts, Norwich's burly centre forward, nips in to score. One apiece. Manchester lose the muse, deficiencies become apparent: lack of real pace, loss of confidence, no buzz or bite midfield; the gap 'twixt frontrunners and midfield yawning like the Grand Canyon. Bishop is now in his mid-30s, a clever, sparky, thinking man's player, but now in the late autumn with legs like old elms. Jeff Whitley is promising but pusillanimous. Kevin Horlock is 'ten to two', flat feet – good brain, but again, off the pace.

Norwich defended deep, fire in midfield stifling and scotching any Manchester ploys. A battler named Malky MacKay, with his skyscraper size, manned the battlements; Mike Milligan, a former favourite of Joe Royle's at Oldham, rattled sabres and skirmished fiercely. Norwich attacks were sporadic – like an Italian infantry division on the advance – in retreat at the first hint of grapeshot. The match is in the doldrums. I dreamed of Haaland of Leeds, Frandzen of Blackburn in City's midfield, Huckerby upfront. Players of quality and fire going cheaply. When suddenly the Puck of the first half hit the ground running. Mark Kennedy materialised in the Norwich box, fastened on the high ball from Wiekens and smashed a super half-volley past an immobile Green in the Norwich goal. Time, 83 minutes. One minute passed – Kennedy again – a daisy-cutter drive, a peach of a shot, a plum of a goal. But what a rotten apple of a game. Manchester need injections, Joe – we are suffering. As *Much Ado About Nothing* ends, so does this advice:

Think not on them until tomorrow. I'll devise thee brave punishments for them. Strike up, pipers. Dance and exeunt!

Manchester City: Nicky Weaver, Richard Edghill, Gerard Wiekens, Kevin Horlock, Ian Bishop, Shaun Goater, Richard Jobson, Jeff Whitley, Mark Kennedy, Danny Granville, Paul Dickov. Substitutes: Nick Fenton, Danny Allsopp, Jamie Pollock, Tony Grant, Tommy Wright.

Norwich City: Robert Green, Daryl Sutch, Erik Fuglestad, Mike Milligan, Shaun Carey, Malky MacKay, Matt Jackson, Iwan Roberts, Paul Dalglish, Daryl Russell, Chris Llewellyn. Substitutes: Andy Marshall, Lee Marshall, Che Wilson, Jean Yves de Blasiis, Adrian Forbes.

BARNSLEY 1 – BOLTON WANDERERS 1
Nationwide Football League, Division One, 26 February 2000

Nick Barmby scored a hat trick at West Ham today in a surprise Everton victory. 'Nick nicks the headlines.' His soul mate, from their days at Middlesbrough, is Craig Hignett who wastes his substance on less than riotous living at Barnsley. A sublime talent, Hignett; like a derby-winner among selling platers: around him some goodish players, Chettle, Eaden, Tinkler, Sheron, Curtis; but not of Premiership quality. And now three points from their last five games not suiting Barnsley's aspirations. Bolton controlled the first half at strolling leisure. Jensen in the hole behind the frontrunners had the freedom of the pitch, Barnsley standing off in admiration. Johansen and Holdsworth flitted around him, puzzled. Forty-two minutes Holdsworth running free was felled in the box by Miller, the Barnsley keeper. It was the merest fairy touch, Holdsworth's drive was triple salchow with pike. Mr Fletcher blew his whistle, for Holdsworth's piece of theatre – no – a penalty! Holdsworth struck the ball past Miller low inside his far post. One minute in the second half, short corner for Barnsley, Eric Tinkler's speculative shot deceived Jaaskelainen, the Bolton keeper, and Barnsley were level. The crowd, normally stolid, as befits their reputation, bellowed, 'We are become a sounding brass or a tinkler's tinkling symbol.' Barnsley, the team, responded with a peck of perk, and the game became lively. Holdsworth struck a momentous volley, the goal of his life; the referee allowed it and was swallowed up by players of both sides. Was Mr Fletcher confused or kerfuffled? The goal did not stand, nor Hristov's bullet header for Barnsley minutes later. The game naturally turned rumbustious, the fustillarian in the audience vocally doubting Mr Fletcher's parentage. Mr Fletcher was escorted off at full time by a posse of large florid bobbies. Bolton Wanderers have not won at Barnsley for 91 years – the age of meat and potato pie, on which I splurged £1.60 while loitering outside the gentlemen's water closet. The concrete pie bar abuts the corrugated iron and whitewashed pee-stone.

'Gourmet's paradise', Barnsley.

Postscript: For itinerants intending to visit. Do not arrive until 13.30 hours.

I arrived at 12.50 hours. Reported with my satchel to reception. Bewildered lady informs me that ground does not allow persons respectable or otherwise into its environs 'til the appointed hour. She returns 10 minutes later.

'Go to gate 33. A steward will let you in.' Once inside I face a stiff mistral; there is always a strange wind blowing at Barnsley, laden with desert sand!

Both doors to the press box were locked, so, to the soigné bobbies await-ing duty, bums down in the main stand, vainly suppressing their joy at my futility, I vainly sought ingress into the hallowed seat. Clambering over seats, impediments and a bit of furniture, I finally plugged in my broadcasting appa-ratus. Time: 13.12 hours. Rather snottily I was informed: 'You have missed your slot.' I was cut to the quick. In a flash, I recalled another embarrassment. A Yorkshire miner, having regaled himself with 10 pints of foaming Yorkshire best bitter, returned home for a little 'diddly doo wi' t'wife'. His member could not rise to the occasion. Sadly, he told me: ''Twere like thumbin' a Pontefract cake into a slot machine.'

Barnsley: Kevin Miller, Nicky Eaden, Eric Tinkler, Craig Hignett, Neil Shipperley, Mike Sheron, Robin Van Der Laan, Chris Morgan, Keith Brown, Steve Chettle, John Curtis. Substitutes: Bruce Dyer, Darren Barnard, Geoff Thomas, Georgi Hristov, Chris Barker.

Bolton Wanderers: Jussi Jaaskelainen, Mike Whitlow, Gudni Bergsson, Michael Johansen, Claus Jensen, Robert Taylor, Dean Holdsworth, Ricardo Gardner, Robbie Elliot, Mark Fish, Dean Holden. Substitutes: Bo Hansen, Steve Banks, Franck Passi, Paul Ritchie, Allan Johnston.

ROTHERHAM UNITED 1 – PETERBOROUGH UNITED 1
Nationwide Football League, Division Three, 25 March 2000

Barry Fry, Posh's manager is writing his memoirs. A touch of Hemingway out of Playboy; when the expletives have been deleted – what is left? This afternoon he could be ballistic – Rotherham beat them five–nil earlier in the season. He will enjoy Millmoor as I do, grateful to find it after circumlocuting Wath on Deane and Greaseborough. Millmoor is tucked away under a railway bridge – a throwback to grass-roots football; the grass is still growing everywhere. Lots of whitewash, corrugated iron; the press box a shack, with a front supported by rusting hooks. My seat, at the far end, came from a 1930s omnibus. When I eventually scrambled past my colleagues, my position at the far end, front row, I dumped my bag on the seat. Clouds of dust rose and choked the inmates. Press programmes had been dispensed, all 12 of them, so I proceeded to the pie shop and splurged £1.80 on a programme and £1.40 on a potato pie. My expenses will break Greg Dyke's budget. Damn it, as I speak free spud pies are being given to the press. I politely demur the offer of a pie. The correspondent from Peterborough next to me is obviously famished. I settle in my seat, light a Silk Cut. A lackey bellows, 'No smoking'. Hell fire; I would be doing them a favour incinerating the place.

To the game. Posh have many injuries; hence a patched-up defence. Rotherham's star striker, Leo Fortune West is absent, hurt. What a romantic name. Hope the Miller's fortunes do not evaporate with him.

I was at Millmoor years ago to observe Wally Ardon's retirement. Remember it well; W.C. Grace smote a century same day. I vaguely recollect Kevin Keegan bagging four goals for Newcastle here in a Cup tie. Nothing at Millmoor has changed; it is quaint, red and white antediluvian. My beard is grey, my eyes purge thick yellow amber and plum tree gum, my wit is diminished, my hams are weak. The game will not be included in Barry Fry's memoirs, though 1,500 Posh fans swelled the gate to 5,000 odd. Rotherham took the lead on fifteen minutes – Paul Hurst – a neat header from a right-wing cross. Jon Cullen equalized on 44 minutes – his first goal for Posh. 'Twas a rollicking first half, a proper joust. Posh put themselves about a bit, Jason Lee with elbows as sharp as John Fashanu's, Andy Clarke, remember him, a Wimbledon all dash and dart.

Rotherham without Master Fortune, played measured football – somewhat above their means, and lacked up-front bite.

The second half was lacklustre and goalless, entertainment sporadic. I did admire Posh's left back young Jelleyman, lots of skill and enterprise, and Zat Knight, Posh's number eight. He is six feet eight inches, like a Harlem Globetrotter crossed with a Masai hunter. Football in the bowels can be fun, y' know!

As I quit the press shoe box, squirming past the Posh scribe writing furiously, I tore the ligaments in my left knee. I am *hors de combat* – on crutches. I shall never forget sublime moments at Millmoor.

Rotherham United: Mike Pollit, Will Varty, Vance Warner, Guy Branston, Kevin Watson, Darren Garner, Chris Sedgwick, Paul Hurst, Paul Warne, Andy Turner. Substitutes: Paul Pettinger, Jason White, Brian Wilsterman, Steve Thompson, Lee Glover.

Peterborough United: Bart Griemink, Richard Scott, Andy Edwards, David Farrell, Zatyiah Knight, Steve Castle, Gareth Jelleyman, Simon Rea, Howard Forinton, Jason Lee, Jon Cullen. Substitutes: Dan O'Connor, Adam Drury, Matthew Gill, Ritchie, Daniel French.

PARLEZ-VOUS ANGLAIS?

Recently I took part in the 'cult' show *Row Z*. It is on BBC Choice, shot on location in the vestry of a London trattoria. Various fans are assembled to air potent views on their own footie teams.

On the Saturday when Manchester United played Vasco de Gama, I presented the entire programme from the Red Café at the heart of the shrine, or in popular parlance 'the Theatre of Dreams'. My fellow presenter was Clare P. Grogan of *Gregory's Girl*, a most delightful, feisty Scottish lass who in a previous life was Robert the Bruce, Robbie Burns, Kenneth McKellar and Doris Day. The show was fun, the talk effervescent, stimulating, cogent, off the wall, immensely satisfying. They all hated Manchester United. Resentful of success, envious of global adoration, disgusted by arrogance, wishing for the crock of gold that United found at the end of the rainbow. It is commercial, lads; it is not football. It is marketing, selling, flogging, milking, soothing, smoothing, merchandise and back to more marketing. Lads – you are fooling yourselves. Fans – Christ, we do not need you. We need share-watchers, the fast buck – who needs whingeing fans when millions of punters ride on the share price?

The mention of Chris Evans and Danny Baker trousering £75 million set the stock market quivering like blancmange. A million Millwall shares were traded at the mere thought that Evans would buy in. They shot up by – hold yer bleedin' breath – by one and a half pence. There's big business for you. Did you miss out? Yes – you were too busy uttering hot air on *Row Z*.

Now the previous week on *Row Z*, a motley crew assembled in London presided over by Matt Smith, the resident compere. One slot featured S J Hall, MA, at Manchester City FC for the game with Swindon on VT. I was dressed in my winter apparel – mink coat and long johns. The mink is 30 years old. I bought it for 200 quid. It is the best buy ever. When all us hacks assemble in the press box, they freeze. I simply roast. Those wild mink knew a thing or two in Canada.

So, the little episode at City was shown in the middle of *Row Z*. In it, I explained that football reporting was a hobby, not a career. I leave that to guys who queue up for gobbets from managers and players. They have wives, families, mortgages and bank statements. I do it for love (have you spotted a BBC cheque unless you're Vanessa Feltz?).

Matt Smith asked the fans, after our little vignette, what they thought of Stuart Hall. Opinions varied among the fellers.

'Different, eccentric, surreal, witty, northern bias, opinionated, *knows* his football, *does not know* his football'. All of which I accept.

Then to a damsel. She despised my mink. She was wearing leather shoes. She thought in sound bites. Not a sentence in sight. She said I *trivialise*d football. My hackles rose. Trivial means commonplace, ordinary, trite, of no significance. Shock, horror, crap! I invoke Shakespeare, Kipling, Keats, Shelley et al in my reports oftentimes to paper over the cracks in what has been a totally negative, dull, featureless game. I search for the beautiful, the witty, the *charmant*, the stimulating. I want to bond with fellow bizarre spirits. Mademoiselle, you are off my Christmas card list. But how's about a snog in my mink?

ON STAGE HE WAS NATURAL, SIMPLE, AFFECTING
'Twas only that when he was off – he was acting.
23 February 2000
I was spreading Tiptree blackcurrant jam on to my toasted and well-buttered hot-cross bun. The knife was poised over a chunk of thick, crumbly Cheshire cheese. Yes, my favourite breakfast – the bun, a layer of wonderful jam with cheese on top. Suddenly my wife interrupted the repast. 'This Beckham stuff – what's going on?'

She knows little of football and its machinations. She once enquired of Matt Busby, at a party, what he did for a living – he promptly invited her to Wembley to spare my blushes. But she does know all about Victoria Beckham, and can even whistle a Spice Girls song. I am impressed, as my musical education finished with the Stan Kenton Orchestra and Mel Tormé, Nelson Eddy and Jeanette McDonald.

'My sympathies are with the Beckhams,' said t' wife. 'If baby Brooklyn was poorly, it's the dad's duty to minister, whether it's night or day, sod turning up for training – that child was ill, and Mr Ferguson was totally in the wrong to fine David, and humiliate him by not playing him.' I was flummoxed. My hottie bun was cold and t' wife was up for a right argument. In my house all argument is titled 'discussion'. If I finish with a black eye or my arse in a sling, the discussion has been somewhat tart and lively. If I decamp from home the discussion has definitely turned sour.

I tread the Beckham issue like a mouse treading on eggs.

'David,' I whispered, 'is a highly-trained athlete, honed to perfection at the United Academy for wayward boys. Millions have been spent on his educashun, to teach him to play football and learn him how to talk proper, like what Victoria does. He is obliged to live a monastic life, closeted with his colleagues, shunning exotic food, fine wines, fun, games, japes, naughty company and dirty thoughts. For this sacrifice he is paid per year what the average guy gets paid in a lifetime.'

'Gonads,' said t' wife. 'You were there when the children were ill. You've had sleepless nights when they had measles, whooping cough, scarlet fever, coughs and colds. And you've had days off when they have been seriously ill.' T' wife won the argument – David was right to put family before football. She took it further. 'Think of all the footballers who frequent low dives, misbehave, consort with lowlife, wreck bars and kick hell out of strangers. David is a great example for the youth of today. He's showing them that being a family man brings responsibilities – and he's shouldering them like a real man, not a wimp.' She is not finished. 'And hark back to your days of George Best, Paddy Crerand, Mike Summerbee and company, roistering till dawn in dark satanic clubs, sinking pints, singing inflammatory songs, dancing on tables and mooning.' I conclude that the tabloids, once again, have put an innocent man in the pillory. David has been slaughtered over yet another minor transgression. He and Victoria are doomed like the Ancient Mariner to sail forever on the shallow sea of vain popularity, the ship piloted by angels. They must live on ambrosia, the food of the gods that made them immortal – but 'Husband and wife must drink from the cup of conjugal life, but they must both taste the same ambrosia or the same gall'.

I hope David and Victoria will survive this ordeal. She is intent on reinventing herself, although to judge from her skeletal form, reincarnating her mind and body. And why not? Since the death of Diana, Princess of Wales, there has not been a single figure on the world stage to replace her. The tabloids have tried – Mein Gott, have they tried – to discover a folk heroine with Diana's appeal, charisma, naivety, simplicity and beauty. All Diana's faults were well catalogued, and some were like the San Andreas – therein lay her appeal. Victoria could be a Diana clone. Maybe Max Clifford could bleach her hair – he has! Choreograph her dance steps, teach her a little French, instruct her how to hold a champagne glass overflowing with Dom Pérignon, persuade her to begat another child and call it Tristram, give David his knighthood, consign Mr Ferguson to Devil's Island, let David play for the Arsenal and be part-time Minister of Sport, ambassador to Northern Ireland, chairman of the Race Relations Board and happiness will pervade.

David is a fine footballer. I saw his first game for Manchester United. I admired first of all his vision, his inclination for the imaginative ball – a sign of true class. He was played wide on the right – I thought if he were central this boy could destroy. Fine right foot, mediocre left, but with practice could become two-footed. On this day he was a yard off the pace. He was caught in possession too often. And you can coach forever and improve skills, but you cannot teach speed – that searing pace over the first five yards that marks a world-class midfield player.

Observe that fantastic creator Giresse, mastermind of Platini's French team, off the blocks faster than Carl Lewis. Colin Bell – the Nijinsky of Manchester City. A whole litany of great midfielders. Zito of Brazil, Cruyff of Holland, Falcao, Neeskens, Rijkaard, Hoeness, Didi again of Brazil, Platini, Schuster, Zidane, Van Himst, Valderrama, Haan, Cubillas. The list is endless of great world players of the last century. Oh! I forgot Martin Peters and Alan Ball – World Cup winners.

Can David ever join the real elite? Can he play that killer one-two centre midfield where cut and thrust be at its height? I write this before the Europa 2000 match. The Argentines were miffed that they outplayed 11 Englishmen only to struggle against 10. Ortega is a wonder player with something to prove.

Alas, the Argies used Wembley as a training stint, hardly breaking sweat.

France, Holland, Spain, Italy, Germany await. The French have flair. In second gear, they humiliated the Scots in a recent friendly. The Dutch have Davids and Seedorf – wonderful players. Has the team the will? The Germans have suffered as England with the influx of foreigners. Their system is proven – not the players. The Italians have superb technique. In Francesco Totti the finest midfielder in the tournament. Have they the stamina? Scotland make up the numbers. England need to establish a pattern, a discipline. Andy Cole must play: with the United caucus of the Neville brothers, Scholes, Beckham and Butt. Europe is terrified of United. Follow Alex.

STANLEY MATTHEWS

His best companions, innocence and health;
And his best riches, ignorance of wealth.

Stanley Matthews, 'wizard of the dribble', died on 23 February 2000. Stanley was born in Hanley in 1915. Joined Stoke at the age of 14. Turned professional at 17. He played 710 games for Blackpool and Stoke City. In 1932 his salary was £5 in the winter and £3 in the summer.

The five pottery towns are today brushed up and fairly spruce; in Stanley's days they were mean, grey tunnels of back-to-backs, smoking mounds of potters' clay and belching kilns. His dad, a barber and part-time featherweight boxer, would take little interest in Stanley's career. I remember him telling me that his dad never saw him play. Truth is that Jack Matthews sneaked out of the tonsorial shop and watched Stanley from the terraces. Jack fought 350 bouts, many of 20 rounds, and lost only five. Stanley honed his skills in Meakin's Square, a rough piece of land adjoining a local pottery. He perfected control, swerve and speed so much that before he was 10 years old he held the locals spellbound – they turned up to watch him even then.

He left school, Wellington, in Hanley, and apprenticed himself to a brick-layer, sharing customers in the evening at the barber's shop. In 1930 he joined Stoke as a grounds-staff boy; cleaning 48 pairs of boots each day. Boots those days were like miner's clogs, almost with steel toecaps. Huge lace-up surgical boots that required washing, drying off and hours of dubbin to soften them

By the 1933–4 season Stanley was a regular first-teamer. Stoke were pro-moted to the First Division. Stanley scored 11 goals – he would never again equal that. He made his international debut for England against Wales in 1934, and played against Italy and Germany. He missed an open goal in the Germany match and was dropped until 1937. His triumphant return was Berlin, 1938. The Nazi Party, led by Göring, Hess, Ribbentrop and Goebbels, unfurled their banners, lit their torches, assembled the serried ranks of brown shirts, and the black of the Waffen SS to gloat. The 'master race' against the 'contemptible little army', as the Kaiser called Britain back in 1914.

The chants were stilled, the banners stayed furled, the smiles turned to growls as Matthews destroyed the German defence. England won six–three.

Matthews even scored. The German magazine *Fussbal* described Matthews as 'wunderbar – he risks everything and can do everything'.

Came the Second World War, which stifled not just Matthews's career but that of sportsmen in other fields. The great Hedley Verity of Yorkshire was killed. Cricketers like Hutton and Hammond, Compton, Miller, Lindwall found themselves in uniform instead of whites. The War Department, unusually for a strict, disciplinary, backward body, allowed famous sportsmen, if they desired, to become physical training instructors of NCO rank, and thus entertain the troops. Which was a slice of enormous good fortune.

I have detailed the facts of Stanley Matthews's life objectively. The story now is subjective. Matthews was posted to Blackpool, where the RAF had a huge base to train flight crews. Stanley thus played for Blackpool during the war. I was a snotty-nosed schoolboy in love with the beautiful game. As Old Trafford had been blitzed, all the football took place at Maine Road, Moss Side, Manchester 14. The Blackpool side was magical: forward line Matthews, Dix, Dodds, Finan, Burbanks. Behind them Farrow, Johnstone, Hayward. Their football was sublime. Matthews, my boyhood hero. Burbanks, from Sunderland, was clever, Ronnie Dix of Spurs a sly inside forward, Jack Dodds the archetypal centre forward of the day. A huge bulk of a man. Face of bruises, thick black hair with centre parting. A heading machine. His duels with Frank Swift were fantastic. Huge Swifty, with hands like frying pans, whipping the ball off Dodds's flying head. The subsequent exchange of patter 'twixt them. Swifty patting the head of Dodds. So many vignettes of those days of true soccer artistry. Stanley, though, was the man the public went to see. He was the matador caping the bull. The bull, the fullback, knew he was part of the play. He would boast for ever that he was mesmerised by the great Stanley Matthews. He knew at 3 p.m. that his reputation would be shattered. He knew he could not contain Matthews.

I picture Stanley in the famous tangerine shirt and baggy white shorts, shuffling towards the fullback. The poor defender, in retreat, desperately hoping that his left half would lend support. The poor fellow trapped like a rabbit in a car's headlights; he knows that Matthews will draw him close, so close that he can make his tackle. Matthews is balanced on the balls of his feet, perfect balance, that of the matador, or Olga Korbut, that balletic grace as if suspended on gossamer. The twinny-toed shuffle continues – Matthews, with the ball curled on his right foot, feints to the left, inside the back. The back counters with a move to follow – Matthews is going inside, the back lunges with the tackle – he is off-balance. On the instant Matthews, with the outside of his right boot, flicks the ball past the back and is in flight. His body has leaned so far to the left that it defies gravity. The fullback vainly gives chase; Matthews is one of the quickest wingers ever, his speed over the first 10 yards phenomenal and so deceptive. Yet he never gave the impression that he was a tearing, run-at-'em flier like Cliff Jones or Garrincha. Matthews, with that lean, slim, balanced body, implied flowing grace like a stalking panther or a

Kittyhawk in for the kill. He was supreme, his art conceived in joy, performed at apparent leisure.

Great artists, in any field, elevate their art to God-given intuitive instinct, like the mellifluous flow of a Versailles fountain. If I make a comparison with motor-racing, Matthews is Fangio; Fangio at one with his machine, part of it, it part of him. His speed was fantastic, his four-wheel drifts defying all motor-racing theories. Yet there was no arm twirling, no histrionics, loss of control. He just flowed. Mere mortals like Hawthorn, Mansell, even Hakkinen, looked fast, gave every indication that they were fast, but never had that impassive balance of mind and body that distinguishes the greats from the rest.

I revelled in Matthews. Nobody was his equal. Pele, Garrincha, Di Stefano, George Best, Tom Finney, Peter Doherty, Bobby Mitchell, Ryan Giggs – all had, or have, the dribbling skills, taking the ball to the opposition's bootlaces and then whisking by, but Matthews was peerless.

1953 was his zenith. 'The Cup Final of all time'. Matthews had all the honours save one – a cup medal. Bolton Wanderers were three – one up with 20 minutes to go. Bolton's pragmatism draining Blackpool skill. Eric Bell of Bolton injured, limping, out of the game. These were the days of no substitutions. Matthews then embarked on the classic finale. The famous shuffle – Banks mesmerised, the cross, Stan Mortensen scores. Mortensen again – this time a ferocious free kick from 20 yards. Three–three. Seconds remaining, Stanley cuts outside, then inside, two defenders gasping for air like stranded sharks, the cross, and Bill Perry hammers the winner. Four–three. An epic – should it be the Mortensen final? Morty would not have it – 'Stan's match', that is it. Morty always referred to me as his twin. I saw much of him and Stanley throughout their lives.

In 1971 I achieved my lifetime ambition. I played number four behind the great Stanley at Burnden Park, Bolton, in a testimonial match for Eddie Hopkinson, the Bolton long-serving goalkeeper.

Our forward line was Matthews, Finney, Lofthouse. I have forgotten our number 10, but number 11 was a very young George Best. At number two was one James Armfield. The opposition a World Cup Eleven featuring Eusebio. Stanley was 56 years old – still living on carrot juice, steaks and early-morning runs. The speed had diminished, the perfect balance remained. He was still quicker than Bobby Moore, although Bobby, the perfect gent, said to Stan: 'I'll go left – you go right.' He wanted to ensure that the maestro gave the crowd what it wanted. Wonderful night. I scored a goal from a Matthews pass, something to treasure for ever.

Subsequently I saw Stanley on a regular basis. He was a very shy, modest man of simple tastes. At the Victoria Ground we would reminisce of the great players past and present. Tony Waddington, the 'Artful Dodger', had assembled Geoff Hurst, George Eastham, Alan Hudson, Gordon Banks, Jimmy Greenhoff, Jimmy McIlroy – no, not assembled, rather snaffled them as 'past their sell-by date'. An anarchic setup. A wilful bringing together of super-talents –

a tapestry of delight that made Stanley smile. His modesty was overwhelming. Two years ago I went to make a TV programme in Scotland; Christie's were holding an auction of football memorabilia. The auction room was overflowing with artefacts, Cliff Jones double-winning Spurs trophies of 1961. George Cohen's England cap from 1966. Medals, trophies, salvers, photographs, international caps of the famous, football programmes and assorted treasures. The buyers were well-heeled businessmen, serious acquirers who spent serious money on the vast collection. A set of Celtic medals of pre-war vintage for £25,000. An Arsenal artefact for £10,000. Cliff Jones memorabilia for £40,000. I was amazed; more amazed when the buyers wished to stay anonymous. Negotiations conducted by stealth, sleight of hand, surreptitious bargaining. Boy! This is big business.

I enquired if international caps of the not-so-famous bring large largesse. What about the Stanley Matthews collection? A small Jewish gentleman with a kind face took me to one side. Stanley, he confided, was married to Betty Vallence in 1935. The marriage finished 40 years later, and Stanley remarried a girl he met in Malta – Mila Winterova. In a fit of pique, Betty sold Stanley's artefacts on Fleetwood Market for flump-pence. In disbelief, I accused him of retelling an apocryphal story. His eyes narrowed. 'You tell me, then, where they are, who owns his 1953 medal, his first international cap.' I never dared broach the subject with Stanley. The only solace is return to the quote whence I began this eulogy.

Postscript: During the Second World War, the League was split into League North and League South. Blackpool were top (1944). Observe Bradford, Northampton, Mansfield and Hartlepool. Shackleton got five goals. Tommy Lawton scored for Everton.

HOME THOUGHTS ON DANNY WILSON

A black Wednesday for Wednesday. I grieve for Danny Wilson, a Wigan lad of some quality. During his career as a player, he was knocked about by Bury and Chesterfield. Brian Clough gave him a rough ride at Forest; 10 games and then out to pasture at Scunthorpe. A spell with Luton and then blossoming at the ripe old age of 30 with Sheffield Wednesday. I adored his bustling play, his adroit passing, his application, his jocular temperament – a fine wing half of the old school. At Barnsley I liked his management style. He took a bunch of less than Premiership players and instilled in them the football ethic of the beautiful game. 'It's just like watching Brazil,' cried the fans. It was never Brazil, but it was smooth, eye-catching, rhythmic, imaginative, but off the pace of the Premier League.

At Wednesday, with higher-quality players, I expected Barnsley ideas at a faster tempo. I saw Wednesday at Bradford on the first day of the season. Bradford aglow in a sea of crimson, yellow and orange. The Symphony Stand packed to its clapboard rafters. The Wednesday band beating out martial music. The sun beaming down. A Yorkshire derby – an occasion. What happened? The team was tepid, flaccid, unmoved by the cacophony around them. Strolling football to little purpose while Bradford buzzed and harried. How could footballers on obscenely high wages treat a match like this with disdain? I marked Wednesday down as relegation fodder. I noted that Wim Jonk, a creative midfielder, elegant and thoughtful he may be but too laid back. Sonner, talented but ineffective. Carbone wanting away could not give a damn. Rudi – a high stepper but out of radar reach with colleagues. Andy Booth – honest Yorkshire yeoman but frankly, a Nationwide player. Niclas Alexandersson lost in the malaise. Gerald Sibon the beanpole, as much pace as a pensioner trotting for his pint. Gilles De Bilde, former Belgian player of the year, clever, takes good positions, makes the play – misses the chances.

All these players were playing a falsehood. They believed they were better than they are. Reputations mean little if form is not revealed on the park. Thome, their best player, was sold. Carbone left. I wrote off Wednesday until they played Leeds at Yelland Road. In an incredible first half they played Leeds off the park. Their football was exciting, played in little triangles, the movement so fluid that Leeds were chasing the game. Wednesday should have been four up at half-time. De Bilde chief culprit, shooting wide and over. Came the defining moment: Martyn pulled off an incredible reflex save from De Bilde that confounded belief. The ball was zapped up-field – Huckerby shot – Srnicek spilled it – Smith tapped in – soft goal. Wednesday finished. Leeds escaped, but that Wednesday style lived on in memory. How could the players be impotent one game and brilliant the next?

I next saw Wednesday at Derby. Three–one up with injury time to play. Kinkladze's genius mesmerised them; Derby bagged two goals in two minutes. Three–three.

Two weeks ago at Everton, Wednesday fought, scrapped, toughed it out at the School of Science. Young Quinn was quicksilver, Des Walker, the old fox, operated the offside trap like Sweeney Todd's chair. Atherton and Briscoe battled. One apiece. Hope is alive. A three–one beating of West Ham revived Danny. Wednesday in a crass first half were outplayed by West Ham intent on swagger and showboat. The game was there for West Ham to win. They had not the will – what a set of underachievers. Wednesday clapped on pace and inspiration, Ferdinand boobed, Wednesday equalized and ran away with the match.

Now to Watford, the watershed. A dreadful match, a Watford winner. Wilson out. Danny a delightful man, a fine coach, an honest lad, let down by his players. The Wednesday boardroom has always had bonhomie and a certain culture. After the West Ham match it was joyous. We talked of Eric Taylor and Harry Catterick, who ran the club yonks ago. Eric, the wheeler and dealer. Catterick, the enigma who decamped to Everton. As he used to tell me, 'The higher up the tree you climb the stronger the winds.' Eric used to say, ''Tis better to travel safely than to arrive.' Eric subsequently was severely injured in a car crash. In other words, Wednesday are a great club. A stadium fit for the year 2000. A loyal support. A club held in affection and esteem by football followers throughout the world. It is history going down the pan. Will Wednesday recover from the trauma? Can Mr Shreeves work the miracle? He once drove a taxi when football shunned him. Can he keep the wheels from falling off at Hillsborough? Or will Wednesday follow Nottingham Forest, Manchester City, Wolverhampton Wanderers, Bolton Wanderers, West Bromwich Albion, Huddersfield Town, Blackburn Rovers and Sheffield United, once members of the elite, into the Nationwide wasteland?

And whither Danny Wilson? He will receive a year's salary as compensation, which is more than a steelworker will save in a lifetime, but Danny is not a money man; his pride is hurt, his reputation damaged. He will mull over his misfortune. Did Carbone and di Canio unhinge his thinking? Could he handle foreign mercenaries? Should have forsaken his principles, discarded pure football and scrapped imponderables?

Be consoled Danny: good managers do not leave the game. Next season you will be back, and I shall welcome you!

SEASON 1998/99: NOTHING IS HERE FOR TEARS; NOTHING TO WAIL
Or Knock the Breast, No Weakness, No Contempt,
No Dispraise or Blame, Nothing but Well and Fair

STOCKPORT 2 – GRIMSBY 0
Nationwide Football League, Division One, 5 September 1998
The Angell of Stockport found the muse, lit up the leaden sky above Edgeley Park – the Brett Angell, giant centre forward of Stockport County, a free spirit, unfolded his heavenly wings, scored two goals, and brought untold happiness to the supporting cherubs.

Season of mists and mellow fruitfulness, close bosom friend of the maturing sun. The sun matured early at Edgeley Park – it always does in Stockport – deep cloud enveloped us, and the match. I was inspired by County's manager, Gary 'Mystic' Megson. As County began sprightly, he exhorted, cajoled, pleaded. As County subsided, he bellowed, screamed, jumped in anger, covered his eyes in frustration. Grimsby's tiny forwards tiptoed through County's static defence, phlegmatic to the point of slumber. I sat on my sultan's throne atop the canopy covering the players' tunnel. It is encrusted with grime, chewing gum, old dog-ends, the detritus of neglectful years. Nobody gives a toss for the press hacks – may I suggest a set of stocks? I also observe that when the canopy was unfolded, it had a bird's nest entwined in its cacky greyness. I exchanged pleasant northern banter, as my throne was in the midst of the County supporters. Interest in the match was waning. County brought on two subs, pressed forward in hope – yes, the Angell of Stockport bundled in the first goal. County's form instantly razor-sharp, and inventive. One minute from time, the Angell bagged a second from a textbook move. Mystic Megson must ponder – does he need a guardian Angell every match? – or consult an agony aunt. One appears in the County programme – yes, a real 'Agony Aunt'. Her name – Gladys Nutter.

Stockport County: Carlo Nash, Sean Connelly, Colin Woodthorne, Paul Cook, Mike Flynn, Martin McIntosh, James Gannon, Chris Byrne, Brett Angell, Ian Moore, Kevin Cooper. Substitutes: Aaron Wilbrahams, Tony Dinning, Wayne Phillips.

Grimsby Town: Aidan Davison, John McDermott, Tony Gallimore, Peter Handyside, Richard Smith, Wayne Burdett, Stacy Coldicott, David Smith, Lee Ashcroft, Jack Lester, Paul Groves. Substitutes: Lee Nogan, Vin Black, Mark Lever.

BLACKBURN ROVERS 1 – LEICESTER FOSSE 0
The FA Carling Premiership, 29 August 1998

The Blackburn motto is *Arte et Labore.* Not so much art as sweated labour at Ewood Park, Jack Walker's steel and concrete sarcophagus. Leicester Fosse are a pragmatic side, tough, resilient, uncompromising. They are to flair what Kevin Keegan is to the English language or Dennis Wise to the art of diplomacy. In Izzet, Lennon, Savage and Zagorakis an engine room of true power. A midfield as strong as any in the Premiership. Elliott and Walsh immense centre backs. Heskey and Cottee the Little and Large of strikers. The parts today were greater than the whole. Like Rottweilers on a short leash. Come on, Mr O'Neill – let them play – unleash them!

Blackburn apace returned to the drawing board – the season a bare two weeks old and nary a win. Sutton twinned with Gallacher upfront, Henchoz and Peacock twinned in central defence. Thirteen minutes' fulfilment with a dash of *arte; ars est celere artum* (the art is to conceal the act). Sherwood's long ball to Duff on the left wing, Duff the little leprechaun looked for the crock of gold wafting into space, Gallacher ghosted in – a lovely neat goal ensued. Gallacher should have stitched Fosse moments later but botched up.

Came then a rash of yellow cards, four to Blackburn, two for the Fosse. All six substitutes came on, including Kevin Davies, the £7 million misfit. He has thunder thighs and a large bottom. He appears overweight and lazy and plays in a blue mood of distraction, overweighed either by the size of his transfer fee or by expectation. As Lincoln, Abraham – not Sincil Bank – once said: 'I claim not to have controlled events, but confess plainly that events have controlled me!' Mr Uriah Rennie, having dished out yellow cards like roubles in a Muscovite bank, mystified the players, drove the crowd apoplectic with erratic behaviour. He was a cross between Attila the Hun and Ivan the Terrible. Maybe he had a poor lunch and mild dyspepsia. Take a Rennie, Mr Rennie! *Erroneous erraticus.*

Fosse shoved Walsh upfront; his mere bulk gave Blackburn the frighteners. Henchoz and Peacock were stalwart as Taggart and Walsh, casting huge shadows, mixed heads, elbows, knees and thighs in bruising encounter. More muscle than a rugby pack. Blackburn hung in; *nul arte*, much *labore*. Maybe we change the motto to *Exitas acta probat* (the end justifies the means).

Blackburn Rovers: Tim Flowers, Jeff Kenna, Callum Davidson, Tim Sherwood, Darren Peacock, Stephane Henchoz, Garry Flitcroft, Kevin Gallacher, Chris Sutton, Damien Duff, Sebastien Perez. Substitutes: Kevin Davies, Jason Wilcox, Billy McKinlay, Christian Dailly, John Filan.

Leicester Fosse: Kasey Kellar, Frank Sinclair, Steve Walsh, Mustafa Izzet, Neil Lennon, Emile Heskey, Steve Guppy, Robbie Savage, Matthew Elliot, Tony Cottee, Theo Zagorakis. Substitutes: Gerry Taggart, Garry Parker, Pontus Kaamark, Stuart Campbell, Pegguy Arphexad.

EVERTON 0 – BLACKBURN ROVERS 0
The FA Carling Premiership, 26 September 1998

Dreams and the light imaginings of men, and all that faith creates and love desires. A romantic idyll at the School of Science, whatever happened to the beautiful game here? Joe Mercer, that wonderful disciple of creative, attacking football, must be choking on his flagon of nectar in the Elysian Fields, that heavenly paradise for artists now departed. Knowing Joe as a former great chum, he will have ignored this awful match and had another nectar with Dixie Dean, Tommy Lawton, TG Jones and Cliff Britton. (Combined worth today £1,000 million).

In mitigation, Blackburn, shorn of Sutton, Gallacher and Davies, played a damage limitation exercise; packed midfield, suffocated the game and reduced Myhre in Everton's goal to an observer role. Midfield stalemate always means minefield – crunching tackles, falling bodies, naughty challenges, compressed play, life squeezed out of promising ideas. Everton foxed me with their tactics. Four central defenders, two fullbacks, Duncan Ferguson standing like the Eiffel Tower, alone as Greta Garbo upfront. He played out of his jersey, hit a post, grazed the bar, brought heroics from Tim Flowers. He needs a striking partner – quickly – Bakayoko, Babayaro, Yoko Ono – somebody who can read his aerial power and not inconsiderable skill on the floor. Two goals in nine games for Ferguson is a poor return. John Collins is worthy of sympathy: a class player, an instigator of the creative, incisive, defence-splitting pass, a superb one – two player, a top act. Today he was like a geriatric lady caught in a revolving door, no room to breathe, no escape from the claustrophobia. Blackburn proceed next week to Lyons in their quest for glory. Walter Smith needs a striker or, as Falstaff would say, 'I'll tickle your catastrophe!'

Everton: Thomas Myhre, Alex Cleland, Michael Ball, Dave Watson, David Unsworth, John Collins, Nick Barmby, Duncan Ferguson, Don Hutchison, Craig Short, Marco Materazzi. Substitutes: Paul Gerrard, Gareth Farrelly, John Oster, Tony Thomas, Danny Cadamarteri.

Blackburn Rovers: Tim Flowers, Jeff Kenna, Callum Davison, Tim Sherwood, Darren Peacock, Stephane Henchoz, Garry Flitcroft, Jason Wilcox, Martin

Dahlin, Damien Duff, Christian Dailly. Substitutes: Billy McKinlay, John Filan, David Dunn, Gary Croft, Sebastian Perez.

LEEDS UNITED 0 – LEICESTER FOSSE 1
The FA Carling Premiership, 3 October 1998

The inspirations of today are the shams of tomorrow – the purpose has departed. The inspiration, George Graham, has departed for Tottenham Hotspur. He decamped under a cloud of financial skulduggery, tainted by a desire for personal fortune and the glitz of the West End.

Armani-suited George was a City boyo: years in the marble halls of Highbury gave him the taste for caviar. Denby Dale pie and chips, the lethargy of Leeds were inadequate. It has left David O'Leary in a quandary. He wears about him a puzzled expression of a simple Irishman cast in a role of sophisticated team manager. Before the match I tested the waters with malice aforethought. Peter Risdale, the Leeds chairman, wanted Martin O'Neill as manager. Armed with this I interviewed Mr O'Leary. Did he want to follow Mr Graham? Not sure. Would he like to manage Leeds? Not sure.

I offer him the job on a whacking salary, intimating that the vast majority of Leeds' cynical fans want him. He is taken aback. Eloquently, he tells me of his wife, his family, the family home outside Harrogate. Of the children settled at good schools. The warmth of the Yorkshire welcome. And of the young players at the Academy, their talent and team spirit. I ask him bluntly: 'Do you want the job?'

'I'll have to ask my wife,' he replies in that soft Irish brogue. A great Arsenal centre half, now an ambivalent Irishman. I warm to him. He is a nice man of some character. I hold ambition of so airy and light quality that it is but a shadow's shadow. But there is a hidden agenda; a plot of Machiavellian intrigue and diplomacy, a little light dancing – a tangled web of sophistry I will unfold later.

Inspiration George gone, team purpose departed. O'Leary came second on the day to O'Neill. If Martin O'Neill had prepared this match as the gold seal on his CV, then it went to plan. From the start Fosse held tactical sway. Ullathorne played sweeper. Elliot and Taggart gargantuan in the Fosse defence.

Midfield, Izzet's spindly legs ran a marathon. Savage was his usual ferocious savage self, snuffing out Lee Bowyer. Lennon and the Greek Zagorakis supplied the craft, sleight of hand, width and speed to outmanoeuvre a tepid, flaccid Leeds side. Lee Sharpe on Leeds' left found it barren. Hasselbaink is talented, but what a whinger. Like a shopper caught in a swinging door he could only spectate as Leicester buzzed around him, starving him of the ball, cutting off supply lines, clattering him to earth like Prometheus. Leeds were hairy-legged, but on the riposte Lee Sharpe sped down the left, crossed, Wijnhard botched the shot. He repeated the error minutes later. Wijnhard's days here are limited. Hasselbaink, the groaner, showed his displeasure at Wijnhard. His confidence collapsed. Sharpe was withdrawn from the left to bolster midfield. Fosse had the muse, the flow, the rhythm. Heskey ran like a gazelle down the right, a gazelle with gorilla muscles. Frightening sight for defender, Heskey at speed. A low cross and like a striking viper Tony Cottee struck – a typical TC goal. O'Leary in desperation threw on the neophytes Granville, Woodgate, McPhail. Youngsters wet behind the ears – this is O'Leary's Rubicon. O'Neill performs a war dance. O'Leary's gamble failed. *Now the denouement.* I persuade Mr O'Neill, despite protestations, to grant an interview. We talk about the game, the tactics, the goal. We dance around the topic of the manager's job. He backs off – it's *sub judice*, cannot comment, off limits, contractual strangulation. Suddenly I say: 'I offer you the Leeds manager's post, salary £1 million a year'.

'Yes, taken'. He says. *Fait accompli.* What transpired the following week is something I cannot disclose. It is Official Secrets Act. O'Leary is the manager. He will clear out the stables and bring in youth. He will challenge for honours and within two seasons bring silver to the Leeds table. He will stay at Yelland Road for life. All in football wish him well. Mr O'Neill negotiated a whopping salary increase from a Fosse board of directors who lack direction. No man's fortune can be an end worthy of his being. Martin, you have missed it. But my runes say: 'You shall go to the ball. You shall have the golden slipper. You shall have the Manchester United job come the year 2001.' An Odyssey! An intelligent man judges the present by the past.

Leeds United: Nigel Martyn, Alf-Inge Haaland, David Wetherall, Lee Sharpe, Clyde Wijnhard, Jimmy Floyd Hasselbaink, Lee Bowyer, Gunnar Halle, Ian Harte, Martin Hidden, Robert Molenaar. Substitutes: Danny Granville, Harry Kewell, Jonathon Woodgate, Paul Robinson, Stephen McPhail.

Leicester Fosse: Kasey Kellar, Gerry Taggart, Mustafa Izzet, Neil Lennon, Emile Heskey, Steve Guppy, Rob Savage, Matt Elliot, Rob Ullathorne, Tony Cottee, Theo Zagorakis. Substitutes: Garry Parker, Pontus Kaamark, Stuart Campbell, Graham Fenton, Pegguy Arphexad.

DERBY COUNTY 1 – MANCHESTER UNITED 1

The FA Carling Premiership, 24 October 1998

I remember an epic between these two way back. Boxing Day 1970. A snow-covered pitch at the ancient ramshackle Baseball Ground. Days of Dave Mackay, that barrel-chested perfection of a wing half. Worth today £40 million. And O'Hare, Gemmill, Hennessey, Roy McFarland, Alan Durban and Hector. Durban epitomised style; so cultured he could dine off the Queen's golden platters. United of Crerand, Best, Charlton, Kidd, Law and Morgan. Derby that day took a two-goal lead, lost it, regained it, lost it again, and the match finished four–four.

Would today's match compare? Are today's players' similar class? Certainly Derby are up for it. Accused of playing 'fancy dan' football, they dropped Carbonari and Baiano; Burton and Stimac came in. Forget style, get real! Style is merely the silhouette of thought. Thought made manifest is Sturridge running like a wounded panther at United's defence, Wanchope baffling United, the spectators and himself, casting spells bewitching all with marionette skills. At the back Stimac repelled the marauders, a rock on which Cole and Yorke foundered. Giggs was anonymous. Beckham, suntanned, wind-blown, honeymooners at last alone, had a touch of Marbellitis. Capacity 31,000 adored it. The rain fell steadily. Derby creaming passes as the pitch quickened. All so different from the clinging mud and the quicksand of the old Baseball Ground of yore. Seventy-five minutes. Wanchope wizardry – he juggles with the ball; like moths drawn to a candle flame United's defence stood motionless. On the blind side Dean Burton slipped into the box, a lightning shot – Schmeichel rooted to the spot. It was audacious, arrogant, an arpeggio of the beautiful game.

The sun burst through and lit up the blasted heath. In the distance I heard the mellow chimes of Repton school. *'Deus nobiscum,'* sang the pink-cheeked choir. Alex Ferguson is not a man for the public school, heavenly choirs, sentiment and culture. His background is the shipyard, the noise of rivets drowning the matins. His scholarship was honed sharpening his elbows, hardening his pate, putting himself about a bit at Rangers. Building a bulldog squad in the Granite City of Aberdeen fit to break the Glasgow monopoly. Mr Ferguson was riled. Ten minutes before time he poleaxed Jim Smith, the Derby factotum. Bald Eagle Smith is tough. A Yorkist bludgeoned by many clubs only to give rise again – another patch, another world: he really is an ascending Atlantis. Off came Butt, Giggs and Gary Neville, three internationals, replaced by Scholes, Blomquist and Cruyff, three more internationals. All the substitutes came on together. I have never witnessed this before; neither had Bald Eagle; more importantly neither had the Derby players. They became chickens with the fox in the roost. Confidence eroded, shape collapsed, panic rife. A masterstroke by Ferguson, it brought a near stroke to Jim. Instructions rattled from the dugout like peas on a drum. United were afire. Cruyff was the ace ghosting into space, the ball delivered to the heart of Derby's box, seconds of pinball panic – Cruyff scored. One apiece, with one minute to play. The Alamo, rough and tumble, ooohs and aaahs, United went for the jugular – bells and bugle stuff. Derby survived – just. Mr Ferguson smiled briefly. Mr Smith, dressed by Oxfam, departed happy. Well – did it compare with 1970? Erumph, yes it did, but I still think Mackay is worth £40 million!

Derby County: Russell Hoult, Stefan Schnoor, Darryl Powell, Igor Stimac, Dean Sturridge, Paulo Wanchope, Rory Delap, Jacob Laursen, Spencer Prior, Lee Carsley, Dean Burton. Substitutes: Mart Poom, Tony Dorigo, Horacio Carbonari, Steve Elliot, Francesco Baiano.

Manchester United: Peter Schmeichel, Gary Neville, Jaap Stam, David Beckham, Nicky Butt, Andy Cole, Ryan Giggs, Phil Neville, Roy Keane, Dwight Yorke, Wesley Brown. Substitutes: Jordi Cruyff, Jesper Blomquist, Raimond Van Der Gouw, Paul Scholes, Henning Berg.

OLDHAM ATHLETIC 0 – MANCHESTER CITY 3
Nationwide Football League, Division Two, 7 November 1998

Four years ago this was a Premiership fixture. But to quote 'Andy Cole Porter': 'When the Premiership congeals, it soon reveals the faint aroma of performing seals.' The aroma is the stench of failure. That City of an illustrious history should be jousting in the basement of Division Two. Losing to such teams as Notts County, Blackpool, Macclesfield Town, Wigan Athletic and Bournemouth: scrambling to escape lying sixth, praying for a play-off place. Another season in this whelk stall means financial ruin. For City today means the seal of approval. For Oldham it is the Dead Sea Scrolls. One point from their last seven games. Lying third from bottom, two points ahead of Lincoln and Wycombe Wanderers. November in Oldham is like Vladivostok in January. It is bitter – at Boundary Park.

Oldham began at a fast lick. John Sheridan is a composed, articulate artist. He loves the ball, caresses it, harbours it, parts with it reluctantly – but always creatively. He is now in the late summer, the brains hyperactive, the legs will not obey the summons. City asserted themselves, marshalled by the blond Dutchman Wiekens and the strapping Morrison. Morrison is a bruiser. Cast off by Huddersfield as a problem boy needing counselling, he now counsels his pals. Clouts them, cajoles them, castigates them. This heavyweight is a real find. His attitude today was: 'If this is what you want I'll stuff it up 'em.' He has a modicum of skill too. If City make it to the premiership, Morrison will make his mark physically and mentally!

Enter then Kevin Horlock, flat-footed but deceptively slow. He has a football brain but oh, those feet! But he can intuitively sniff out the main chance. When on 16 minutes, Edghill's cross flew across the Oldham box like one flew over a cuckoo's nest 'twas Horlock who put the boot in – a simple, tap-in, far post.

On the half-hour 'twas Horlock again. A storming free kick hustled into the Oldham net. Two–nil. A warlock, Horlock, seismic shock double. He celebrated long – like a winning presidential candidate. Mr Tiffin, the assistant referee, waved his yellow flag. For an infringement or merely time for tiffin. The result – a yellow card for the Warlock. He kicked the ball straight over the stand in disgust. City's 4,188 fans in the 10,000 strong audience chanted nonstop; a blinkered faithful or inspired troupe. Seventy minutes Andy Morrison, this Chopper Harris lookalike, thumped a 30-yard half-volley. Match won. Joe Royle's triumphant return to his old stomping ground.

At last City have the pulse of this league and will depart it 'ere long. Not as champions. I am sure that Fulham have the players and resources. City have the will and the fantastic support. Oldham, I am afraid, will be departing and may never meet City again.

Oldham Athletic: Gary Kelly, Nicky Spooner, Ian McLean, Shaun Garnett, Stuart Thom, Lee Duxbury, John McGinlay, Andrew Holt, Paul Rickers, Steve Whitehall, John Sheridan. Substitutes: Adrian Littlejohn, Mark Allot, David McNiven.

Manchester City: Nicky Weaver, Richard Edghill, Tony Vaughn, Andy Morrison, Gerrard Wiekens, Lee Crooks, Ian Bishop, Gary Mason, Shaun Goater, Michael Branch, Kevin Horlock. Substitutes: Paul Dickov, Michael Brown, Danny Allot.

LIVERPOOL 1 – LEEDS UNITED 3
The FA Carling Premiership, 14 November 1998
Mon Dieu, coup d'état complet. Roy Evans, Evans the coach, part of the furniture and fittings at Anfield, has departed. The umbilical cord linking Evans to the balmy days of Shankly severed. The family at Anfield dismembered. Gerard Houllier, the Anglophile Frenchman, is in sole charge. The bespectacled schoolmaster who once stood on the Kop has, like Alexander the Great, performed the impossible, with a mighty sweep of his sword cut the Gordian knot of Greek mythology in twain. Some of us, sentimental old fools are we, rue the passing of this great empire where the Crown was passed down to loyal members of the family. Shankly, Paisley, Fagan, Ronnie Moran, Kenny Dalglish, Graeme Souness, Roy Evans. All those apostles, disciples, worshippers at the Colosseum became a Clochemerle. Will Liverpool resound to cries in foreign languages? Can foreigners blend into a strident, determined fighting force, each man playing for the others: the Corinthian spirit?

Monsieur Houllier's reign began with a crisis, a farce of Jacques Tati proportions. A three–one defeat from deep rivals Leeds. David O'Leary has been manager at Leeds for six weeks. It must seem like six years. O'Leary has blossomed, replaced established players with pink-cheeked youngsters, been fearless, almost ruthless in management. It was crystallised today. For 65 minutes the match was goalless. Then Nigel Martyn, the Leeds keeper, almost decapitated Riedle – penalty. Robbie Fowler smashed the ball past Martyn. One–nil. The Kop, in a vacuum of dismay, sympathy and sorrow for Evans, burst into song, chant and highly-charged encouragement. Mr O'Leary took off Wijnhard the Dutchman and bunged 18-year-old Alan Smith into this heaving, plunging, sweating, bruising confrontation. Smith is a Yorkist; he relishes the physical even though he is slightly built. Within minutes he had scored, calmly picking up a rebound off James, the Liverpool keeper from Hopkin's fierce drive. One–one. Time now for Jimmy Floyd Hasselbaink to strut his stuff. Hitherto, he had spent the afternoon practising Wagnerian drama, a soul tormented by rough seas and tempest – the 'Non-Flying Dutchman'. One minute after Smith's goal (eighty-one to be precise on the clock) Hasselbaink transfixed the immobile Liverpool defence like a stoat on a rabbit, a gleeful shot. Two–one to Leeds. Four minutes later he was one to one on Staunton: no contest, Hasselbaink is lightning-fast, possessed of a beautiful athletic grace, round Staunton rooted to the spot where Jimmy had been – thumping shot, three–one, game over.

Liverpool did protest at rough play before those goals – Mr Gallagher the referee unmoved. Liverpool exposed by weakness at the back. Staunton, Carragher, Heggem and Bjornebye unable to deal with high crosses, fallible to fast-moving attackers getting goal-side of them. James is goal-wary of coming off his line: he needs a commanding heading machine at centre half. Paul Ince no longer has the strength and pace to disturb quality midfielders; Bowyer reduced him to chasing shadows. Leeds will only improve as O'Leary builds team spirit, culls old-timers and inveigles new young players to join the crusade. Liverpool face a massive rebuild under Houllier. '*Malheur ne vient jamais seul*' (misfortunes never come singly).

Liverpool: David James, Steve Staunton, Robbie Fowler, Jamie Redknapp, Karl Heinz Riedle, Vegard Heggem, Patrick Berger, Paul Ince, Stig Inge Bjornebye, Jamie Carragher, David Thomson. Substitutes: Brad Friedel, Bjorn Tore Kvarme, Phillip Babb, Oyvind Leonhardsen, Danny Murphy.

Leeds United: Nigel Martyn, Clive Wyjnhard, Jimmy Floyd Hasselbaink, Ian Bowyer, David Hopkin, Gunnar Halle, Harry Kewell, Ian Harte, Martin Hiden, Jonathon Woodgate, Robert Molenaar. Substitutes: Alf-Inge Haaland, David Wetherall, 'Vimto' Ribeiro, Paul Robinson, Alan Smith.

EVERTON 0 – CHELSEA 0

The FA Carling Premiership, 5 December 1998

The sun beamed down from a clear sky at the School of Science. The azure blue crisscrossed with jumbo vapour trails to Elysian Fields. ''Tis the bright day that brings forth the adder – and that craves wary walking.' Dennis Wise walks warily on a tightrope in perpetua. He lasted 35 minutes, two yellow cards, a red, and then off! Chelsea, by then already knocked off their elegant stride, looked ready for fleecing. Alas, 13 minutes from time, Dunne of Everton was dismissed, and in those final minutes Chelsea found strength, determination and their Bolshoi Ballet style. Flo, as is his wont, missed three chances to win it. Matteo hit the bar. Had Chelsea triumphed it would have been a travesty.

Everton's football was a revelation. So much of this season's home matches have seen them struggle as if anchored in quicksand, real talent sinking under a weight of doubt. This was from the School of Science textbook. Collins was at his productive best – magnificent in midfield. Grant and Hutchison, the support players to Collins's lead violin, were *allegro in tempo*, the savage passages played with fire and passion. If this were the *1812 Overture* – Cadamarteri clashed the cymbals; Bakayoko the brass section, which he played like a whirling dervish with the witch-doctor's spell cast on him. Duncan Ferguson has departed for Newcastle to joust with hot head and elbows – will he open a charm school? The aerial route has gone with him; today was two feet; pure class and entertaining. Everton still lack a goal poacher, a natural goal scorer to sniff out the opportunities, capitalize on quality build-up. When Chelsea staged their competitive finale, it was Walter Smith in torment. Thirty-six thousand are puzzled; if Everton can raise their game to their heights against class opposition, why can they not devour the artisan teams? Let's rejoice; today is ephemeral but it is worth a smile.

Everton: Thomas Myhre, Alex Cleland, Michael Ball, John Collins, Don

Hutchison, Craig Short, Tony Grant, Marco Materazzi, Ibrahima Bakayoko, Richard Dunne, Danny Cadamarteri. Substitutes: Olivier Dacourt, Michael Branch, Mitch Ward, Slaven Bilic, Steve Simonsen.

Chelsea: Ed De Goey, Dan Petrescu, Celestine Babayaro, Frank Le Boeuf, Marcus Desailly, Gustavo Poyet, Dennis Wise, Roberto Di Matteo, Albert Ferrer, Tore Andre Flo, Gianfranco Zola. Substitutes: Bjarne Goldbaek, Michael Duberry, Kevin Hitchcock, Mark Nicholls, Jody Morris.

DERBY COUNTY 2 – CHELSEA 2
The FA Carling Premiership, 12 December 1998
'Night's candles are burnt out and russet dawn stands tiptoe on the sleepy mountain tops.' The russet dawn is the championship, Chelsea are tiptoe as genuine contenders. Aston Villa lead with 30 points, Manchester United have 29, Chelsea 28. Chelsea are here on the back of an injury-time victory over Villa last Wednesday. Flo scoring the winner. Today the Rams gave them a physical and mental workover. Chelsea are resilient. Critics accuse them of brittleness under pressure, loss of focus in white-heat combat, and smug superiority against inferior teams. Self-belief is paramount, but to lose to inferior forces as Chelsea do is simply waste. Mr Vialli is hairless as a result!

Before kick-off Chelsea players formed a magic circle and bonded. It was a trifle namby-pamby and frightfully Knightsbridge but it laundered them into Shaftesbury Avenue, a scenario of elegant, pacy, controlled football as Derby defended too deep. A Derby goal rocked them out of kilter. Twenty-seven minutes, Carbonari, the Argentinian, smote a low free kick from twenty-five yards. The ball took deflections like a pinball machine and ricocheted past De Goey. De Goey was slow to get down, not surprising as he is 10 feet tall. But De Goey is the weak link in this multinational galaxy. Great sides have great keepers. Schmeichel is worth 15 points a season to Manchester United. Seaman likewise. Martyn is essential to Leeds. Tim Flowers is available – sign him, Luca!

County finished the first half on the rampage. Then two goals turned the match on its head. Fifty-three minutes Jody Morris, the tiny tot in midfield, Chelsea's star player and he is English – *mon Dieu!* – quick feet, quick brain, chipped over the Derby defence. Flo chested down and with another exquisite chip beat the flailing Poom, the Derby keeper, for a potent goal.

Four minutes later Gustavo Poyet, head down, blasted a blazing right footer – a goal from the second the ball left his foot. Poom gasping air like a stranded flounder. Chips are down. Derby gunning for equality. Jim Smith played three jokers in the final minutes. Schnoor, Sturridge, Harper. Dean Sturridge has Ben Johnson pace, unlike Wanchope, who has the pace of Dr Johnson's dog. Sturridge is not favoured by the 'Bald Eagle'. Rumour hath it that Sturridge cannot 'hold up' the ball, and he is not a tactical little grey cells player, but he is a flier; he covers the ground like a centipede on speed. So, at speed, Sturridge arrives in the Chelsea box, a mêlée ensues – Sturridge scrambles the equalizer. Just end to a cracking match. Chelsea on tiptoe. They will lose Wise through suspension for Christmas. What is new?

Che cosa significa questo por Chelsea? Primo, secondo or terzo? (What does this mean for Chelsea. First, second or third?)

Derby County: Mart Poom, Horacio Carbonari, Darryl Powell, Tony Dorigo, Paulo Wanchope, Rory Delap, Lars Bohinen, Jacob Laursen, Spencer Prior, Stefano Eranio, Francesco Baiano. Substitutes: Russell Hoult, Stefan Schnoor, Dean Sturridge, Kevin Harper, Steve Elliot.

Chelsea: Ed De Goey, Frank Le Boeuf, Bjarne Goldaek, Gustavo Poyet, Dennis Wise, Michael Duberry, Graeme Le Saux, Tore Andre Flo, Bernard Lambourde, Gianfranco Zola, Jody Morris. Substitutes: Dan Petrescu, Celestine Babayaro, Kevin Hitchcock, Roberto Di Matteo, Mark Nichols.

EVERTON 0 – DERBY COUNTY 0
The FA Carling Premiership, 26 December 1998
Encore égalité, mes amis.

I know a bank whereon the wild thyme blows,
Where oxlips and the nodding violet grows;
Quite over-canopied with luscious woodbine,
With sweet musk-roses, and with eglantine.

My pastoral thought during a first half which numbed the mind. I lit a luscious Woodbine in a wind as stiff as Peter Mandelson's upper lip. Litter fluttered as if the School of Science was a giant dustbin. We consign this match to that giant dustbin. Derby put five in midfield, retreated at the first hint of danger and compressed the match into the channels. I have never seen a match so boa-constricted as this. Derby had one shot, a Carbonari free kick, the rebound missed by Powell. If the first half lacked pattern, rhythm, style, class or any semblance of football, the second was even worse. Everton cannot score. Three goals at Goodison this season. Seven matches scoreless. Expensive players, huge overdraft. Upfront, Bakayoko and Cadamarteri must feel like inmates at Alcatraz, in isolation, a huge gap 'twixt them and their midfield. Bakayoko is a disastrous expensive buy, another Amokachi. Put him in the veldt among the African Karoo, give him the ball and let him demonstrate his solo pyrotechnics – for fun. He is not a team player and has little tactical awareness. Plus Everton do not possess wide players to unlock massed defences. It was all tumbling bodies, schoolboy howlers, aerial ball borne on the wild wind. The Everton parts – Collins, Dacourt, Barmby, Hutchison look excellent; the sum is bitterly disappointing. Thirty-nine thousand file away deep in pastoral thought. This is the worst match I have ever seen. Farewell from windswept Goodison. I shall seek not the wherefore, race of human mind. I wonder what Sharon Stone's doing tonight?

Everton: Thomas Myhre, Michael Ball, Olivier Dacourt, Dave Unsworth, John Collins, Don Hutchison, Marco Materazzi, Ibrahima Bakayoko, Richard Dunne, Slaven Bilic, Danny Cadamarteri. Substitutes: Steve Simsonsen, Nick Barmby, Craig Short, Tony Grant, Michael Branch.

Derby County: Mart Poom, Horacio Carbonari, Darryl Powell, Paulo Wanchope, Rory Delap, Jacob Laursen, Spencer Prior, Lee Carsley, Steve Elliot, Stefano Eranio, Robert Kozluk. Substitutes: Russell Hoult, Dean Sturridge, Kevin Harper, Mark Bridge-Wilkinson, Jonathan Hunt.

MANCHESTER CITY 2 – STOKE CITY 1
Nationwide Football League, Division Two, 28 December 1998
A Tale of Two Cities, the swish of the guillotine, the roll of the tumbrels and Brian Little of Stoke loses his head – not literally, but now three defeats in a row suggest that Joe Royle has done a far, far better thing.

In truth this was a cracking match. The Theatre of Base Comedy crammed with 31,000 faithful. The sun beamed down. Manchester needed the win. Off the blocks rapido, Stoke defending deep. But 33 minutes, Sugurdsson headed Stoke into the lead. The sun disappeared; no justice for Manchester – muscle is the reality. Neat football, sincere commitment and one down. Crowd deflated, pensive and stilled. Out of the blue, 50 minutes, Stoke hashed a clearance, Dickov tapped in the equalizer. Crowd alight, Wembley atmosphere. Stoke's poise at the back evaporating. Discipline disappearing. Five yellow cards flourished.

Just before time, here come the cavalry, yet another Manchester attack down the left. Cross far post. Gareth Taylor headed in. Crowd rejoiced, such ecstasy at a Second Division match. No matter. At the Theatre of Base Comedy the faith has returned.

Manchester City: Nicky Weaver, Richard Edghill, Lee Crooks, Andy Morrison, Gerard Wiekens, Gary Mason, Michael Brown, Jamie Pollock, Shaun Goater, Gareth Taylor, Craig Russell. Substitutes: Danny Tiatto, Danny Allsopp, Paul Dickov.

Stoke City: Carl Muggleton, Chris Short, Bryan Small, Larus Sugurdsson, Phil Robinson, Stephen Woods, Kevin Keen, Richard Forsyth, Simon Sturridge, Kyle Lightbourne, David Oldfield. Substitutes: Dean Crowe, Ray Wallace, Ben Petty.

EVERTON 0 – LEICESTER FOSSE 0
The FA Carling Premiership, 9 January 1999
Encore égalité, nul–nul. Yes, I am at the School of Science again. This is masochism. I have been immunized against football. I have taken the pill and become, as they say in Lancashire, 'happy daft'. I intone:

> *If you your lips would keep from slips*
> *Five things observe with care:*
> *To whom you speak, of whom you speak,*
> *And how, and when, and where.*

Another 33,000 feel affinity with me. Throughout this tedious, ordinary match they were silent onlookers, Micawbers – hoping, praying, pleading for something to 'turn up'. Everton played five at the back; Watson, Dunne and Unsworth, three centre halves, the destroyers; Ball and Cleland the frigates.

Four in midfield, Bakayoko yet again in isolation up front. His contribution was so inept he would have been just as effective contemplating his navel in his Ivory Coast village. Everton were constructive but pedestrian and pre-dictable. Keller warmed his palms twice. Myhre saved a couple of Fosse shots brilliantly. Leicester Fosse are the complete enigma. They have an abundance of talent. Lennon and Izzet a couple of angry hornets, Elliot and Walsh in shape and gesture proudly eminent. Fosse play mind games better when Savage, a mobile time bomb, and Zagorakis, a crafty, devious Greek, join Lennon and Izzet in a combative midfield. Today Savage was missing. Zagorakis stayed on the bench. Fosse went through the motions; if they had clapped on pace, pushed up, accelerated a gear Everton could have suffered. Whoa – Elliot with a free kick on the stroke of time brought a fantastic save from Myhre. Why not earlier? Now, dear listener, I have spectated here, on your behalf, 550 minutes of football without a goal. My lips are sealed. I am suffering night starvation and seek a rapid cure.

Everton: Thomas Myhre, Alex Cleland, Michael Ball, Olivier Dacourt, David Watson, Dave Unsworth, Don Hutchison, John Oster, Ibrahima Bakayoko, Richard Dunne, Danny Cadamarteri. Substitutes: Steve Simonson, Nick Barmby, Tony Grant, Michael Branch, Mitch Ward.

Leicester Fosse: Kasey Keller, Frank Sinclair, Robert Ullathorpe, Matthew Elliot, Steve Walsh, Mustafa Izzet, Neil Lennon, Andrew Impey, Steve Guppy, Tony Cottee, Emile Heskey. Substitutes: Pegguy Arphexad, Gerry Taggart, Stuart Campbell, Theo Zagorakis, Ian Marshall.

EVERTON 1 – WIMBLEDON 1
The FA Carling Premiership, 27 February 1999

The only way to render old age vigorous is to prolong the youth of the mind. This adage sprang instantly to mind as Dave Watson, the Everton captain, committed a huge blunder to gift Wimbledon a goal after a mere 14 minutes. A mischievous, blustery wind came off the Irish Sea and swirled around the School of Science. Watson, the last man, looked up to the leaden sky, was mortified to see the ball looping over his head weaving like a kite in a Skegness gale. Ekoku, son of tribal chief, stabbed the ball past Myhre, the hapless Everton keeper, as if hurling a spear. If you had speared Watson's entrails, he could not have been more hurt. A lethal blow which caused 32,000 scholars to beat their breasts, wail in sorrow and eat their children. Two hundred Wimbledon supporters uttering vile imprecations, celebrated with a war dance. Everton's resources are stretched thin. Despite a huge playing staff, Oster, Cadamarteri and Jeffers are young boys learning the trade. Relegation battles are quicksands where talent is sucked in and suffocated. They played to feet, ideas present, execution abysmal. Sullivan, in Wimbledon's goal, had match practice picking cherries from trees. Everton's shooting was fey. Apace, Wimbledon were their usual pragmatic selves putting it about a bit, roughing up the neophytes. Robbie Earle was perfection box to box. If only he had played for a fashionable club, he would have masterminded an England team. Michael Hughes was a crackerjack. Everton fans lost patience; they have had it stretched for many seasons. Then Jeffers restored the faith. A magnificent far post header from Cadamarteri's cross. Excitement aplenty in the closing minutes. Unsworth, the barrel-chested central defender, discovering hitherto unknown midfield skills, like a young bullock after the heifer. It availed not. One apiece. Not good enough, cried the faithful. The relegation dogfight is on again.

Everton: Thomas Myhre, Michael Ball, Olivier Dacourt, Dave Watson, Dave Unsworth, Nick Barmby, Marco Materazzi, David Weir, John Oster, Danny Cadamarteri, Francis Jeffers. Substitutes: Steve Simonsen, Craig Short, Michael Branch, Phil Jevons, John O'Kane.

Wimbledon: Neil Sullivan, Kenny Cunningham, Chris Perry, Dean Blackwell, Ben Thatcher, Robbie Earle, Efan Ekoku, Andy Roberts, Marcus Gayle, Michael Hughes, Jason Euell. Substitutes: Alan Kimble, Neal Ardley, Paul Heald, Mark Kennedy, Carl Court.

DERBY COUNTY 3 – LIVERPOOL 2
The FA Carling Premiership, 13 March 1999

What a glorious, exciting, storming match, a panoply of the beautiful English game. Worth a panegyric, certainly a paean of praise. Derby's football in rhapsodic first half was a revelation: cultured, fluent, inspired. A tapestry woven by international artists. Baiano, Eranio, Bohinen and Wanchope in wondrous form – one touch, deft, elegant and pure. Eleven minutes Liverpool's glass-jawed defence laid low with a Dean Burton header. There will be a public enquiry on this one: how could Burton, all five feet seven inches, out-head the beanpoles of Liverpool?

A record audience of 33,000 leaned forward like a string section under Bernstein's baton. Thirty-five minutes Owen ran at the Derby defence in his usual tearaway style – his little legs a blur. Prior fouled him. Fowler tucked away the resultant penalty. Justice made manifest on 43 minutes; Stimac's free kick – Wanchope, a whirling millipede of elbows and stringy legs, headed in. Half-time, two–one. Owen did not appear for the second half. Riedle replaced him. Four minutes into the half 'twas Paulo again. Liverpool's defence square and toothless, Paulo ran at it like a gunrunner pursued by the Peelers. What a gait this man has: like a broken-kneed cab horse over the Aintree jumps. A marionette hop, skip and jump and a joyous thumping shot that James in Liverpool's goal could only admire as it passed his hair. Three–one to Derby and then, to Jim Smith's apoplectic consternation, Derby go on cruise control. Jim's Yorkshire patois was eclipsed by Phil Thompson. He verbally abused his charges in pure Toxteth. That, plus his protruding proboscis, inflamed Liverpool. On the hour, Fowler scored his second from Matteo's low cross. The match became a rampage, a Cup tie, the thunder of cavalry, the stench of cordite, the blast of the blunderbuss. What a super match. I must hie me to a dark corner.

Derby County: Russell Holt, Stefan Schnoor, Darryl Powell, Igor Stimac, Paulo Wanchope, Lars Bohinen, Jacob Laursen, Spencer Prior, Stefano Eranio, Dean Burton, Francesco Baiano. Substitutes: Mart Poom, Horacio Carbonari, Kevin Harper, Malcolm Christie, Vass Borbokis.

Liverpool: David James, Rigobert Song, Steve Staunton, Phil Babb, Robbie Fowler, Michael Owen, Jamie Redknapp, Vegard Heggem, Patrick Berger, Dominic Matteo, Steve Gerrard. Substitutes: Bjorn Tore Kvarme, Oyvind Leonhardsen, Karlheinz Riedle, Brad Friedel, Stig Inge Bjornebye.

BLACKBURN ROVERS 3 – WIMBLEDON 1

The FA Carling Premiership, 20 March 1999

If this Rovers team is a scratch one, then Brian Kidd is an alchemist – base metal into gold. No – maybe gold-plated. As my dear dad used to say when he inserted a teaspoon of California syrup of figs in my child's mouth: 'This is not a silver spoon, Kiddywinky – it is EPNS.' As I protested at this evil-smelling potion, he gave the upstairs maid a playful slap and gave the dictum: 'Open bowels lead to open mind'.

I have an open mind on Brian Kidd. Blackburn are third from bottom. Forest are doomed. Southampton have 26 points. Blackburn 27, Charlton 28. Perm three from four. Blackburn's form is stamped 'relegation'. Seven games without a win. A dressing-room like some scene from *Mash*. But Mr Kidd himself has brought super-league ideas and concepts from Manchester United to a provincial club. Like forcing your grandma into a basque and joining the Spice Girls. Players, no matter what quality or experience, like to be reassured that they are first teamers. They bond as a team, think as a team, respect each other, live and die for each other. At Blackburn it is apparent that some individuals are not in the team ethic. Mr Kidd needs help – quickly. Today is resolution day. Wimbledon in the comfort zone lying eighth. They have achieved their yearly objective – survival.

Blackburn's 21,000 fans, realising that Doomsday was nigh, vocalised. It gingered the team. They scintillated in the first half of concise, tight bright football of some quality. Matt Jansen was inspirational. Twinkling-quick feet on the left, low cross Ashley Ward tapped in, time eight minutes. Ten minutes later Sutton won the ball in the air, a little fracas on the goal line, Thatcher and Kimble dwelt, cursed each other – Jansen nipped in to score, or was it Kimble own goal? Twenty-five minutes Ashley Ward's shot parried by Sullivan, Jansen crashed on the rebound. Three–nil. Ewood in bemused shock. The last time the fans had witnessed three goals was last autumn against West Ham. Wimbledon had been mugged. Joe Kinnear will suffer a fit of vapours at this inept Wimbledon performance. They attempted football to feet elevated above their class. Whatever happened to blood and thunder, highball at the gallop, ball in the box pronto? It was like watching Vanessa Feltz in a tutu, lap-dancing. John Hartson came off preserved in aspic, sweatless. Ekoku, off-spring of a Nigerian chieftain, replaced Hartson, assegai at the slope. At last, the old Wimbledon we know and unlove. Kimble's lofted cross to the area of trepidation, Jason Euell contorting to a classic goal. Blackburn declared. Wimbledon huffed, puffed, blew strong and finally expired. The ides of March torment Mr Kidd. His mentor, the soothsayer 'Alex of Govan', has already expressed doubts on his sibling's ability as coach and man manager. This really is the Black Spot. I ask Mr Kidd for clarification. He declines with some grace. 'Search for a Star,' he intones. Unable to find one I accost Ashley Ward. Ward is a dashingly handsome young blade. Tall in the saddle, a black mane like Samson, a Hollywood buck. I ask him innocently if, yclept as he is, Ashley, would he play Ashley in the remake of *Gone with the Wind*, which I plan to direct in my spare time. Victoria Adams as Scarlett O'Hara, David Beckham as Rhett Butler. It is a silent movie shot in Moss Side. Alas, the fee could not compare to his salary at Ewood. I ask, in all innocence, have Blackburn's survival chances gone with the wind? He smiles enigmatically: 'Better ask Mr Kidd.'

I summon my chauffeur. 'Home, James, and don't spare the horses. See you in the Nationwide, Ashley.' Exit – pursued by a glare.

Blackburn Rovers: John Filan, Callum Davidson, Darren Peacock, Stephane Henchoz, Chris Sutton, Jason Wilcox, Dario Marcolin, Damien Johnson, Ashley Ward, Matt Jansen, Jason McAteer. Substitutes: Kevin Davies, Damien Duff, Martin Taylor, Keith Gillespie, Alan Fettis.

Wimbledon: Neil Sullivan, Kenny Cunningham, Alan Kimble, Dean Blackwell, Ben Thatcher, Robbie Earle, Marcus Gayle, Neal Ardley, Michael Hughes, Jason Euell, John Hartson. Substitutes: Ceri Hughes, Efan Ekoku, Andy Roberts, Mark Kennedy, Paul Heald.

SHEFFIELD WEDNESDAY 1 – COVENTRY CITY 2

The FA Carling Premiership, 3 April 1999

'For lo the winter is past, the rain is over and gone, the flowers appear on the earth, the time of the singing birds is come, and the voice of the turtle is heard in our land.' The voice is not the turtle; it is *relegation*. This match did not have the taint of the drop – it had the stench.

Hussle, tussle, scuffle, crunching ruffle. Tackles were biffo, nil artistry, just stifling rough and tumble. Like the Eton wall game, the ball was incidental. Wednesday were stunned on 18 minutes. Thome's appalling back header released Huckerby on one of his mad, careering chases; he is like a coursed hare, the pack of hounds in pursuit. Srnicek, the Wednesday keeper, could not stop Huckerby, so he simply threw himself at him. A noble sacrifice like the heroine Pearl White and the runaway train. Mr Burge was a trifle cross. He awarded a penalty to Coventry in pure spite. McAllister stroked the ball past Srnicek with panache. I have always admired McAllister. His zenith was with Leicester Fosse and Leeds United. A footballer's footballer. Economic with his passing, fantastic vision and use of space – total awareness of his own skills and lack of them in colleagues. Wednesday were fuming. Carbone, the Wizard of Oz, all flash and flying boots, executed yet another whizz-bang in his armoury. A brilliant overhead kick left Rudi loitering on the goal line like a footpad awaiting a victim. Rudi stretched his leg – the ball struck it – the equalizer. One apiece. Both sides settled for the draw as the match died in the evening sun. I was contemplating my drive home through the Peak Forest; communing with nature, the tame herd of yak, the pack of armadillo, the friendly iguana, when I spotted Huckerby lurching up the right; he slung in a speculative cross – Noel Whelan leapt in and scored the winner. Whelan of the master mariner's gait. He swaggered in celebration. Coventry fans sang the 'Eton Boating Song' in exceedingly jolly fashion, despite the fact that in the boat race only one Etonian was in the Cambridge crew. The rest were Johnny Foreigners. Whatever happened to John Bull? Wednesday are in deep water. Five consecutive defeats, and Danny Wilson is such a nice man.

Sheffield Wednesday: Pavel Srnicek, Peter Atherton, Wim Jonk, Des Walker, Benito Carbone, Ritchie Humphreys, Lee Briscoe, Richard Cresswell, Emerson Thome, Petter Rudi, Niclas Alexandersson. Substitutes: Kevin Pressman, Jon Newsome, Philip Scott, Junior Agogo, Danny Sonner.

Coventry City: Magus Hedman, Paul Williams, Richard Shaw, Gary Breen, Darren Huckerby, Noel Whelan, Gary McAllister, George Boateng, Paul Telfer, Steve Froggatt, Marc Edworthy. Substitutes: Mohammed Konjic, Stephano Gioacchini, Trond Egil Soltvedt, Phillipe Clement, Chris Kirkland.

LIVERPOOL 0 – ASTON VILLA 1
The FA Carling Premiership, 17 April 1999

The Shankly gates festooned with flowers and wreaths. Mourners shuffling by in silence. Many in tears as recollections of the Hillsborough disaster overwhelmed them. Ten years have passed since the disaster when ninety-six died at Sheffield Wednesday. Grief is tangible on Merseyside. They are not afraid to display emotion here and unite in a common bond to sustain them, 'And thus the heart will break and brokenly live on.'

The entire Kop stood and held red and yellow cards covering their faces as their hymn, 'You'll Never Walk Alone', echoed round the Colosseum. Villa fans understood, kept respectful silence and broke into spontaneous applause as the last note died away. One minute's silence at six minutes past three was observed with religious piety. The spirit was still alive.

Alas, the match was anticlimax. Grief hung like a pall over the first half. Villa almost apologetically controlled the game. Composed, articulate, laid-back, they swept forward as if on rollers. Domination yielded a goal on 34 minutes. Ian Taylor is keeping with the occasion, nudging the ball into the net. Young Hendrie showed lovely, velvety touches. Draper, Taylor and Stone grafting in midfield. Leonhardsen came on for the second half to buttress midfield, and Liverpool gingered their play.

McManaman roamed the range, Ince snapped out of his trance and snapped into tackles. Redknapp rose to the combat. The sun blazed down to add heat. The fans found heat and voice. Villa stood firm, Southgate at the helm. Liverpool lost one–nil. Whither now the Colosseum? The season is fallow. Monsieur Houllier will dismantle this team. Fowler has already bid adieu, Owen lies hurt. Ince will depart to ply his boots and ill temper possibly at Middlesbrough. Bjornebye looks forlorn and a misfit. The family ethic at the Colosseum has gone.

The 'Boot Room', that oracle of Delphi, the epicentre of football wisdom, is no more. The miracles of Shankly, Paisley, Fagan, Moran, Evans, Saunders forgotten on the winds of change. Masked forces now rule; sentiment, humour, kindness, once the hallmark and bed-rock of this great club, swept away. Will Monsieur Houllier crack the whip, inspire, decamp to Paris, or rebuild a team worthy of the Colosseum?

Liverpool: David James, Rigobert Song, Phil Babb, Steve McManaman, Robbie Fowler, Jamie Redknapp, Karlheinz Riedle, Paul Ince, Stig Inge Bjornebye, Dominic Matteo, Jamie Carragher. Substitutes: Steve Staunton, Oyvind Leonhardsen, Sean Dundee, Jean Michel Ferri, Brad Friedel.

Aston Villa: Mark Bosnich, Alan Wright, Gareth Southgate, Watson, Taylor, Mark Draper, Julian Joachim, Dion Dublin, Lee Hendrie, Steve Stone, Colin Calderwood. Substitutes: Paul Merson, Michael Oakes, Gareth Barry, Darius Vassell, Mark Delaney.

LIVERPOOL 3 – TOTTENHAM HOTSPUR 2

The FA Carling Premiership, 1 May 1999

May Day at the Colosseum. Mayday, mayday for distress. Liverpool and Spurs languish mid-table, European football unobtainable, unacceptable for Liverpool fans who expect and desire the best. Forty-four thousand and '007' turned up under a blazing sun. Lions versus Christians, a meaningless encounter points-wise, the only hope blood and thunder, severed limbs, personal vendettas, a red card or two. The Kop was in savage mood; they want revenge for Spurs' win here in November in the League Cup. They demanded a spectacle and got it.

Spurs smashed two goals in the first half-hour. The first on 14 minutes in the lion's den of Liverpool's penalty box. Carragher of Liverpool, Armstrong of Spurs locked paws with pride – Carragher turned the ball into his own net. The second a beautifully-flighted free kick from Anderton, turned in from Iversen.

Spurs on cruise control, Liverpool in mayday distress. The referee Lodge sent off Taricco for a second bookable offence. Ho, ho – now for a spot of blood-letting!

The second half was explosive. The Roman legion advanced on Spurs in full muster, Redknapp the centurion inspiring the legionaries. Redknapp smote a penalty after Riedle was cruelly felled. Liverpool on the flood tide, the crowd baying for blood. Spurs, so poised and gritty in the first half, fell apart in full retreat, shapeless, hapless. Spurs threw on three subs, Fox, Sherwood and King. That son of Gaul, that wandering minstrel, that poetic genius Ginola stayed rooted to the bench. His consummate artistry could have lit the scene. The battering continued. Seventy-six minutes Redknapp's cross – Ince headed the equalizer. Two minutes later Rigobert Song, the all-singing, dancing entertainer, pranced down the right – crossed – McManaman lashed the winner. Monsieur Houllier's holiday. A new dawn or *le commencement de la fin*.

Liverpool: Brad Friedel, Bjorn Tore Kvarme, Steve Staunton, Steve McManaman, Oyvind Leonhardsen, Jamie Redknapp, Karlheinz Riedle, Paul Ince, Dominic Matteo, Jamie Carragher, David Thompson. Substitutes: David James, Rigobert Song, Sean Dundee, Stig Inge Bjornebye, Steve Gerrard.

Tottenham Hotspur: Ian Walker, Steve Carr, Steffan Freund, Allan Neilsen, Darren Anderton, Chris Armstrong, Steffan Iversen, Maurico Taricco, José Dominguez, Sol Campbell, Stephen Clemence. Substitutes: Ruel Fox, Epsen Baardsen, David Ginola, Tim Sherwood, Ledley King.

EVERTON 6 – WEST HAM 0
The FA Carling Premiership, 8 May 1999

The School of Science is in shock; a six-goal thrashing of West Ham; a Kevin Campbell hat trick, a tidal wave of glorious football, an oasis in what has been a goalless desert of a season. The kick-off was delayed – trouble at t' mill. At 3 p.m. a piper played 'Scotland the Brave'; a sea fret off the Irish Sea soaked his sporran; Everton sported a new retro kit; it was Sir Philip Carter's birthday; West Ham had been nobbled, drugged or counselled by Glenn Hoddle's soothsayer. In other words, I am searching for the reason for Everton's metamorphosis – inexplicable. The first half was School of Science textbook: sublime, assertive football to feet, flowing rhythm, quicksilver movement. Dacourt was the fulcrum tackling like a pampas bull; rumour hath it he is exiting Goodison – he must stay – he is vital. Round him Gemmill, Hutchison, Jeffers and Campbell rolled on to a tepid, flaccid West Ham. Razor Ruddock found himself stropping fresh air, not his razor, as Everton streamed by his flailing legs in a blue tide. Ferdinand so laid back, at times he was horizontal, his sang-froid is sometimes sadly misplaced. Ian Wright was booked early, was estranged from his colleagues like Man Friday on the desert isle. Reduced to vain impotence, he was replaced in the second half. As he crossed the touchline he aimed a kick at the trainer's liquid refreshment – a can of isotonic potion; it flew 20 yards: his only kick of the game, bellowed the partisans. Trouble was, it was 'Gatorade' and it got up and bit him; I think that was the scenario, as he instantly disappeared into the bowels of Goodison. Enough of West Ham, now to the goals.

Kevin Campbell opened the scoring on 15 minutes from Gemmill's corner. Twenty-four minutes Gemmill felled by Ruddock. Ball smote the penalty. Thirty-five minutes Hutchison volleyed the third. Everton, scenting a West Ham debacle, upped the tempo in the second half. Campbell hit number four after a scintillating move between Gemmill and Hutchison and bagged his third with a thumping shot in off a post. Nine goals in seven games. An inspired signing by Walter Smith. Jeffers knocked in number six two minutes from time.

Forty thousand fans jubilate. Standing ovation at the whistle. West Ham slunk off, whipped and cowed. Another season, another wasteland. Everton the revelation of today, the sadness of yesterdays in a barren first half of the season. Take solace in the maxim 'only the mediocre are good all the time'.

Everton: Thomas Myhre, Michael Ball, Olivier Dacourt, Dave Watson, David Unsworth, Kevin Campbell, Don Hutchison, Scot Gemmill, Craig Short, David Weir, Francis Jeffers. Substitutes: Steve Simonsen, Nick Barmby, Ibrahima Bakayoko, Mitch Ward, Peter Degn.

West Ham: Shaka Hislop, Rio Ferdinand, Neil Ruddock, Scott Minto, Trevor Sinclair, Frank Lampard, Steve Lomas, Marc-Vivien Foe, Eyal Berkovic, Paolo Di Canio, Ian Wright. Substitutes: Craig Forrest, Marc Keller, Chris Coyne, Scott Mean, Gary Alexander.

A CHRISTMAS CAROL
Old Loves, Old Aspirations and Old Dreams

More Beautiful for Being Old and Gone

A PROLOGUE TO LOURDES: THE SANCTIFICATION OF GLENN HODDLE

I have admiration for Glenn. He was a fine player, an exponent of the beautiful game. His vision light years ahead of his time.

David Davies is a colleague and a personal friend. He joined the BBC and was a reporter on the Manchester-based regional programme *North at Six.* He specialised in crime and sport. As the two are siamesed, David was well groomed in the black arts. In those far-off days, we had a thoroughbred stable.

Nick Clarke, now the most intelligent, articulate presenter of the media.

Felicity Goodey who now rules Manchester. John Humphries, whose special interests were brucellosis, anthrax and foot and mouth. He believed in mulch. Muck-spreading on politicians comes naturally.

Gerald Harrison. The superman of reportage. He turned down the Moors Murders as beneath him. Brady and Hindley went on to notoriety. Gerald is now an advanced ski instructor in Austria.

Bob Perrin, who reported the Moors Murders, made a fortune in expenses, rose to fame and is probably running a gambling joint in Vegas.

We had a football team. Nick was 'Billy Buttocks'. A striker of immense power but, really, no finisher.

Steve Ireland, the editor, built close to the ground. Steve blinked a lot; he was trained as an upstart on the *Daily Mirror.* To overcome this dreadful handicap he immersed himself in gobbledegook, a BBC speciality. He became by rote unintelligible, disorientated and sycophantic. We threw sand in his face to make him blink. He became blinkered. Last I knew he was running UK Gold.

Davies, though, was loved by all. He ran around in our football games until he dropped. He was a trier. He then dabbled in religion. He has a beatific countenance which can change, in an instant, from somnolence and deep grief to high glee. The zenith was presenting *Songs of Praise*. He became known as 'the Bishop'. Thus, I could not resist writing Lourdes. I mean no offence to persons living or departed. I have a tongue between both cheeks, if you see wot I mean, Harry!

LOURDES, CHRISTMAS EVE 1998

Hi, *Match of the Day* surfers. Yes, I'm in Lourdes, not Lords. LOURDES. The snow is falling gently, the candles are guttering low. We are holding them as Cleopatra might have held the asp – close to her breasts. We are here at this vast shrine to sanctify Glenn. A glittering vignette of VIPs, Tony, Alistair, Mandy, representing Cool Britannia. Roger Cook's away playing Grumpy in *Snow Black and the Seven Gnomes*. Incidentally Ron Davies is playing Sleazy, and Bill is playing Gropey in the same production at Dukinfield Empire.

I will not dwell on the cast list here in Lourdes. As a toff, bourgeois upstarts and Johnny Come-latelies reduce me to common casuistry or cyclical cynicism. But behold Bishop Davies and Father Kelly are present for the FA (Fathers Anonymous). Bishop Davies is on his knees as Glenn's arrival is announced. He spent years on his knees in supplication to Graham Taylor. Any incumbent to the throne of England's manager demands a genuflect from the Bishop. Father Kelly clutches Baron Hardacre's Bible, 'How to Eunuch the Honest Pro'.

The Bishop, his and Glenn's latest ghostwritten text, 'How to Eunuch England'.

'Off your knees, you cassock,' murmurs Kelly.

'Don't you mean hassock?'

'No, pillock – you *ad hoc*.'

'*Annus mirabilis*,' muttered the Bishop in reply.

'Shut your anus,' yapped Father Kelly. 'Saint Glenn appeareth.'

The floodlights snapped on. The entourage shuffled before the great edifice. The icy-blue waters in flood rushed by as the cruel east wind blew from the Pyrenees.

Glenn was haggard. Swathed in a white robe embossed with those three little lions. His shoes were bespoke Jesus boots in red, yellow, blue and black. Insignia proliferated, so many that it was confusing. 'Pumike, Filadibok.' Is this a sanctification or a photo opportunity? On his head a crown of thorns courtesy of Umbro. Across his shoulders the enormous oaken cross. Suddenly he stumbled. His disciples rushed forward.

Paul Gascoigne sporting his AA badge (he'd driven from Middlesbrough). Steve McManaman, his left foot bandaged heavily. Apparently, he'd been learning to kick with it for the first time. Alan Shearer, his anaconda thighs gleaming under his toga, wearing his Mona Lisa smile. David Batty, the Yorkshire impassive: 'Say nowt, give nowt, kick it if it moves'. We muttered sympathy for Batty. He'd just been fined £20,000 for appearing in the opposition's penalty box and offering Mr Elleray communion wine. David Beckham, clad in Armani loincloth, was surrounded by gendarmerie. He'd offended the French. Becks thought the ECU was a bird and had imported £80,000 to buy a trinket or two for his bird's Christmas. Also, he described his profession on his passport 'Profeshunal Futbaler'. Try telling the French that he neglected Educashun. They thought he was extracting the pissoir. Michael Owen cherubic, beatific choirboy, a halo atop his shaven head, was singing in his falsetto 'All Things Bright and Beautiful'. Dion Dublin tootled on his tenor sax 'Oh, Come All Ye Faithful'. Le Saux was carrying his leg – not his Dennis Wise's appendage. It had become detached in a rather exuberant training clash. Eileen's presence was everywhere, incandescent. A loving, healing, gentle St Bernadette. She dispensed the holy water from exquisite engraved three lions glasses, Bishop Davies having blagged a crate from HM the Queen. God, those knees must be calloused. Gazza had an exigence. The 'Holy Water' had reached parts that even Gazza didn't know. He cartwheeled to the *gentilhommes*, followed by a large St Bernard, an equally large flask around its neck. The St Bernard guffawed. It was Bernard Manning in drag.

'Have I told you about them three nuns?'

'Shut up,' we cried. Glenn wept: 'It's them free points was needed.' Darren was in a miasma of self-pity: 'I need healing hands.'

Berti Vogts appeared from the shadows: 'Look Darren, no Hans.' Darren fell into Eileen's bosom.

This was no sanctification. It was pantomime!

'Twas time for speeches. Ken Bates read a few programme notes. Swedes, Poles, Turnips received honourable menches. We were all crap, said Ken, apart from Ken. Kevin, on behalf of 'Save the Aitch' campaign, was eloquent: ''onest, 'istoric, 'ippodrome, 'oddle at the 'elm, 'onourable, 'onest, 'ealthy.'

Trevor spoke on behalf of the English Speaking Society: 'Brookin,' he observed, ''ad 'somethin' goin' happin' comin' battin' and bowlin'!'

A straitjacket was procured. Trevor encased and whipped back to Desmond's boudoir. Andy Gray grabbed the mike and, wearing Mick Jagger's lips, harangued us. A fringe of Swedes applauded madly; he was speaking their language. Poor Neophytes us could not understand a word – we never do. Alistair murmured to Tony, 'I'd incarcerate the lot in Clapham Common. I'd arrange for the media to be there, and I could manage England in my spare time.'

Tony flushed. 'But Alistair – I already do that.'

The Bishop, on his obsequious knees, enquired of Mandy: 'How's the Millennium Dome?'

'Keep your head out of this,' barked Mandy, his nose having extended another six inches.

Amid this gallimaufry, the ghosts of Christmas Past appeared like wraiths.

Joe Mercer beamed his omnipresent smile. Joe the disciple of the beautiful game. As England manager he had blind faith in God-given talent. The ability to express those talents unfettered by coaching manuals, drab systems and fear of losing. A sublime entertainer in an era when negativity was negated.

'Give me the Spurs of 1961, not the Spurs of today.'

'Give me the Cliff Jones, Len White, Terry Medwin, Dave Mackay, Danny Blanchflower.'

Joe evoked the spirits like smoke drifting from St Peter's chimney. Peter Docherty, Raich Carter, Willie Steel, Stan Mortensen, Jock Dodds, Cliff Burton, Alex Young, Cliff Bastin, Duncan Edwards, Roger Bryne, Dixie Dean, Tommy Lawton, Albert Stubbins.

Great managers drifted before our bewildered eyes. Bill Shankly, Bob Paisley, Matt Busby, Jock Stein, Don Revie, Arthur Rowe, Bill Nicholson, Alf Ramsey, none were bitter about the obscene salaries of today's players. They were happy sipping their nectar in the Elysian Fields.

In a working-class era, £20 a week was better earned on the football field than down the pit or at the factory lathe. The lament was that the fun, the joy, the beauty were disappearing from the game.

Lourdes by now was swollen by other ranks. Gullit, Rijkaard, Van Basten, Gento, Puskas, Zoff, Giresse, Platini, Beckenbauer, Pele, Socrates, Maradona, Batistuta, Salas, Zidane, Baggio, Kluivert, Davids, Bergkamp, Seedorf, Cruyff.

We were in awe. Glenn's sainthood had become a pilgrimage – homage to the beautiful game. Glenn staggered forward, bent double with the weight of the cross. A choir, 1,000 strong, began 'Nessun Dorma'. Then a miracle. The cross slowly rose from Glenn's tortured shoulder. Higher and higher into the frosted air, above the throng and into the stars disappeared the cross. Like Excalibur into the lake. To await a real king. The telephone rang. It was Ian Wright requesting a one-to-one with Martin Loofah King. I explained he was out. It was nearly midnight. I'm not in Lourdes at all. It was a dream. Tomorrow is my birthday. Claret is my undoing. I must to bed. I take my latest tome, *Great Lovers of the World* by Don Juan Lynam, and repair to my kip. Merry Christmas, everyone! It was only a dream, remember…

IN DEFENCE OF STANLEY

Stanley Collymore is a trifle more complex than hitherto we understood. Obviously a troubled soul standing alone like Lear on the blasted heath; a torrent of diatribe, invective, spurious gossip, even hatred, threatens to engulf him. His misdemeanours are well catalogued. Two lady friends accused him of a little GBH – he was cleared. Ulrika suffered a little in Paris, but was he provoked? There have been two reported incidents of racial abuse, one in Cannock, the other in Liverpool. I have never been racially abused, so I am not able to judge whether Stanley is rational when applying his fists to some verbalizing nutter's jaw. My sympathies are with the flying fists, not the broken jaw.

I observe Stanley at close quarters during his stay at Liverpool. 'Twas like observing a lifer in a state penitentiary. Introspective, friendless, fretful, feckless, fearful; his mind a farrago of wild thoughts and frustrated emotion. A tormented soul.

I remember in one match at the Colosseum, a five–nil drubbing of Middlesbrough; he made four goals for colleagues. In a match against Forest, he flung himself into a one-man cavalry charge at the Forest defence which simply melted under the sheer weight and heat. Stanley crossed to Fowler, who tapped in. Stanley stood awaiting the usual back-slaps, loving embrace, mouth to mouth, semi-shagging which is *de rigueur* in today's footie. Fowler ran to McManaman, his best buddy, and they hugged each other. Stanley eventually ambled over to Fowler and shakes his hand.

Little wonder that Stan's mind is like that of Hamlet. Whether 'tis nobler in the mind to bear the slings and arrows of outrageous fortune. Sod the meek inheriting the earth. Let us, by opposing, end the slings and arrows. Hand me my burning bow – let us have a little imbrue.

More sinned against than sinning. That is Stanley. All the popular scribes have railed at the La Manga fire extinguisher jape. Was there a fire? Did some sycophantic, half-sizzled damsel ignite her knickers to inflame Stanley's fires? Were they stoked by excessive alcohol imbibed by onlookers? Did somebody suggest that fire extinguisher liquid gave a wicked cocktail that lethal dash of testosterone? Maybe Stanley's cure would be a tincture of oestrogen in his Horlicks. Calm that sudden urge which apparently overwhelms him. He, like many of us, succumbs to 'that moment of danger'. Even the Duke of Edinburgh has been accused of that. Headstrong, impulsive, fearing nothing, disdaining discipline, a bull in a china shop; and then the awful realisation – 'I've done it again'.

I am guilty, m' Lud' of the offence. Once in the early 1970s I made a promotional film for Ford. The location – the Algarve, Portugal; the team base a very posh hotel in Albufeira. Shooting finished, we repaired to the hotel at nightfall. I went upstairs to my room to pack for a presentation back in London early the following day. My room was under water, all my clothes floating on top. My shirts were on the bed, covered with shaving foam and toothpaste. An act of total bloody vandalism. I hurled myself down to the very, very posh lobby to confront the manager. Gripping him by the jowls, I demanded the identity of the culprit. Anti-British feeling was rife in Portugal, the Communists painting everything red. The guy was terrified. He pointed, not at his staff, but my team, the camera crew and producer. I ran to the cameraman, who blurted that it was a joke. A joke, a joke – to destroy somebody's belongings. I hit him straight through the plate-glass window of the bar. I turned just in time to see a glass of brandy flung at me by the producer. With the strength of Samson and the expertise of Bruce Lee, I caught the glass and hurled it back into his hideous face. Within seconds I was alone in that bar. All save he had fled in terror at this mad Englishman. A salutary tale for all those who are quick to judge.

Stanley, go forth and play. All the attributes. Two-footed, strong, sprinter quick, good awareness, excellent in the air if he wants to be. If I were a centre half with Stan bearing down on me at full chat, I would wear rubber knickers. Prove them wrong, Stan! Grab a dozen goals for Leicester Fosse. Mr O'Neill is as good as it gets, manager-wise. He knows men; he is a real man himself. If he cracks the riding crop on yer buttocks, he is only practising for the hunt.

And to all Stanley's critics: 'Let he who is without sin cast the first stone.' Bible fanatics and troubled souls can pop something in the confessional box on 'Church Hall', my new web site.

SEASON 1997/98: I HOLD AMBITION OF SO AIRY AND LIGHT A QUALITY, THAT IT IS BUT A SHADOW'S SHADOW

EVERTON 1 – CRYSTAL PALACE 2
The FA Carling Premiership, 9 August 1997
'Dreams and the light imagining of men and all that love creates and faith desires.' The thought of 35,000 fervent fans as they trudge away from the sunlit School of Science. The start of a new season; expectation crackling through the stands at 5,000 volts, millions expended on new players of some pedigree. All eclipsed by Attilio Lombardo, a son of Rome; balding pate, bandy legs, stooping gait – the antithesis of the Italian super-hero. On 34 minutes he strutted down Everton's left flank, leaving them like pillars of salt. He instincted Warhurst to put the ball into space. Warhurst obliged. Attilio whipped the shot past Southall. Imagination made manifest. Attilio embarked on his triumphal flight, swooping like an eagle with outstretched wings – the Juventus repertoire. Thirteen minutes from time, he was skipping through a lax Everton defence when he was felled by Graham Stuart. Bruce Dyer rammed in the resultant penalty. Everton stunned. Defenders Thomsen and Thomas hauled off, Nick Barmby and Michael Branch propelled on. At last Everton cracked on pace, and they relied on classical studious football; the fans here will accept nothing less, breeding demands it. Oster has style and quality but he is a mere stripling, Farrelly has promise, Speed, the captain, has an impressive Leeds curriculum vitae but cannot inspire the troops. Barmby is class, but he needs a definite role just behind the front two. Ferguson is a one-man 'Black Watch', but a foil for his belligerence must be found. Palace did things simply and well. Their plus, Attilio, the Bald Eagle. Howard Kendall has mega-problems – how to make the parts fit the sum.
Everton: Neville Southall, Tony Thomas, Terry Phelan, Claus Thomsen, Dave Watson, Slaven Bilic, John Oster, Graham Stuart, Duncan Ferguson, Gary Speed, Gareth Farrelly. Substitutes: Paul Gerrard, Earl Barrett, Craig Short, Nick Barmby, Michael Branch.
Crystal Palace: Kevin Miller, Kevin Muscat, Dean Gordon, Andy Roberts, Andy Linighan, Marc Edworthy, Attilio Lombardo, Paul Wharhurst, Bruce Dyer, Simon Rodger, David Tuttle. Substitutes: Carlo Nash, Hermann Hreidarsson, Neil Shipperley, Carl Veart, Jamie Fullarton.

BARNSLEY 0 – ASTON VILLA 3

The FA Carling Premiership, 13 September 1997

Onomatopoeic Barnsley. B is for Brazilian football, B for bravery. Alas, there is no such thing as bravery – only degrees of fear. At Oakwell the fear factor is off the Richter scale. Franklin Delano Roosevelt once said: 'The only thing we have to fear is fear itself.' But fear manifests itself in devious ways. It erodes confidence in one's own abilities. Limits expressions and expels optimism. I sympathize with Barnsley. Their deliberate, crafted football was blown away by Villa's professional performance based on speed in thought and deed. Villa's first away win since April, and smiles are broad. Barnsley opened with a warlike drumbeat but gradually were forced back by Collymore and Yorke playing at a fast clip. Ehiogu scored Villa's first goal on 27 minutes, a merry header from a corner kick.

Mark Draper bagged the second five minutes into the second half – a Villa breakaway – Draper one to one with Leese, the Barnsley keeper; whites of the eyes confrontation. Leese advanced; he is German. Draper advanced; he is English. Draper calmly drove the ball between Leese's legs.

What is German for 'nutmeg'? Villa's third was simply embarrassing, a flurry of one twos, Ian Taylor flicked the ball in the net like a child with his Subbuteo kit. Stan Collymore did not 'score' on the pitch, but one breathtaking pass brought a cry of 'Eureka, Eureka' from the sidelines. Recording his scoring elsewhere, it could be construed as 'Ulrika'. Stan's nickname is 'Width', so Eureka! Villa's bench sported four internationals, Barnsley's two Bullocks. Enough said: Barnsley face a harsh winter; reality, like hoarfrost, will set in.

Barnsley: Lars Leese, Nicky Eaden, Matty Appleby, Adie Moses, Arjan De Zeeuw, Neil Redfearn, Andy Liddell, Eric Tinkler, Georgi Hristov, Darren Barnard, Ashley Ward. Substitutes: Darren Sheridan, Martin Bullock, Laurens Ten Heuval, Ales Krizan, Tony Bullock.

Aston Villa: Mark Bosnich, Steve Staunton, Gareth Southgate, Ugo Ehiogu, Ian Taylor, Mark Draper, Dwight Yorke, Stan Collymore, Alan Wright, Fernando Nelson, Simon Grayson. Substitutes: Savo Milosovic, Julian Joachim, Michael Oakes, Sasa Curcic, Riccardo Scimeca.

WIGAN ATHLETIC 2 – FULHAM 1

Nationwide Football League, Division Two, 27 September 1997

If you are strolling through St Peter's Square or trolling round the Trevi in the Eternal City, spare a thought for the faithful at Springfield Park. This relic of Wigan's industrial past was never a thing of beauty and joy forever. It is grim, grey, tatty, almost derelict. I allude to Rome, as Kevin Keegan is my hero of Rome 1977. Sporting two black eyes, he took a pounding from Berti Vogts, never flinched, was wonderful leading Liverpool's line and emerged a true Brit – with a European Cup medal. Transitory thoughts as I gaze at 200 Fulham fans scattered on an open terrace bearing flags of the Union and St George. A solitary drummer beat the 'Dead March from Saul'. Wigan Pier does not compare with the Tiber. I wonder if Kevin knows what really lies before him. To take Fulham on that voyage of discovery that so enchanted Newcastle, and indeed the football world.

Kev was on his feet early. Hayward scored on 18 minutes. Gavin Johnson equalized for Wigan five minutes later. Colin Greenall, Wigan's captain, won the match with two minutes to go, bullet header from a corner kick. Fulham languish mid-table with Wigan. Mr Fayed is bankrolling Fulham, much wealthier Dave Whelan 'sugar-daddies' Wigan. Does Kev have present assets? Hayward looks like Neil Webb, Herrera like Mickey Thomas, Glenn Cockerill is still a playmaker. Thought is there, but not deed. There is little pace in the team. Kev will have to raid Harrods, tackle its owner Herod, and spend. Maybe he will sign a lookalike Beardsley, but who would dare admitting it?

Dave Whelan, by contrast, is a Lancashire toughie. He is planning a super-stadium, super-players, super-dooper-troopers. The big drum, the wipeout, Wigan is on the map, folks – but I wonder how is la vie on the Via Veneto tonight?

Wigan Athletic: Lee Butler, Scott Green, Gavin Johnson, Colin Greenall, Pat McGibbon, Roberto Martinez, David Lee, Graham Jones, Brendan O'Connell, Kevin Sharp, David Lowe. Substitutes: Paul Roger, Paul Warne, Andy Saville.
Fulham: André Arendse, Richard Carpenter, Rob Herrera, Rod McAree, Danny Cullip, Matt Lawrence, Glenn Cockerill, Steve Hayward, Mike Conroy, Simon Morgan, Paul Moody. Substitutes: Rob Scott, Nick Cusack, Neil Smith.

BLACKBURN ROVERS 1 – SOUTHAMPTON 0
The FA Carling Premiership, 18 October 1997
Ewood Park of yesteryear was one of my favourites. Old oak, corrugated iron, hot Bovril, Holland's pies, flat 'ats, warm Lancashire vowels and a cracking team – Matt Woods, Ronnie Clayton, Billy Eckersley, Brian Douglas *et al*. The boardroom was solid mahogany, a coal fire roared up the mantelpiece, a table was laid with steak and kidney pudding, home-made apple tart, buttered scones with blackberry jam. We quaffed draught Guinness with elderly gentlemen in rough tweed; portly ladies busied themselves waiting on. Oh, the change! Today concrete and steel. A reception woman in uniform (they are all in uniform) greets you like Rosa Klebb. Is the poisoned boot to be withdrawn swiftly from under her desk to deliver the fatal jab? Does she wear regulation black locknit knickers under her clouts? I furtively secrete my Silk Cut for fear of incarceration. No incineration at Ewood – Christ, in a modern stadium so bleak, bare, minimalist, cheerless, what is combustible? The pies, too, have gone. It's coteletta alla milanese, boeuf en croûte, Chianti and Montrachet. Does Continental style suit traditional Lancashire palates? The flat 'ats have gone, but the folks are the same, by background, as their forebears. Stolid, slightly cynical of the outside world, conservative but optimistic. Roy Hodgson, a man of Europe, a fluent speaker of Italian, manages Blackburn with style. They are third in the table. Southampton next to bottom; perennial

stragglers. The audience anticipate a goal fest. Blackburn off the blocks to wipe out the opposition.

Tim Sherwood scored on 25 minutes after a little Kevin Gallacher magic. Right, lads – turn up the wick. They did just that. Damien Duff a leprechaun on Blackburn's left, quick feet, gazelle speed, pure class.

Monkou and Lundekvam at the head of Southampton's defence held the bridge. Lundekvam reading Chris Sutton, nullifying his physical presence, quelling every move. Blackburn their own enemy. Shots blazed wide when cool head was needed. Sutton, Gallacher, Bohinen wasting chances. Southampton, sowing profligacy, made Blackburn sweat on the break. Tim Flowers beating the ground in anguish as his defence, Colin Hendry apart, took deep slumber. David Hirst, the St John's Ambulance man's dream, so often is he injured, had a couple of moments then became anonymous. What malady will strike him next – BSE or e-coli? He has had everything else.

On the hour, Southampton introduced 'Dell Boy' Andy Williams. He is very nippy and on the fast track. If he can croon 'Moon River' as well – then he will be a star. Stardom is a universe away for his team, five away defeats, bottom of the league; surely their tenuous grasp on the premiership will be loosed this season?

Blackburn Rovers: Tim Flowers, Jeff Kenna, Tim Sherwood, Colin Hendry, Stuart Ripley, Kevin Gallacher, Chris Sutton, Lars Bohinen, Gary Croft, Stephane Henchoz, Damien Duff. Substitutes: Tore Pedersen, Martin Dahlin, Garry Flitcroft, Billy McKinlay, Alan Fettis.

Southampton: Paul Jones, Jason Dodd, Carlton Palmer, Ken Monkou, Claus Lundekvam, Robbie Slater, Francis Benali, Kevin Davies, Simon Charlton, Kevin Richardson, David Hirst. Substitutes: Lee Todd, Matthew Oakley, Andy Williams, Stig Johansen, Maik Taylor.

MANCHESTER UNITED 7 – BARNSLEY 0
The FA Carling Premiership, 25 October 1997

Andy Cole's golden day. Fifty-five thousand supplicants at the Shrine, many doubting Cole's ability, including, if rumour hath it, Alex Ferguson. Facts are clear. Fifteen games United have played so far this season. Cole three goals. He is not a regular in the team. Cruyff, Solskjaer, Sheringham and Poborsky are the permutations. So the scenario. A pristine pitch, a golden autumn day, Barnsley third from bottom playing in virgin-white shirts, hearts pounding, knees knocking, at the sheer volume of noise rising from the stands. Intimidating – I imagine dry throats, nape hairs rising among the Barnsley lads.

Cole knew it was his day. His body language spoke it. Shoulders back, touch of arrogance, lithe, powerful, like a cheetah poised for the prey. Quicksilver in his boots, adrenalin pumping, intent on savagery. United began with majestic football, intuitive, one touch, rhythmic, two yards quicker than Barnsley. Their movement off the ball breathtaking. Seventeen minutes a flurry of passes sliced open Barnsley yet again – Cole in full flight whacked his first goal. Fist clenched, arm raised, he glared at Mr Ferguson and the doubters in the stand. He was then engulfed by the entire team. They rushed to embrace him, to claim him, to celebrate that he was one of them – their own hero. On this day, United paraded the home-grown, the product of the production line that grooms base metal into gold. Gary and Philip Neville, David Beckham, Paul Scholes, Nicky Butt, John Curtis and Ryan Giggs, the 'daddy' of the intake. The air was electric. Barnsley were about to be slaughtered.

Eighteen minutes and Cole's second goal, a diagonal run from Solskjaer's unselfish pass. His third came just before half-time – a right-foot boomer.

The hugging and kissing, prancing and dancing followed the script like an Oscar ceremony. Ryan Giggs, the old man of the team, tormented Barnsley down the left, tore at them like a wounded stag. His first goal on 43 minutes left Barnsley's defence wide open. Half-time, four–nil.

Giggs again wanting centre stage bagged the fifth goal on 57 minutes. Match over as a contest. In truth it never was. Danny Wilson, Barnsley's manager, has spent a mere £5 million to assemble his team. Krizan the Slovenian, De Zeeuw a Dutchman, Hristov from Macedonia, Marcelle from Trinidad, Darren Barnard from Bristol, and Ashley Ward at £1.3 million his biggest splurge. To their credit, they played neat football. It was crisp, with a touch of imagination, their heads never dropped, but they must have felt like novice skiers enveloped by an avalanche.

Deep in the second half United turned off the turbos, introduced Wallwork, Cruyff and Poborsky. Wallwork yet another off the production line; it never ends – and they get younger.

The final goals from Scholes and Poborsky completed the rout. It was Cole's day. Even Mr Ferguson smiled his wry smile. Was it all a plot to stir Andy's loins, a Celtic ruse to bond Cole to the master plan? We cogitate. Matters are that it was 'Manchester United International Mega-Store' versus 'Barnsley Market'. The stallholders will remember their whirlwind entrance and exit through the swing doors.

Manchester United: Peter Schmeichel, Gary Neville, Gary Pallister, David Beckham, Nicky Butt, Andy Cole, Ryan Giggs, Philip Neville, Paul Scholes, Ole Gunnar Solskjaer, John Curtis. Substitutes, Teddy Sheringham, Brian McClair, Jordi Cruyff, Karel Poborsky, Ronnie Wallwork.

Barnsley: Dave Watson, Nicky Eaden, Darren Sheridan, Arjan De Zeeuw, Neil Redfearn, Neil Thompson, Martin Bullock, Georgi Hristov, Ales Krizan, Darren Barnard, Ashley Ward. Substitutes: Arian Moses, John Hendrie, Clint Marcelle, Lars Leese, Jovo Bosnacic.

SHEFFIELD WEDNESDAY 5 – BOLTON WANDERERS 0

The FA Carling Premiership, 8 November 1997

David Pleat, Wednesday's manager, peers up and observes the sword of Damocles swinging on his unprotected neck. A threatened football manager has few friends in failure, yet he is a fine man, intelligent, articulate in football matters, if a trifle wayward with his syntax and choice of friends.

His teams down the years, including Luton Town and Tottenham Hotspur, have reflected his philosophy and belief in the beautiful game with players of class and style. Today, in a fall from grace, he placed his faith in Atherton and Booth, a couple of yeomen journeymen of good heart, calloused palms, iron lungs who in a previous life would have manned the bellows in a village blacksmith's. Needs must when devil drives.

'I fear not when they return,' uttered Mr Pleat. Today they returned. A five–nil victory ensued. Mr Pleat was sacked. Booth, missing for the last 11 games, bagged a hat trick. Wednesday's football was glorious one touch, at times sublime. Stolid Bolton were mesmerized, demoralized, resembling creaking, rusting old mill machinery from Lancashire facing Grand Prix Ferraris. Di Canio was incandescent, brilliant, impudent, arrogant, his vision light years ahead of colleagues. Rudi, the Norwegian, was his alter ego, high-stepping and fluent. Booth relished the space they created.

Wednesday were two–nil up in twenty minutes, Di Canio a bending, wicked right-foot shot, Guy Whittingham a brave header. Enter then Andy Booth, the archetypal English centre forward. Tall, raw-boned, fearless, feckless, built like Hadrian's Wall. Three goals in fifteen minutes. Two poacher's goals near post and a flying header among upraised Bolton boots that Nat Lofthouse would have been proud of. Bolton were in tatters, blasted away by those five first-half goals. Mr Todd, their manager, inculcates Derby County style; he was a stalwart in Mr Clough's heady days. But style alone will not keep Bolton in this league. Blake and Holdsworth never broke sweat. Pollock is labouring with advancing years. Thompson was flash but ephemeral. Set fire to their jockstraps, Colin, or nemesis will set in.

So, whither Wednesday? The Pennine leaves have turned gold, the forests prepare for deep winter, loneliness returns to the Snake Pass. Today, though, Hillsborough is wreathed in smiles. Pure football ruled. Whither David Pleat, pure man? As Oscar Wilde observed, 'To the pure everything is indecent' – including the sack.

Sheffield Wednesday: Kevin Pressman, Peter Atherton, Ian Nolan, Mark Pembridge, Jon Newsome, Des Walker, Guy Whittingham, Andy Booth, Paulo Di Canio, Jim Magilton, Petter Rudi. Substitutes: Graham Hyde, Matt Clarke, Patrick Blondeau, Wayne Collins, O'Neill Donaldson.

Bolton Wanderers: Keith Branagan, Per Frandzen, Jamie Pollock, Nathan Blake, Alan Thompson, Gudni Bergsson, Jimmy Phillips, Mark Fish, Mike Whitlow, Dean Holdsworth, Arnar Gunnlaugsson. Substitutes: Peter Beardsley, Michael Johansen, Gavin Ward, Andy Todd, Franz Carr.

BURY 1 – SHEFFIELD UNITED 1

Nationwide Football League, Division One, 20 December 1997

For world travellers and the cognoscenti, Bury is a Lancashire mill town famous for its bustling, unique market. The European Union says 'Non' to great delicacies like black tripe, elder, slut, pig's dick, chitterlings, chunks, wezel, lambs' fries and black pudding. Stalls at Bury market are laden with banned substances. Sheer delight, plus that iconoclastic Lancashire humour from the vendors. Make the pilgrimage and savour.

Less famous is the football club – the 'Shakers'. Governed by Mr Neville Neville, matron in charge Mrs Neville Neville. Between them they spawned brothers Gary and Philip. Gigg Lane thus has the atmosphere of a medieval tavern, florid faces, much banter and comfort food.

Alas, grey fog engulfed Gigg Lane, and the Shakers were decidedly shaky in a lively Sheffield opening spell. Illustrious names Brian Deane, Graham Stuart, Dean Saunders, Vassilis Borbokis, Jan Aage Fjortoft strutted their stuff. The Blades have recently floated on the stock market. They aspire to the Premiership. Largesse has been dissipated on these stars. They bear a superior style in the dingy surrounding of Gigg Lane. Thick fog, 6,000 supporters scattered around the bare terraces. Superstars need super-stadia, huge crowds, swelling anthems, atmosphere. Apathy dulls the soul, saps the will. Sheffield distracted – unfocused. Bury hit them. Johnrose, Bury's number ten, latched on to a loose ball, his looping header soared over Kelly in the Sheffield goal, nestling gently in the net. Bury grew in stature and confidence. Half-time, one–nil.

Second half – the Blades much sharper. Energized by a dressing-room tirade, they enfiladed. Steam rose from sweating bodies like a team of oxen on a steep incline. Bury being rolled over. Paul Dalglish came off the substitutes' bench to the delight of his dad Kenny sitting morosely in the stand. Paul infused a little skill, but Sheffield were determined. Twelve minutes from time the equalizer from Deane. A scrambled, untidy goal. His long sinewy shank snaking through a ruck of players and the merest touch. A draw trifle unjust for Bury, a black spot for the Blades. A gutsy, roistering match savoured by the 6,012 who forsook the vicarious pleasures of Bury market.

Bury: Dean Kiely, Andy Woodward, Gordon Armstrong, Nick Davis, Chris Lucketti, Paul Butler, Chris Swailes, Tony Ellis, Peter Swan, Lennie Johnrose, Andy D. Gray. Substitutes: Paul Dalglish, Adrian Randall, Tony Battersby, Jason Peake, Ronnie Jepson, Andy Gray.

Sheffield United: Alan Kelly, Vassilis Borbokis, Roger Ford, Michel Vonk, Dean Holdsworth, Dean Saunders, Nicky Marker, Jan Aage Fjortoft, Brian Deane, Graham Stuart. Substitutes: Marcelo Cipriano, Andy Walker, Don Hutchison, Gareth Taylor, Curtis Woodhouse, Simon Tracey.

EVERTON 3 – BOLTON WANDERERS 2
The FA Carling Premiership, 28 December 1997

One win in nine matches, a barren wasteland livened only by the win against Leicester Fosse last week, bottom of the table with Barnsley – the School of Science patrons are losing patience with Howard Kendall. Today's bender gender, 'the Toffees' versus 'the Trotters', was no pig's ear of a game; rather they filled their bellies with the husks that the swine did eat; husks being precious points to lift them up the table lorded over by – guess who? – Manchester United! In a pulsating, thrilling, absorbing match, 'twas the Trotters who became the Gadarene swine. (Remember those poor porkers who threw themselves over the cliff?) Duncan Ferguson was the bastion; returning as captain, he bagged a hat trick: two in the first half, one in the second. His first an arms and legs akimbo header from a Tony Thomas cross. The second a super shot after a neat *pas de deux* 'twixt Farrelly and Barmby. His third, the winner on 67 minutes, was another braveheart header, diving into the flailing boots on to a right-wing cross. The Trotters, meanwhile, trailing by two goals after half an hour essayed for a School of Science degree with some classic football. Per Frandzen, Scott Sellars, Gudni Bergsson and Peter Beardsley crafting moves to feet, finding gaps between Everton's central two, working over Tony Thomas down the flanks. It really was exhilarating, cultured, purest football. And it turned the game upside down with two goals in forty-five seconds before the interval. First Bergsson with a fierce header from Sellars' free kick; then Sellars himself – a venomous strike from 25 yards. The scrap intensified in a fantastic second half; the crowd almost regurgitating Christmas fare, nails bitten to the quick. Bolton threw Franz Carr, Michael Johansen, Gunnlaugsson into the battle. Then the *coup de grâce* – the Ferguson winner.

When I take the motes from my eyes and assess the merits of these two sides, I consider that Bolton play too much football for a cynical Premiership; they need more steel and a powerhouse goal scorer. Everton have too much untried talent: Farrelly, Ball, Oster, Cadamarteri, Thomas, all young neophytes who could be overwhelmed dogfighting in the basement. Happy New Year, Howard Kendall.

Everton: Thomas Myhre, Tony Thomas, Richard Dunne, Carl Tiler, Andy Hinchcliffe, John Oster, Nick Barmby, Gareth Farrelly, Michael Ball, Danny Cadamarteri, Duncan Ferguson. Substitutes: Paul Gerrard, Earl Barratt, Claus Thomsen, Graham Allen, Francis Jeffers.

Bolton Wanderers: Gavin Ward, Per Frandzen, Jamie Pollock, Chris Fairclough, Scott Sellars, Nathan Blake, Gudni Bergsson, Peter Beardsley, Neil Cox, Mark Fish, Mike Whitlow. Substitutes: Michael Johansen, Jimmy Phillips, Arnar Gunnlaugsson, Jussi Jaaskelainen, Franz Carr.

MANCHESTER CITY 2 – BRADFORD CITY 0
The FA Cup – Third Round, 3 January 1998
The third round of the FA Cup. City are sliding down Division One faster than tallow from a lighted candle. Above them are Crewe, Port Vale and Oxford. They have won six games from twenty-five matches. The likes of Middlesbrough, Sunderland, Charlton, Ipswich, Wolves, Nottingham Forest, Sheffield United still to play. Alarm bells not just ringing at the Theatre of Base Comedy but falling from the Campanile onto Frank Clarke's head. Mr Clarke is Baron Hardup. He seldom smiles, wears a hangdog expression, is doleful as if

grief were a permanent bedfellow. He is the Micawber of David Copperfield. Projector of bubble schemes leading to fortune always ending in grief. Hoping for something to turn up. Thirty thousand regular inmates are happy today. Baron Hardup still occupies centre stage. City beat Bradford by two comic goals – what do you expect? – comedy was invented in Moss Side.

Rösler, the German, bagged the first, a gift from Jacobs, Bradford's number five. He attempted a clearance, as if 30,000 had tugged the magic carpet, slipped and fell in a heap. Rösler rounded the keeper Walsh and popped the ball into the empty net. Chris Kamara, Bradford's manager, was apoplectic. His normal voice is equal to the foghorn on the QE2. Amplified in the dugout, the decibel level was so far off the meter that it brought down a passing Lufthansa flight, *and* a flock of cormorants.

Half-time approached – another pantomime goal for City. Michael Brown's hopeful drive was bound for row 20 in the Kippax when Youds struck out his boot and deflected the ball past a stranded Walsh. Walsh threw himself to the ground and beat it in frustration. A passing bobby asked him to guard his language. Kamara was kinetic, kinkajon, kinderspiel with knallgas. Two volumes of hydrogen, one of oxygen. He simply imploded. Lord help us if he deserts management and favours the 'media'. He will dispense with effete devices like microphones; there will be a rush for earplugs! Bradford responded – 'Fiery Jack' in their jockstraps. (Fiery Jack is an unction applied to limbs: keep away from orifices. Do not try this at home!) Beagrie, a City old boy tantalized with ball skills. It is all left foot but it is of snake-charming proportion. Jamie Lawrence was swift and sinewy. Bradford finished the half in the ascendant.

The second half was pure theatre. The sky turned black. The gale blew fierce and chill, corner flags bent double. Kamara had disturbed the gods. Thunderbolts were hurled, lightning flashed, rain lashed the faithful. City showed form. Kinkladze scintillated with close control. Rösler threw off his ill temper. Chances came abegging. Bradford chief culprits: up and over, far and wide, woodwork smitten. City followed suit – a litany of spurned chances. Two–nil to City, another pantomime for the Theatre of Base Comedy. Kamara retrieves his tonsils from the centre pitch. Baron Hardup is ambivalent. City are alive and in the velvet bag for the fourth round.

I ask Baron Hardup what he will do when the sack eventually arrives. He breaks into a smile. 'I'll join a skiffle group.' We break into Lonnie Donnegan's 'Rock Island Line'. You do not support City and lose your sense of humour.

Manchester City: Tommy Wright, Ian Brightwell, Murtaz Shelia, Michael Brown, Jeff Whitley, Gerard Wiekens, Ged Brannan, Craig Russell, Paul Dickov, Georgie Kinkladze, Uwe Rösler. Substitutes: Jason Van Blerk, Martyn Margetson, Tom Scully, Jim Whitley, Chris Greenacre.

Bradford City: Gary Walsh, Chris Wilder, Wayne Jacobs, Shaun Murray, Eddie Youds, Andrew O'Brien, Jamie Lawrence, Nigel Pepper, Robert Steiner, Robert Blake, Peter Beagrie. Substitutes, John McGinlay, Mark Prudhoe, Craig Midgley, Dennis Sepp, Ian McLean.

MANCHESTER CITY 3 – FULHAM 0
Nationwide Football League, Division Two, 16 January 1998

> *'My traffic is sheets. When the kite builds, look to lesser linen. My father named me Autolycus, who being, as I am, littered under Mercury, was likewise a snapper-up of unconsidered trifles. With die and drab I purchased this caparison, and my revenue is the silly cheat.'*

The winter sun glinted on the frozen snow-capped Alps distant beyond the stands at the Theatre of Base Comedy. The nobility skied down the black runs to Gstaad (hard by Oldham), doffed their Armani, loosened their Versace, quaffed Glühwein as the goals rattled in. A Winter's Tale. Fulham sophisticated, poised, svelte as Leontes for all of 20 minutes. Then, out of the sky blue to a sky blue – Lee Crooks's cross – Shaun Goater's header – Autolycus? Fulham down one–nil. Thirty-two minutes Fulham's defence advanced like a Roman Square for offside, the last man Symons failed to notice City's Gareth Taylor infiltrating as a spy. Taylor's twenty-five-yard boomer – Fulham two down. Kevin Keegan, king of the aspirate, was not 'appy – rather 'apless and 'angdog. The aspirate does not feature with Kevin. Joe Royle, king of aspiration, was joyful. City began a romp. Confidence surged through chilled limbs. They tore into Fulham, roughed 'em up a bit – the chances came. Fifty-five minutes Kevin Horlock hammered the third from a free kick. Fulham, in despair, piled on three subs, Smith, Peschisolido and Horsfield. To no avail. 'Blue Moon' rent the darkening sky, the inmates trolled off to neighbouring public houses, the nobility popped the Dom Pérignon and popped snow tyres on their Porsches. Mr Hall, the referee, on his first visit here, popped 11 yellow cards. So to you, Mr Hall, the most famous goodbye of *A Winter's Tale* – exit, pursued by a bear.

Manchester City: Nicky Weaver, Lee Crooks, Richard Edghill, Gerard Wiekens, Tony Vaughan, Kevin Horlock, Michael Brown, Jamie Pollock, Gareth Taylor, Shaun Goater, Terry Cooke. Substitutes: Paul Dickov, Ian Bishop, Jim Whitley.
Fulham: Mark Taylor, Alan Neilson, Rufus Brevett, Steve Hayward, Chris Coleman, Kit Symons, Steve Finnan, Paul Bracewell, Dirk Lehmann, Matty Brazier, Barry Hayles. Substitutes: Neil Smith, Paul Peschisolido, Geoff Horsfield.

BOLTON WANDERERS 1 – COVENTRY CITY 5
The FA Carling Premiership, 31 January 1998

Reebok, knees knock, seismic shock, schlep shmok. Tears for souvenirs, all schmaltz after Bolton's humiliation, pomp and circumstance before it. Bolton were schnooked.

A virtual ram raid by Coventry – they have scored only four away goals, and won one in twenty-three games played this season. Bolton are second from bottom with 22 points, eight games now without a win, doomed, the Damocles sword of the Nationwide League descending on their bared necks.

The first half was dominated by Bolton playing swanky, swaggering, sashaying football of high quality. Sellars gave them the lead on 22 minutes with a tap in. Noel Whelan, he of the rolling mariner's gait, equalized five minutes later. Half-time, one apiece.

Gordon Strachan's managerial peroration in the Coventry dressing-room was pure Aberdonian flecked with Anglo-Saxon invective, riper than figs burnt under a Mediterranean sun.

Coventry played furious football; they clapped on a yard of pace, a ton of application, a tanker-load of perspiration and gave Bolton a fearful tonking. Bolton's defence – a tattered veil was torn asunder on 58 minutes; Fairclough hesitated, Huckerby, head down, in a red mist, scored. Sixty-five minutes Dion Dublin's glanced header to Huckerby's right boot – Huckerby's second goal. Seventy-three minutes Dublin's shaven pate rose above the rest in Bolton's penalty box – a clinical header. Four–one to Coventry.

Dublin was by now in seventh heaven; supreme in the air, he revealed ball skills of subtle richness and balletic grace; like Katarina Witt – without the ice. Seventy-nine minutes Phillips, the hapless Bolton defender, ballooned the ball – it fell to Dublin, who in high glee popped it past Branagan for number five. Bolton had received a public flogging; will the scars heal before next week's away game at Old Trafford?

They have won one away game all season, the first day of it, at Southampton (August last year). At the close, a forlorn announcer summoned a gentleman to return to base as his wife was in labour. I imagine Colin Todd, Bolton's manager, to join him.

Bolton Wanderers: Keith Branagan, Neil Cox, Per Frandzen, Jamie Pollock, Scott Sellars, Nathan Blake, Andy Todd, Jimmy Phillips, Chris Fairclough, John Sheridan, Bob Taylor. Substitutes: Michael Johansen, Peter Beardsley, Dean Holdsworth, Mark Fish, Gavin Ward.

Coventry City: Magnus Hedman, Richard Shaw, David Burrows, Gary Breen, Darren Huckerby, Noel Whelan, Dion Dublin, Paul Telfer, Tronde Solvedt, George Boateng, Roland Nilsson. Substitutes: Marcus Hall, Viorel Moldovan, Gavin Strachan, Scott Howey, Willie Boland.

BARNSLEY 2 – EVERTON 2
The FA Carling Premiership, 7 February 1998
The lights have just gone out at Oakwell. Another 10 pence in the meter would have saved us, but this is Yorkshire, and as you are well aware Yorkists are Scotsmen with deeper pockets. Lights out means *lights out* for little Barnsley. Bottom of the league; won six games from twenty-four, conceded fifty-nine goals, scored only twenty. Arsenal took them for five, West Ham for six, Manchester United for seven. They have sampled the high life; reality is setting in. Oakwell is at altitude; the zephyr blows like a hurricane; the pie shop abuts the pissoir; the media centre is a moth-eaten Portacabin. But for antediluvian entertainment it is Las Vegas.

In a feisty first half, little Barnsley, against the wind, blew Everton off the park, Bullock playing as if he had been caped in the Corrida. I wished to place a rosette in his ear. Bosancic hashed an open goal; Ashley Ward reprieved him – crossing for Fjortoft to head a spectacular goal. Time 27 minutes. Alas for Barnsley, Ferguson replicated the goal for Everton – this from a Mitch Ward cross. Time 43 minutes. Just after half-time Tony Grant, Everton's assiduous midfielder, hit a speculative shot. The capricious wind blew the ball like a child's kite at the seaside; Watson, Barnsley's keeper, mesmerized and off-balance, fumbled that ball into his own net. Barnsley chins dropped, Everton engaged another upward gear. Barnsley regrouped: being bottom means there is nowhere else to go but up, or, more succinctly – there is no such thing as bravery – only degrees of fear. Sixty-three minutes Ashley Ward thumped the bar, Barnard scrambled home the rebound. Two–two, scant reward for Barnsley skill and style. They can play, as their fans insist: 'It's just like watching Brazil.' Trouble is, it is too pedantic and pedestrian to trouble the Premiership. Talking of style, I was fascinated by referee Martin Bodenham's running style. His knees bound for the knacker's yard.

Barnsley: David Watson, Nicky Eaden, Adie Moses, Arjan De Zeeuw, John Hendrie, Neil Redfearn, Martin Bullock, Jovo Bosancic, Darren Barnard, Ashley Ward, Jan Aage Fjortoft. Substitutes: Lars Leese, Eric Tinkler, Georgi Hristov, Peter Markstedt.

Everton: Dave Watson, Mickael Madar, Nick Barmby, Duncan Ferguson, Craig Short, Tony Grant, Gareth Farrelly, Mitch Ward, Michael Ball, Thomas Myhre, John O'Kane. Substitutes: Paul Gerrard, Claus Thomsen, John Oster, Graham Allen, Danny Cadarmateri.

EVERTON 1 – DERBY COUNTY 2

The FA Carling Premiership, 14 February 1998

Paulo Wanchope is Costa Rican. Little is known of Costa Rica. It is in Latin America, famous for volcanoes, coffee, the odd revolution, giant iguanas and eating of hats. An amazing country. It has spawned an amazing species in Paulo, a gangling beanpole, a cross between a Harlem Globetrotter and an anaconda. He is idiosyncratic, eccentric and diverting, like a Lipizzaner stallion at dressage. Today, at the School of Science he was the villain of the piece. On 16 minutes he wrapped himself, like turkey foil, around Duncan Ferguson in the Derby penalty box. 'Red mist Fergie' struck out with venomous elbows. Wanchope fell like a pile of rags. Ferguson red card: match ruined as a spectacle. The audience, some 35,000-strong, was incensed. At the first whiff of smelling salts, or some other potent unguent, Paulo was up like a trampolinist, all eager beaver. Everton down to 10.

Bilic, the Croatian lawyer, came off the bench. His first action was to gift Derby a goal. He met Rowett's corner with his intellectual head at the far post and diverted the ball, at some speed, into his own net. That goal fanned the flames. It had Messrs Smith and Kendall, rival managers, bobbing from the dugout. Two bald heads flashing in the floodlights like two monks at evensong.

Wanchope, Sweeney Todd, the demon king, tortured Everton and the loyal audience. Even worse, he scored on 50 minutes. Sturridge's low cross scudding across the Everton box – Paulo, all whirling arms and legs, tucked it past a flailing, impotent Myhre.

Is Paulo nonchalant or arrogant? Everton's 10 chased the game. Tony Grant, a peripheral figure, retired. Madar had no appetite for cut and thrust and was replaced by Allen, a callow youth.

Five minutes from time, Thomsen scored for Everton – a rebound from Carsley's shins but to no avail. Everton lost again. Relegation looms; Kendall's P45 is being prepared yet again. But I wonder what Duncan is saying to Paulo right now – another volcano in Costa Rica? Or, 'That Costa Pointa'?

Everton: Thomas Myhre, Tony Thomas, Craig Short, Dave Watson, Carl Tiler, Michael Ball, Gareth Farrelly, Tony Grant, John Oster, Mickael Madar, Duncan Ferguson. Substitutes: Paul Gerrard, Slaven Bilic, Claus Thomsen, Danny Cadamarteri, Grahan Allen.

Derby County: Mart Poom, Gary Rowett, Chris Powell, Igor Stimac, Dean Sturridge, Paulo Wanchope, Rory Delap, Ron Willems, Lee Carsley, Stefano Eranio, Christain Dailly. Substitutes: Russell Hoult, Darryl Powell, Marc Bridge-Wilkinson, Steve Elliot, Robert Kozluk.

BOLTON WANDERERS 1 – WEST HAM UNITED 1

The FA Carling Premiership, 21 February 1998

I am now habituated to centre forwards receiving red cards. Last week Duncan Ferguson in a mistral of red mist, today John Hartson, West Ham's wild bull of the pampas. Hartson is primitive man, a massive physical presence, a wild Celtic temperament, complete disdain for law and order. A Boeotian of ancient Greece. These rude, unlettered, agricultural peasants were classified by the Athenians as blockheads. Hartson's elbows are as sharp as knives on Boudicca's chariot. He chopped Jamie Pollock. Pollock was poleaxed. Off went Mr Hartson, Mr Redknapp venting his spleen as Hartson went by.

Engagingly, the event galvanized West Ham, especially Berkovic, a sly, devious, skilful inside forward of Israel. Berkovic broke out, ran 40 yards, gesticulated to Trevor Sinclair exactly where Sinclair should be. Sinclair obeyed the instruction, received the pass on his instep, rounded the keeper Branagan, and scored a sweet goal. Ten men, one up.

Bolton had to react. Up to this point they had been timorous, anxious, defensively minded, cowed and overawed. West Ham, oozing class, had rippled the futuristic Reebok Stadium with futuristic moves, unruffled in defence, cultured in attack. Moncur was insolent and incisive, calmly dissecting Bolton's defence. Berkovic incinerated them. Together they are hegemony. Bolton, lacking real pace, could not launch an offensive. Holdsworth's two-minute goal was disallowed for offside. Bolton suffered inferiority from that moment. So off came Fairclough, on roared Gunnlaugsson firing from the hip. Four minutes from time he skinned Pearce on the left, crossed deep – Nathan

Blake headed the equalizer. Now muck and nettles Bolton. A Redknapp rollicking for Hartson.

Bolton Wanderers: Keith Branagan, Neil Cox, Alan Thompson, Andy Todd, Chris Fairclough, Gudni Bergsson, Jamie Pollock, Michael Johansen, Per Frandzen, Nathan Blake, Dean Holdsworth. Substitutes: Gavin Ward, John Sheridan, Jimmy Philips, Scott Taylor, Arnar Gunnlaugsson.

West Ham United: Craig Forrest, David Unsworth, Ian Pearce, Rio Ferdinand, Frank Lampard, John Moncur, Eyal Berkovic, Stan Lazaridis, Andy Impey, John Hartson, Trevor Sinclair. Substitutes: Bernard Lama, Ian Bishop, Steve Potts, Lee Hodges, Scott Mean.

EVERTON 0 – NEWCASTLE UNITED 0
The FA Carling Premiership, 28 February 1998

Cynics say history is but a distillation of popular beliefs. History at the School of Science is tangible. I did not cull it from gentle whispering in the cradle. I saw it, savoured it, revelled in it. Preserved in aspic for all time. And so it came to pass that this awful match will have the heavenly wraiths of Goodison choke on their nectar. Dixie Dean, Tommy Lawton, Cliff Britton, Joe Mercer, divine masters of their art, will twitch the royal purple and return to tiddlywinks. This match was truly a dogfight in the bowels of the Premiership.

Ferguson was absent. He is always absent with his diverse ailments or suspensions, so Everton missed his red mist presence. They played three centre backs terrified of Shearer's combative spirit, and left themselves lightweight in attack. Shearer unleashed a minor salvo of shots early in the game, and then disappeared under a mantle of Bilic, Tiler and Short. Gary Speed, returning to Goodison, was derided from start to finish. Batty flattened everything in sight. Pearce's thunder thighs were always in conflict. 'Psycho' relishes the battle like a wild boar in mud. He hauls his knickers up to reveal his anaconda thighs. Once at Oldham a brave but foolhardy peasant uttered the cry: 'Pull yer shorts up, yer big Jessie.' 'Psycho' ran to the touchline, shot the inmate a disembowelling glare, and attempted to vault the retaining wall. It took a posse of weather-beaten bobbies to restrain him. Madar, a French itinerant in Everton colours, blanched as Pearce thundered like a Panzer corps: '*C'est magnifique, mais ce n'est pas la guerre.*' Madar, casting nervous thoughts back to Waterloo, played like Edith Piaf, the six-stone waif of Paris. Tackles flew in, bodies littered the pitch in casualty-clearing station propensity. 'Twas all negative, redolent of hare coursing at nearby Waterloo. Madar almost fainted at the mention of the word.

Nil–nil the non-score. So depressing that the entire Newcastle squad, 21 in number, and yes, including Shearer, emerged at five o'clock for further exercise. Military jankers, I suppose. But their 15 minutes' callisthenics to promote heath and beauty were far more absorbing than the previous 90.

To the gods of Goodison I implore: 'Forgive them: for they know not what they do.'

Everton: Thomas Myhre, Mitch Ward, Michael Ball, Craig Short, Slaven Bilic, Carl Tiler, John O'Kane, Gareth Farrelly, Don Hutchison, Mickael Madar, Danny Cadamarteri. Substitutes: Paul Gerrard, John Oster, Phillip Jevons, Dave Watson, Graham Allen.

Newcastle United: Shay Given, Warren Barton, David Batty, Steven Howey, Robert Lee, Alan Shearer, Gary Speed, Stuart Pearce, Keith Gillespie, Phillippe Albert, Andreas Andersson. Substitutes: Shaka Hislop, Darren Peacock, John Barnes, Temuri Ketsbaia, Jon Dahl Tomasson.

CREWE ALEXANDRA 0 – CHARLTON ATHLETIC 3

Nationwide Football League, Division One, 21 March 1998

Gresty Road, Alexandra's tight little ground, lies in the shadow of Crewe Station, that vast junction of endless lonely platforms, nasal announcers, soulless buffets and winking signals. Trains from distant parts trundle in, then thunder away to Never-Never. Crewe Station still strikes a chill, as I recall hours I spent there as a young national serviceman in khaki. Hours of stag amid dense fog and thick black smoke ascending from huge weather-stained locomotives. Wisps of steam, the stench of hot oil, the slamming of carriage doors. Like countless other would-be graduates, I served king and country fighting the enemy in hot spots like the drill hall, Aldershot, and Quaglino's, London.

Gresty Road, after today, I shall rename Crest Fallen Road. Alex were shunted by Charlton on to a blind branch line. Charlton on the fast track to promotion. Charlton this week paid £350,000 for fullback Danny Mills. He shattered Crewe when after a mere three minutes he ghosted into the Crewe penalty box and headed a goal. The Mills grind fast, not slow at Charlton. Crewe with a posse of scouts in attendance regained their poise, played attractive football of winsome style, forced Charlton on the back foot, but wasted divine opportunities to capitalize. Forty-three minutes Clive Mendonca, the Shylock of Charlton, flipped a pass to Shaun Newton. This lad is a flier in the Carl Lewis mode – he simply flowed into a rhythmic stride and finished with a blockbuster shot. Two–nil at half-time. Crewe reminded me of early Barnsley. Studied, sweet football but at funereal pace. Charlton overwhelmed them second half. Old heads Mendonca and Bright used space and played into it for the fleet of foot. Sheer speed and positive thought on the rampage. Seventy-six minutes Paul Mortimer, lithe and languid, played a ball to Kinsella's bootlace. Kinsella nodded grateful thanks and lashed the third goal.

Mr Curbishley, the Charlton manager, was a stylish craftsman with West Ham. His visage is Squirrel Nutkin. His team remind me of spring squirrels, quicksilver and muscle. They will reach the Premiership, but do they have the pure quality to survive? Curbishley is learning. Dario Gradi, the Crewe coach, will return to the drawing board. The scouts departed, nuggets of gold like Murphy, Hignett and David Platt will not be unearthed in this current crop. And me – back to Cold Compost Farm on draughty Crewe Station. The 6.31 p.m. to Oswaldtwistle beckons.

Crewe Alexandra: Jason Kearton, Marcus Bignot, Shaun Smith, Mark Foran, Dave Walton, Phil Charnock, Jermaine Wright, Gareth Whalley, Steve Guinan, Seth Johnson, Colin Little. Substitutes: Steve Anthrobus, Kenny Lunt, Lee Unsworth.
Charlton Athletic: Sasa Ilic, Danny Mills, Mark Bowen, Keith Jones, Phil Chapple, Stuart Balmer, Shaun Newton, Mark Kinsella, John Robinson, Clive Mendonca, Mark Bright. Substitutes: Paul Mortimer, Kevin Lisbie, Paul Konshesky.

WEST BROMWICH ALBION 3 – SUNDERLAND 3
Nationwide Football League, Division One, 13 April 1998

Easter Monday in the Black Country. The hawthorn in bud, but what is blooming at the Hawthorns, home of perfidious Albion? The 'Baggies' languish mid-table, Sunderland are second. Peter Reid, their manager, with his jug ears, pepper-and-salt hair, master of the Anglo-Saxon, is assembling a fine team. To think Manchester City sacked him for being merely fifth in the top flight. The vicissitudes of football management.

''Tis a bright day, but 'tis the bright day that brings forth the adder – and that craves wary walking.' Michael Gray, Sunderland's number three, did not heed. He was dispatched from the fray on 35 minutes for a spot of GBH. Referee Lomas fell under the spell – he retired lame at half-time. Nipped by the adder or simply a fit of the vapours. I cannot enlighten you dear listener – I was too idle to enquire.

But to the meat – what a game – a rollicking rigwiddy romp in the sun. Sunderland were two down in twelve minutes. Hughes and Kilbane catching Sunderland's defence in deep snooze under the noses of 5,000 of their travelling troubadour fans. Eighteen minutes Niall Quinn, yards offside, nicked a goal. Twenty-eight minutes Summerbee's lofted cross, Albion's defence cross-legged in fear of Quinn's towering presence, Kevin Phillips stole in for a classic poacher's goal. Phillips must be the steal of the century. Bought from Watford for flump-pence, he is a flying ferret. Low centre of gravity, highly nimble, he flits into space and simply grabs vital goals.

Quinn is the enigma. He looks top-heavy, appears clumsy and awkward with the ball at his feet, but he is imperious in the air. Why did the Arsenal release him? Why did Manchester City waste him? And off the pitch he is articulate, intelligent, witty – and a perfect gent. Two apiece, then Gray's red card reduced Sunderland to ten!

Fifty-four minutes Quinn the paradox – cunning footwork, a solo run and a cheeky chip over the Baggies' keeper Adamson. Albion were incensed; three–two down to ten men. The Alamo in the burning sun. Albion on ferocious charge. Lionel Perez – remember him of the Shirley Temple locks? Gosh – remember Shirley Temple? Well, he has shorn off his tonsorial tresses and discovered hidden depths of goalkeeping talent. He was heroic. Alas, as the seconds ticked down, Albion equalized on 93 minutes – Lee Hughes, his second of the match. Peter Reid waggled his ears, a passing pachyderm waggled back. Dennis Smith, manager of West Brom, awaits his P45.

To coin a cliché – an Easter egg of a match.

West Bromwich Albion: Chris Adamson, Andy McDermott, Jason Van Blerk, Sean Flynn, Paul Beesley, Matthew Carbon, James Quinn, Steve Nicol, Andy Hunt, Lee Hughes, Kevin Kilbane. Substitutes: Stacy Coldicott, Richard Sneekes, Shaun Murphy.

Sunderland: Lionel Perez, Chris Makin, Michael Gray, Lee Clark, Darren Holloway, Darren Williams, Nicky Summerbee, Kevin Ball, Niall Quinn, Kevin Phillips, Allan Johnston. Substitutes: Dan Dichio, Alex Rae, Jody Craddock.

BOLTON WANDERERS 2 – LEEDS UNITED 3
The FA Carling Premiership, 18 April 1998

Rough justice at the Reebok. But justice is a concept – muscle is the reality. Leeds had the pragmatic muscle, Bolton the style, the passion, the Kultur, but, mystifyingly for a side packed with Nordics, the Viking ethic was missing – nil raping, pillaging and burning. They exhibited English naivety, gifting Leeds two first-half goals that left Bolton chasing the game.

But what a chase – nail-biting, controversial, exciting. Haaland and Halle scored those Leeds goals. Are the Nordics appropriating the Premier League? Bolton, on the riposte, hit the post twice – all oohs and aahs. Then Alan Thompson, he of the Charlie Mitten–Bobby Charlton School of Howitzer Shot, struck a free kick straight, strong and low. Super goal, Bolton back in the game, and with style – Todd style. The referee, Mr Winter, made bizarre decisions. Mr Graham, the Leeds manager, clad in Armani, restrained by his assistant, Mr David O'Leary, clad by Oxfam.

The crowd, all belligerences, bellowed: 'Now is the *Winter* of our discontent.' Mr Winter stood unabashed. Eight-six minutes Jimmy Floyd Hasselbaink scored a breakaway goal for Leeds. Mark Fish a desperate goal on ninety-two minutes for Bolton. Colin Todd is a forlorn figure, contemplating life in the bowels of next season's Division One. Leeds show great promise of heady days to come – but will Gorgeous George be leader? A siren song emanates from the cockerel at Tottenham Hotspur. Watch this space.

Bolton Wanderers: Keith Branagan, Neil Cox, Mark Fish, Alan Thompson, Jimmy Phillips, Gudni Bergsson, John Sheridan, Andy Todd, Per Frandzen, Nathan Blake, Bob Taylor. Substitutes: Jussi Jaaskelainen, Michael Johansen, Gerry Taggert, John Salako, Gaetano Giallanza.

Leeds United: Nigel Martyn, Gary Kelly, Alf-Inge Haaland, Lucas Radebe, David Wetherall, Jimmy Hasselbaink, Lee Bowyer, Gunnar Halle, Harry Kewell, Ian Harte, Martin Hiden. Substitutes: Mark Beeney, Robert Molenaar, David Hopkin, Mark Jackson, Rod Wallace.

MANCHESTER CITY 2 – QUEENS PARK RANGERS 2
Nationwide Football League, Division One, 25 April 1998

The last home game of the season. The last home game in Division One. City are doomed. The Stygian cave of Division Two is now reality. Joe Royle has been at the Theatre of Base Comedy for two months. He is helpless. Hubris has prevailed here since the heady days of the 1960s. 'Tis now nemesis – divine retribution. Joe is Hercules; three-headed dogs await him at outposts like Macclesfield and Wycombe. City have to beat QPR today. The foot of the table reads: Reading 42 points. Portsmouth 43. Manchester City 44. Stoke City 46. Port Vale 46. QPR 48.

Two seasons ago City were in the Premiership, third from bottom, needing to beat Liverpool to stay up. Liverpool did everything possible to ensure City's survival. They played with ennui, disdain – total disinterest. City idiotically played for a two–two draw and went down.

Could history repeat itself today? Relegation is a disaster. City have bankrolled on flimsy hopes of success. The bankroll is a spider's web. City have always been in hock. Bank borrowing to horrific levels. High-priced, non-delivery players. An abyss. The audience, though, is incredible. Thirty-two thousand singing 'Blue Moon', waving giant bananas, on a flood tide of emotion.

At 2.50 p.m. the players held aloft a banner with a strange device: 'Thank you for your loyal support!' It is a lachrymose farewell to the good times. City gave their all throughout the match. Committed, passionate, bristling for action. And what action.

Kinkladze, the folk hero restored by demand, gave them a sensational start. A free kick in the first minute low inside the far post. Seven minutes later Mike Sheron, a City old boy, equalized for QPR. Maine Road was a crucible, not for the faint heart or those of nervous disposition. Then nobody could invent a plot like this. Twenty-one minutes Margetson, the City keeper, lunged off his line to intercept a QPR cross. He did not inform Pollock, his captain, who headed the ball back over Margetson's despairing body into his own net. Margetson, playing with broken knuckles, stranded, helpless and furious. City needed the cavalry: this was Little Big Horn.

The troops mounted fierce attacks – hit the bar twice, Lee Bradbury missed golden chances. Razor Ruddock at the heart of QPR's defence was the hatchet man thumping everything above grass height. Vincent Jones, hod carrier turned superstar, shanghaied City players, mugging and blagging. Four minutes in the second half, hopes raised. A sly pass from Goater, Bradbury atoned for profligacy and, with the goal gaping, scored. Two goals apiece. QPR were battered. The crowd urging, pleading, crying, bellowing for just one more City goal. Quashie was sent off five minutes from time – more hope – no avail. Two–two. QPR are safe. City retired with a fond farewell and to plaudits. One game to come at Stoke, but we all realize that this is the nadir. Farewell to giant stadia, fame, fortune and silverware. Hello scrattin-sheds, chicken runs and the Stygian cave.

Manchester City: Martyn Margetson, Richard Edghill, Kevin Horlock, Ged Brannan, Kit Symons, Tony Vaughan, Jim Whitley, Jamie Pollock, Shaun

Goater, Georgie Kinkladze, Lee Bradbury. Substitutes: Paul Dickov, Craig Russell, Ian Bishop.
Queens Park Rangers: Lee Harper, David Bardsley, Ian Barraclough, Vinnie Jones, Danny Maddix, Neil Ruddock, Steve Yates, Nigel Quashie, Mike Sheron, Kevin Gallen, Steve Slade. Substitutes: Matthew Rose, Antti Heinola, Gavin Peacock.

BLACKBURN ROVERS 1 – NEWCASTLE 0
The FA Carling Premiership, 10 May 1998
The last match of the season at Ewood Park. Newcastle play in the Cup Final next week; Blackburn reflect on an appalling last 10 matches. Two wins, seven defeats, Roy Hodgson's future in jeopardy; Mr Walker the munificent, Uncle Jack the benefactor not best pleased. Shearer has sheared Jack of his fleece, departing Ewood for the Palazzio. Likewise David Batty, the gritstone mill of Yorkshire – he, too, took the Newcastle shilling and deserted Uncle Jack.

False bonhomie was ever present at 4 p.m. on this Sunday. Fireworks, speeches, balloons to light up this drab corner of East Lancashire. Ewood Park, for all its concrete and steel kitsch splendour, sits awkwardly among the Victorian back-to-backs. Alan Shearer has been headlined recently for blatantly kicking an opponent's head. Rumour hath it that Mr Shearer has turned to Kipling, no, not the maker of fine cakes, but Kipling the bard!

'If you can keep your head when all about you are losing theirs and blaming it on you, you'll be a man, my son.' Mr Shearer is a man of deeds, not words; roundly booed, he smiled a grim reaper's smile and put himself about a bit. So did David Batty; he was sent off early in the second half for a silly retaliation foul, in fairness more sinned against than sinning. Astonishing, really, as prior to this conflagration the match had failed to ignite. Newcastle rehearsing Wembley moves at leisure, Blackburn muted, inhibited, lacking thrust and bite.

Blackburn roused themselves; the 30,000 crowd demanded a cavalry charge on Newcastle's 10. It was the bum's rush, never a charge. Three minutes from time a Blackburn free kick outside the box; Chris Sutton, who always looks ill-tempered and tetchy, extracted vengeance on the poor match ball lying on the greensward in all innocence. His run reminiscent of Darren Gough, 15 yards at the double. The poor ball flew from Sutton's foot, blasting its route through Newcastle defenders and into the net. Those defenders nodded at each other, grateful that none had impaired his sexual prowess, or neutered himself attempting to halt the missile's progress. Sutton's eighteenth goal of the season. It propels Blackburn into Europe via the back door. Hodgson can breathe again, rumbles of Sutton's discontent muffled. Newcastle off to Wembley. Mr Walker to his counting house.
Blackburn Rovers: Tim Flowers, Colin Hendry, Stuart Ripley, Kevin Gallacher, Chris Sutton, Jason Wilcox, Billy McKinlay, Garry Flitcroft, Stephane Henchoz, Damien Duff. Substitutes: Martin Dahlin, Anders Andersson, Gary Croft, Martin Broomes, John Filan.

Newcastle United: Shay Given, David Batty, Alan Shearer, John Barnes, Gary Speed, Temuri Ketbaia, Stephen Watson, Alessandro Pistone, Phillippe Albert, Nikolaos Dabizas, Andrew Griffin. Substitutes: Ian Rush, Stuart Pearce, Des Hamilton, Andreas Andersson, Shaka Hislop.

A MAN IS BADLY IN NEED OF ADVICE WHEN HE HAS MANY ADVISERS

'Sit thee in the chair of Hiram the Bith. First artificer of Solomon. I shall build thee a temple hundreds of cubits high. I shall use thousands of slaves. Use tons of finest Italian marble.' A temple of supplicants to worship their heroes, dwell in Olympian success and return to their mundane lives, to live shallow existence in their tiny houses.

'The inherited glory go with thee and shine upon thee.'

It began with Bob Lord, the Burnley butcher. Turf Moor was his personal temple. Gruff, uncultured, maybe uncouth. His manner was a cross of Rottweiler with Margaret Thatcher. A total despot. A ruthless manipulator, yet a benefactor. He typified the local dignitary who ruled the town. Built like a pampas bull, deaf as a post – unless you uttered something derogatory. Then you were banned. Yet he, and his like, built football teams *par excellence*. His Burnley of Pilkington, Adams, McIlroy, Miller, Pointer, Coates won championships and cups.

Industry thrived in the Rossendale Valley. Wakes week took place. The workforce traipsed to Blackpool. Roistered along the promenade. Complete, if naive, in happiness.

Then there was Albert Alexander, the diminutive chairman of Manchester City. Dapper, charming, high-pitched voice, bespoke-suited, worth a bob or two.

Good Friday 1963. Manchester City at home in the bowels of the Football League. A hopeless case, George Poyser an inept manager. In the BBC newsroom, Manchester, above the National Westminster Bank, a message flashed: 'Riot at Maine Road.'

I rushed down to witness hundreds of angry fans smashing windows, fighting the Peelers and crying lustily for the head of Albert. The directors were cowering inside. I approached Albert. 'Alberto, 'tis time for an interview.' White-faced, he agreed. That was the good news. The bad was – I had no lights for filming indoors. It had to be outside, with the madding crowd baying for blood.

I appeared on the steps. The audience, realizing that they were to witness an extraordinary happening, attempted to touch the hem of my robe. I brushed them aside and spake: 'Hear ye the word of Albert. It is of mighty import.' Thus, Albert stepped forward. The crowd pressed forward. It was intimidating, frightening foolhardy on our part.

'Silence, silence, give ear.' Silence descended. A new era, a fresh dawn, the clouds roll by after the rain. Silver from Tarshich, gold from Uphaz. The silver is Malcolm Allison. The gold is Joe Mercer.

Eight thousand fans rejoiced, fears allayed, hope restored. They cheered. They hoisted little Albert on their shoulders. Tears filled his eyes and coursed down his cheeks. What a brave little man. And what an era was spawned that day. The flame shall not be quenched, and all faces from the south shall be burned therein.

Present-day chairmen are a different breed. Despots exist like Ken Bates, a brontosaurus with a real sore arse. Loveable, romantic, waspish, idiosyncratic, maverick, Machiavellian, but clever enough to hearken to accountants and lawyers. At Oldham he walked on water. Then some infidel put nails through his feet.

David Moores of Liverpool. Poacher turned gamekeeper. He came to Liverpool when Liverpool was a family. Bob Paisley, the greatest manager ever in the world. Joe Fagan, Ronnie Morgan, Roy Evans, Tom Saunders, Peter Robinson and *paterfamilias* John Smith.

John Smith, the meeter and greeter. All teeth and smiles. Downstairs the 'Boot Room'. Gin and tonic with ice and lemon. Yes, they installed a fridge in that hallowed 'Boot Room' to shut me up. Liverpool was a total family. The players honoured to be part of it.

David Moores, with Scouse vowels and Beatle hairdo, was raised in that bountiful tradition. Today David is bewildered. The family is no more. Commercialism, player power, greed, disloyalty, the TV bandwagon. It is rolling over David like a storm-lashed sea. Granada TV have rolled in too. They know a ripe lemon ready to be squeezed. Ask Rocco Forte. Even the pips squeak when Gerry puts the boot in. Will Anfield, the Colosseum, rise again with gladiatorial cries, or degenerate into French farce?

'And he looked up and saw the rich man casting their gifts into the treasury. And he saw a poor widow casting in two mites. Of truth I say unto you, that this poor widow hath cast more than they all'. He is Martin Edwards. My tennis partner. Played two, won two. He is anything but a poor widow and, brethren, seen rich men bestow upon the Shrine much gold and silver. And the riches stayed in the Shrine. It became Solomon's temple. Solomon Edwards attracted disciples. One of them Rowland, son of Smith. An academic with a fierce commercial bent. Such men are dangerous. They wield power.

He spake thus: 'Thou wilt walk in my ways, keep my statutes and my commandments. Thou shalt buy the best artisans, nay artists, from the world's cauldron and win the treble.'

Alex, son of Ferguson, a warlike Celt, came south. A fearsome yeoman from the bowels of that strange kingdom of Scotland. He spake 3,000 proverbs, his songs were 1,000 fires. Alex was wise in the ways of men. When the sardine followed the trawler, he shot the seagull and sank the trawler. Alex is omnipotent. He overlaid the temple with gold. His United is worshipped throughout the world. Solomon now has several temples in many countries. They speak not our language but pay for the fleece of United. It changeth colour from season to season, but doth it matter? They must have the fleece and be, to be frank, fleeced.

And so it came to pass that Alex, when the Kidd grew to be fatted calf, slaughtered it and gave it to Blackburn, a settlement in the Lancashire lowlands.

There a Pharisee, Jacob Walker, had turned base metal into gold. He was no alchemist. He simply dug iron from the ground and fashioned it into steel. Desiring to emulate Solomon Edwards, he built a small edifice at the bottom of a hill and lavished his fortune on gladiators.

Yet another Celt, chieftain Kenny of the Dalglish tribe, bought famous jousters and, against all soothsayers' and prophets' dire warnings, won the silver pot. Kenny was clothed with camel's hair, with a girdle of skin about his loins. He did eat locusts and wild honey. He was profound with his niblick. Alas, Blackburn jousted badly in Europe. Battles were lost against a Viking team of Rosenbourg. Ewood became a mausoleum – a garden of Rosenbourgs – of remembrance. Jacob Walker was displeased. The veil of Ewood was rent in twain. The earth did quake. The rocks rent. Kenny was cast into the wilderness. Artisans, disenchanted, left also. Shearer, Batty, Sutton, Flowers, Ripley, Le Saux. Dross remained. Jacob to this day ponders the fates. He reads the runes. Consults the soothsayers.

Brian of the Kidd, condemned by Alex of the Ferguson, is now in the wilderness, grasping defeat from the jaws of victory. Jacob Walker cannot see the Ewood for the trees. Moral of story: 'All that glisters is not gold.' St Souness now wears the purple. He never came second. He will triumph.

At Leeds, hard by Jericho, is Peter Ridsdale, their chairman. He wanted a Celt from the Irish north, failed, and thus appointed a Celt from the south, yclept David. Many shekels flow in Leeds. And David said unto his men: 'Gird ye on every man his sword.' And David also girded on his sword: and there went up after David about 40 men and boys, 20 abode by the stuff. David is in envy of Solomon Edwards and Alex of Govan but, alas, young excellence is not enough. Silver will be seen in 2001.

Alan Sugar, purveyor of new cymbals, or symbols to the multitude. Furthermore, he speaketh a strange tongue and hath a strange philosophy. He hath cut off those that have familiar spirits and cast the wizard Venables out of the land. The burning spear handeth to George, son of Graham, winner of many battles as foot soldier and leader. Spurs shall rise with each season passing.

David Dein, Lord of the Arsenal, he sayeth to Arsene: 'Gird up thy loins, and take my staff in thine hand and go thy way. If thou meet any man from Britannia, salute him not, but men of Gaul salute and enslave.' So it came to pass that Viera, Petit and Henry unfold the Tricolour and put away the raiment of St George. Truth shall spring out of the earth: and righteousness shall look down from heaven.

Deadly Doug of the Villa. Then arose Doug and made all chief priests, the Levites and all Brummagem to swear that they should do according to his word. And they sware. And it came to pass that Ronald of Atkinson and Brian of Little, on hearing the word, sat down and wept, and mourned certain days and fasted. Defy the statues of Deadly Doug and thou shalt be cast into the wilderness.

THE HABIT OF AGREEING SEEMS TOO DANGEROUS AND SLIPPERY

The wages of sin is death. Is it a sin, brethren, to earn £4 million of a year? Let me speak unto you – if you were Roy Keane, a humble son of the soil of Cork, living off potatoes, wearing woad, lashed by the wild Atlantic Ocean, would you refuse a mountain of gold? Nay, nay, 1,000 nays.

'Let us erect an altar to greed. Make stars of shittim wood, and overlay them with brass. Hangings of fine linen a hundred cubits long.' The hooks of silver. The sockets of brass. Tons, tons of brass. Footballers love brass.

Once upon a time footballers retired at 30, married hairdressers and opened a pub. Remember John Higgins? He played centre half for Bolton Wanderers in the 1950s. The phrase 'a brick outhouse' was coined for him. I always imagined him holding up the Forth Bridge with one hand. He was a colossus. Behind him were Hartle and Banks. Fullbacks whose tackles began at knee height and worked their way up. Going to Burnden Park in those days was akin to visiting a bear pit in Berne.

Big John had a large round face. To call it florid would be an injustice. It was like a mandrill's arse. All colours: red, puce, purple, orange. He had large pearly-white molars. If you were not caught up in his reaper and blinder tackles, he would gnash you to pieces.

At Burnden the keeper of opponents' houses shall tremble, the strong men shall bow themselves, the grinders cease because they are few, and those that look out of dressing-room windows be darkened.

Off the pitch, John was a 'beaut', as the Aussies say. A man's man. A barrel of mirth. A wheeler-dealer in the Arthur Daley mode. Fond of his ale. Then he opened a pub. It never closed. 'Twas in the foothills of Derbyshire, closeted among sheep farms and piggeries. What a hostelry! In those days we had licensing laws. The local bobbies would enter the front door ostensibly to call time. Then tiptoe round the pub to re-enter by the back door, and roister until dawn.

I remember one carouse vividly. I have always been a petrol-head fascinated by motorcars. I shall write more on my 50-year stable subsequently. Suffice to say that my mount that night was an Armstrong Siddeley Star Sapphire. A huge cream and gold pose-mobile. Mushroom leather. Cocktail cabinets front and rear. A tartlet trap. I had taken t' wife to Big John's. Stayed until dawn, literally. I drove at a sedate pace through the Hope Valley. Suddenly the sun rose and flooded the valley with a roseate, incredibly beautiful light. You could almost smell the lushness of the fields. Inhale the pines. The world in bloom. I was overcome by the mystery of nature. Breathlessly I exclaimed:

'Night's candles are burnt out, and russet dawn stands tiptoe on the sleepy mountaintops.' I threw the automatic gearbox into reverse. The cogs screamed for mercy. Much graunching and grinding. The car lurched drunkenly backwards and forwards, eventually settling on its haunches. Now, brethren, there is a golden rule. Do not mess with automatic boxes. They bite back. The dawn euphoria died. I fumbled with the lever. The only gear I could select was first. We crawled home at 10 mph. Rolls-Royce made the gearbox. A replacement cost £450, roughly £4,000 in today's money.

That is roughly equivalent to 20 minutes' play from your superstar footballer.

'Are they worth it?' I hear you asking. Of course not, I reply. For £1 million a year Big John is apoplectic, musing into his heavenly nectar. He never earned that in his lifetime.

And what happened to Big John? Alas, he drank the proceeds. Led the bibulous sessions from the front, behind and on the bar. He bade us fond farewell from the bottom of a pint pot.

A million pounds a year. I suppose for that money, in any walk of life, you are entitled to a top professional. A man or woman with brains, expertise, training and, above all, application.

My son Danny set his stall to become a lawyer. A slog at school for twelve GCSEs, four A-levels at A grade, a top degree at university. Years of articles and, at 24 years old, fully qualified, ready for the job. Now, at 37, he is senior partner with Eversheds, one of the world's leading law firms. His salary, excellent in lay terms, simply does not stack up with that enjoyed by footballers. And he is number one in the merit list.

Take McManaman – I am glad they have. Like most British footballers, John Charles and Denis Law apart, McManaman has not the quality to succeed in world football. I have watched his play down the years and likened it to a fox loose in a chicken coop. Running wildly into blind alleys. Little tactical awareness. No subtlety in the play. Coltish in the extreme. His display in Warsaw crystallized all his faults. Playing down the left. Even the dimmer fans, let alone international managers, know that Mac is a right-footer. His left is standing room only. Show him the touchline, and he is finished. Surely, a professional could hone up? Practise, practise with his left foot? Three hours every afternoon is all it would take. Every professional has to practise. Concert pianists, golfers, tennis stars, basketball players, motor-racers, athletes dedicate their lives pursuing perfection. Is it too much to ask that the pro footballers eradicate gross faults? If McManaman was in ballet he would not even make the chorus. (A member of the corps de ballet earns £200 a week.) And yet McManaman represents England. It is like an albatross wearing the three lions. Get real, Real. A week is a long time in politics; it is even shorter in football. Bill Shankly would have sorted him. Holding Liverpool to ransom. Refusing to move mid-season knowing that a free transfer was available is reprehensible. Shanks would have had him down the road quick sticks, never to return.

Main picture: The Baker's Boy. Would butter melt in my mouth? I won 2nd prize with this outfit. I've been coming second ever since!

Right: Doris Jackson, my first teacher. Sublime, sympathetic Doris. Can you fall in love at four years old?

Below: We know whence we came. Traditional dress in Hadfield, a small hamlet in Derbyshire. Breakfast was wild elk on the hoof with poached weasel slain with bow and arrow, or the jaw bone of an ass.

Left: 1 March 1968 – Nuptials at St Andrew's Church, Hadfield. I've never attended a wedding so full of joy and happiness. A full church; a splendid choir; a gay vicar; all my pals in great voice. Hazel a beautiful wife. Could a man ever be so lucky? Although … weak men believe in luck; strong men believe in cause and effect!

Right: The family Hall. The old fart on the right; Danny, in his Brideshead mode, on the left. Hazel in the middle; Francesca in demure mode at the base.

Below: Red Book Time. Grandson Ben, the star of the show. I thought he was abed, being but two years old. He ran down the set like Concorde. Made the night. PS He is two-footed. Offers please in writing!

Right: My passion – clocks!
Lesson one: never hold them
by the handle – support them
with the loose hand. One day
I didn't – the clock fell and
smashed to smithereens.
I slashed my wrists.

Below: An eccentric – nay,
mad – collector. A magpie
Capricorn building his nest.
Fifty clocks; antique furniture;
knick-knacks infest my house.
Give me timeless pleasure;
infuriate Hazel.

Above: *It's A Knockout* for Lord's Taverners. HRH Princess Anne – a clever, feisty lady who doesn't mince words; a doughty opponent; disdains frippery; suffers fools with horror; should be Prime Minister. A Knockout. Gennaro bows low; my Union Flag sweater was nicked; Eddie Waring awaits.

Right: The halcyon days of *Knockout*. A way of life for me, the family, Eddie, Arthur and Barney. The BBC ruled!

Below right: Rifleman Aspel of the Rifle Corps accosts Col Hall of the ACC. 'It's Jankers for you, Hall,' says Aspel, brandishing the red book on the Moll Flanders set at Granada Studios. I was pitching for £50,000 worth of *Knockout* business at Microsoft. I refused to realise that Aspel was serious. My *K.O.* friends in the background were overjoyed.

Above: Great men are modest, unassuming and kind. Insecure as the rest of us but happy in their own skins. Gennaro Olivieri, the fellow madman who refereed *Jeux Sans Frontières*. Harry Secombe – simply a wonderful chap. Eric Morecambe – peerless comic.

Right: 'I wandered lonely as a cloud/That floats on high o'er vales and hills ...' Was I lonely? Marooned on a pontoon on a bathing pool, compèring a televised beauty competition. The wind blew Force Eight. The cameramen on similar pontoons retired – seasick!

Above: Blanco the Lion took a real shine to me. Hugged me, kissed me, simulated sex. Gorgeous animal, though his breath was like a rugby forward's jockstrap. A favourite at Belle Vue Zoo, when it closed Blanco was apprenticed to a circus. During one act, he mauled the trainer, savagely tearing him to pieces. Blanco was shot.

Above right: Bill Roache, alias Ken Barlow – the longest-serving actor in a soap (*Guinness Book of Records*). The greatest guy in the business. Straight, honest, kind. If Bill says he'll do something for charity, he does it, no matter what the cost. He never lets you down.

Right: 'The wild, outre, louche, decadent days' – outside the Georgian pad in Glossop. The TVR – too fast to be tamed, like a night out with Sharon Stone. The Jaguar S – nerves filled the E-type's boots. The Blydenstein bomb – the 'Droop Snoot' Firenza. It required the might of Samson, the strength of Garth to tame it. A crazed, hairy beast. I've always loved bikes. When falling off, the brain says, 'This is going to hurt.' The brain is always right!

Bishop Davies wearing my hair and some of the tinware we accumulated.

Shanks was a great buddy, straight, honest, teak-tough. He demanded discipline and trust. He would regale me with stories, strictly not for airing publicly. Once at Melwood I sat, as usual, with a mug of tea, listening avidly. Suddenly I saw a tiny tot footballer doing incredible things. 'Who is that black-haired, short-arsed player, Shanks?'

'Just signed him for 39,000. Name's Keegan; no brains, but fast and bloody brave.'

Yes 'twas Kevin, king of the aspirate.

Kev went on to be one of the great centre forwards. A natural footballer – it was obvious on that first glimpse. But – no brains, according to the oracle of Merseyside. I must confess I saw little tactical awareness in the subsequent years, but Kev was above all the blackboard posturing. He knew his job, got on with it, picked up his wages, moved on, and became rich and happy. At Newcastle, as manager, he gave free rein to natural talent. It was exciting football. Nothing sterile, only positive 'seat-of-the-pants' *Swallows and Amazons*. Newcastle won nothing but gave unlimited enjoyment.

As England manager, Kevin is in the stocks, maybe even the guillotine. The tumbrels roll. The old hags knitting, awaiting his severed head. In today's parlance, read old hacks for old hags.

The memory of Warsaw will live long. Flawed tactics. A misplaced belief in players not of international standard. A failure to adjust when the master plan disintegrates.

Was Shanks right, or will Kevin progress, escape the baying hounds and become one of Europe's top managers?

IF SLIGHTED, SLIGHT THE SLIGHT, AND LOVE THE SLIGHTER

'Oh, that mine head were waters, and mine eyes a fountain of tears.' Referees are masochists. Self-flagellation. A death by stoning and slander. Trust ye not any brother on the field. Brothers will deceive, have taught their tongues to speak lies, and weary themselves to commit iniquities. There has only been one referee: Arthur Ellis.

Arthur Ellis died on 23 May 1999. He was 84. Born 8 July 1914. Arthur was the first football referee to achieve public acclaim in this country and international fame abroad. He really desired fame as a footballer but, alas, he was never good enough.

Born in Halifax, he was innately proud of his Yorkshire roots. In between bouts of refereeing he sold foaming Yorkshire bitter for a traditional Yorkshire brewery.

He refereed more than 70 international matches. The first European Cup Final between Real Madrid and Rheims in 1956, the first West German international versus Switzerland in Stuttgart in 1950. His zenith came in 1954, though, when he refereed the 'Battle of Berne', Hungary versus Brazil. He sent off Santos of Brazil and Bozsik, a Hungarian MP, for fist-fighting. He dismissed another Hungarian and gave two penalties. The Brazilian centre half was clouted by a bottle thrown from the bench. Arthur, sanguine as ever, determined the game would finish – and it did. He blew for time. The Brazilians invaded the Hungarian dressing-room. A brawl ensued. Arthur sipped his tea unconcerned.

I remember him recalling his difficult times. He had a bad day at Bolton in the 1950s. He gave wrong decisions. The Bolton centre half descended on Arthur in a blind rage. Arthur defused it all.

'Has tha cum to match by tram?' Bolton defender shook his head from side to side, indicating, 'No'.

'Has tha cum be bus?' Defender nods yes.

'Then tha's best behave thi'senn.' Defender, bemused, backs off. The crowd murmur approval. They imagined Arthur had chastised the bear.

I knew him best as the referee in *It's a Knockout*. The 'Custard Pie' Olympics. Famous with his dipstick, and his insistence on fair play. He was inspirational. A man of total integrity and honesty. He was ever cheerful. I never, in thirty years, saw him lose his temper. He was a man in his own skin. Grateful that life was everything he had dreamed about. He never grumbled, even though the British weather taxed us all. At Ashington an inch of rain fell like a waterfall on our *Knockout* heads. Arthur never wilted as the games sluiced away. His beaming smile an inspiration. I wished to be on the next tram home.

Abroad, his Yorkshire bluntness cut through sometimes strained international relations. Once in Passeriano a delegation visited a famous villa owned by a celebrated marquesa. The villa was celebrated as a producer of fine Barolo and the finest Grappa. The Grappa was distilled in enormous copper vats that had remained untouched for 200 years. The copper pipes were of ancient gold colour. As she intoned in broken English, the supplicants nodded sagely, *très bon, magnifique, fantastique*. All neophytes, bar Arthur. In his stentorian Yorkshire voice he proclaimed: 'Ah'll tell thee wot, marquesa – if them pipes hat bin in t' brewery – tha cud see thee face in 'em.'

The marquesa demanded an instant translation, provided by Eddie Waring. Bemused, she declared that she must take an instant course in colloquial English. We retired to a magnificent lunch.

Later I gave Arthur a lift in a borrowed Alfa Romeo. We battered down the autostrada and turned off into a small town. I drove down a street bearing the sign SENZO UNICO.

'What's yonder sign mean?' queried Arthur.

'One-way street.'

'Oh ta. I'm comin' to Italy for me 'olidays.' Arthur, you see, was never fazed. He knew he would succeed.

His wife Kathleen died before him. He leaves two sons with happy memories.

Arthur was unique. A national treasure from the days when national treasures were revered, not vilified.

SEASON 1996/97: 'I AM NOT A MAN SCRUPULOUS ABOUT WORDS OR NAMES OR SUCH THINGS'

Oliver Cromwell, ex-Nantwich Town

BLACKBURN ROVERS 0 – TOTTENHAM HOTSPUR 2
The FA Carling Premiership, 17 August 1996

The first match of the 1996–7 season, bright with hope, crackling with expectation, the footsteps quicken, the pulse races. The dross of the previous season forgotten, the excitement of a new term and a satchel bursting with good intention. Alas, I feel a cold chill of apprehension at Ewood Park: to lose David Batty is a tragedy, to lose Alan Shearer smacks of carelessness. When good players desert ship, who knows who will follow? As Chaucer (ex-Rovers) put it: 'If golde ruste, what shall irone do?' Mr Dalglish, 'Lord of all Being', and his cohort Mr Harford will ponder who is next – Tim Sherwood, Graeme Le Saux, Chris Sutton. Mr Walker, 'Uncle Jack the Benefactor', may jump back on the gold standard should predators lurk.

To the plot. Who can replace Shearer, now with Newcastle? Kevin Gallacher tried; he bungled two chances that Shearer would have plundered. Then Ian Pearce, a centre back, was flung in; another failure. Lastly, Paul Warhurst, a utility player, attempted to fill Shearer's boots: lamentable. Faint hopes are now fears realized. How can you replace the Colossus of Rhodes, that giant of a sun-god, with a pickled sheep from Damien Hirst? Blackburn were suffering at the back, Ruel Fox proving too slippery for Kenna, Teddy Sheringham teasing Colin Hendry with sleight of foot on the ground, subtle headers to bring Sinton and Anderton into play. Mabbutt and Nethercott retired in the first half-hour; Mabbutt's was serious, yet he attempted to play on – I fear something is broken in his body, you can never break his spirit. Spurs showed character and class. A spate of elegant football brought a goal on 33 minutes: Anderton's looping cross – Armstrong's diving header. Sixty-eight minutes Spurs, with imagination and poise, prised open a brittle Blackburn defence – Fox speeding to the by line – low cross – Chris Armstrong whipped the ball past a furious Tim Flowers. When Tim has the dogs on him, he shows it, livid style! Easy for Spurs. Two–nil. Blackburn in the toils. A-Donis, the debutante flying Greek, prometheused for them down the right – his colleagues squandered his work. Adonis, as you know, was the beautiful Greek youth beloved by Venus, regrettably killed by a boar while hunting. This A-Donis will be killed off by boredom afore long. Blackburn have acquired a new sponsor in CIS. (CIS is not the Soviet Union, merely the Co-op.) They could demand a destroyer or two from Boris Yeltsin.

As I floated back from Ewood through Darwen and the East Lancashire tundra, I mused with deep pleasure at a meeting 'twixt Blackburn and Spurs in 1960. Those Spurs were gods. The cultured maestro Danny Blanchflower, the Silver Ghost John White, the mercurial Cliff Jones, the mobile power station Bobby Smith, the dynamic duo Baker and Henry. A sublime team. Blackburn, a more prosaic team, beat Spurs three–one. An idiosyncratic lot. Peter Dobing could have been great but was not, Bryan Douglas an out-and-out running winger, Ronnie Clayton and Matt Woods tough guys – when the opposition was tackled, it stayed tackled – and Derek Dougan, a mad Irishman who kissed the Blarney Stone and found it was really Medusa. (Medusa, you mythology fans, was the gorgeous tartlet who violated Athena's temple [Ovid]. Athena promptly transformed Medusa's long hair into serpents: her Joan Collins looks made her so hideous that all who looked at her turned to stone.) Joan Collins has the same effect! Dougan led a rebellion before the Wembley final against Wolves. I had observed him, and was benignly envious, engulfed in the arms of a femme fatale, the Mata Hari of Manchester, a well-known concubine, and it was not Joan Collins. Suffice to say, Blackburn were palsied at Wembley. Were accused of simply not playing. Wolves devoured them. Dougan never recovered. Blackburn's phlegmatic public never forgave its team. The stench lingers today. Dave Whelan broke his leg. With his compensation he started a business in a tiny Preston street. Today he is a billionaire. Spurs continued with the Beautiful Game; signed Dave McKay, the most complete footballer of all time, and won the Majestic Double in 1961. Blanchflower got the silver spoon – Dougan the wooded ladle.

I stopped for a pint of Guinness in Darwen to reflect on this unleavened bread of a match I had just witnessed at Ewood, and uttered to a fellow imbiber:

> This is the place. Stand still, my steed.
> Let me review the scene,
> And summon from the shadowy past
> The forms that once have been.

'You're a nutter,' said my imbibing friend.

Blackburn Rovers: Tim Flowers, Chris Coleman, Jeff Kenna, Tim Sherwood, Colin Hendry, Stuart Ripley, Kevin Gallacher, Graham Fenton, Henning Berg, Georgios Donis, Garry Flitcroft. Substitutes: Nicky Marker, Paul Warhurst, Ian Pearce, Gary Croft, Shay Given.

Tottenham Hotspur: Ian Walker, Justin Edinburgh, David Howells, Colin Calderwood, Gary Mabbutt, Ruel Fox, Darren Anderton, Teddy Sheringham, Chris Armstrong, Sol Campbell, Andy Sinton. Substitutes: Jason Dozzell, Stuart Nethercott, Clive Wilson, Ronny Rosenthal, Espen Baardsen.

LIVERPOOL 0 – SUNDERLAND 0

The FA Carling Premiership, 24 August 1996

Newly-promoted Sunderland were imagined to be neophyte Christians, to be slaughtered by rampaging lions of Liverpool at the Colosseum. The lions played like lost sheep baffled by Little Bo Peep – Peter Reid and his collection of selling platers and shire horses. A motley collection: Coton in goal, injury-prone, and discarded by Manchester City; Kubicki of the creaking legs, a flump-pence buy from Aston Villa; Paul Bracewell and Kevin Ball almost grasping bus passes. Paul Stewart a flop at Spurs and Liverpool, another free transfer. Maybe it is Peter Reid's command of the English vernacular that has corralled all these loose cannons on the Roker quarterdeck. It certainly is salty prose. The scene was set by the Sunderland support attired in the famous red and white stripes. They sang 'You'll Never Walk Alone', the Kop anthem, and 'Can't Help Falling in Love with You' – sacrilege. The Kop replied tartly, casting their Roker ancestry into question.

On the pitch, Liverpool's passing game was inept, always in second gear grinding along. Sunderland gobbled it up, processed it like ripe grapes trodden in a vat – Sunderland had the 'jus', Liverpool the spent skins. McManaman is a player, and there are many like him, whose self-belief is entirely misplaced. He was a headless rooster tearing round the pen. Fowler and Collymore played blind man's bluff – correction, had they been blindfold they could have eventually found each other. I detect a frisson developing 'twixt them – and the season a bare two weeks old. John Barnes looked a man running down a fast escalator going up. The game was strangled. Sunderland's Quinn missed a couple of chances. Paul Stewart, never a favourite in his tenure here, was hissed and booed and had a great chance for nemesis – a gaping goal was overawed, and missed. Was chagrined when he was booked. A bleak day for Liverpool, the only beacon Dominic Matteo, a replica Alan Hansen, a Rolls-Royce in a rally of Ford Populars.

Liverpool: David James, Jason McAteer, Mark Wright, Phil Babb, Steve McManaman, Stanley Collymore, Robbie Fowler, John Barnes, Michael Thomas, Stig Inge Bjornebye, Dominic Matteo. Substitutes: Tony Warner, Neil Ruddock, Jamie Carragher, Lee Jones, David Thomson.

Sunderland: Tony Coton, Dariusz Kubicki, Martin Scott, Paul Bracewell, Kevin Ball, Andy Melville, Michael Gray, Richard Ord, Paul Stewart, Steve Agnew, Niall Quinn. Substitutes: Craig Russell, Gareth Hall, Michael Bridges, Sam Aiston, Lionel Perez

BOLTON WANDERERS 2 – CRYSTAL PALACE 2
Nationwide Football League, Division One, 16 November 1996

Burnden Park, the shed: antebellum 1914 clapboard and corrugated iron, floodlights one candlepower, destined for the knacker's yard, or yet another superstore. Steeped in classical history, romantic thoughts flood the memory. Wembley 1923, the first Cup Final there, the peeler on the grey horse controlling 125,000 cloth-capped fans. The disaster here in 1946 when 33 fans died on the terraces as Stanley Matthews sought refuge from the carnage. The lion of Vienna, Nat Lofthouse, the folk icon of Bolton. Today, 16,000 faithful, weaned on traditional English football, wove their warm and homely tapestry of Lancashire life. Hot Bovril, tea with proper leaves, not teabags, pies and peas – nowt fancy.

Bolton's football is a paradox: shabby surroundings, but the play elegant, symmetrical, free-flowing, contoured from imagination. Bolton top the Nationwide League, Palace are second – a cut-and-thrust match to savour.

John Sheridan, on his home debut, scored on 12 minutes with a rapier thrust volley. Blake hit a post. The football rippled. Johansen a flying felucca, McGinlay a pouncing wild cat, Sheridan a preening, elegant ocelot. Palace indulged in heavy breathing on the ropes, taking stock, assessing. Twenty minutes John McGinlay whacked home a penalty kick. Two–nil. Bolton strove for the third goal to kill the match. 'Twas Palace who exploded, David Hopkin with his flaming hair and toothless grin, a fearsome sight, become more fearsome – his 40th-minute drive was mighty. Dyer and Freedman soared on eagles' wings, swooping on Bolton; Shipperley looks like a hippo, plays like a mad rhino. Just before half-time Freedman walloped the equalizer. Two–two.

The first half was a roister, the second anticlimax. Palace with 41 goals in the season's bag virtually declared innings closed. Bolton rolled forward without conviction; the spark had died. We had time to appraise the referee, Mr Kirkby, in his bizarre attire: an Armani-speckled negligee with fetching cummerbund. 'Ee-up, yer big Jessie,' cried one fan dressed by Oxfam.

Bolton Wanderers: Keith Branagan, Andy Todd, Jimmy Phillips, Gudni Bergsson, Gerry Taggart, Chris Fairclough, Michael Johansen, Scott Sellars, Nathan Blake, John McGinlay, John Sheridan. Substitutes: Scott Taylor, Scott Green, David Lee.

Crystal Palace: Chris Day, Mark Edworthy, Kevin Muscat, Andy Roberts, David Tuttle, David Hopkin, Robert Quin, Neil Shipperley, Dougie Freedman, Bruce Dyer, Carl Veart. Substitutes: Dean Gordon, Leon McKenzie, Paul Trollope.

LIVERPOOL 4 – NOTTINGHAM FOREST 2
The FA Carling Premiership, 17 December 1996

A cold misty night at the Colosseum. But in from the cold, one Stanley Collymore. Stanley, until last Saturday a figure alone, from a foreign land, Cannock. Anywhere outside Toxteth is a foreign land to Liverpudlians. And Stan, like Ruth amid the alien corn, has been in exile. A pariah, an outsider, almost shunned by colleagues. Last Saturday, against Middlesbrough, he made four goals for Fowler in a five–one thrashing. After each goal I observed that Fowler embraced McManaman, his bosom pal, despite Stan's old-style runs at defences, which directly led to all four goals. Poor Stanley was left ruminating, eventually having to amble to Fowler, to give his congratulations. Tonight I wish fervently – accord Stan some generosity. He could be fired up against his old club, Forest.

Liverpool, if they win, will go top. They are on 34 points to Arsenal's 35. If Forest lose, they go bottom. Beset by financial woes, they looked doomed. Worse still, Hillsborough hangs over the Colosseum like a pall. Forest were Liverpool's opponents in that 1989 semi-final. A campaign called 'Justice' has been formed; a crusade for a moral judgement on what really caused football's most terrible tragedy. A debate in the House of Commons takes place this very night. Shades of Hillsborough, battle fatigue, a touch of influenza? Whatever,

Liverpool were a mix of lacklustre and brilliance. Stanley was electrifying. On five minutes his perfect lob deceived Crossley for Liverpool's first goal. Fowler neatly tucked in the second after 20 minutes. Kevin Campbell scrambled a goal just before half-time to keep Forest in the match at two–one. Fate intervened on 50 minutes, Des Lyttle scoring an own goal. Minutes later, Stuart Pearce, thunder-thighs Psycho, hit a leviathan free kick that David James, Liverpool's keeper, never glimpsed, turned to stone by sheer power. Three–two, game on.

Then Stanley's academy award-winning goal on the hour. Berger, on for Fowler, crossed low behind the Forest defence. Lyttle, Pearce and Cooper flailed at the ball, Collymore was in there – deadly – a wonderful striker's goal. Four–two. Forest fought against fate and flashes of superb skill. A mountain to climb, like scaling the north face of the Eiger. At the whistle, I looked for Stanley's attitude, his body language. He acknowledged the plaudits from 36,000 fans but trudged off alone, his contribution mighty – his thanks none.

Liverpool: David James, Jason McAteer, Mark Wright, Phil Babb, Steve McManaman, Stanley Collymore, Robbie Fowler, John Barnes, Neil Ruddock, Michael Thomas, Stig Inge Bjornebye. Substitutes: Jamie Redknapp, Tony Warner, Patrick Berger, Mark Kennedy, Dominic Matteo.

Nottingham Forest: Mark Crossley, Des Lyttle, Stuart Pearce, Colin Cooper, David Phillips, Dean Saunders, Kevin Campbell, Ian Woan, Chris Allen, Alf Inge Haaland, Vance Warner. Substitutes: Scot Gemmill, Jason Lee, Alan Fettis, Stephen Howe, Bryan Roy.

OLDHAM ATHLETIC 2 – MANCHESTER CITY 1
Nationwide Football League, Division One, 21 December 1996

At 3 p.m. the sunshine dappled the Pennines. The mighty Monarch Mill cast its shadow on Boundless Park. The hoarfrost sparkled on those well-trodden paths leading down from the Rochdale Road. A cherubic brass band blew festive Christmas carols. I half-expected Scrooge, Bob Cratchit, Tiny Tim and Marley's ghost to materialize. The players, characters from Dickens: there is for ever an antediluvian air about Oldham.

'Gentlemen of the free-and-easy sort, who plume themselves on being acquainted with a move or two, and being usually equal to the time of day, express the wide range of their capacity for adventure by observing they are good for anything from pitch and toss to manslaughter!' Pitch, toss, bear-baiting, bullfighting, hare coursing, fox-hunting – near manslaughter – this was the match. End of Christmas cheer, time to shelter in the bunker. 'Twas pandemonium on the pitch, nonstop cacophony off it. Both sides hit the bar. Kinkladze had a penalty saved. Tackles began at grass height and finished shoulder height; not just a local derby but a deadly scrap to stay in the league. Oldham third from bottom. City two places above. Steve Lomas and Ian Brightwell relished this bare-knuckled fight, Paul Dickov and the German Uwe Rösler hid in the trenches. Kinkladze, the pocket genius, carefully, artistically twinkled through the falling bodies as a young ensign at the Charge of the Light Brigade. The maestro struck a super goal on 38 minutes. Dickov blundering through savage tackles, a 20-yard pass to Kinkladze, who advanced another 10 yards, cocked his lethal left foot. One–nil to City.

The battle raged. Sixty-four minutes Nicky Henry bowlegged down the right like a bosun after the rum ration, crossed high – beanpole Ormanroyd headed the equalizer. '*Limbus fatuorum*,' (fools' paradise) bellowed the Oldham faithful. Hope exists in Oldham, but it is fragile. Not today, though. Nicky Banger rhymes with Ranger, not banger of the explosive sort. Banger emerged from the manger (well, 'tis Christmas time) off the substitutes' bench and cracked the winning goal. A whizz-bang of a shot from 15 yards as Ormanroyd towered over City's defence like a giraffe eating acacia leaves.

So to a brainstorming finish. Latics' character and muscle. City's fragile skills. Temperature on the pitch white-hot, off it polar. Mark Twain (ex-Latics) once said: 'The coldest winter I ever spent was summer in Oldham.' So to tiny tots everywhere, I wish you a frostbitten Yuletide.

Oldham Athletic: Gary Kelly, Craig Fleming, Carl Serrant, Nick Henry, Shaun Garnett, Steve Redmond, Scott McNiven, Paul Rickers, Ian Ormanroyd, Stuart Barlow, Lee Richardson. Substitutes: David Beresford, Richard Graham, Nicky Banger.

Manchester City: Martin Margetson, Eddie McGoldrick, Simon Rodger, Steve Lomas, Kit Symons, Ian Brightwell, Nicky Summerbee, Jeff Whitley, Paul Dickov, Georgie Kinkladze, Uwe Rösler. Substitutes: Mikhail Kavalashvili, Lee Crooks, Gerry Creaney.

LIVERPOOL 1 – BURNLEY 0
The FA Cup – Third Round, 4 January 1997

The third round of the FA Cup. The season starts here for the poor relations, the tiny tots, the minnows, the once League champions fallen on hard times. Market forces, as Thatcher proved, bring severe casualties. Burnley FC are one such. Founder-members in 1882, champions of Division One in 1960. Names are historical. Miller, Adamson, Pointer, McIroy, Pilkington, Cummings, Blacklaw. Claret and blue the colours – they wore a fascinating tapestry of sophisticated football that defied the homeliness of Turf Moor. Harry Potts, their manager, swept-back hair, nut-brown visage, always in a fawn raincoat. Adamson a taciturn yeoman of the north-east. Short on words, high on class. Today a Third Division side with anonymous players, they come to be devoured, innocents from the snow-capped Rossendale Valley, by the lions of the Colosseum. Eight thousand Burnley fans came to the spectacle, and like a Roman audience uttered a deal of noise. The Kop replied with stony silence. Why? Beats me. Liverpool top the Premiership, five points ahead of Manchester United, Arsenal and Wimbledon. Stan Collymore silenced the Burnley throng 12 minutes into the match. Berger and Bjornebye exchanged sweetness and light down the left, Stanley popped in the goal. Would it herald an onslaught? Burnley defied them. Defended in fathomless depth, held their shape and frustrated an out-of-sorts, lacklustre Liverpool team. Burnley's number nine stuck to McManaman like a limpet, Makkers was brassed off: number nine's name is Chris Brass. Stanley Collymore is the total enigma. Tall in the saddle, heavyweight build, a Carl Lewis turn of speed, he plays like a seven-stone weakling. His touch is missing. His mind is missing. He is a loner. I observed that when he scored he was not engulfed by team-mates. Not for Stanley the hugging, kissing, diving on turf, saluting the audience. The team does not play for him; he does not play for the team. It is not terminal, but sticks of gelignite up the orifice would help. A little ginger, boys! Does Caesar Evans have the power, the resolution, the steel, the ruthlessness of Shankly and Paisley? Wield it now, Caesar, or you could fall on your own sword. Burnley not only survived, but blossomed. Adrian Heath, their manager, used this match as research and development. His team raised the biggest cheer and laughs. His tiny trainer, with duck's disease, ran on the pitch to minister to the fallen so fast that his little Ernie Wise legs almost caught fire. Roadrunner of Burnley – you are famous.

Liverpool: David James, Jason McAteer, Mark Wright, Phil Babb, Steve McManaman, Stanley Collymore, John Barnes, Patrick Berger, Stig Inge Bjornebye, Dominic Matteo. Substitutes: Tony Warner, Mark Kennedy, Lee Jones.

Burnley: Marlon Beresford, Gary Parkinson, David Eyres, Gerry Harrison, Mark Winstanley, Jamie Hoyland, Paul Weller, Paul Smith, Chris Brass, Paul Barnes, Nigel Cleghorn. Substitutes: Steve Thompson, Glen Little, Andy Cooke.

MANCHESTER CITY 1 – CRYSTAL PALACE 1
Nationwide Football League, Division One, 11 January 1997

The first match of the New Year at the Theatre of Base Comedy. City are lumped with Southend, Grimsby and Bradford rooted at the foot of Division One. They have lost their last three games to Barnsley, Port Vale and Oldham. Francis Lee looks like Polonius stabbed through the arras – his investment turning turtle. Desperate times dictate desperate measures so – appoint a new manager.

Frank Clarke, a one-time dour fullback with Newcastle and Forest, is the fourteenth appointee charged with the resurrection of this moribund body at Maine Road, Moss Side, Manchester 14. Frank, alias Baron Hardup, relished the pantomime; arms akimbo, he received an exultant welcome from 28,000 inmates, revelling in the cacophony. He was like Moses in the tabernacle charged with leading the children of Israel, the tribe, out of the wilderness and into the Promised Land. The moment of truth is nigh. The audience fell silent as Palace, a strong-running pragmatic side, gave City a bit of stick. Kinkladze was battered and roughed up. Rösler was Cumberland wrestled into submission. City looked fragile, trepidation ruled, Baron Hardup concerned, nay, worried, his forehead wrinkled like an old army blanket. The ecstasy –

Kinkladze's wicked curling free kick was blasted into his own net by Palace's number five, David Tuttle: nothing subtle about Tuttle. The audience raised the roof. City relaxed: frayed nerves calmed, they were resolute. Palace, though, play like stags at bay, brandishing antlers as if rutting – to hell with finesse. Dave Bassett is our manager, give them the bludgeon. Kinkladze retired to embalm his bruised limbs in aspic – anguish set in. Neil Shipperley, Palace's number nine, is a battling, battering ram – Lomas and Symons flattened in the ruck. Palace thundered forward, George Ndah headed a stupendous goal. Harry Bassett will never adhere to the script.

City's cage severely rattled, they hung on like a prim spinster holding on to her skirts in a high wind. One apiece. As Wellington said about Waterloo, true could be said now: 'It was a damn close-run thing.'

Baron Hardup is now aware that the pantomime will run despite his grip on the poisoned chalice. He hopes that shortly his fairy godmother, Steve Boler, the entrepreneur who bought half of Botswana for a back garden, will fly in bearing millions for new players. 'Til then is the Theatre of Base Comedy Aladdin's cave or a cobwebbed, desolate Sleeping Beauty's castle?

Manchester City: Martyn Margetson, Eddie McGoldrick, Rae Ingram, Steve Lomas, Kit Symons, Ian Brightwell, Nicky Summerbee, Gerry Creaney, Neil Heaney, Georgie Kinkladze, Uwe Rösler. Substitutes: Lee Crooks, Jeff Whitley, Mikhail Kavelashvili.

Crystal Palace: Chris Day, Marc Edworthy, Dean Gordon, Andy Roberts, David Tuttle, David Hopkin, Andy Cyrus, George Ndah, Neil Shipperley, Bruce Dyer, Carl Veart. Substitutes: Leif Andersen, Hayden Mullins, Leon McKenzie.

A CHRISTMAS PARABLE SET IN GAUL (FRANCE), AD 42

Once upon early Roman times a child was born in a manger. The crib lay on damp straw in this manger. The boy child's father was a swineherd and a tender of sheep. His mother a tiller of the soil. Yes, a Tiller girl. The boy child grew, his loins, at three years old, covered with hair. His physique akin to a Michelangelo sculpture. The Romans introduced football to Gaul. It was played with the heads of Christians. Those heads that had not been chewed by lions at the Colosseum. Eric, as the child was yclept, one day entered the Roman football game. He carried an inflatable pig's bladder. Booting aside the heads, he proceeded to baffle the simple, soulless Roman legionaries with his sublime skills, combative spirit, naked aggression and total arrogance.

Juventus, the Roman legion, chronicled forth that Eric was immortal. From the gods. The son of Jupiter. Brethren from continents travelled to observe. All nations upon horses, and in chariots, and in litters and upon swift beasts.

'Eric,' they cried, 'your bones shall flourish like a herb, your heart shall rejoice, you will come with fire, render your anger with fury, and your rebuke with flames of fire.'

Eric thus desired fame. He spake thus to his father: 'Father, give unto me thy portion of goods which falleth to me.' In other words, 'Part with the dosh you've made taking side bets against those crass followers of Juventus.' As Eric had been suckled in the mountains by a lioness, Father did not quibble.

'*Limbus fatuorum*,' cried Father (fools' paradise), to which Eric replied, *mot à mot*: '*Mens agitat molem*' (a mind informs the masses). In simple words: 'Bollocks, Dad.'

But it was Eric who dropped the 'goolie'. In southern Gaul he was God. In northern Gaul he was the prodigal son. He was three years short of a score in age. And three scores was his total for the year. And two of those were with Sharon Pebble, the Romans camp's bicycle whom everybody rode. He had wasted his substance on riotous living. And began to be in want. There arose a famine in that land. He would fain have filled his belly with the husks that the swine did eat. No man gave unto him. And when he came to himself, he said:

'I will arise and return to the Romans and say I have sinned against Jupiter and in thy sight, and am no more worthy to be called thy son.'

The Romans, meanwhile, had annexed the downtrodden little island called Anglia. The native Angles were peasants, ruled by an even simpler peasant called Majore Majore. Stringent taxation, harsh laws, a feudal aristocracy had reduced them to forelock-touching, whingeing supplicants to a temple of emptiness. Into this void, the Romans brought fussballium. The centre was Mancunium, whose skies rained ink, whose rivers were black and whose populace were satanic.

Eric thus played for Mancunium Arhaprody, a cornucopia, an allegro in excelsis. The Mancunium chief was a fierce Celt, Alex Fergusonium, whose sole motto was '*Fortes fortuna juvat*' (Fortune favours the brave). In English, 'Stick this claymore up your sporran.' Eric found kindred spirits in a weird Viking shot-stopper, Pietro the Dane, who, standing six cubits high, was a giant among pygmies. He and Eric defeated the mighty in battle. The red shirts of Woolwich were drenched with their blood. The black and white stripes worn by a straggling bunch of marauders from the north were overcome, again with many casualties. Among them Kevin Keegonomus, a wayward spirit who believed in art, and beauty, and heavenly gifts, bestowed on his players. Alas, this swain of Scunthorpe confessed: '*Dulce bellum inexpertis*' (war is sweet to those who have not tried it). In short, 'Sod this for a game of soldiers. I need 11 David Battys.'

Gold and silver cups, chalices and salvers flowed in the Shrine, as the house of Mancunium Unitedus were yclept. Until, one day, disaster struck. An infidel intruded at the Palace of Crystal. Eric, mistaking an opponent's head for the pig's bladder, was dismissed from the field of play. The infidel cried out '*Lupus est homo homini*' (you ain't nothing but a wolf man).

Eric, in frenzied rage, launched himself horizontally at the infidel. '*Nemo me impune i acessit*' (no one provokes me with impunity). In simple English: 'Here's my boot in your tripes'.

107

Eric was in exile again. He repenteth. Taught young Angles, Saxons, Picts, Scots and Celts to play fussballium. Succoured a fey, dark Gypsy, Giggsium, to success. Became a philosopher extraordinaire.

'When the seagull follows the trawler it expects to be thrown a sardine' became the touchstone of the masses.

A fellow Gaul – Deschamps, a centurion with Juventus – was described by Eric as 'a water carrier'. Again the world was mesmerized. Does Deschamps play with a full bladder? Is he a mobile aqueduct? Zidane, another Juventian, is a perfumed fairy. Eric succeeded mumbling Major as the leader of men. 'Tis now wicked winter in Anglia. Mancunium waits now until spring. When the clouds roll by after the rain. The silver cord be loosed, the golden pitcher at the fountain of hope to be won.

Mancunium rejoiced that three coveted trophies were won in a unique season. A feat never to be repeated. While the evil days come not, nor the years draw nigh when thou shalt say, I have no pleasure in them. Vanity of vanities, saith the preacher; all is vanity. Eric seweth the seed, put forth green figs, and the vines with the tender grapes give good smell.

Vivat Eric!

Voilà tout.

SEASON 1995/96: CENSURE IS THE TAX A MAN PAYS TO THE PUBLIC FOR BEING EMINENT

EVERTON 2 – SOUTHAMPTON 0
The FA Carling Premiership, 26 August 1995
Andrei arrived at the School of Science greeted by 34,000 as a latter-day Rasputin. Does Kanchelskis possess the magic power and influence to convert the dogs of war, as Everton are, to the balletic exponents of the beautiful game that Goodison desires? On 34 minutes he did just that, the revelation. A meandering run, arms pumping, a flick to Rideout. Limpar lurking outside the box finished the move with a glorious goal. Amokachi, another genius, popped up eight minutes later. A bouncing ball, a joust with Benali. A little samba; amazing vision, a swivel of the hips and a nod of the ball over the advancing Beasant. Two magical moments: the game won. But in truth Everton have to establish a permanent pattern of play. Today their midfield two, Horne and Parkinson, were overrun by Southampton's willing, battling midfield four. Horne played out of his jersey as red and white stripes buzzed round his boots. Le Tissier loafed around with that peculiar sailor's gait, but despite commanding 60 per cent of the play, their lack of a striker could put them in the Endsleigh League. Everton will eye a trophy or two when the Rasputin blend is right.
Everton: Neville Southall, Earl Barratt, David Unsworth, Dave Watson, Gary Ablett, Paul Rideout, Barry Horne, Anders Limpar, Daniel Amokachi, Andrei

Kanchelskis, Joe Parkinson. Substitutes: Jason Kearton, John Ebbrell, Stuart Barlow.
Southampton: Dave Beasant, Jason Dodd, Francis Benali, Jim Magilton, Richard Hall, Kenneth Monkou, Matthew Le Tissier, Gordon Watson, Neil Maddison, Tommy Widdrington, Simon Charlton. Substitutes: Bruce Grobbelaar, Alan Neilson, David Hughes.

NORTHWICH VICTORIA 1 – SCUNTHORPE UNITED 3
The FA Cup – First Round, 11 November 1995

Like Francis Urquhart, I have been putting myself about gathering propaganda. Northwich is an old Roman town built on salt. The Drill Field is the oldest football ground in the world, saved from the developer's supermarket aspirations – by of all bodies the Brazilian FA. But what is recent history is that Scunthorpe were too strong and resourceful, as befits league players, opposed by Victoria's part-time jousters. I enjoyed the thought and deed of the match – perhaps the execution and pace were lacking. A first half of Northwich one-twos starred a young feller called Walters. But he and his green-shirted colleagues felt the blast as Scunthorpe upped the wick. Tony Ford, he of 700 matches, scored the Scunthorpe first goal. Andy McFarlane, the strapping centre forward, the second. Cooke briefly gave Victoria hope with a goal eight minutes from time, but then Greygoose, the Victoria keeper, fiddled with un-sublime knavery – he gave the ball to McFarlane. Three–one. Greygoose cooked the Northwich goose on the Drill Field and home of the Cheshire Regiment – 14 days' jankers for you, Greygoose.
Northwich Victoria: D. Greygoose, W. Simpson, M. Jones, D. Tinson, D. Burgess, S. Walters, C. Williams, B. Butler, I. Cooke, P. Clayton, C. Duffy. Substitutes: H. MacAuley, S. Holden, D. Vicary.
Scunthorpe United: M. Samways, S. Housham, P. Wilson, T. Ford, A. Knill, C. Hope, S. Thornber, W. Bullimore, A. McFarlane, J. Eyre, J. Patterson. Substitutes: M. Nicholson, M. Walsh, S. Young.

MANCHESTER CITY 1 – ASTON VILLA 0
The FA Carling Premiership, 25 November 1995

The Theatre of Base Comedy today revealed a bronze bust of Joe Mercer, that great manager and gentleman who brought Malcolm Allison the maverick, Lee, Bell, Summerbee, Neil Young, Tony Coleman and other assorted wayward souls to Maine Road, Manchester 14, and fashioned one of England's memorable postwar teams. Joe was a lifelong friend, a man who really cared. Yes, he was devious, could duck and dive, bob and weave with the worst characters in the football sewers: but those sewers are long, deep and wide; it is a case of strong swimming or swift drowning. I saw Joe Mercer play during the War, his legs so bandy that he could not stop a pig in a ginnel. He could work the ball, lean into the pass like a top-class snooker player, caress it like a newborn child. He could will his body to run when the rest had flagged; he inspired fellow men. He played in the army team against the RAF and the Civil Defence. The RAF were the dandier; their centre half was Bernard Joy – unlike the rest, a commissioned officer. He was an amateur with the Arsenal in peacetime. Flight-Lieutenant Joy received a less-than-joyful kicking from those army NCOs. A wartime international was played at Maine Road. England versus Scotland. England thrashed Scotland eight–one. I treasured the programme, filed it with my other artefacts in the attic, along with my Flying Scotsman Hornby gauge '0' 4472 locomotive and Pullman coaches, my first teddy bear (a Steiff) and various wartime relics. Alas, my mother, a maverick Irish Aquarian, is a soft touch. One Christmas, an itinerant Gypsy knocked on her door pleading for gifts for his children. She gave the bastard all my treasures; my autograph album of famous footballers, my beautiful programmes, my train set, down to the last porter and baggage.

'Mother,' I cried. 'How could you? Apart from the fact that I loved them, you've just blown about £60,000. That's the value of the train and the teddy bear.'

As I write this, I feel a tension spreading through my shoulders. I am still bitter that 'knockers' can deprive innocent, generous old ladies of treasured possessions. Littered as I am under Saturn, aspected by Mercury, born on Christmas Day, I am a true Capricorn. We collect things, hoard them away like a magpie in the nest. Our main fault is unswerving loyalty to fellow men, sometimes completely misguided. So, dear reader, details of the match are lost. The romance of it lingers. The Scottish fullbacks Carabine and Beatty were overwhelmed. The great Tommy Walker of Hearts anonymous. England's halfback line ruled. Cliff Britton, Stan Cullis, Joe Mercer. All three divine ball players. Britton was as divine as Donatello's David; lean, svelte, swift, his passes measured to the centimetre. Sergeant-Major Cullis crouched over the ball like a Comanche unleashing a quiver of arrows into the Yankee masses. Joe shuttling up and down selling dummies to gullible Scots. The War over, Joe resumed his career, but five years had blunted his talent, like so many other sportsmen – Ted Drake, Tommy Lawton, Tom Finney, Stanley Matthews, Walter Hammond. When I survey Britain today, they paid a high price. Rolls-Royce and Bentley owned by Germans, industry propped up by Japan – white goods made in Italy. Maybe it is better to lose a war than win a Pyrrhic victory. Cynically, I presume that all those whose careers were terminated or shortened by war could sue the government for loss of limbs or earnings. Litigation is the growth industry of our times.

Meanwhile, Joe played for the Arsenal until old age and arthritis stopped him. He managed Aston Villa and flopped. Now, in 1963, he was in desperation pitch, then forked into restoring glory. I was with the BBC in Manchester, and having, as Sky TV would say, 'sole and exclusive' access to the Good Friday riots at Maine Road, and the exclusive interview with tiny Albert Alexander revealing the Mercer-Allison axis the following Monday, I journeyed thus to interview Joe. He was incarcerated in a small office. After a mug of tea, it was down to the filmed interview. Joe was trembling and flushed, a ragbag of tattered nerves. The interview was a stumbling, hesitant, vacuous nonstarter. I asked the cameraman and sound recordist to leave.

'Joe, you are my childhood hero. I come to praise, not to denigrate. I'm here as a catalyst between you and the City fans, to build, not to demolish.' He confessed that he was suffering from hypertension, low self-esteem and a genuine fear that he was tempting fate here. I said if it took 12 hours I would not leave without the firebrand, onward and upward vision that Joe really wanted. It took three hours of takes and retakes. Joe regained composure, realized that goodwill and kindness were hallmarks of Manchester life. The rest is history. I shall write of Malcolm Allison elsewhere. This is a eulogy to Joe. We shared a love of the beautiful game, a flagon of claret, a fine supper, epicurean Manchester delights, roistering in maverick company, sharing family life. One of the greats.

Could Joe's bust inspire today's City, third from bottom with Bolton and Coventry? A six–nil beating at Anfield in October still hurts. This match is a watershed. Bert Trautman, the German POW, the greatest goalkeeper of postwar Britain, opened the new Kippax super-stand. A double inspiration. Alan Ball, City's manager, himself an inspiring firecracker, is on a learning curve; abrasive and combustible, his style, or lack of style, upsets sensitive players who need a friendly arm around the shoulder, not the neck. Lomas and Flitcroft, the young midfielders, are still adapting to the genius of Kinkladze. Ball expects more from his players than, at the moment, they are capable of delivering. Kinkladze with his close control contrives the openings, splits defences and is still directing fledglings exactly which course to pursue. Meanwhile, City languish. Nora, Joe's widow, is present, a wonderful lady, a bountiful, kindly presence. The scene is set.

Brian Little has a head of premature grey, testimony to the grim reaper, 'Deadly Doug' Ellis, who makes Joe Stalin look like Dale Winton. Gulag Villa Park. Little has bought and sold players like Supermarket Sweep (a defunct game show of rather high-speed, low-camp shopping). Steve Staunton, Gareth Southgate, Gary Charles, Alan Wright to bolster defence. Ian Taylor and Mark Draper, Draper an inventive, underrated player, £3.25 million from Leicester Fosse, and Andy Townsend make up the revamped midfield. Three and a half million pounds was splurged on Savo Milosevic, all left foot and suspect temperament; Dwight Yorke, a slippery youth from Trinidad, twins with Savo, and Tommy Johnson a £2 million buy from Derby. Little has raised £7 million selling Ray Houghton, Kevin Richardson, Garry Parker, Dean Saunders, Dalian Atkinson, Earl Barrett, Shaun Teale, Graham Fenton, John Fashanu, Nii Lampety and Phil King; 'swing-door trading'. The stagecoach of Villa is rolling, but who would be the driver? A loose cannon or a whiff of grapeshot – wear your upholstered leather chaps, Brian, it is going to be a rough ride. With 'Deadly Doug' as shotgun, he is liable to down the Indians, the cavalry, the posse, the passengers and *you*.

That is the subplot of this match. To the play.

Kinkladze cost a mere £2 million; his first goal for City was a gem from Georgia, millions of roubles worth. A little snitcher of a back heel from Niall Quinn, Kinkladze's left foot whopped the ball past Bosnich, Villa's Australian goalkeeper. Bosnich looked as if a kangaroo had punched him. That goal was the winner exactly five minutes from time. The Theatre of Base Comedy erupted – rightly so; it was a moment of passion, a fulfilment of hope in a match of total commitment, brilliance and magic. There was a brightness and confidence in City's play; Flitcroft and Lomas dovetailed as Kinkladze wove a mesmerizing tapestry. Even Curle's appalling penalty miss did not stop the adrenalin flow. Curle and Symons like Mont Blanc at the back. Villa are a fine team; Draper was hyped up, a vision master of midfield, he operates by stealth with the strength of a commando. Ian Taylor was ubiquitous and dangerous. Yorke sinuous and volatile, a great player in embryo. Milosevic, the strange mix of spectacular and inane, missed an open goal after 30 seconds but brought thrilling saves from Immel in City's goal. Ugo Ehiogu, arms and legs flailing like a witch-doctor casting spells, threatened both City and his own mates, a whirling dervish. In contrast, Paul McGrath, dodgy knees and all, covers the ground like an antelope. Villa, to be fair, deserved a draw, but the day, the glory, the rekindling of spirit, the recollection of days gone but ne'er forgotten belong to City and 28,000 joyous inmates. I shall seek out Mr Ball to confirm euphoria, bestow a loving kiss on Nora Mercer's cheek, and raise a glass to Joe, whose memory shall never fade.

Manchester City: Eike Immel, Steve Lomas, Keith Curle, Georgie Kinkladze, Niall Quinn, Garry Flitcroft, Ian Brightwell, Kit Symons, Nicky Summerbee, Uwe Rösler, Michael Brown. Substitutes: Gerry Creaney, Alan Kernaghan, Martin Phillips.

Aston Villa: Mark Bosnich, Gary Charles, Alan Wright, Ugo Ehiogu, Paul McGrath, Gareth Southgate, Ian Taylor, Mark Draper, Dwight Yorke, Savo Milosevic, Tommy Johnson. Substitutes: Steve Staunton, Nigel Spink, Riccardo Scimeca.

MANCHESTER CITY 1 – COVENTRY CITY 1

The FA Carling Premiership, 20 January 1996

The Theatre of Base Comedy is subdued. Coventry chasing shadows should have been flayed alive, escaped, virtue of Quinn's profligacy in front of goal, and Ogrizovic's peerless goalkeeping. One save deep in the second half saw him lying prone one second and leaping on t' other side of goal a second, defying gravity and middle age, later. The match was colourless, lifeless, the very antithesis of a relegation fracas until Manchester scored on 55 minutes.

Young Phillips, a pocket genius to be, was flung into the fray five minutes after half-time. His sheer energy and exuberance lit up the match. From his work sprang the goal – a Quinn back-header – scored. Rösler removed his jersey in glee. His hairless chest did not excite the masses, so he swiftly put it back on. Sixty-eight minutes Dion Dublin equalized. Marcus Hall drove down

the left, Whelan took the pass – crossed. Dublin a simple header. Coventry held the line, 'Oggi' impassable. Big Ron in his Mafia gear grinned. Mr Ball grimaced. Gordon Strachan, patrolling the touchline as sub, was severely admonished by the referee Hart. A heart-to-heart in the right vein – so to say.
Manchester City: Eike Immel, Steve Lomas, Keith Curle, Georgie Kinkladze, Niall Quinn, Garry Flitcroft, Ian Brightwell, Kit Symons, Nicky Summerbee, Michael Brown, Uwe Rösler. Substitutes: Gerry Creaney, Alan Kernaghan, Martin Phillips.
Coventry City: Steve Ogrizovic, Brian Borrows, Kevin Richardson, Paul Telfer, Peter Ndlovu, Dion Dublin, John Salako, Noel Whelan, Ally Pickering, Marcus Hall, Richard Shaw. Substitutes: John Filan, Gordon Strachan, Willie Boland.

CREWE ALEXANDRA 2 – PETERBOROUGH UNITED 1
Endsleigh Insurance Football League, Division Two, 30 April 1996
Alexandra, surely the quaintest and most romantic of football names. Alexandra conjures visions of ancient Egypt, of science, philosophy, literature, with a dash of barbarism. Gresty Road, hard by that labyrinth of railway lines known as Crewe Station, swiftly brings you down to earth. On a dank dark night, its fusty, peeling painted wooden structures invoke Trevor Howard, Celia Johnson and *Brief Encounter.*

Alexandra are in the play-off zone with Blackpool, Notts County and Bradford City – so Alexandra, you shall go to the play-off ball. Yes, they have grace, style, élan: they entertain their public – a mixture of the mature cloth-capped and ebullient youth. Dario Gradi is not so much Alexandra's manager – he is a breeder of footballers, a trainer of thoroughbreds: Gresty Road is a stable. David Platt is an example. A castoff of Manchester United, Platt blossomed under Gradi's tuition, sought fame and fortune elsewhere, and brought largess to Crewe's coffers. Southgate, Hignett, Murphy, Adelbola. A nonstop bloodline. The pitch was sodden, a damp mist hung in the air – aptly, Rivers scored Alexandra's first goal on 40 minutes. Colin Little, a snip signing for £50,000, bagged the second just before half-time. Alex had the muse, they do entertain in thought and deed – they adhere to football principles, disdain the 'get rid of it, high ball into box' theories. Two–nil, half-time. Posh held sway second half, Posh with the power, the muscle, the first time ball, the braggadocio. A San Siro moment on the hour, a vignette of Posh ping-pong football, Grazioli scored. Fluent Italian flowed from the terraces:

'*Ho chiesto una camera con bagno.*' (I asked for a room with a bath.)

'*Alora, bello. Grazie, è stata una magnifica serata,*' (How now, beautiful? Thank you, it has been a beautiful evening) I cried, caught up in the San Siro atmosphere. I could hardly breathe as the game ebbed and flowed like the Tiber in full flood.

The final whistle heralded joy. All 35,000 of us thumped our seats in appreciation. I have not had as much fun since I was a national serviceman doing stag on Crewe Station.

Crewe Alexandra: Mark Gallie, Wayne Collins, Shaun Smith, Chris Lightfoot, Brian McAllister, Gareth Whalley, Colin Little, Rob Savage, Steve MacAuley, Danny Murphy, Mark Rivers. Substitutes: Lee Unsworth, Ashley Westwood, Lee Ellison.

Peterborough United: John Sheffield, Mark Blount, Simon Clark, Neil Le Bihan, Mark Foran, Greg Heald, Lee Power, Marcus Ebdon, Giuliano Grazioli, Ken Charnley, Niall Inman. Substitutes: Sean Farrell, Ben Sedgemore, Tom Meredith.

LIVERPOOL 2 – WEST HAM UNITED 1
Aggregate: Liverpool 4 – West Ham United 1
The FA Youth Cup Final – Second Leg, 17 May 1996
First Sighting of Michael Owen.

Talent spotting begins in the cradle. Dads everywhere are launching their male offspring into orbit as soon as they can walk.

'Don't put his name down for Eton, Esmerelda,' cried Granville de Trubshawe. 'He's bound for Chelsea.' Forget the little grey cells; far better if you have been banged up in one clad in grey. Makes a man of you, lad. A drop of GBH, a spot of dangerous driving in your Ferrari, a drop of spittle aimed at a fan, a drop of your knickers in protest at some decision with which you disagree. Josh around with some starlet. Knock her about a bit and, hey presto, you are a star. Tabloids will fawn, Tony will toss you an MBE, TV companies will entice you with millions, *Hello!* will tip another mil. The lush life. Why burn the midnight oil, study until double vision sets in, scrimp, save, cadge, budget until midlife? No. Sod the degrees, doctorates and all that bilge. Be a footballer. And no! This is not heresy. My own grandson Ben, star of *This is Your Life*, is now two years old. He is out on the lawn with me kicking with *both feet*. I have got his name down not for Repton – oh no! He is enlisted in the MUFC academy. And he will be Prime Minister in his spare time!

I thus journeyed to the Colosseum with ulterior motive. I want to see how the babes are weaned. 'Twas the second leg of the FA Youth Cup. Liverpool had beaten West Ham two–nil at Upton Park on May Day without Owen. Tonight he was playing. The boy prodigy about whom they whispered names like Pele, St John, Keegan, Shearer. Twenty-one thousand peppered the stands. The Kop a mass of cherubic faces, a forest of scarves and banners, a choir of high-pitched screaming voices.

Momentarily quelled when West Ham took the lead within two minutes. Frank Lampard, son of the famous Frank, walloped a shot from 20 yards – blink and you would have missed it. Young Lampard is England material. Stylish, crafty, powerful – he needs an extra half-yard of pace. West Ham one, Liverpool two on aggregate.

Enter Michael Owen. Small, whippety, low centre of gravity, superb acceleration – the sign of a natural-born striker. Speed out of the holds, the first five yards off the blocks – straight from the coach's manual. The lad is fearless. He runs full tilt at defences. They hate this. Which way will he go – left or right? Owen does not care – he does what he does naturally – came from the cradle, and milk from Romulus and Remus!

Forty-three minutes total reflex, great perception – the ball rebounded from a free kick – Owen simply headed the ball into goal. *Kinderspiel.* Fifty-three minutes Owen won the match with a surging solo run, West Ham defenders trailing in his wake – a cracking shot hit the post – Stuart Quinn, flowing up, scored. Four–one on aggregate, game over.

I picked over the remains of the West Ham team for future stars. Rio Ferdinand is a cool customer; class oozes, but he is inclined to self-belief and hence distraction. Lampard, of course, and maybe Chris Coyne. Liverpool had David Thompson, a small urchin of combative spirit; Jamie Carragher – a flavour of Alan Hansen about him – obviously loves style, and young Owen. Note his name now; he is destined for greatness, although his diminutive size may twang his hamstrings.

Steve Heighway, that high-stepping flier, can be proud of his fledglings. *Liverpool:* Roy Naylor, Lee Prior, Gereth Roberts, Phil Brazier, Jamie Carragher, David Thomson, Stuart Quinn, Mark Quinn, Michael Owen, John Newby, Jamie Cassidy. Substitutes: Andy Parkinson, Ian Dunbabin, Eddie Turkington. *West Ham United:* Neil Finn, Jason Moore, Joe Keith, Chris Coyne, Rio Ferdinand, David Partridge, Manny Omoyimni, Frank Lampard, Anthony McFarlane, Lee Boylan, Lee Hodges. Substitutes: Justin Bowen, Alex O'Reilly, Chris Sains.

STRANGE TIMES AT THE COLOSSEUM

Strange times at the Colosseum. The other day I laughed with John Barnes and quizzed Caesar Evans at their training ground. The sun was high, merriment and revelry the tone. The following day, deep gloom. Sunderland, a team of serving platters and drayhorses, had reduced Liverpool's gladiators to impotent wimps. Sunderland's blanket defence, as thick as a 1930s London fog, defied Liverpool's vain attempt to improve their close passing game on the match. John Barnes like a man trapped on a fast escalator. Michael Thomas a man in quicksand. McManaman a headless rooster pursued by the fox – in this case his marker Ball. McAteer, the strong runner, was deployed at right back, his hands full with Bald Eaglet Agnew. Somewhere in the midst of blind chaos were Fowler and Collymore. Perfect strangers and non-communicators. I observed that not only were they not playing but not even speaking to each other. A wag overheard and pithily observed: 'I don't f***ing care if they don't f***ing speak or f***ing play – we want f***ing goals.' How crisp, how succinct.

Something has happened to Stan on his way to the Forum. He is a lovely chap. Affable, likeable, a superb runner on to the through ball, a great shot in either foot. But now he's like a stag at bay. Bemused by cerebral football, he's lost the plot. He needs goals. Liverpool have to play over the top, and at some pace. Give the stag a charge; use his physique – biff and bash.

Two goals up, lads, and we will return to culture. More steel, less epée. The Cup Winners' Cup is the ideal rehearsal room. The least attractive European tournament. Liverpool wanted the UEFA Cup. But they've a chance to atone for that appalling, inept performance last May at Wembley. They have the talent, the backstage know-how to tread the European stage as winners. Meanwhile, in the wilds of Finland, danger lurks. MyPa 47, a backwoods side of little pedigree. A hundred miles from Helsinki. A ground that holds 4,500. Is there a hotel there? Will it have hot and cold running water? Do we need a bowser of pure water or lager? Shall we take steaks or is there a McDonald's? A party including Caesar Evans, Virgil Robinson *et al* is, as I speak, exploring the tundra of Finland with backpacks, crampons, pitons and emergency rations. Will they suffer snow blindness or merely hypothermia? Whatever – MyPa 47 is Stan Collymore's show. 'Stan the Man', in Richie Benand's immortal words – 'Stuff it up 'em.'

PS Stuart Hall is suffering from amnesia.

THIRTY-NINE THOUSAND AT THE COLOSSEUM

Thirty-nine thousand at the Colosseum for a foregone conclusion. How astute to lower the admission price and field Patrick Berger, the Czech mate of the Kop. Hollywood visage, long sensual locks, tall, willowy, easy on the ball with both feet, and a predator for goals, he's the archetypal Anfield hero. A sensational signing. Compare the 30 million ducats or crowns or marks paid for Berger, then look askance at Chelsea, Middlesbrough and West Ham. Berger will either force 'Stan the Man' to play to his enormous ability, or simply leave. Liverpool have always retained the 'boot room' egalitarian approach. Insouciance to temperament. Tumescent egos lanced like boils. Berger fits in with the other internationals, and grafts for a living. The philosophy handed down by the late Bob Paisley, the greatest and most successful manager the game has known. It riles me when sycophants laud Busby, Stein, Shankly, Revie and omit Paisley. Three European Cups. A master tactician and psychologist. And so down to earth. Roy Evans (Caesar) now bestrides the Colosseum. When will he call legionaries Redknapp, Scales, Razor, and the half-dozen fledglings in the youth ranks to the fray? Scales and Razor replaced Wright and Matteo against the Finns – this will be the pattern. Poor Wright, the best centre half in Britain – speedy recovery to you. And to Matteo, the Hansen clone – make that England place yours. As Byron once said (ex-Tranmere): 'While stands the Colosseum, Liverpool shall stand. When falls the Colosseum, Liverpool shall fall. And when Liverpool fall – the world.'

SEASON 1994/95: HOW BEAUTIFUL UPON THE MOUNTAINS ARE THE FEET OF HIM THAT BRINGETH GOOD TIDINGS, THAT PUBLISHETH PEACE
LIVERPOOL 3 – ASTON VILLA 1

The FA Carling Premiership, 8 October 1994

The Colosseum in the blazing sun. The boardroom crammed with VIPs, a posse of earnest young men in immaculate suits and cravats buzzing attentively round an equally young Labour MP, Mr Tony Blair. Radio Five had arranged an interview for 2 p.m. At 1.45 p.m. I tugged the sleeve of a spin doctor. He rushed off and quickly returned.

'Mr Blair must have your list of questions.'

'I don't know. It's *ad hoc*. Does he want to win the next election? I'm unpaid by the BBC and frankly it is not the high watermark of my career.'

'It's the hope of reward that sweetens labour,' says the Bible. Will a Tory defeat sweeten Labour?

Mr Blair and I left the sanctuary and sat in the directors' box. He had a rapid speech pattern with spasmodic hand movement as if taught by a palmist. His eyes bright and crusading; if he dropped his voice an octave and obliterated a certain hesitance he would be a fine speechmaker. He confessed to admiring flair, denigrating the functional and purely pragmatic. (I wondered at this point why J. Prescott Esq. was running mate. If the New Labour is Aston Martin, why have a Ford Popular?) Flair player, the beautiful game, pure football – yes, he loved all of that. Will he, if elected, appoint a Sports Minister with brains and real clout, someone to work with industry and clubs to ensure that our children can play on a site earmarked, yet again, by greedy developers for supermarket housing or, worse, supermarket stores? I advanced the credentials of Tom Pendry, an old chum who once boxed for Oxford, played football on my lawn with a bunch of ragamuffins, and sank a few clarets afterwards. Mr Blair was noncommittal. Could we have an integrated transport policy as the Germans have? Trains that run efficiently and promptly? An Underground system in every major city, freedom from quangos and powerful anti-car lobbies? Blair is a man of zeal. Blair the flair. To win the election, he admits, will be to ditch old Labour dogma, pay lip service to the housing estate minds who will vote Labour if the candidate is a chimpanzee, and persuade Middle England that the New Labour beacon shines for them. I thank him and return him to his cohorts, by then worried sick that I had lured Mr Blair into a mantrap. I mused that Mr Blair had appropriated Mrs Thatcher's policies and modified them, rinsed them of acerbity, ventilated the arcane to mollify detractors, and present a platform to ensure success. Mr Blair will win. With a fair wind, a little foul play, a dash of common sense, he will be a success. At least it is a wind of change from that grey vacillator, Mr Major.

To the game. 'Blair the Flair' lit up the game as if all the players were racing to the hustings. Ball to feet, elegant use of space from Liverpool. Imaginative frisky play from Ron Atkinson's team. Is Ron still on the gold standard or is he a Labour voter? Molby was insolent in languidity; McManaman a high-stepper; Rob Jones marauded down the right.

The first goal was bizarre. Bosnich, the Villa keeper, handled a back pass – free kick. Razor Ruddock blasted the ball through the Villa wall, Bosnich parried, Fowler picked up the rebound and flashed it by Bosnich's left ear. Liverpool relaxed; Guy Whittingham nicked a Villa goal just before half-time. The second half never scaled the heights of the first. Robbie Fowler, though, relished his second goal on the hour. A yard of space t' aim for, sheer power beat Bosnich on his near post. Staunton's drive made it three–one just before full time. Liverpool's defensive trio of Babb, Scales and Ruddock are still playing 'Getting to Know You'. Babb seems overawed at the Colosseum, Scales, despite his Wimbledon upbringing, is a little too cultured, Ruddock for all his aggression not the force in the air that a 'stopper' centre half should be. We enjoyed it. 'Blair the Flair' never stopped smiling that number ten smile.

Liverpool: David James, Rob Jones, Phil Babb, Ian Rush, John Barnes, John Scales, Jan Molby, Steve McManaman, Stig Inge Bjornebye, Robbie Fowler, Neill Ruddock. Substitutes: Michael Stensgaard, Nigel Clough, Jamie Redknapp.

Aston Villa: Mark Bosnich, Earl Barrett, Steve Staunton, Paul McGrath, Ray Houghton, Dean Saunders, Andy Townsend, Garry Parker, Ugo Ehiogu, Dwight Yorke, Guy Whittingham. Substitutes: Nigel Spink, Nii Lampety, Phil King.

HYDE UNITED 1 – DARLINGTON 3
The FA Cup – First Round, 12 November 1994
> *True hope is swift, and flies with swallow's wings;*
> *Kings it makes gods, and meaner creatures kings.*

Non-League Hyde versus the Quakers, with League status. I am emotionally drained, I am filling up, as they say around these parts. Hyde, my birthplace, now made unlovely by hideous building, ugly roads, the closure of industry, the decline of quality shops. My first recollection was the smell of hot muffins, custard pies, crusty bread and coke fumes from my dad's baker's shop, a mere free kick from Ewen Fields. We have lived with the stigma of losing twenty-six–nil to Preston North End for a hundred years. My Uncle George, who was a tripe dresser in Bacup, vaguely remembers it. Wags say I follow in his footsteps, dressing tripe in words. Three thousand of us, including the Shadow Minister of Sport, MP for Stalybridge and Hyde, Tom Pendry, were fervent, even babes in arms chucked away their dummies and spoke: 'Runs not this speech like iron through your blood?' (They age quickly in Hyde.) The pitch is plastic, as threadbare as my granny's nightie. We took the lead on eight minutes through Phil Chadwick, Chaddy, first to a ball that bounced on the plastic so high that it came down with frost on it. Bernie Slaven – remember him with Middlesbrough? Still clever, still scoring crucial goals – he controlled a capricious ball and calmly side-footed the equalizer. Darlington are a strapping side, tall in the saddle, as subtle as a Sherman tank. They gave the ball fearful wellie and tonk, threatening human passers-by and the windows, nay structure, of the little Leigh Street School, my first *alma mater*. Pygmy Hyde versus Juggernaut Darlington. Jason against the Argonauts. We were superb, supple and lithe, a samba Brazilian style on the plastic. We lost five balls as Darlington gave them hefty boots over the retaining walls. That's a week's take at the gate gone! Then, two goals in two minutes undid us late on. The first scored by Warboys, another six-footer, the other I could not recognize as tears flooded my eyes and coursed down the cheeks. Three–one to Darlington. We bungled a penalty kick, I will not name him; the Hyde inquisition is notorious for thumbscrews; and the one-candlepower floodlights dimmed the scene. We gave blood this day. The night air is hot with our steaming breath and the vapour from hot pies and mushy peas.

> Hope tells a flattering tale,
> Delusive, vain and hollow.
> Ah, let not hope prevail
> Lest disappointment follow.

Oh well, back to tripe dressing!
Hyde United: Anonymous *et al*
Darlington: *Ad libitum...* (as one pleases...)

EVERTON 0 – TOTTENHAM HOTSPUR 0
The FA Carling Premiership, 17 December 1994
Sixteen years ago Joe Royle and Gerry Francis were in England's team at Wembley. They beat Northern Ireland four–nil. The team was Ray Clemence, Colin Todd, Mick Mills, Phil Thompson, Brian Greenhoff, Ray Kennedy, Kevin Keegan, Gerry Francis, Stuart Pearson, Mick Channon and Peter Taylor with substitutes Joe Royle and Towers. Eleven of those players went on to coach or manage at the top. Mick Channon coached horses and, with that Hampshire brogue, defied logic and bred winners.

Joe and Gerry meet again today as newly-appointed managers. Everton in the trap door of relegation, 18 games, 18 points. Tottenham 18 games, 25 points. It is Christmas – the School of Science welcomes us with festive joy.

A bevy of shapely damsels wore blue bonnets proclaiming: 'Santa Claus is an Everton fan.' I thought Santa played in Coca-Cola red, or was not that the bitter east wind from Siberia that blued the bonnets and blewed this match to tatters? It promised fulsome fare, School of Science versus the grand masters of the beautiful game. Alas, the ball was capricious. Close control impossible, the weighted pass unthinkable. Everton nowadays tear about the pitch as if possessed; fireworks attached to their buttocks. Barry Horne the principal stick of dynamite. Walker saved a Barlow shot in the opening salvo, Spurs thus defended in rumbustious fashion. Mabbutt, Calderwood, Howells the new breed of Gerry Francis steel bludgeon replacing the Ardiles rapier of old. As the litter flew over the park, so the match degenerated. Illuminated by Andy Hinchcliffe's dead ball kicks that raised panic; Anders Limpar's fanciful runs, David Unsworth's immense promise at centre back, Spurs never forced Neville to make a save. Though they hit a post from a free kick. Typical was the larrikin game of the keepers Walker and Southall – who could kick furthest? Neville the dishevelled won. Santa is blue after all.

Everton: Neville Southall, Matt Jackson, David Burrows, Barry Horne, Dave Watson, David Unsworth, John Ebbrell, Joe Parkinson, Paul Rideout, Stuart Barlow, Andy Hinchcliffe. Substitutes: Jason Kearton, Anders Limpar, Graham Stuart.

Tottenham Hotspur: Ian Walker, Dean Austin, Sol Campbell, Gheorghe Popescu, Colin Calderwood, Gary Mabbutt, Darren Anderton, Ronny Rosenthal, Teddy Sherringham, David Howells, Nick Barmby. Substitutes: Chris Day, Justin Edinburgh, Stuart Nethercott.

EVERTON 4 – IPSWICH TOWN 1

The FA Carling Premiership, 31 December 1994

Oh, dear! For the School of Science read School of Militant Warfare. Joe Royle's dictum: 'Once more into the breach, blue shirts, or shore the wall up with Joseph's dead; imitate the action of the tiger; follow your spirit and upon this charge cry, "God, Joe Royle and England".' Bellicose, gung-ho, John Bull, fire and brimstone up your bum, white-hot passion, this is war, lads, and we are the dogs of it. Ipswich were bludgeoned, blown away like Christmas decorations in a gale. 'Twas like a cattle stampede in Calgary. Ipswich breathless and faint until the tenth minute: they worked with stealth through the steam-rolling midfield, Steve Sedgeley stole up on the blind side and sneaked a clever goal. We were stunned, astonished, no rapier ever vanquished broadsword. Duncan Ferguson cried, 'Why, then, the world is mine oyster, which I with sword will open,' and fell upon Ipswich's rearguard. Came a Jackson low cross, Duncan bullet headed the equalizer. The crowd bayed for blood and guts; the fearful among the spectators averted their gaze. This was Agincourt. Everton tore into Wark, Linighan and Yallop. Three blue shirts into every ferocious tackle. Ipswich miraculously survived until two goals in two minutes ripped out their hearts; Paul Rideout, underrated by many, adored by some, scored both. The first a rip-roaring drive, the second a subtle flick on the goal line after Hinchcliffe had somehow wormed to the by-line and crossed low. Dave Watson headed the fourth exactly on time. He had missed three chances; this was atonement. Dave is the platoon sergeant here, leather lungs, fearless temperament, a thirst for battle, scant regard for his own wellbeing. I would want him on my beaches if ever we go to war; Gary Lineker can be the pay clerk. Dogs of war they be, no doubt Joe Royle will continue their diet of brimstone and treacle; it is a desperate battle in the nether regions. Ipswich are milk and water, fey and non-combative. They are doomed.

Everton: Neville Southall, Matt Jackson, David Burrows, David Unsworth,

Dave Watson, Barry Horne, Joe Parkinson, John Ebbrell, Andy Hinchcliffe, Duncan Ferguson, Paul Rideout. Substitutes: Stuart Barlow, Jason Kearton, Anders Limpar.

Ipswich Town: Craig Forest, Tony Vaughan, John Wark, David Linighan, Paul Mason, Frank Yallop, Steve Palmer, Chris Kiwomya, Steve Sedgeley, Claus Thomsen, Bontcho Guentchev. Substitutes: Stuart Slater, Clive Baker, Phil Whelan.

TELL IT NOT IN GATH

Tell it not in Gath. Whisper it not in the streets of Askelon lest the daughters of the Philistines rejoice that I, as a Manchester City fan, admire most the Shrine, known to the vulgar as the Theatre of Dreams. An edifice to mass commercialism. A temple of capitalism. A worldwide marketing exposition. And home to the finest football team in Europe.

Much have I travelled in the realms of gold and dross. I have stood agape at the modern monstrosities of steel and concrete devoid of the very soul of football. I remember ancient wooden stands wherein sat nobility. Grocers, fishmongers, bakers and fruiterers in bowler hats. Their wives wearing upturned chamber pots alive with floribunda. The fans flat caps smoking Woodbines at sixpence for twenty. One shilling to stand on the terraces. Two pence for a hot Bovril, four pence for a pint of warm mild beer.

The soul, brethren, of the beautiful game. The heroes for £20 a week. My eyes mist, I clutch my surplice or surplus, in tender loving memory. My tablet of stone says:

My name is Ozymandias, king of kings;
Look on my works, ye mighty, and despair!'
Nothing beside remains. Round the decay
Of that colossal wreck, boundless and bare,
The lone and level sands stretch far away.

The sands of time, brethren. But I revel in anachronisms. Old dinosaur grounds enchant me.

BARNSLEY IS ONOMATOPOEIC

It is what it is and ere will be. Steel, iron, coal, Scargill, tough-as-teak Yorkshire. Not having visited Oakwell for a quarter of a century, I dispatched there on a March day for a joust with Birmingham City. Barnsley *en fête*. I wandered lonely as a cloud o'er hills and dales until I found Pattpong Road (or similarly yclept). You *will* get lost. Acquire an English-Yorkshire dictionary and accost a local.

'Tha turns reet, reet again, allreet then, tha does a left darn t' road – up t' hill, down t' hill. Allreet.' This is Dickie Bird country. All foreigners come from Mars.

So down Pattpong Road, down the steep hill at the bottom of which stood a posse of Yorkist bobbies. (What is the collective noun for policemen: fandango of fuzz, cornucopia of coppers, plumage of police?) All the peelers have florid, cherubic, beatific countenances.

'Tha can't park thi car theer. You can't park anywheer,' observed a large blue bottle with a choirboy's visage. You must approach Oakwell by tram, bus, horseback or shanks's pony. I abandoned the Hupmobile on high ground for fear of locusts. Number one bobby: 'Has't getten thissen a pass?'

'No,' I gasped. 'The BBC don't bother.'

'Tha goes to gate 42.' I look blank. 'Ah'll tek thi.'

I was led to gate 42 and handed over to a steward.

'I need a pee.'

'Thru' t' hamburger bar and it's theer.'

Dying for a leak, I fought my way through the jostle, the smell of onions hitting the larynx like mustard gas. I dived into the urinal. The pee-stone was Jacques Tati's Clochemerle – Pop Gothic. Corrugated iron and guess your weight! Having relieved myself, most of it splashing back off the iron, I was led to the press box cheek by jowl with the audience. By now I was in fits of laughter – this is football as it should be. I felt at home after a Pop Gothic pee!

The charladies had been a trifle lax. My seat had sweet wrappers, old newspapers, chewing gum, layers of desert sand. Oakwell is atop a mountain; the Yorkshire mistral is blowing at 80mph. As I swept my workplace clean, the gale blew in another mountain of debris. I had come to witness Barnsley's Brazilian-blend football and to pay homage to Danny Wilson, a wonderful wing half of his day. I laughed a lot. Rustic gaiety. Here at Oakwell amid Brazilian footie and flat Yorkshire vowels lies the grass roots of the beautiful game. Alas, the plot went awry. With the gale at his back the Birmingham full-back blasted a 60-yard free kick through the Barnsley net and into Grimethorpe Colliery. Blow wind and cataract. Barnsley's poise evaporated and Birmingham did the business. One–nowt to Brum.

Afterwards, I mused with Danny Wilson, an open-faced lad of the soil, an honest, straight gent. He loved the fact that I'd loved the day. A tight, spruce, little ground. A board of directors brewed locally. A fan's football club. We chuckled and relished the thought of Chelsea's stretched luxury limo crawling down Pattpong Road. Ken Bates and his sophisticated cronies incredulous. Le Boeuf, Di Matteo, Emile Zola, Vialli and Tore singing 'Waters over Troubled Bridge' (apologies to Simon and Garfunkel). Those pansy yellow and blue pyjamas that Chelsea sport will be heckled off the pitch. From San Siro to Oakwell. From larks' tongues in aspic with quails' eggs to baked beans and Bovril. It's Don Quixote time. I love it. Romance lives in Barnsley.

SEASON 1993/94: 'MONEY IS THE MOST IMPORTANT THING IN LIFE... EVERY TEACHER OR TWADDLER WHO DENIES IT, OR SUPPRESSES IT, IS AN ENEMY OF LIFE. MONEY CONTROLS MORALITY.'

George Bernard Shaw, ex-Villa

LEEDS UNITED 4 – CHELSEA 1

The FA Carling Premiership, 6 November 1993

Leeds United were League Champions in 1991–2. The gloss rapidly wears off. Mr Wilkinson, the multi-worded Elijah, is confounded. Five games played in October; only one win, against Wimbledon. David Batty, the Yorkshire terrier, has been sold to Kenny Dalglish at Blackburn. Leslie Silver, the Leeds chairman, a bomber pilot in the Second World War, has been bombed out by furious Leeds fans. Never mind the facilities, do not sell your best players. Chelsea have Glenn Hoddle as player/manager, one of the great inventive thinkers England have ever possessed; one Hoddle pass worth ninety minutes of dross elsewhere. His team is enigmatic, extrovert and bubbling one game, pale and introspective the next.

Meteorologically-wise it was a dank, dark, drizzly day at Yelland Road. Yorkshire greyness equals matt black on the swell boulevards of the King's Road. Yorkshire pudding versus carciofi alla romagna. Chelsea were a damp squib extinguished by a Leeds roaring inferno. Bonfires of joy light up this scene at 4.45 p.m.

A first half of Leeds rampage, blanket defence from Chelsea, Hitchcock in goal performing minor miracles. McAllister primed his team for onslaught as the teams emerged after half-time. Two minutes into it, the 35,000 exulted – acclaimed Brian Deane's first goal at home, only his third for the club. He shrugged off Sinclair, like a heavyweight boxer, held his nerve and slugged the shot past Hitchcock. Three minutes later Deane, now on a roll, crossed from the right – Rod Wallace bundled the ball in. Fifty-six minutes Fairclough's header forward, Chelsea's defence appealed for offside – Wallace sprinted forward – super shot, three–nil. David Rocastle, the Batty replacement, high on adrenalin, high on confidence, weaved past three defenders and walloped number four. Shipperley sneaked in five minutes from time for a token Chelsea goal, but today Glenn Hoddle, laying tactics like a chess master – Peacock in the hole, three at the back, Newton deep – must have felt like a country clergyman in a New York revolving door. The pace and commitment from Leeds was nearly championship style.

Leeds United: Mark Beeney, Tony Dorigo, Chris Fairclough, Rod Wallace, Brian Deane, Gary McAllister, Gary Speed, David Rocastle, Jon Newsome, David Wetherall, Gary Kelly. Substitutes: John Lukic, Steve Hodge, Jamie Forrester.
Chelsea: Kevin Hitchcock, Erland Johnsen, Frank Sinclair, Tony Cascarino, Gavin Peacock, Dennis Wise, Eddie Newton, Glenn Hoddle, Mark Stein, David Hopkin, Jakob Kjeldbjerg. Substitutes: Mal Donaghy, Neil Shipperley, Nick Colgan.

BOLTON WANDERERS 3 – GRETNA FC 2
The FA Challenge Cup, 13 November 1993

The Queen Mother has never visited Bolton, a town halfway between Gothic Renaissance splendour and Thatcher super-drab, nor, to my limited knowledge, officiated at nuptials in Gretna Green, that village seven miles north of Carlisle whose marriages are made, not in heaven, but over the anvil. Gretna had a home tie but decided to opt for a sack of loot, thus playing at the Shed, Burnden Park. This clapped-out, crumbling ruin is destined for the knacker's yard, but I love it. It is part of my sporting life.

I have played here; number four behind peerless Stanley Matthews. Icons Higgins, Banks, Hartle, Gowling, Bill Ridding, George Moir and Nat Lofthouse are or were mates. History whispers from the rafters: four times FA Cup winners, Wembley 1923, Lions of Vienna, the 1953 Final. Down to earth this Bolton side is, struggling in the Endsleigh League, fourth from bottom, only Peterborough, Oxford and Barnsley below them. A Cup run stimulates the fans, distracts them from sorrow; we are all lemmings at least. The humble Gretna side ran out to ringing applause. Police Constable J.B. Priestley in goal. In front of him fitters, joiners, a security guard, a sandwich seller, a confectioner, plus the ubiquitous publican. Bolton are swells by comparison.

A dream scenario unfolded. Gretna one up after 11 minutes. Derek Townsley, their six-feet four-inch defender, soared upwards and onwards – great goal. Oops – one minute later he conceded a penalty. McGinlay, the gimlet, converts. One–one. Twenty-four minutes Mark Dobie, our sandwich seller, sold Bolton a rye with mustard and put Gretna two–one up.

The rain teemed down, a bitter wind blew off the East Lancashire steppes, the pitch looked like a home for Highland cattle. We were on tenterhooks – could Gretna hold on? Mike McCartney, player/manager ex-West Bromwich Albion, Southampton, Carlisle and Plymouth, discovered muscles that even Heineken could not reach. Thick mud clung to his clogs; he should have worn galoshes. Bolton whipped up the pace. Jason McAteer energized the charge, the all-action man, McGinlay o'Gimlet leaving spray in his wake, David Lee, scarce of hair, whippety of foot, scaring the part-timers. Alan Stubbs – what a fine centre half, quality player; 'twas too much for Gretna. PC Priestley was Hannibal in goal, Horatio on the bridge, or is it on the beat? The ball was taken into protective custody on anything but flat feet.

'Letsby Avenue,' the cry. Weariness set in, the ball weighed a ton, oxygen was scarce. The game stretched like a strumpet's knicker elastic. Owen Coyle, the Bolton centre forward, blasted the equalizer on 78 minutes. Seven minutes to go, Gretna grasping for air, on the ropes, when Coyle ploughed through the middle and thrust in the winner.

Bolton triumph three–two. Standing ovation for Gretna Green and a resounding rendition of the 'Anvil Chorus'.

Bolton Wanderers: Aidan Davison, Phil Brown, Jimmy Philips, Jason McAteer, Alan Stubbs, Mark Winstanley, David Lee, Scott Lee, Owen Coyle, John

McGinlay, Alan Thompson. Substitutes: Tony Kelly, Mark Seagraves, Russell Hoult.

Gretna FC: Jason Priestley, Lee Armstrong, Mike McCartney, Paul Gorman, Wayne Gardiner, Derek Townsley, John Halpin, Derek Walsh, Andy Walker, Mark Dobie, Chris Potts. Substitutes: Anthony Monaghan, Mark Eagling, Stuart Sweeting.

EVERTON 0 – QUEENS PARK RANGERS 3
The FA Carling Premiership, 20 November 1993

Bradley Allen scored all three QPR goals. Littered from the same family tree as the famous Clive, scoring goals is nature's gift. They were born wearing football boots; they spat their dummy and sold one instead. Their first words were not 'Mummy' and 'Daddy' but 'On mi 'ead, son'.

But how could Everton, renowned for the beautiful game, be so outclassed and embarrassed by QPR? There were 17,000 at the School of Science; flabbergasted, dismayed, then angry; loud boos, jeers, taunts and Toxteth industrial language at the whistle. Disenchantment rended. How could Everton, led by the midget Cottee, throw so many high balls into the penalty box, then in desperation dispatch Watson, their centre back, supreme in the air, to a battering ram role upfront? It spelt failure – did from the first minute when Ablett failed at a goal chance. He could have scored with any part of his anatomy, as the stevedore behind me succinctly pointed out.

QPR punished them cruelly. Twenty-six minutes Bradley Allen scored his first, a simple tap in, as Everton suffered meltdown. Fifty-two minutes the second, tucking away a rebound off a post. The third, six minutes from time, beautifully conceived: a Wilkins pass wide to the charging Bardsley, a thumping cross – Allen steered the ball wide of a distracted, distraught Neville the Dishevelled.

QPR were fast on the button, physical, and kept the game simple. Ferdinand was powerful, enormous upper body strength, omnipotent in the air. Sinclair, a recent signing from Blackpool, effervesced, only 20 years old, a real prospect. The star was Ray Wilkins the venerable, strolling arrogantly like a Parisian boulevardier eyeing courtesans on the Champs-Elysées. He could have played in a Bath chair and been magnificent. The forlorn have departed. One hundred and two folk remain on the terraces for a charity match between a team of MPs and a side of journalists. The Commons versus the common, hot air versus harsh words. It is only a game, after all.

Everton: Neville Southall, Paul Holmes, Gary Ablett, John Ebbrell, Dave Watson, Matt Jackson, Preki, Mark Ward, Tony Cottee, Stuart Barlow, Peter Beagrie. Substitutes: Barry Horne, Jason Kearton, Graham Stuart.

Queens Park Rangers: Jan Sjeskal, David Bardsley, Clive Wilson, Andrew Impey, Simon Barker, Ray Wilkins, Les Ferdinand, Bradley Allen, Trevor Sinclair, Steve Yates, Darren Peacock. Substitutes: Ian Holloway, Tony Roberts, Rufus Brevet.

MANCHESTER CITY 0 – TOTTENHAM HOTSPUR 2
The FA Carling Premiership, 11 December 1993

At five o'clock, a small knot of vociferous, angry fans was dispelled by the bobbies. Storm clouds are back at the Theatre of Base Comedy. The team, under Brian Horton, is once again in relegation quicksand. The saviour, Niall Quinn, is sidelined with cruciate ligaments. One win in their last eight games. A mere eight goals for, 15 against in those matches. Ozzie Ardiles brings a talented, well-schooled Spurs team for the joust. Ardiles with mixed thoughts – Ardiles the player was finished here by a grotesque foul by Hutchinson, City's most pusillanimous player. Outgoing chairman P.J. Swales was absent with fear. Rumour hath it that Mr McDonald, the would-be incoming chairman, was sitting in the Kippax stand. I sympathize with Peter Swales. He has been victimized, vilified, threatened, his family maltreated by an underground Mafia intent on forcing Swales out. The methods stink. It is foul play from the gutter. There is scum in Manchester.

There was no pre-match demonstration, the minute's silence for Danny Blanchflower observed with decorum. Decorum continued with the football match. Both sides, with many absent stars, fielded reserves of scant acquaintance with the big time. In this first half, City's Lomas and Flitcroft played attractive, neat football. Spurs, with Samways nursing an injury, playing a holding pattern. It was gentle, gentlemanly, no contact, no passion stuff.

Second half Spurs emerged with girded loins and upped a gear – Samways and Hazard, relaxed and comfortable, brought the best from Caskey, Anderton and Dozzell. So it became Dozzell's match. Sixty-five minutes Anderton's long cross, Dozzell's simple stab past a furious Coton. Curle the City marker at fault. And it was Curle again misjudging the play that allowed Dozzell to nip behind the City defence three minutes from time and tuck the ball away for his second goal. Thorsvedt, delighted, threw his gloves to the Spurs fans. Came the small demonstration; an uneasy peace now at Maine Road but no sign yet of Francis Lee.

Manchester City: Tony Coton, Terry Phelan, Keith Curle, Michel Vonk, David White, Mike Sheron, Garry Flitcroft, Carl Griffiths, Mike Quigley, Steve Lomas. Substitutes: David Brightwell, Carl Ingebrigtsen, Andy Dibble.

Tottenham Hotspur: Erik Thorsvedt, Dean Austin, Justin Edinburgh, Vinny Samways, Colin Calderwood, Gary Mabbutt, Darren Anderton, Teddy Sheringham, Jason Dozzell, Micky Hazard, Darren Caskey.

SEASON 1992/93: I HAD RATHER A FOOL MAKE ME MERRY THAN EXPERIENCE MAKE ME SAD

EVERTON 1 – SHEFFIELD WEDNESDAY 1
The FA Carling Premiership, 15 August 1992

The School of Science celebrates its centenary. Howard Kendall rules. It is

aspiration time; Goodison bright, shining, the greensward blindingly fast and lush. The Everton toffee girls in their Edwardian long frocks and frilly bonnets are tossing sweeties to a fawning audience. I am always reminded of my junior school days when classes were mixed. Innocent charming little girls with monstrous, recalcitrant, atavistic, Neanderthal boys. The dictum:
'Keep your hand on your halfpenny until you get your sweeties.' Was this to be a sweetie game? Howard has signed Barry Horne, a highly-intelligent foot-baller who can inspire. Mo Johnston, Peter Beardsley, Peter Beagrie are Everton's entertainers. Chris Waddle will strut his stuff for Wednesday.

Twenty-eight thousand are present. Five thousand Wednesday fans unfurl a giant blue and white flag for a Mexican wave. When Wednesday scored after 15 minutes a huge flag of St George was flourished. Maybe Neville Southall was the slain dragon in the scenario; 'twas he who dropped Nigel Worthington's corner ball right on to Nigel Pearson's boot. Nigel scored. Much flag-waving ensued from Wednesday's travelling troubadours. The draught from these endeavours caught Wednesday's sails – they began to rampage. David Hirst loves the rampant, a true cruiserweight prizefighter. Carlton Palmer towered. Well, he would with a name like a Manhattan tower block! Worthington's left foot was like sticky toffee pudding – everything adhered to it. Everton misread the game, Horne and Ward flitting fitfully to little purpose. Rideout was lost in the prairie, riderless Rideout.

Fifteen seconds to half-time, Peter Beagrie demonstrated his sole art – feinting inside the back, charging up the line and crossing – all with the left foot. Peter, if only you had a right pedal extremity you would be world-class. But Nilsson, the Wednesday fullback, was suckered in, left sprawling, Beagrie's cross, Barry Horne volleyed the goal. One–one at half time.

The second half was bizarre, bouts of zany back passing to excited goal-keepers, bags of highball, a complete breakdown of pattern.

Chris Waddle, out of sorts and form, retired. Barry Horne followed him up the tunnel, injured. Polish Bob, so yclept because nobody can pronounce his name, replaced Horne. His surname Warzycha: get your tongue round that, delving into your cornflakes! Bob is a flier on the right wing. Trouble is, where he flies no Everton player goes. They must feel like trainspotters watching the Orient Express go by. Bob turned on the borscht, hot pepper style. Peter Beardsley hashed a chance. Rideout had the ball on his boot two yards out and failed. The whistle: frankly welcome relief. Aspirations – sorry, Howard Kendall and Trevor Francis; nothing for you this season.

Everton: Neville Southall, Matthew Jackson, Andy Hinchcliffe, John Ebbrell, Dave Watson, Gary Ablett, Mark Ward, Peter Beardsley, Paul Rideout, Barry Horne, Peter Beagrie. Substitutes: Mo Johnston, Rob Warzycha, Jason Kearton.
Sheffield Wednesday: Chris Woods, Roland Nilsson, Phil King, Carlton Palmer, Nigel Pearson, Paul Warhurst, Chris Waddle, Graham Hyde, David Hirst, Paul Williams, Nigel Worthington. Substitutes: Gordon Watson, Chris Bart-Williams, Kevin Pressman.

OLDHAM ATHLETIC 5 – NOTTINGHAM FOREST 3
The FA Carling Premiership, 22 August 1992

The Premier League of 1992 is bizarre, Norwich City and Coventry at the top, Manchester United at the bottom. Latics have two draws from their first two games against Chelsea and Crystal Palace. Brian Clough has rebuilt his side. He paid £2 million for Teddy Sheringham from Millwall, and £10,000 for Roy Keane, a wild Irish lad from Cobh Ramblers. Keane has legs like oak trees and a brain, some say in Cork, like an acorn.

Oldham, apace with the times, have erected a brand-new stand in 90 days. I lament the passing of cherished landmarks. My view of Monarch Mill, that huge grey monolith, the constant reminder of Oldham's golden period of Victorian prosperity. The cruel demolition of Millhench's shed, dingy and tatty, it provided shelter for the frozen peelers tired of fractious fans and Pennine hurricanes. Gone the days of bleached tripe and parched peas, potato pie and Bovril. Lasagne has wormed its way here from Milan.

To the match. Joe Royle likes attacking football. Brian Clough savours the pure. We had a fine open game of classic style, a dash of imagination, a whiff of the beautiful. For Oldham Ian Marshall, a centre forward who looks like a market trader less than shevelled, played sweeper. Gunnar Halle, a fullback, played right wing. Henry, Bernard and Milligan a feisty, florid, think-tank of a midfield. For 30 minutes the game was for the technical, both sides incising, probing, taking the pace, showing respect for each other. There was talent galore for the neutral, gnawing impatience for the fans. On the half-hour Redmond essayed down the right, Neil Adams thrashed the ball past Crossley. Crossley was cross. A silly goal that opened the floodgates. Thirty-eight minutes Terry Wilson, the Forest centre back, boobed like an unfrocked bishop; divest of raiment, he allowed Sharp to dispossess him and put away goal number two. Within minutes Nicky Henry's blistering left-foot drive put Oldham three–nil up.

Seconds after half-time Stuart Pearce, having a nightmare against pace, miskicked. Gunnar Halle side-footed the fourth. On the hour Paul Bernard's peach of a goal, five–nil. Oldham on the rampage, Forest reeling, Nigel Clough an emergency defender.

Latics then declared. The body language indicated 'We've done enough; we can relax'. Mr Clough, incensed as it was, became more incensed; he was puce, impure vitriol, imprecations hit the desert air.

Sixty-six minutes Pearce struck a penalty so fierce that the ball finished in nearby Rochdale. Eighty-six minutes Gary Bannister's shot. Five–two.

Eighty-eight minutes Gary Bannister's header. Five–three.

Latics now hanging in – the force with Forest. A great game for the pure in heart, for the romantic. A memorial, really, for the Oldham diehard fans. They know that Joe Royle will move upwards: that when this present team disbands, through ambition or old age, these moments will be treasured, never forgotten. *Oldham Athletic:* Jon Hallworth, Steve Redmond, Neil Pointon, Nicky Henry,

Richard Jobson, Ian Marshall, Gunnar Halle, Paul Bernard, Graeme Sharp, Mike Milligan, Neil Adams. Substitutes: Roger Palmer, John Keeley, Craig Fleming. *Nottingham Forest:* Mark Crossley, Brian Laws, Stuart Pearce, Terry Wilson, Steve Chettle, Roy Keane, Gary Crosby, Scot Gemmill, Nigel Clough, Teddy Sheringham, Ian Woan. Substitutes: Kingsley Black, Andrew Marriott, Gary Bannister.

LIVERPOOL 2 – WIMBLEDON 3
The FA Carling Premiership, 26 September 1992

The Colosseum is in turmoil. Caesar Souness feared histrionics from the Romans, knives from Cassius and Brutus, a horde of Goths baying for his blood. The divide between him and the Liverpool public as wide as the Red Sea. Ian Rush, John Barnes, Ronnie Whelan absent. A patched-up team with lost intentions. Four goals conceded against Chesterfield last Tuesday in the Coca-Cola Cup. James in goal having a personal nightmare; Grobbelaar returns today. Souness knows, and this he cannot handle, that there are players wearing red shirts who are not Liverpool players but masqueraders. Istvan Kozma, Paul Stewart, Don Hutchison, Phil Charnock, Mike Marsh, David Burrows – all fall short of the pinnacle that the Colosseum demands. Piechnik, another misfit, is drafted to replace another misfit, Nicky Tanner. Rosenthal runs like a coursed hare – into the trap.

Mark Walters flatters to deceive. It was always going to be torrid; the Crazy Gang thrive on embarrassing the elite. So it came to pass. Wimbledon two goals up in 25 minutes. John Fashanu, 'Fash the Bash', pinged in the first after a sweet one-two with Robbie Earle. Fashanu really is a reaper and binder, a combined harvester, all threshing and thrashing; tackling him is virtual suicide under his blades. The second was a Grobbelaar clanger; punched out to nowhere, Robbie Earle lobbed him. The crowd howled derision – poor Brucie – he will be remembered forever, not as a brilliant keeper, but as a fallible instigator of those daft errors that TV will highlight. Liverpool were stung (maybe another win bonus down the drain). Redknapp, Rosenthal, Molby, Hutchinson shot wide or over with golden opportunities. Thirty-five minutes Molby converted a penalty kick after a foul on Rosenthal. Thirty-nine minutes Rosenthal's shot cannoned off the bar, McManaman cleverly half-volleyed the equalizer. Roger Milford, the referee, is a jolly fellow, but he filled his notebook as the temperature rose to white hot. The energy expended by both teams would light New York City for a week; a two–two draw seemed fair. Not to Robbie Earle, a class act in a workhorse team. As Mark Wright and Piechnik slumbered, Earle ran through them and blasted the ball past Brucie. Three–two to the crazy gang; it was their Cup Final. Vincent Jones led the lap of honour to much whooping. Backstage is Caesar Souness. We are friends; I coined the pseudonym Caesar for leaders at the Colosseum. I am no Cassius, I am merely an apostle.

Caesar Souness stayed in the dressing-room until 6.15 p.m. I know because I waited for him in an anteroom. One by one, the players filed by, heads bowed low. Thick depression hung like storm clouds. The boot room, normally alive, cheerful, the think-tank of English football, was dead. The Kop does not sing any more. The Liverpool public now disenchanted and critical.

Liverpool is unique. Since 1964 and Shankly it has belonged to the public. As Liverpool's (the city's) fortunes waned, the football club was dream fulfilment. The hopes, the aspiration, the sheer success kept morale high.

Bill Shankly and Bob Paisley were simple men, not derogatory; they were footballers, not ambitious for anything but football's success.

The chairmen, Sid Reakes and John Smith, and secretary Peter Robinson handled all the affairs like benevolent despots backstage. *The club belonged to the public* – now apparently it does not. David Moores of the Littlewoods family is a different animal. A boardroom coup ousted Sir John Smith. Noel White, a bewildered nice guy, was dragooned into the job and bartered for David Moores to succeed. Executive boxes and plush restaurants now take precedence to the Kop. Do not blame David Moores; this is, of course, the path that football clubs tread. It is no longer a working man's game. It is for the entrepreneur. Big bucks, big returns.

The working lad is distanced from the club, his heroes earning more per week than he gets paid per year – if he is lucky to have a job. Twenty-thousand soundless Kopites bear out the truth.

On the pitch, Graeme Souness, Caesar, is a footballer with a brain. Married into enormous wealth, expressed in Majorcan, nouveau riche, gold-plated ostentation, he nurtured burning ambition. A piece of the action. Personal wealth, children at public school, large mansions, exotic cars. The ultimate high profile. Caesar ruling the senate, making the laws, exiling those not faithful; to the cause. His private life he thought was private. The Sun newspaper demolished it. Public opinion turned; so did the local press. Both have been treated with disdain by Caesar.

Injuries have decimated the team. But unanswered questions remain. The Liverpool philosophy was: bring on fledgling talent like Keegan, Heighway, Tommy Smith; blend with inspired signings like St John, Alan Hansen, Kenny Dalglish. The pattern in tablets of stone. A heritage trail.

Now the pattern is blown away. Why do internationals like Dean Saunders and Mark Wright play like novices? Do the seasoned players want to play for Caesar? When they do return, will Rush, Barnes, Whelan be the players they were? Shankly's sign, 'This is Anfield', does not intimidate visiting teams. It inspires them.

A victory today over Wimbledon was absolutely crucial. The spirit of the team monitored by the world. The Colosseum is not a football arena; it is a crucible and cauldron. Caesar will survive the heat. I have a great personal affection for this unique club and its servants.

Graeme Souness was one of the great wing halves of all time. He was well aware of his superior talent over lesser mortals. He is an honest, straight man whom I admire; but in today's shifting sands of football, can honest men survive?

Honour and money are not found in the same purse.

Liverpool: Bruce Grobbelaar, Mike Marsh, David Burrows, Torben Piechnik, Jamie Rednapp, Mark Wright, Ronny Rosenthal, Steve McManaman, Don Hutchison, Jan Molby, Mark Walters. Substitutes: Istvan Kosma, Nicky Tanner, David James.

Wimbledon: Hans Segers, Warren Barton, Justin Skinner, Vinnie Jones, John Scales, Scott Fitzgerald, Neal Ardley, Robbie Earle, John Fashanu, Dean Holdsworth, Andy Clarke. Substitutes: Lawrie Sanchez, Paul Miller, Neil Sullivan.

MANCHESTER CITY 2 – NOTTINGHAM FOREST 2
The FA Carling Premiership, 3 October 1992

Away from the Anfield cauldron, football-watching today was like peaceful pasture after Slaughterhouse Five. To purr with pleasure at the pure quality of Forest's football. It flows like vintage burgundy of velvet taste, matured in style. Their running and first touch, their wit and intelligence all pluses. Their minuses – lack of a quality striker and a replacement for Des Walker; Roy Keane too fine a midfielder to play centre back.

City responded with commitment and muted aggression and of course Niall Quinn's eponymous head. A ball to that head precipitated City's first goal on 18 minutes. A mint cavalry charge in Forest's box. Rick Holden's half-volley.

Fifty-seven minutes Forest's equalizer from the textbook. Orlygsson's pass sliced through City. Crosby on the sprint. His cross tickled across goal by Clough. Ray Wilkinson far post, fine goal.

Sixty-five minutes Terry Phelan, City's sprightly left back, hared down the left. High cross – Niall Quinn out-headed goalkeeper Crossley. Fitzroy Simpson's shot. Two–one. Eighty-three minutes silky Forest football, Bannister's instinctive pass. Stuart Pearce on a fearsome gallop slammed the equalizer seven minutes from time.

A moment of humour. Peter Reid's callisthenics as sub before appearing: like a lethargic, rheumy brigadier emerging from his Bath chair – antithesis of Anfield.

Manchester City: Tony Coton, Ian Brightwell, Terry Phelan, Steve McMahon, Keith Curle, Andy Hill, David White, Mike Sheron, Niall Quinn, Fitzroy Simpson, Rick Holden. Substitutes: Peter Reid, Adie Mike, Martyn Margetson.

Nottingham Forest: Mark Crossley, Brian Laws, Stuart Pearce, Ray McKinnon, Carl Tiler, Roy Keane, Gary Crosby, Scot Gemmill, Nigel Clough, Gary Bannister, Thorvaldur Orlygsson. Substitutes: Steve Chettle, Lee Glover, Andrew Marriot.

LEEDS UNITED 3 – SHEFFIELD UNITED 1
The FA Carling Premiership, 17 October 1992

Could this be Leeds United's European Cup year? Howard Wilkinson has assembled a fascinating conglomerate of pure footballers, sweating journey-men, and the gods in Cantona and Strachan to give the team immortal status. On 16 September they lost three–nil to Stuttgart, the home of Porsche. On 30 September they beat Stuttgart four–one at Yelland Road. They were forced to replay the tie on 29 October on neutral territory, the Nou Camp, Barcelona. Stuttgart had been concealing the fact that they fielded four foreign players. Bill Fotherby flew to Stuttgart into a UEFA trial. Leeds versus Stuttgart. Round a table, headphones at the slope, four different languages, heavy Germanic influence. They beat Stuttgart two–one before 7,000 bemused spectators and now meet Glasgow Rangers at Ibrox in a week's time.

Before the match in the plush Leeds executive suite – Harry Basset the Sheffield manager and I listened in awe to the full Stuttgart saga from the Leeds managing director. A John le Carré yarn with overtones of the Gestapo and Nuremberg. The Leeds players dwelt on that, and the Ibrox affair to come, for half an hour. The skills, the shape, the technique present – motivation absent. All bar Strachan, a supercharged Peter Pan. By example, he raised the game's tempo. His corner far post, swung back to goal by Cantona, Lee Chapman's textbook header. The stuff of Chapman's dreams. And Leeds on song.

But Sheffield are dismissive of reputation. Their football is boisterous, foot up the jumper, aerial, 'bandits at five o'clock' variety. Paul Beesley equalized from a corner kick on 54 minutes. A rash of bookings. The superb battler Batty after a linesman ratted on him to the referee. Cantona for over the ball. Littlejohn for a foul on Strachan. And here the little man intervened to plead Littlejohn's case, to no avail. Still buzzing, Strachan virtually set up the win. Seventy-five minutes Newsome's free kick to the underbelly of Sheffield's defence. Speed's fulminating drive. Two–one. Seventy-nine minutes McAllister's chip forward; Whyte hit the bar with his header – nonchalantly headed in the rebound.

Now for Ibrox – *Achtung, Auf Wiedersehen*, Leeds.

Leeds United: John Lukic, Jon Newsome, Tony Dorigo, David Batty, Chris Fairclough, David Whyte, Gordon Strachan, Eric Cantona, Lee Chapman, Gary McAllister, Gary Speed. Substitutes: Carl Shutt, Scot Sellars, Mervyn Day.

Sheffield United: Alan Kelly, Mitch Ward, Tom Cowan, John Gannon, Brian Gayle, Paul Beesley, Carl Bradshaw, Paul Rodgers, Adrian Littlejohn, Brian Deane, Glen Hodges. Substitutes: Charlie Hartfield, Simon Tracey, Ian Bryson.

OLDHAM ATHLETIC 1 – ASTON VILLA 1
The FA Carling Premiership, 24 October 1992

A platoon of bobbies huddled against Milhench's shed as Lancashire's icy rain swept like a curtain over Boundary Park. But on the pitch both sides generated white heat in a lusty encounter. Villa, lacking Parker's imagination and Froggatt's width, were congested, allowing Jobson, Oldham's centre back, to present his poise and élan for Mr Taylor's approval.

As Oldham played three centre forwards, the channels, as the professionals name them, were like trenches in the First World War. A set piece was the answer. Nineteen minutes, Steve Redmond's corner on the right, Ian Olney's brave spectacular header in the forest of claret and blue.

Oldham burgeoned. Milligan, Henry and Bernard dovetailing and breaking from midfield. Teale and McGrath grafted in Villa's heart. Teale a muscular barrelhouse buffeted Sharp like a punchbag. Sharp, though, should have punished Teale and Villa, but missed a gaping goal with a glanced header 15 minutes from time. But Oldham became so *distrait*. Eighty-two minutes Houghton's floated cross, Dalian Atkinson's bullet header. Out of jail Villa, total chagrin for Latics.

Oldham Athletic: Jon Hallworth, Gunnar Halle, Neil Pointon, Nick Henry, Richard Jobson, Steve Redmond, Ian Olney, Ian Marshall, Mike Milligan, Paul Bernard, Graham Sharp. Substitutes: Neil Adams, Neil McDonald, John Keeley.
Aston Villa: Nigel Spink, Earl Barrett, Steve Staunton, Shaun Teale, Paul McGrath, Kevin Richardson, Ray Houghton, Dwight Yorke, Dean Saunders, Dalian Atkinson, Brian Small. Substitutes: Mark Blake, Dave Farrell, Mark Bosnich.

MANCHESTER UNITED 0 – WIMBLEDON 1
The FA Carling Premiership, 31 October 1992

Night's candles are burnt out at the Shrine and russet dawn does not stand tiptoe on the sleepy mountaintops. Deep gloom among the supplicants suffering famine, a goal famine. United's last win was 12 September, knocked out of the Coca-Cola Cup by Aston Villa; torpedoed by Moscow in the UEFA tournament; a mere six goals scored in eleven games. For the mountains will I take up a weeping and wailing, and for the habitations of the wilderness a lamentation, because they are burnt up?

Burnt up, disappointed, disenchanted. Martin Edwards is a flagellated soul; he failed to sign Alan Shearer, has awarded himself a £45,000 pay rise, and is under constant fire from impecunious fans at the rising cost of the offertory at the Shrine. Only the sacred cow of the championship will silence them: it is the Marie Antoinette school of diplomacy: 'No bread – let them eat cake.' McClair, or 'Choccy' as he is yclept, could be the sacrificial lamb. One solitary goal in 19 appearances, even Steve Bruce at centre back has scored three. Mr Ferguson is worried: 'Why can't my strikers pop the ball in the onion bag?' A wag replied: 'Because they are blinded with tears at their crap form.'

Mr Ferguson is content with his defence; Peter Schmeichel is the best keeper in Europe, Pallister and Bruce like Hadrian's Wall in central defence. Kanchelskis can fly, Ryan Giggs flies even higher. Midfield is the weakness, Paul Ince is willing, Bryan Robson and Neil Webb injured, Phelan out of form, today Darren Ferguson, son of Alex, plays number five. Darren, alas, is not Premiership quality, much as I admire Alex's love for his sibling.

Wimbledon, of course, relish an occasion like this. Southern League clod poles, upstarts of every football league division, the Crazy Gang, love to impart a good, thumping boot in the goolies, bastinado precious celebrity teams.

At 3 p.m. a solitary fan sat in the now-demolished, newly half-built Stretford End. At half-time he had disappeared; was he evicted or did he decamp in disgust at United's insipid, flaccid non-performance? Wimbledon, without John Fashanu: more legs and arms than a thrashing octopus, is out injured; perforce they had to play to feet Dean Holdsworth partnering tiny Terry Gibson. They relish turning on the style; Robbie Earle is the cleverest box-to-box player in the land – he was majestic, the controller of midfield. At the back Warren Barton ran like a frightened impala, McAllister and McLeary snuffed out Hughes and McClair. United's midfield palsied: Ferguson fey, Ince inadequate, inadhesive, inanimate. Giggs embarked on his speciality runs, in full flight, with his fluent close control, one of football's delights, but Barton is no slouch and ran shoulder to shoulder – a bewitching battle.

'Twas 75 minutes before Hans Segers, the Wimbledon keeper, made a save; prior to that it was 'LOOK, NO HANS'. Wimbledon served notice that if United lacked ginger and heart, they had plenty of sting; Gibson and Holdsworth carved up United's back four like a Christmas turkey – Schmeichel made the art of goalkeeping look child's play. Could Big Peter ever be beaten? He destroys the opposition's confidence with sheer size, athletic ability and simple psychology. Forwards wilt in his presence. Ten minutes from time Terry Gibson took a free kick on the left. Lawrie Sanchez met it low near post and deflected the ball past the impregnable Schmeichel. One–nil to the Crazy Gang. Vinnie Jones led the carnival celebration. High fives – salutations and blown raspberries to friend and foe. The announcer at the Shrine drily announced to Don's fans: 'Your bus is at the back of the stand.' Vincent raised two fingers to acknowledge the insult; words have never hurt him – maybe sticks and stones.

Mr Ferguson now has selection problems. Denis Irwin must be his regular number three. Blackmore is not Premiership material. Paul Parker is a bag of nerves at right back – he was best fighting for QPR in central defence. Kanchelskis has lost the muse. Gary Neville has played one game – he will play many more. The youth team is awash with talent, one of them a child named David Beckham, who is photographed in the programme as winner of the 1987 Skills Final. His hair is brunette, his face alight with toothy grin – a set of mashers straight from Crocodile Dundee. Youth will have its fling – Captain Marvel will school them – championship, here we come.

Manchester United: Peter Schmeichel, Paul Parker, Clayton Blackmore, Steve Bruce, Darren Ferguson, Gary Pallister, Andre Kanchelskis, Paul Ince, Brian McClair, Mark Hughes, Ryan Giggs. Substitutes: Bryan Robson, Gary Walsh, Mike Phelan.

Wimbledon: Hans Segers, Warren Barton, Roger Joseph, Vinnie Jones, Alan McLeary, Brian McAllister, Terry Gibson, Robbie Earle, Dean Holdsworth,

Lawrie Sanchez, Gerald Dobbs. Substitutes: Andy Clarke, Neil Sullivan, Steve Cotterill.

LIVERPOOL 0 – MANCHESTER CITY 1
The FA Carling Premiership, Christmas 1992

Bitterly cold at the Colosseum, must be – John Barnes wore red tights and black gloves. Even chillier for Wright, Stewart and Thomas – dropped by Caesar Souness in his quest for the Golden Fleece – the championship. So with two Scando-Vikings at the back, Piechnik and Bjornebye, battle was joined. City took a 30-minute buffeting, the ball zooming over the bar – Coton living dangerously, City's back four impressive. Phelan and Earle fast and flashy. Andy Hill resolute, steadfast Liverpool though were playing a naive offside game sprung thrice by City. Flitcroft, as his name implies, is a flitter of a foot-baller – he flits into space with invention but he smote a post. White scored – no! Offside! Then on 42 minutes Brightwell and Sheron down the right – the ball whipped in – Niall Quinn headed past a flailing Mike Hooper. Nil–one at half-time.

Five minutes into the second half at last a Liverpool move of sweet sim-plicity. Jones out wide to McManaman, first time low cross, Ian Rush's stun-ning electric volley. The game white hot.

As you all know, the modern game is all youth, pace and movement. So into the fray steps Peter Reid, the venerable warrior. Pepper-and-salt hair, legs so battered and bent they should be on Eastbourne seafront in a Bath chair. I had visions of the trainer abandoning the magic sponge and rushing forth with a Zimmer frame.

Alongside Reid, Steve McMahon a mobile gun emplacement. He dismem-bered Ian Rush – yellow card. He disembowelled Redknapp; the referee merely grimaced and gave succour to Redknapp. At the whistle, the City fans applauded Steve – the Kop cheered him off. Reidie and Macker – youth in its prime.

SEASON 1991/92: POWER GRADUALLY EXTIRPATES FROM THE MIND EVERY HUMANE AND GENTLE VIRTUE

MANCHESTER UNITED 2 – SHEFFIELD UNITED 0
Barclays Football League, Division One, 2 November 1991

Forty-three thousand attended the Shrine, grey drizzle, stiff breeze, slippery pitch notwithstanding. Sheffield opened in typical bellicose style, found Schmeichel in the United goal a trifle vulnerable. Blackmore headed off his line; a goal-bound shot hit a forest of Manchester limbs. Manchester, disorganized by injury, gradually regrouped. Thirty-five minutes Ryan Giggs out swinging corner, Steve Bruce headed the ball back to the Sheffield heart – poor Paul Beesley, Sheffield's number six, put through his own goal. A grave misfortune,

Sheffield disheartened. But deep in the second half they mounted their charge. The high ball, the pack in pursuit. Mr Ferguson, one eye on the championship, the other on Athletico Madrid, his third eye on the United share price, flung Pallister and Robson semi-cocked off the substitutes' bench into the buffeting gallimaufry. A little desperation appeared in the Manchester play. Agana was felled – no penalty. Umpteen corners – all Sheffield, but enter on 80 minutes Paul Beesley, own goaler. On the halfway line he lost the ball to Kanchelskis, who was off like the hare – a jink left and right – a sizzling shot past Tracey's left ear. Sheffield's supporting thousands never lost voice – let the same din be heard at Bramall Lane to precipitate a miracle or two. Sheffield are in the toils, bottom of the league, played 14, won two, lost ten, eight points. Will the Manchester invalids be fit for next Wednesday at Old Trafford? They have to overturn a three–nil deficit against Athletico Madrid in the Cup Winners' Cup. The shareholders bate their breath, clutch their wallets, review their share certificates.

Manchester United: Peter Schmeichel, Paul Parker, Clayton Blackmore, Steve Bruce, Neil Webb, Mal Donaghy, Andrei Kanchelskis, Paul Ince, Brian McClair, Mark Robins, Ryan Giggs. Substitutes: Bryan Robson, Gary Pallister.

Sheffield United: Simon Tracey, John Pemberton, Tom Cowan, John Gannon, Brian Gayle, Paul Beesley, Ian Bryson, Jamie Hoyland, Tony Agana, Carl Bradshaw, Dane Whitehouse. Substitutes: Mike Lake, Colin Hill.

MANCHESTER UNITED 1 – SHEFFIELD WEDNESDAY 1

Barclays Football League, Division One, 8 February 1992

Forty-seven thousand and seventy-four at the Shrine. Apprehension at 3 p.m., cold shock at 3.03 p.m. as Wednesday took the lead. Wednesday awarded a free kick three yards outside the penalty area. Graham Hyde, the tearaway ragamuffin, ran over the ball and dallied; Danny Wilson tapped the ball to David Hirst, who smashed it past Schmeichel. Hirst did not cavort or rejoice – he simply smiled. The Stretford End was traumatized. United soared into rampant attack. Breathless fomenting football; tackles flew in; bodies fell. Roger Milward, the referee, he of Hollywood glamour, booked Hyde to draw the sting. A different sting happened on 13 minutes. From the left a United attack; Hughes leapt, McClair dwelt and scored. He looked two yards offside. The linesman said nay. One apiece.

I awaited the second half like a child at Christmas. 'Twas anticlimax. Chris Woods in goal was brilliantly intuitive. The Wednesday back line held. Hereabouts Hughes was aggressive, Kanchelskis fleet of foot, Robson, however, like others, seemed to fade. Too much football, or is the texture of the team not firm enough? The return of Steve Bruce is vital – then the pure football will flow again. Meanwhile, it is still tops at the Shrine. It is Leeds or United for the championship.

But now here is a little gem. Alex Ferguson appealing in the programme for a sense of humour at the Shrine. The fear of failure, he says, is corrosive. Keep your nerve, it is a terrific season.

It is 25 years since United won the championship; so long, says Alex, that half the supporters do not know what it looks like. That is the supporters without heads, Alex! The sense of humour is at the Theatre of Base Comedy down the road. Inmates there know they will never win it again.

Manchester United: Peter Schmeichel, Ryan Giggs, Denis Irwin, Mal Donaghy, Neil Webb, Gary Pallister, Bryan Robson, Paul Ince, Brian McClair, Mark Hughes, Andre Kanchelskis. Substitutes: Mike Phelan, Lee Sharpe.

Sheffield Wednesday: Chris Woods, Roland Nilsson, Phil King, Carlton Palmer, Nigel Pearson, Paul Warhurst, Danny Wilson, Graham Hyde, David Johnson, Nigel Worthington, David Hirst. Substitutes: Paul Williams, John Harkes.

MANCHESTER CITY 1 – TOTTENHAM HOTSPUR 0

Barclays Football League, Division One, 1 February 1992

As Vincent Jones once said: 'Agree with thine adversary quickly while thou art in the way with him!' The Theatre of Base Comedy adopt it as their text.

Maine Road inmates are blessed – or cursed – with a redoubtable sense of humour and great fortitude. In a first half of exemplary textbook football, City probed and teased enigmatic Spurs, yet spurned a multitude of chances. David White, of Olympian build, today at centre forward, Quinn still suspended, was chief culprit. Twice he blasted over or wide. Brightwell headed past the post from merely a few yards. At last, White atoned. A free kick from Hughes swung into the overcrowded Spurs penalty area. White rose above the throng, super header, one–nil. Time, 30 minutes. McMahon, patrolling centre circle, pumped long balls to the flanks. Alongside, Peter Reid picked up the spare and loose, releasing little Hughes to torment Edinburgh, the Spurs number two. Hughes the pick of City's future hopes, low centre of gravity, fast with the ball, perky and swervy. The prospect. But consider McMahon and Reid, the greying elder statesmen – like senior Mafiosi. No violin cases – just battered legs. 'Twas Reid who retired 10 minutes from time. McMahon carried his injury – pride kept him going.

Tottenham were neat, concise but tepid. They applied more heat in the second half. Stewart and Durie roused from somnambulance. Walsh drafted in 13 minutes from time to support Lineker playing a lovely, lonely Garbo role upfront. More profligate shooting from White. City, who should have been five up, were suddenly paralysed as Coton saved from Stewart – only Coton knows how. A draw at that stage purely farce. So, City ride bemusingly high. But, gentlemen, observe Spurs' timorous league position. The ides of March are upon us.

Manchester City: Tony Coton, Andy Hill, Neil Pointon, Peter Reid, Keith Curle, Steve Redmond, David White, Ian Brightwell, Mike Sheron, Steve McMahon, Michael Hughes. Substitutes: Gary Megson, Mike Quigley.

Tottenham Hotspur: Ian Walker, Justin Edinburgh, Terry Fenwick, Steve Sedgley, David Howells, Gudni Bergsson, Paul Stewart, Gordon Durie, Vinny Samways, Gary Lineker, Paul Allen. Substitutes: Paul Walsh, Nayim.

LIVERPOOL 1 – COVENTRY CITY 0

Barclays Football League, Division One, 26 October 1991

The spectre of Auxerre hung over Anfield for the first half-hour of this match. Young Rob Jones on his home debut embarrassed Brucie with a back pass and there were hot claims for a penalty. But a goal on 35 minutes exorcized that spectre. Rush's lofted ball over the Coventry defence to Walters on the left, Walters' cross and Ray Houghton on the goal line shovelled the ball into the net. Few smiles – there could have been a Coventry assist. Coventry, meanwhile, looked an artisan outfit; Gallacher and Smith mobile and at times inventive. But Liverpool should have impacted them. Midfield, Molby, back in the side, has the style but appears to be on a diet of steamed jam roll. McMahon still does not have the old-time fire in his boots. Houghton is fitful. Upfront there is effort from Rush and Saunders, but with Liverpool you are looking for those balls to feet, triangular play, one-touch imaginative football.

Despite this, Liverpool stage-managed the second half. Walters had two amazing misses. Rush teed up as the Kop uttered prayers – then ballooned over. Ogrizovic had two inspired moments. Finally, Brucie had to dive to avoid an embarrassing Coventry equalizer. That would have been farce.

Liverpool: Bruce Grobbelaar, Rob Jones, David Burrows, Glenn Hysen, Jan Molby, Nicky Tanner, Dean Saunders, Ray Houghton, Ian Rush, Mark Walters, Steve McMahon. Substitutes: Ronny Rosenthal, Steve Harkness.

Coventry City: Steve Ogrizovic, Brian Borrows, Lloyd McGrath, Stewart Robson, Andy Pearce, Chris Greenman, Ray Woods, Michael Gynn, Paul Furlong, Kevin Gallacher, David Smith. Substitutes: Robert Rosario, Dean Emerson.

OLDHAM ATHLETIC 1 – ARSENAL 1

Barclays Football League, Division One, 16 November 1991

The last time Oldham met the Arsenal 'twas 1923, when they danced the black bottom in London's West End, and Oldham's dark satanic mills ground the capital for those rich revellers. From the marble halls of Highbury to rustic Boundary Park. And the football today was rustic, rumbustious, raw, rapido, brimful of incident, loaded with excitement, typically English – hugely enjoyed by the crowd of 16,000. Both sides gave the ball some whack. Ian Marshall did not on the second minute. An exquisite chance blasted wide. Amid the hurly-burly Paul Merson was bombing shots on Hallworth in Oldham's goal. Hallworth was brilliant.

Then on 66 minutes Palmer, the Oldham number seven, cleverly held the ball in play, crossed at 500 mph. Andy Barlow, his number three, met the ball on the meet – far post. Seaman merely blinked. One–nil. The battle raged on. Hillier booked for petulance, Wright for a late tackle on Barrett. Barrett and Wright had scuffled – lovely word, scuffle – all afternoon like fractious school-boys. Wright felled Barrett again. 'Off,' said the masses. 'On,' said the referee.

And so it came to pass that three minutes from time under the one-candle-power floodlights, Perry Groves, recently on as substitute welted in a cross, the 'Demon King' Wright rose high – superb header. One apiece.

Oldham Athletic: Jon Hallworth, Neil McDonald, Andy Barlow, Nick Henry, Earl Barrett, Richard Jobson, Roger Palmer, Ian Marshall, Graeme Sharp, Mike Milligan, Rick Holden. Substitutes: Neil Adams, Craig Fleming.

Arsenal: David Seaman, Lee Dixon, Nigel Winterburn, Dave Hillier, Steve Bould, Andy Linighan, David Rocastle, Ian Wright, Alan Smith, Paul Merson, Colin Pates. Substitutes: David O'Leary, Perry Groves.

OLDHAM ATHLETIC 2 – NOTTINGHAM FOREST 1
Barclays Football League, Division One, 28 December 1991

Joe Royle is a high roller. On Boxing Day he gambled on forward play and lost to Manchester United. Today he gambled on Ian Marshall, his centre forward, at centre back and thrust fledgling Paul Bernard, a Scottish under-21 international, up with Graeme Sharp. For the first half-hour Oldham were in shock, traumatized by Forest's sheer quality. Svelte ideas and superb one-touch football scythed open an Oldham defence still adjusting, like Gorbachev, to major change.

At last Forest scored. Stuart Pearce, running like a golden pheasant before the beaters, materialized in the Oldham penalty area. The ball whizzed to his awesome left foot, and he walloped the goal. Ian Liversidge, the Oldham physiotherapist, obviously muttered 'offside' to the linesman. The muttering was spicy by nature. The referee, angry as a cockerel awakened before dawn, booked him.

That was the cockspur for the Oldham revival. Nerve, sinew and muscle were thrust at Forest. On the forty-sixth minute Rick Holden's cross, Graeme Sharp's immaculate glancing header: one–one.

We could not wait for the second half. It opened with a Sheringham palsied miss at goal. Forest paid dearly. Down the left ripped Holden; he turned his fullback Charles – lofted the cross – Bernard in his first full game in the First Division bullet-headed a goal. Two–one. Atmosphere like a Cup tie. Forest on a high. The magnificent Walker, the aggressive Keane in the van. Oldham's vice-president is with me behind the memorial pillar – trembling with anxiety. Oldham held. Joe's gamble a winner.

End on a sartorial note. Stuart Pearce's short shorts exposing his beer barrel thighs, was implored by a spectator: 'Lower your shorts, you big Jessie.' From 50 yards away that was the bravest gesture of 1991.

Oldham Athletic: Jon Hallworth, Gunnar Halle, Paul Bernard, Nick Henry, Earl Barrett, Richard Jobson, Neil Adams, Ian Marshall, Graeme Sharp, Mike Milligan, Rick Holden. Substitutes: Roger Palmer, Craig Fleming.

Nottingham Forest: Mark Crossley, Gary Charles, Stuart Pearce, Des Walker, Carl Tiler, Roy Keane, Kingsley Black, Scot Gemmill, Nigel Clough, Teddy Sheringham, Ian Woan. Substitutes: Darren Wassell, Lee Glover.

SEASON 1990/91: PAIN AFTER PAIN, AND WOE SUCCEEDING WOE – IS MY HEAD DESTINED FOR ANOTHER BLOW?

MANCHESTER UNITED 2 – COVENTRY CITY 0
Barclays Football League, Division One, 25 August 1990
At 2.55 p.m. the Shrine was full, thousands locked out. Forty-six thousand, seven hundred and fifteen supplicants in multicoloured hue basked in euphoria as their gladiators paraded the FA Cup and their half of the Charity Shield. Alas, euphoria evaporated, the silver tarnished, in a first half of baffling tactics, muffled, sporadic big-name displays and an aggressive, ebullient approach from Coventry. United had five at the back, and little support for McClair and Hughes, who still gel like Thatcher and Kinnock. Coventry fans even burst into the Eton Boating Song, which was gentlemanly.

Enter the cavalry on 58 minutes. Denis Irwin, ex-Oldham thoroughbred, whistled in a corner from the right. Steve Bruce met the ball on the meat. The header flew in far post. Seventy-two minutes. Denis Irwin again, sleight of hand and foot on the right, a whipped cross. Neil Webb's diving header. Two–nil. The sun burst through. And it is off to Europe for Pecsi Monkash or, as the locals have it, Poxy Monkey.

Manchester United: Les Sealey, Denis Irwin, Mal Donaghy, Steve Bruce, Mike Phelan, Gary Pallister, Neil Webb, Paul Ince, Brian McClair, Mark Hughes, Clayton Blackmore. Substitutes: Russell Beardsmore, Mark Robins.
Coventry City: Steve Ogrizovic, Brian Borrows, Paul Edwards, Lloyd McGrath, Brian Kilcline, Trevor Peake, Kevin Gallacher, Tony Dobson, David Speedie, Kevin Drinkell, David Smith. Substitutes: Cyrille Regis, Kevin Macdonald.

EVERTON 1 – ARSENAL 1
Barclays Football League, Division One, 8 September 1990
The School of Science can be re-yclept the School of Retard Skills. Those bygone artists who sepia-gaze from framed photographs on the wall of the inner sanctum would quail at the crudeness and artisan sweat of famous names in those illustrious blue shirts. Everton are bottom of the league, three games played, nul points. Arsenal are behind Liverpool and Leeds at the top. Colin Harvey is Everton's beleaguered manager, a member of that class triumvirate halfback line of Ball, Kendall and Harvey that, like treasured Lalique glass, remains a hallowed heirloom of Goodison. How ephemeral are names and the glory they brought. If only one could preserve them in aspic, or freeze them like butterflies in a frame. Down-to-earth emotion from the audience, contrasted with desperation from the team.

The first half was an Arsenal amble. Compound, comfortable, almost an essay in arrogant strolling. Concise control to feet. Everton's midfield anonymous. McCall, that fiery fighter, lacked mobility after injury, Ebbrell ran in blind alleys, Mike Milligan, signed from Oldham during the summer, seemed dumbstruck, almost inferior in body language to the majestic players around him. They reminded me of three bird-watchers, peering anxiously at the sky awaiting the blue-plumed tit warbler, as the ball zoomed over their heads propelled by Watson and Hinchcliffe to the hopeful head of Mike Newell. David Seaman, George Graham's new signing, a laconic Rotherham lad, was untroubled in the Arsenal goal. On the hour, Arsenal came off the leash, Anders Limpar the Swede ploughed through the turnip field of Everton's defence, unleashed a vicious shot; Southall parried – Perry Groves headed in as Neville struggled to retrieve lost ground. Atteveld, Ebbrell and Bould were booked for naughtiness. Tony Cottee, injured since the start of the season, came off the bench to replace McCall, who, to be fair, had his knee encased in plaster 48 hours before the game. Tony Cottee pepped up the Everton attack, playing to feet. Graeme Sharp and Mike Newell predominantly headers of the ball.

The equalizer 10 minutes from time summed up their football. Hinchcliffe corner to the near post, Adams and Bould flapped, Mike Newell glanced the header. Scruffy match – the Arsenal in contention, the School of Science – lessons begin 9 a.m. sharp Monday morning.

Everton: Neville Southall, Ray Atteveld, Andy Hinchcliffe, Kevin Ratcliffe, Dave Watson, Mike Milligan, Pat Nevin, Stuart McCall, Graeme Sharp, Mike Newell, John Ebbrell. Substitutes: Tony Cottee, Neil McDonald.

Arsenal: David Seaman, Lee Dixon, Nigel Winterburn, Michael Thomas, Steve Bould, Tony Adams, David Rocastle, Paul Davis, Alan Smith, Paul Merson, Anders Limpar. Substitutes: Andy Linighan, Perry Groves.

MANCHESTER UNITED 2 – SHEFFIELD UNITED 0

Barclays Football League, Division One, 17 November 1990

Another 45,000 at the Shrine, 5,000 outrageously vocal blunt Yorkshire folk, 40,000 relishing the prospect of Manchester, on a high, devouring a demoralized, palsied Sheffield side still playing blind man's buff with First Division football. Manchester opened with brisk, high-stepping, almost swaggering play. Ince, Webb and Phelan surged through Vincent Jones and company like galleons in full sail against canoes. Hughes was electric upfront, McClair rumbustious. Manchester rolled Sheffield over. But Tracey in goal was magnificent – his positioning exemplary, as shots, headers, deflections *et al* rained in.

Manchester frustrated. Ince dived into Vincent Jones like a dyspeptic rhino. Vincent fell on him like a reposed bedroom suite. Master Ince, yellow card. Enter Neil Webb's genius. Genius is nothing but a great aptitude for patience. Webb is steeped in it. Sixty-five minutes Ince to Webb on the left, a swivel turn, a low cross that eluded all but Steve Bruce on the far post. Bruce swept the ball in, cavorting in gleeful relief. Danny Wallace trotted from the substitutes' bench, as Sheffield United hashed a solitary chance. Deane then missed another. The crowd suffered the frighteners. But Webb again – down the right – low cross, flicked on by Wallace, Mark Hughes's intuitive goal. Eight games unbroken for Manchester. Four hundred and fifty minutes goalless for Harry Bassett.

Manchester United: Les Sealey, Denis Irwin, Clayton Blackmore, Steve Bruce, Mike Phelan, Gary Pallister, Neil Webb, Paul Ince, Brian McClair, Mark Hughes, Lee Sharpe. Substitutes: Mal Donaghy, Danny Wallace.

Sheffield United: Simon Tracey, John Pemberton, Michael Lake, Vincent Jones, Mark Morris, Paul Beesley, Brian Marwood, John Gannon, Tony Agana, Brian Deane, Wilf Rostron. Substitutes: Bob Booker, Dane Whitehouse.

MANCHESTER CITY 2 – TOTTENHAM HOTSPUR 1

Barclays Football League, Division One, 15 December 1990

Memorable match at the Theatre of Base Comedy. Banished fear, sterility and negation. Cherish two sides who played with schoolboy abandon at mercurial speed, blazing attack, full-blooded defence.

Spurs, lying third behind Liverpool and Arsenal, without a share quote, millions adrift on a bear market, went bullish on the pitch. Three centre forwards – Paul Stewart, Paul Walsh and the peerless Gary Lineker. City, enveloped by this artistic fog, let Lineker advance on an open goal after 45 seconds. Hendry booted off the line. A goal of genius ignited an already megawatt match on 25 minutes. Gascoigne took off, arms flapping like a giant swan erupting from a lake, past three immobile City defenders. More arm flapping, this time the swan was on the wing, into another posse of blue shirts; Gazza emerges with the ball, an eyeball confrontation with Coton, the City keeper, Coton transfixed, Gazza side-foots in. One–nil. A goal of the season – a nugget. City totally stunned in disbelief.

Enter Peter Reid; he inspired; City plundered. Crablike Reid scrabbles all over the park, his legs battered like ancient Roman ruins, his brain as cool as Napoleon's, his spirit that of Olympus. Gary Megson, a tearaway, blossomed, Mark Ward burgeoned. Reid the master general. Meanwhile, Gazza and the referee had a nonstop repartee. (Peter Swales once said his manager and the Maine Road audience had repartee – rapport was never mentioned.) Mr Key was the referee. He put padlocks on the effervescent Gazza verbalizing, a wagging finger here, a pat on the head there, a muttered oath or two; finally booked for naughty petulance. One–nil at half-time. The second half was a reprise, full throttle, full throated, the player's hot breath like steam that rises from New York manholes. Seventy-seven minutes Adrian Heath stretchered off, Wayne Clarke off the bench to his first game with City after a loan spell at Shrewsbury. Clarke's first touch – a thundering shot deflected past Thorsvedt by Redmond, City's centre back. One–one.

Eighty-one minutes Van Den Hauwe handled in the box – penalty. Mark Ward roared on by 32,000 blasted the ball past Thorsvedt. Two–one for City. An amazing, wonderful match – all present will talk of it for years.

Manchester City: Tony Coton, Ian Brightwell, Neil Pointon, Peter Reid, Colin Hendry, Steve Redmond, David White, Adrian Heath, Niall Quinn, Gary Megson, Mark Ward. Substitutes: Hugh Harper, Wayne Clarke.

Tottenham Hotspur: Erik Thorsvedt, Mitchell Thomas, Pat Van Den Hauwe,

Steve Sedgley, David Howells, Gary Mabbutt, Paul Stewart, Paul Gascoigne, Nayim, Gary Lineker, Paul Walsh. Substitutes: Paul Allen, Vinny Samways.

OLDHAM ATHLETIC 1 – NEWCASTLE UNITED 1
Barclays Football League, Division Two, 1 January 1991
The Monarch Mill, which abuts Boundary Park, shuddered to its foundations as the Latics faced defeat. The team had played insipid, indecisive football. Gone behind to a Mick Quinn goal on 64 minutes. Quinn, a former Latic, sprang the offside trap and swept the ball past Hallworth.

Newcastle, faced with a mini Oldham rally, hung on like Kitchener's army. Thirty seconds away from a famous win, Rick Holden, the Oldham number eleven, tore down the left. Roger Palmer nodded down the cross. Mark Stimson, the Newcastle number three, passed the ball back to Burridge, his keeper. In mortification Burridge, wrong-footed, observed the ball trickling into the net for the Oldham equalizer. Poor Stimson. Poor Newcastle. They played controlled plastic-pitch style football, Peacock and Brock holding up the ball, short passing, outpacing Oldham's vapid defence. Roy Aitken gener-alled midfield, and a 16-year-old lad, Steve Watson, playing his Newcastle debut, will savour the day. A leggy boy with lots of guts – more will be heard. But an abiding memory of luckless Newcastle. The sight of Burridge attempt-ing a goal kick with the ball capricious in the wind, digging a divot to place the ball – on a plastic pitch.

Budgie Burridge, one of football's enduring characters, absent in body but present in spirit.
Oldham Athletic: Jon Hallworth, Paul Warhurst, Andy Barlow, Nick Henry, Earl Barrett, Richard Jobson, Roger Palmer, Paul Moulden, David Currie, Neil Redfearn, Rick Holden. Substitutes: Neil Adams, Will Donachie.
Newcastle United: John Burridge, Ray Ranson, Mark Stimson, Roy Aitken, Kevin Scott, Bjorn Kristensen, Kevin Brock, Gavin Peacock, Mick Quinn, Scott Sloan, Steve Watson. Substitutes: Liam O'Brien, Lee Clark.

MANCHESTER UNITED 3 – SUNDERLAND 0
Barclays Football League, Division One, 12 January 1991
The Shrine reverberated to the sounds of joy, appreciation of quality, 45,934 in full voice, including those marvellous loyal Sunderland fans who love pure football. United's first half was memorable. Lee Sharpe irrepressible. Within one minute of the start, he put Sunderland in deep shock. His pace left his full-back Williams like a pillar of salt. Alas, Sharpe's goal was disallowed. Williams was to suffer a traumatic debut – he did not appear in the second half. The goals were inevitable as Robson, the maestro, controlled the pace and direc-tion with his charmed left foot. Ince, Webb, McClair and Hughes fired by Robson's example and sheer enthusiasm. Sharpe, on hype, now a favourite son. Eight minutes Webb's floated corner kick – headed on by Pallister, Mark Hughes's spectacular overhead kick. Fifteen minutes Lee Sharpe's sizzling

pace, exotic ball control destroyed Sunderland down the left – Brian McClair side-footed in the cross. Forty-three minutes Mark Hughes's second blustering finish. Sunderland lost David Rush with injury. Ince and Webb at half-time retired hurt. United thus lost their brilliant shape as McClair bolstered mid-field to accommodate Robins. Sunderland came on the riposte, Bracewell, Owers and Bennett refusing to capitulate. But United today were vintage. A little silverware somewhere, methinks.

Manchester United: Les Sealey, Denis Irwin, Clayton Blackmore, Steve Bruce, Neil Webb, Gary Pallister, Bryan Robson, Paul Ince, Brian McClair, Mark Hughes, Lee Sharpe. Substitutes: Mark Robins, Mike Phelan.

Sunderland: Tony Norman, Paul Williams, Richard Ord, Gary Bennett, Kevin Ball, Gary Owers, Paul Bracewell, Gordon Armstrong, David Rush, Marco Gabbiadini, Colin Pascoe. Substitutes: Warren Hawke, Paul Hardyman.

LIVERPOOL 1 – WIMBLEDON 1
Barclays Football League, Division One, 19 January 1991

Tell it not in Gath, whisper it not in the street of Askelon lest the daughters of Philistine football rejoice, but this fixture, abhorred by Mr Dalglish, detested by the Colosseum audience, lived up, or down, to its prediction. The ball suffering from frostbite, aching necks craning to observe its flight. The Battle of Little Big Horn. Wimbledon football is the teak sideboard variety. Tough, uncompromising, bruise but not break; hewn from tree trunks, get the ball to the opposition where it hurts – in their penalty area. Even Barnes's red tights, and Brucie's green pair, could not add colour. Nor a pitch invasion at 3 p.m. by a two-year-old boy – inspire. Liverpool, sensing the mood, began with a mini stampede. Rush and Gillespie heading wide. Then Gibson brought a marvellous save from Brucie, and Liverpool doubt began. This was eased when John Barnes scored. A basic, simple Wimbledon-style goal. Long ball from Staunton, Barnes hooking the ball over Segers's head. But Liverpool never had time to dwell, to indulge in elegance. Their first touch deserted them. Absent stars sadly missed. Jimmy Carter revealed dash and sweet control, but Wimbledon's cavalry charge dismissed niceties. Seven minutes from time their number four, Warren Barton, smote a free kick past Grobbelaar with great ferocity. The 1988 Wimbledon jinx lives on. A chill wind blows.

Liverpool: Bruce Grobbelaar, Gary Ablett, David Burrows, Steve Nicol, Steve Staunton, Gary Gillespie, Jimmy Carter, Jan Molby, Ian Rush, John Barnes, Steve McMahon. Substitutes: Ronny Rosenthal, Jamie Redknapp.

Wimbledon: Hans Segers, Roger Joseph, Terry Phelan, Warren Barton, Dean Blackwell, Keith Curle, Paul McGee, Detzi Kruszynski, John Fashanu, John Scales, Terry Gibson. Substitutes: Lawrie Sanchez, Alan Cork.

SHEFFIELD UNITED 2 – ASTON VILLA 1
Barclays Football League, Division One, 2 March 1991

Hello, hello, your worships. At 3.05 p.m. a blonde female of tender years, wearing naught but a wide smile, invaded the pitch. Embraced Agana on the bench; Agana may have blushed. She then impeded Deane. McGrath gave her the brush-off. The referee awarded a dropped ball. 'Twas the only eye-opening experience of a flaccid first half. No beavering away here! Four minutes into the second half Hodges flung a long ball to the heart of Villa's defence. Gage hashed a clearance, Ian Bryson gleefully walloped the ball past an enraged Spink. Villa had to grasp the nettle. Cowans, anonymous until this set piece, thumped a corner far post. Derek Mountfield bullet-headed the equalizer.

Sixty-two minutes, from another corner, Brian Deane's brilliant goal, his 14th of the season. And Deane today was superb. His pace tore Villa apart. His power in the air an insoluble problem. Around him a revitalized team. Hodges with class redolent of Tony Currie. John Gannon a pocket battleship in midfield. Even Vincent Jones is playing scientific football, albeit like a trip hammer. And Villa; uninspired without Platt and Daley; McGrath still mobile and brainy, Mountfield poised, laid back. But upfront lightweight despite Cascarino's bulk. Cowans is off-colour, like his team.

Meanwhile, I ponder what happened to our streaker with goose pimples like marbles.

'One hand in the bird is worth two in the bush!'

Sheffield United: Simon Tracey, Chris Wilder, Bob Booker, Vincent Jones, Paul Beesley, Colin Hill, Carl Bradshaw, John Gannon, Glyn Hodges, Brian Deane, Ian Bryson. Substitutes: Tony Agana, Mark Todd.

Aston Villa: Nigel Spink, Chris Price, Kevin Gage, Paul McGrath, Derek Mountfield, Kent Nielsen, Dwight Yorke, Mark Blake, Tony Cascarino, Gordon Cowans, Stuart Gray. Substitutes: Ian Ormondroyd, Ian Olney.

LEEDS UNITED 2 – COVENTRY CITY 0

Barclays Football League, Division One, 9 March 1991

George Bernard Shaw once uttered: we have in England a curious belief in first-rate people, people we do not know. This consoles us for the undeniable second-rateness of the people we know. So 'tis with our football. Xenophobia blinds us to deficient technical skills and lack of charisma. This match registered on the Richter scale, one for entertainment, ten for boredom.

The first half was Coventry desperation versus Leeds skill. Keystone Cops, pie in face, swinging boots, harrying, chasing, spoiling, falling bodies. Hurst and Batty booked. Could have been an episode of *Casualty*. 'Incredible Hulk' Kilcline retired, heavily bruised. Thirty minutes, Mel Sterland thundered down the right like a steaming Suffolk dray. He flattened the opposition, crossed, Strachan dummied, Ogrizovic saved McAllister's drive, Davison scored. First full game, first goal for him.

The second half lasted two hours. Strachan 'Archy Nimble' looked strained, protecting ageing limbs. Chapman missed a gaping goal. Big Cyrille Regis put himself about, Michael Gynn looked like a footballer. McAllister appeared disdainful of thump and thwack. Batty relished it, mixing it with glorious simple classic play. As I consulted my watch for the hundredth time. Chris Whyte tonked Leeds second after yet another goalmouth scramble. Was Mr Shaw a cynic – or a realist?

Leeds United: John Lukic, Mel Sterland, Mike Whitlow, David Batty, Chris Fairclough, Chris Whyte, Gordon Strachan, Bobby Davison, Lee Chapman, Gary McAllister, Gary Speed. Substitutes: Carl Shutt, Jim Beglin.

Coventry City: Steve Ogrizovic, Brian Borrows, Lee Hurst, Dean Emerson, Brian Kilcline, Andy Pearce, Ray Woods, Michael Gynn, Cyrille Regis, Kevin Gallacher, David Smith. Substitutes: Stewart Robson, Lloyd McGrath.

EVERTON 0 – NOTTINGHAM FOREST 0
Barclays Football League, Division One, 23 March 1991

'Beware the ides of March,' said the soothsayer to Julius Caesar, warning that he was to be assassinated. March 15 passed and Julius, strolling into the senate house, spoke merrily to the soothsayer: 'The ides of March is come.'

'So be they,' softly whispered the soothsayer. 'But yet are they not past.'

Howard Kendall has returned to the senate house at the School of Science. It is another fallow season. Mid-table, six points above the relegation dogfight. Forest also marooned with them, but Wembley bound. Mr Clough as usual took his daily constitutional, walking across the River Mersey, muttering: 'The quality of the Mersey is not strained.' He has celebrated his silver anniversary as a football manager winning two League Championships (one with Derby County), two European Cups in consecutive years and four League Cups. He is a legend, a maverick, an iconoclast and football sage. He is a staunch Labour acolyte with a Tory bank balance. He begins every sentence with, 'Look, young man,' and then escalates to a severe drubbing. When interviewing Mr Clough 'tis best first to genuflect; get on your knees and deliver an oblation. If football is the new religion, Mr Clough is father confessor. He is a total outrage, but loveable. Forest are noted for textbook football. It is their ethos; a eurhythmic euphony, like Jerome Kern's wonderful music. (If you have never heard of Jerome Kern, dig out a CD of the musical *Showboat*. That will wean you off Val Doonican.)

Forest thus were the Pipers of Pan; Jemson, Parker and Crosby in unison leading Everton a merry dance. Everton forced eight corners in two minutes; I cribbed that from Denis Lowe, a statistician. I am afraid I never tabulate corners, goal kicks, or throw-ins. Cottee shot over the bar; I reflect another barren goalless day. Everton looked off-balance. Warzycha – Polish Bob to his pals – fluent in Russian, French and Polish, looks fast, intelligent and skilful, but wide on the right was incommunicado in English. Nevin on the left resembled an antipodean mother searching for an expatriate father – lost! Forest awhile, marshalled by the excellent Des Walker, buttressed by the ebullient, forceful Roy Keane – what a monster buy he was – absorbed Everton's huff and puff. Keown, with his beetle-browed, half-crazed, head down, up-yer-jumper style, created a little havoc, he and Keane having a little stand-off, but the match stumbled under a blazing sun. A save or two from Crossley. Newell the substitute falls over twice, cocking his boot to score. Neville dives at Crosby's boots for a courageous save. Tired legs, Forest looking to Wembley in May, if they win their semi-final. Wassall, their number five, did not wassail a merry tune at the start, a doleful dirge at the finish.

Everton: Neville Southall, Martin Keown, John Ebbrell, Kevin Ratcliffe, Dave Watson, Mike Milligan, Robert Warzycha, Kevin Sheedy, Lee Sharpe, Tony Cottee, Pat Nevin. Substitutes: Neil McDonald, Mike Newell.

Nottingham Forest: Mark Crossley, Gary Charles, Brian Laws, Des Walker, Darren Wassall, Roy Keane, Gary Crosby, Terry Wilson, Nigel Clough, Nigel Jemson, Garry Parker. Substitutes: Tommy Gaynor, Phil Starbuck.

LIVERPOOL 2 – TOTTENHAM HOTSPUR 0
Barclays Football League, Division One, 11 May 1991

The final match of the season at the Colosseum. So many hidden agendas that Somerset Maugham could write a novel. Graeme Souness, the newly-enthroned Caesar, has been manager for four games. Beat Norwich and Palace three–nil. Lost to Chelsea four–two and Forest two–one. Souness is a winner, and coldly rebukes his team in his programme notes. Ian Rush has 37 goals in the bag, John Barnes 29; they still gifted the championship to Arsenal, tops with 80 points to date, Liverpool second with 73. Palace third with 66. Caesar Souness is a winner; he will not countenance defeat. He bears a grudge against Tottenham Hotspur; in December 1972 he was sold off by them to Middlesbrough for £35,000 – flump-pence. Even then he had that arrogance, that divine belief in his abilities. A world-class player, he and Kenny Dalglish were Bob Paisley's inspired signings. To refresh you, here is the line-up for his first game at Anfield, 21 January 1978: Ray Clemence, Phil Neal, Alan Hansen, Phil Thompson, Ray Kennedy, Emlyn Hughes, Kenny Dalglish, Terry McDermott, David Johnson, Graeme Souness, Ian Callaghan.

What would that team be worth today?

At 2.30 p.m. we pondered the Spurs team. Terry Venables is manager. They play Nottingham Forest in the FA Cup Final next week. Venables, the Cockney wit, the cheekie chappie, the market trader, in-yer-face Don Quixote – the tilter against windmills – the defier of authority – the naughty schoolboy – the brilliant manager.

Will he play his final team or play the reserves? At 3 p.m. it was his Wembley side: game on! As Terence says: ''Tis as hard and severe a thing to be a true politician as to be truly moral.'

A full house, the Liverpool gladiators playing for their futures. Will Souness have an end-of-season sale, a clear-out of the unwanted to finance the gigantic purchases he has in mind? Spurs began smoothly, rehearsing Wembley moves amid the hot embers of Liverpool's firebrands. Gascoigne ambling, strolling, grinning, grimacing his way against a backcloth of black Kop humour. He beats the opposition merely by flapping his arms like an albatross, a little dink here, another dink there, a move into space – a wall pass to Lineker, the perfect foil, the return from Lineker, Gazza again and then Lineker's shot. They gel like Crosby and Hope, Morecambe and Wise. Two highly-gifted players enjoying and revelling in superb skills. Lineker took a whack from Ablett; he fell like a ton of concrete. Gary does not relish the physical. When Horatio manned the bridge, I cannot imagine Gary assisting him. Gary's limbs are cherished, a protection order stamped on each leg. Play thus stopped, the Spurs trainer broke the Olympic record for the 50-metre dash. The magic spray efficacious, Gary was sprightly. Subsequent manhandling, and Terry removed Gary from the fray midway through the second half. Gary, a self-effacing gentleman, disdains rudery, he is efflorescent, effulgent, effervescent – a toff.

Liverpool by then had the game by the epiglottis. On 42 minutes Ian Rush thwacked a typical Rushie goal, courtesy of Staunton's cross. Three minutes into the second half Ray Houghton, the Artful Dodger of midfielders, cunningly lobbed into space, David Speedie speedily sped into it and delivered an extraordinary volley, the ball thundering past Thorsvedt – the keeper barely twitched. Gascoigne by now was loitering with non-intent. Vinny Samways shimmied and shallied to no avail. A wasted talent is Samways, one moment a diamond, the next a zircon. Gary Mabbutt tried to infuse the spirit, but Spurs were running down the clock. Young Mike Marsh surprised me with his neat, precise play; I never rated him, but he was today the ideal fulcrum for the runners around him. Maybe he, like his colleagues, was playing for Souness; new faces though will be seen at the Colosseum. Souness never came second.

Liverpool: Bruce Grobbelaar, Gary Ablett, David Burrows, Steve Nicol, Glenn Hysen, Steve Staunton, Mike Marsh, Ray Houghton, Ian Rush, John Barnes, David Speedie. Substitutes: Peter Beardsley, Steve McManaman.

Tottenham Hotspur: Erik Thorsvedt, Justin Edinburgh, Pat Van Den Hauwe, Steve Sedgley, David Howells, Gary Mabbutt, Paul Stewart, Paul Gascoigne, Vinny Samways, Gary Lineker, Paul Allen. Substitutes: Paul Walsh, Colin Hendry.

GODS OF THE SHRINE AT WHOSE SIGHT ALL THE STARS HIDE THEIR DIMINISHED HEADS
CHARLIE MITTEN

A quicksilver down the left; a soldier of fortune. His left foot legendary. One icy, frosty Sunday afternoon he smote a free kick at 100 mph. We were playing Foden's ladies. Their number four attempted to breast the ball down. Her 36B became 28E in the instant. A kiss of life revived her.

JACK ROWLEY

Dark, glowering, saturnine. His visage spoke of animosity, black secrets at odds with himself and the world. The Vincent Price of centre forwards who struck terror in opposing centre halves.

DUNCAN EDWARDS

A man mountain with the agility of a gazelle, the predatory instincts of a lurking panther, the heart of a lion, the charge of a rampaging bull elephant. Cut down in his prime. An all-time great.

DENNIS VIOLET

A violet by a mossy stone, half-hidden from the eye. Fair as a star when only one is shining in the sky. A player's player in the Len White magical mould. He was just there on the spot when needed. Never received the accolade.

DENNIS LAW – AN ICON

Eponymous mercurial arm-waving mobile windmill. Littered under Mercury. A snapper-up of unconsidered trifles. A back heel made him infamous. Playing for Manchester City at Old Trafford, his goal consigned Manchester United to Division Two.

PADDY CRERAND

A twinny-foot Celt. He could thread a needle at 100 miles. A Hotspur, a red-blood. When cool, he was a master of the through pass. Favourite touch a one-two with Best – Best would simply cannon the ball off Crerand's shins. Paddy never moved.

BOBBY CHARLTON

His locks were of legend. Sir Robin of Locksley. Flamboyant, never elegant but a shot like a howitzer. Failed in management – no, it was not Southend, but now enshrined as one of the chosen.

JOHNNY CAREY

An Irish gentleman, the forerunner of the Busby legend. As smooth and svelte on the park as Sharon Stone's waxed thighs. Off it as charming as David Niven. In management, he fell foul of the high echelons – in a black cab. (Sacked by Sir John Moores at Everton.)

PHILIP NEVILLE

Martin Edwards and I agree. This player is a Rolls-Royce. His acceleration is so smooth, so powerful, so elegant, so swift that he defies gravity. I came not to Bury but to praise. His mighty deeds are still to come. Euro 2000 is his watershed.

DAVID BECKHAM

I witnessed his first game in the third team. Almost anorexic, spindly legs, enormous feet – the very antithesis of a professional footballer. But that day his vision, that peripheral instinct born only in the great, personified itself. Today it has added Spice.

JAAP STAM

He arrived either from Alcatraz or the Waffen SS. Prison hairdo. Humphrey Bogart profile, as happy as *One Foot in the Grave*. Limited, slow, tactically unaware in the World Cup. He is now Alex's favourite son and number one in Europe. Nice one, Alex.

GEORGE BEST

The sorcerer's apprentice. The Houdini of football. I once played with him in a charity match versus the England World Cup team. Alan Ball watched his amazing virtuosity and exclaimed: 'I thought I could play – I know nowt.' A world great alongside Pele and Stanley Matthews.

GORDON HILL

Impish, roguish, a will-o'-the-wisp fly-by-night – fly by the seat of your pants winger. A cockney wit straight from the music halls of old Islington. A complete maverick.

JIMMY GREENHOFF

His yellow hair flew in the wind. A wing half who leant over the ball like a crack professional snooker player on the first red of a maximum break. A potter's man in truth.

SEASON 1989/90: AND IT CAME TO PASS, WHEN THE KING HEARD THE BOOK OF THE LAW – HE RENT HIS CLOTHES.

MANCHESTER CITY 1 – QUEENS PARK RANGERS 0
Barclays Football League, Division One, 9 September 1989
Mark Twain said, 'I had to swallow suddenly or my heart would have got out.' Mr Twain spoke volumes for the hearts of 23,000 City fans who have run the whole gamut of emotion this afternoon. To distil the action: 43 minutes, *Clive Allen's first goal for City*. He was left solitary in front of goal after the QPR defence melted before an up and under. With great élan, Allen struck a sweet goal. The terraces were *en fête*, Allen dancing a celebration as if Bordeaux had declared a vintage. Half-time euphoria evaporated as QPR, with substitutes Stein and Maddix like ferrets up a drainpipe, ran amok. Sansom and Parker controlled a fiendish offside trap, pushed up on City. Spackman and Reid, the foxes, pumped high balls to the City heart where Cooper, their diminutive goalkeeper, was sorely pressed. Sinton, the QPR number eleven, hit the post. Redmond and Gayle, hardly beanpoles, had to joust with Clarke, a fearsome power in the air. McNab and Bishop in City's midfield, so dominant in the first half, were now trampled on. But wait – here comes the cavalry. Young Brightwell, bred of Olympic stock, came on, stemmed the tide, restored order. The final whistle was balm to all.

Oh! Oh! Oh! City's first win of this 1989/90 season. The Theatre of Base Comedy will not witness a renaissance. Clive Allen cannot sustain the force, Trevor Morley is a yoked ox, David White a brainless express train. A new forward must be bought, mined, discovered, appropriated. They need a Scarlet Pimpernel.

Manchester City: Paul Cooper, Gary Fleming, Andy Hinchcliffe, Ian Bishop, Brian Gayle, Steve Redmond, David White, Trevor Morley, Clive Allen, Neil McNab, Paul Lake. Substitutes: Neil McNab, David Oldfield.

Queens Park Rangers: David Seaman, Justin Channing, Kenny Sansom, Paul Parker, Alan McDonald, Nigel Spackman, Simon Barker, Peter Reid, Colin Clarke, Paul Wright, Andy Sinton. Substitutes: Mark Stein, Danny Maddix.

MANCHESTER CITY 5 – MANCHESTER UNITED 1
Barclays Football League, Division One, 23 September 1989
In Gath is a man of great stature, whose fingers and toes were four and twenty, six on each hand, six on each foot. The son of a giant. David slew him.

Stop the world, sing aloud unto God our strength: make a joyful noise. Take a psalm, bring hither the timbrel, the pleasant harp with the psaltery, blow up the trumpet in the new moon. This is our feast day. Manchester City have trounced their bitter rivals. Five–one. City, until now, one win in six games: bottom of the league with Spurs and Sheffield Wednesday. United, by their standards, are weak: halfway up the table, three wins, three defeats, and calls from the cowardly for Alex Ferguson's head. It is the 111th Manchester derby – could it be '666' for Mr Ferguson or Mr Mel Machin, City's manager? Peter Swales, the City chairman, is a whelk stall wheeler-dealer selling wet fish with one hand and blanking his bank manager with the other. By skulduggery and dubious diplomacy, control of City was whisked away from the naive Alexander family and now reposes with Mr Swales. He wears built-up shoes, a Mona Lisa smile; thinning black hair with a parting that begins at his left ear. His rise to power is shrouded in mystery, a thick cloud of Machiavellian unscrupulous statecraft, cunning intrigue, and a ruthless streak with enemies. A plausible prevaricator: 'And, after all, what is a lie? 'Tis but the truth in masquerade.'

Sir John Smith, the affable gent who, again by sleight of hand, inherited Liverpool FC, hated Mr Swales. I lunched with Sir John at Anfield prior to a City match.

'Observe,' said aforesaid Sir John, 'Mr Swales when he enters the board-room with his entourage: he will stroll up to the cigar box, empty it, proceed to the champagne and canapés, satisfy himself and then deign to say hello. No class, no money, no scruples.' In mitigation I said, 'Mr Swales loves his club, and maybe that transcends all.'

Football is sometimes grubby and tacky backstage; the machinations classified 'top secret'. I make you aware of this, dear listener, to fully acquaint you of this, a seemingly innocuous local derby.

To the game. Alas, it was stopped after three minutes as 2000 marauding United fans had infiltrated the North Stand: how they got there among the City faithful is one for the inquest 'twixt police and stewards. They were forcefully evacuated, screaming, brawling, sprawling and distinctly hostile. They rioted, invaded the pitch, fought the police on foot until the cavalry charged: mounted peelers on massive horses corralled the recalcitrants and restored order. Horse of the Year show in microcosm.

On the restart, City savaged United with two goals in a minute. Oldfield volleyed the first, Morley struck the second. Time, 11 and 12 minutes. Thirty-four minutes, Ian Bishop, the tiniest man afield, headed the third. Three–nil at half-time. Mike Phelan, United's new signing from Norwich, wished he were back in the Cathedral City. He and Gary Pallister were whispering vespers as City rushed by in a whirlwind. Viv Anderson, no slouch himself, was a yard off David White's pace. Paul Ince was baffled by Bishop and McNab in midfield, reduced to scowling, irascible impotence.

Mr Ferguson, renowned for rattling of teacups, must have shattered the entire Wedgwood year's output at half-time. Rumour hath it that dressing-room two was redecorated subsequently.

United resumed, chastened but abrasive. Mark Hughes hit a spectacular volley seven minutes into the second half. City, though, were rampant. They battered the opposition. Oldfield side-footed his second – City's fourth. Then the sensational goal of the season: Ian Bishop, first time out, to White lurking with intent on the right, White, again first time across the box – Andy Hinchcliffe on the run, like Carl Lewis, threw himself at the ball – his header of tremendous velocity left Leighton, in the United goal, a helpless pile of rags. United were outrun on the flanks by White and the superbly talented Paul Lake; outplayed in midfield. Donaghy, Duxbury and Beardsmore, lost sheep in a wilderness, missing the strength and crook of Captain Marvel, Bryan Robson, an absentee today with injury. Five–one to City left the Theatre of Base Comedy inmates delirious. Swales lives.

Back at the Shrine, Old Trafford, Mr Edwards will fight tooth and nail for Mr Ferguson. They will ask whether the pitch invasion unfocused the team, disturbed concentration. They will comb the country for better players; shake out the talent from the youth team, a never-ending production line of pure class, the cream of Britain's youth. City, for all this bravura, are not this good. They scaled Everest today, and this, *for certain, will never happen again.*

But for now,
The rosy-fingered morn appears
And from her mantle shakes her tears
In remembered promise of a glorious day.

Manchester City: Paul Cooper, Gary Fleming, Andy Hinchcliffe, Ian Bishop, Brain Gayle, Steve Redmond, David White, Trevor Morley, David Oldfield, Neil McNab, Paul Lake. Substitutes: Gary Megson, Jason Beckford.

Manchester United: Jim Leighton, Viv Anderson, Mal Donaghy, Mike Duxbury, Mike Phelan, Gary Pallister, Russell Beardsmore, Paul Ince, Brian McClair, Mark Hughes, Danny Wallace. Substitutes: Lee Sharpe, Clayton Blackmore.

SHEFFIELD WEDNESDAY 0 – COVENTRY CITY 0
Barclays Football League, Division One, 30 September 1989

Your faithful correspondent had a contretemps with a sewer in the Pennine foothills. I dropped my orange Jensen Interceptor right in it, 6.7 litres of wallop in the dollop. I thus missed the first 10 minutes of this encounter. At half-time the sewer presented the aspect more pleasant. I endured a shapeless, ragbag of first half that sorely tired the Sheffield public renowned for ascetic stoicism, spurning vulgar emotion. Surely, the second half would titillate. Alas, tempo was allegro, artistry was absent. Coventry are a slippery team; they move the ball to feet with some style, but, Speedie apart, they seemed throughout content with a point. In goal, Ogrizovic pulled off three excellent saves. And Wednesday. Difficult to analyse any pattern. The back four clattered in like earthmovers. Speedie and Gynn retired with bruised limbs. The playmaker is Carlton Palmer. Sounds like a luxury hotel. He is six feet two inches, and finds lovely positions. The Harlem Globetrotters would prize him a jewel, but Wednesday require fundamentals. Upfront, Hirst and Atkinson plunged willingly, but it is now three games without a goal. Big Ron, now off the gold standard, needs luck, but as the sage said: 'Happiness or misery generally goes to those who have most of the one or the other.'

Sheffield Wednesday: Kevin Pressman, Jon Newsome, Nigel Worthington, Carlton Palmer, Peter Shirtliff, Lawrie Madden, Mark Taylor, Steve Whitton, Dalian Atkinson, David Hirst, Craig Shakespeare. Substitutes: Dave Bennett, Alan Harper.

Coventry City: Steve Ogrizovic, Brian Borrows, Tony Dobson, Kevin MacDonald, Greg Downs, Trevor Peake, Micky Gynn, David Speedie, Steve Livingstone, Gary Bannister, David Smith. Substitutes: Keith Thompson, Craig Middleton.

OLDHAM ATHLETIC 2 – BARNSLEY 0
Barclays Football League, Division One, 7 October 1989

Boundary Park lies down a little ginnel, nestling in a hollow. In the distance the glowering Pennines, under a leaden sky foretelling a primeval winter. Fretted by a thin drizzle, a foreboding view. Like my view of the match from the vice-presidents' box. Alas, a gigantic rusting girder completely obscured one half of the affairs. But peering round it, rubbernecking, I observed Oldham devouring Barnsley as if they were the Denby Dale pie (the biggest pie in the world, the size of a house). Frank Bunn blasted the first, Mike Milligan the second, both rebounds from the hapless Barnsley reserve goalkeeper. The game ten minutes old. Such quality, pace and imagination from this free-flowing Oldham team. Andy Ritchie laying off the ball, with his head, like Steve Davis laying snookers. The vice-presidents and old rubberneck – me – chortled with glee. But Barnsley spoilt the party. Paul Futcher settled them at the back. They pushed up, marked tight, denied Oldham space, and the game degenerated into bouncing ball, anaconda thighs, bare knees, shin guards, muscle and sinew, honest endeavour and sweat. Six thousand seven hundred fans settled into disappointment. Salt of the earth, resilient, and full of faith.

Talking of faith, at 4.17 p.m. the Barnsley number 14 entered the fray. The name Archdeacon. Alas, he was not bearing a silver chalice, nor wearing a dog collar. I smite my girder in mock rage.

Oldham Athletic: Andy Rhodes, Denis Irwin, Andy Barlow, Nick Henry, Willie Donachie, Earl Barrett, Roger Palmer, Andy Ritchie, Frank Bunn, Mike Milligan, Rick Holden. Substitutes: Gary Williams, Scott McGarvey.

Barnsley: Ian Wardle, Malcolm Shotton, Paul Cross, Jim Dobbin, Julian Broddle, Paul Futcher, Ian Banks, Steve Agnew, Steve Cooper, David Currie, Darren Foreman. Substitutes: Carl Tiler, Owen Archdeacon.

LEEDS UNITED 1 – WOLVERHAMPTON WANDERERS 0
Barclays Football League, Division Two, 21 October 1989
> *'They saw there was much money in the chest,*
> *Silver, snuffers, basons, trumpets, vessels of gold and silver.*
> *The King's scribe and the High Priest came up,*
> *And they put money in bags.'*

The Plot: The Leeds Revival.
The Players:
High Priest: Howard Wilkinson.
The Scribe: Vincent Jones.
The Apostle: Gordon Strachan.
The Enemy: Marauding Wolves.

Leeds, led by the arch 'Goth' Vincent Jones, are favourites to win Division Two. Top of the table with Sheffield United, 23 points from 12 games. Howard (never use one word if 12 will do) Wilkinson has built a solid foundation team. Mel Sterland to crunch at fullback, Chris Fairclough to solder the iron at centre half, David Batty to graft and sweat midfield, Gordan Strachan to leprechaun his magic wherever he wishes, and Vincent to exhibit his flair.   Vincent, the one-time bricklayer's hod carrier who tipped up for training in hobnail boots and overalls, led out the team sporting an Alcatraz hairdo with a badger on top. Twenty-eight thousand fans aching for olde times gave him a rapturous ovation. They want glory, they love Vincent; if the press vilify him, accuse him of cynicism, arraign him as a hired assassin, then what do the press know? They have never been fond of Leeds since Don Revie was elevated to sainthood. Rousing rock music, a well-grassed pitch, a beautiful cloudless day – let's rock along-a-Vinnie. The roof of the stand blew off with hot air as Yelland Road celebrated an eighth-minute goal. Gordon Strachan's floated corner far post, Bobby Davison's header. Leeds set about Wolves with high-stepping pace, quick one-twos, an aerial ball or three and gave them a severe pounding. Westley, the Wolves number five, committed a gross professional foul, was booked, fortunate to stay on the pitch. Bennett and Downing earned the referee's displeasure – the old gold shirts of Wolves distinctly tarnished as the white shirts of Leeds flashed by like a Persil commercial. Vincent's long throws tended to dazzle them, hurled like grenades into the pillbox of the Wolves goalmouth. Mark Kendall, in the Wolves goal, by sheer brilliance kept Wolves alive.

Wolves were disappointing. Andy Mutch, their playmaker, was elbowed out by Batty: Steve Bull was shackled by Fairclough. In fact it was 72 minutes before the first Bull shot, and I choose my words carefully.

Wide players were absent. Leeds operated a simple, disciplined offside trap. On one occasion the entire Leeds team raced from penalty box to halfway line like a flock of St Trinian's fillies, frocks held high in fright at a mouse. One goal was scant reward for Leeds. Wolves escaped a flaying.

At the close, Vincent applauded his team, the audience, the referee and linesmen, the ball boys, the aristos in the plush seats, the hoi polloi in the two and nine penny, the stewards, and a flight of wild geese happenstance on the wing. I applaud Vincent, 'For what are riches, empire, power, but larger means to gratify the will?'

Leeds United: Mervyn Day, Mel Sterland, Mike Whitlow, Vinnie Jones, Chris Fairclough, Peter Haddock, Gordon Strachan, David Batty, Ian Baird, Bobby Davison, Andy Williams.

Wolverhampton Wanderers: Mark Kendall, Tom Bennett, Mark Venus, Phil Chard, Shane Westley, Nigel Vaughan, Andy Thompson, Keith Downing, Steve Bull, Andy Mutch, Robbie Dennison.

MANCHESTER UNITED 2 – SOUTHAMPTON 1

Barclays Football League, Division One, 28 October 1989

Serendipity. One of my favourite words. The making of happy and unexpected discoveries by accident (Oxford Dictionary).

A serendipity match if ever there was. But at 3 p.m. the Shrine was grey. A grey wind blew grey litter in the chilling grey drizzle. Thirty-seven thousand supplicants shuffled in, shrouded in a grey blanket – a League Cup hand-me-down from Spurs. The lowest gate of the season. Southampton opened with a brilliant, blistering spell of old-fashioned football. Two wingers – Le Tissier and Wallace – playing wide, Le Tissier's silky elegance wreaking chaos, Wallace's sheer speed leaving Donaghy a peeled banana, Pallister a monolith in the United defence. Then, on 15 minutes, Robson, clearly stung by this pink-cheeked, arrogant, youthful Southampton, came on the riposte. An inventive through ball to Hughes, Hughes swift ball to McClair, McClair's strike – one–nil. One minute later an identical move by Southampton, Robson tried to head clear – merely skimmed it on to Le Tissier, who with glee hooked the ball past Leighton.

At half-time I beamed with joy at 45 minutes of brilliant, pulsating, attacking football. And the tempo stayed allegro.

Hughes was peripatetic, in terrific form. His knock-on gave McClair his second goal – a walloping drive. United's throng gave voice – their team responded, rising to the Southampton challenge. Pallister at last looked the part. Phelan uncorked his football brain. Robson the action man. Manchester United, gain heart. They are back in the frame. And serendipity – the joy of discovering something entirely by chance. Thank you, both teams. And I do believe that a crock of gold lies at the rainbow's end. And, yes, I do believe in fairies.

Manchester United: Jim Leighton, Mal Donaghy, Lee Martin, Steve Bruce, Mike Phelan, Gary Pallister, Bryan Robson, Paul Ince, Brian McClair, Mark Hughes, Lee Sharpe. Substitutes: Clayton Blackmore, Guiliano Maiorana.

Southampton: Tim Flowers, Jason Dodd, Francis Benali, Jimmy Case, Neil Ruddock, Russell Osman, Matthew Le Tissier, Glenn Cockerill, Alan Shearer, Paul Rideout, Rodney Wallace. Substitutes: Graham Baker, Ray Wallace.

MANCHESTER CITY 3 – CRYSTAL PALACE 0

Barclays Football League, Division One, 4 November 1989

The City follower is a resilient animal, a life of highs and lows, a roller-coaster that rises high, like the five–one defeat on Manchester United four weeks ago, then cascades down to a four–nil whacking at Highbury. One week it is *Les Miserables,* the next '*Allo,'Allo.* Today it was frolic and farce. Farcical refereeing by Jim Ashworth for starters. Hope his judgement is better than his day job – he is an air traffic controller. Today he was like a diner eating, or chasing, jelly on a red-hot plate – he never caught up with the action. Pemberton of Palace and Clive Allen of City had a verbal *tête-à-tête* straight from the Café René. McNab of City, Pardew of Palace had a fierce taproom scuffle with handbags, the language hardly French. Mr Ashworth, like an impotent gendarme, waved his arms, booked the verbal duo, and ignored the GBH.

To the gist. City were ahead after five minutes: David White with a thunderous shot as Palace defenders were still uttering 'Allo, 'Allo to each other. Forty minutes Andy Hinchcliffe rocketed a free kick across the Palace goal, Trevor Morley cracked the ball into the net. Fifty-eight minutes Paul Lake sped down the left, whammed in the shot, Suckling parried, Clive Allen poached the rebound. Three–nil. City hit a post, Allen struck the bar, had a legitimate goal disallowed by Mr Ashworth, for whom the word 'foible' was coined. City today were on form: Bishop and McNab imposed themselves midfield, Lake is a huge talent sure to represent England, Redmond and Fleming, so hesitant recently, were brimming with *sang-froid.* The inmates at the Theatre of Base Comedy will hit the *trottoir* cafés in sun-baked Manchester and sip their Vermouths and Pernod in rejoicing. Alas, Palace: Wright and Bright apart, the fallen Madonnas – with the big boobies.

Manchester City: Andy Dibble, Gary Flemming, Andy Hinchcliffe, Ian Bishop,

Brian Gayle, Steve Redmond, David White, Trevor Morley, Clive Allen, Neil McNab, Paul Lake. Substitutes: David Oldfield, Ian Brightwell.

Crystal Palace: Perry Suckling, John Pemberton, Richard Shaw, Andy Gray, Jeff Hopkins, Alex Dyer, Eddie McGoldrick, Geoff Thomas, Mark Bright, Ian Wright, Alan Pardew. Substitutes: Rudi Hedman, Phil Barber.

EVERTON 0 – CHELSEA 1
Barclays Football League, Division One, 11 November 1989
At 4.45 p.m. smoke billowed from the stand occupied by the jubilant Chelsea following. 'Twas not a fire – merely punters burning betting slips on Everton's championship. Chelsea, attired in horizontal red-and-white stripes à la Hull KR, played not 'up under' but a sophisticated, rhythmic, one-touch game that used to be the hallmark of the School of Science. Graham Roberts, Kenneth Monkou and the mercurial Tony Dorigo insolently blocked out the Everton attack. Peter Nicholas, Mick Hazard, Alan Dickens and Kevin Wilson were ubiquitous, industrious and telepathic with controlled passing. Everton's first half was anonymous. Pat Nevin not a single run, Sheedy and McCall overrun. A rash of corners and some super saves from Neville were scant reward for Chelsea's first half. At last, the goal on 50 minutes. Kevin Wilson shot, the ball ricocheted to fullback Steve Clarke – with Neville unsighted, Clarke's shot rattled by him. On the hour, Everton made a substitution. Nevin, anticipating the worst, ran to the line, but to Cottee's chagrin 'twas he, not Nevin, replaced by Sharp. What glimmers for Everton with a scratch back four? For excuse, McDonald was excellent, Beagrie, on his debut, a sorcerer. Man of the match Dorigo – the Sardinians will bless him as Garibaldi's own, come next summer. '*Forza Italia*'.

Everton: Neville Southall, John Ebbrell, Neil Pointon, Martin Keown, Neil McDonald, Peter Beagrie, Pat Nevin, Stuart McCall, Mike Newell, Tony Cottee, Kevin Sheedy. Substitutes: Graeme Sharp, Ray Atteveld.

Chelsea: Dave Beasant, Steve Clarke, Tony Dorigo, Graham Roberts, David Lee, Kenneth Monkou, Alan Dickens, Peter Nicholas, Kerry Dixon, Kevin Wilson, Mick Hazard. Substitutes: John Bumstead, Kevin McAllister.

MANCHESTER CITY 0 – NOTTINGHAM FOREST 3
Barclays Football League, Division One, 18 November 1989
Is this a valediction for Jimmy Frizzell, the resident host at the Theatre of Base Comedy? Thumped six–nil last week by Derby County, third from bottom in the First Division, now by Nottingham Forest, a team that Brian Clough is rebuilding in his own autocratic, didactic, dictatorial manner. Frizzell, already demoted to general manager, has Mel Machin as team manager. City came up from Division Two last season with Chelsea and Crystal Palace; to City's chagrin Chelsea are top, unbeaten after 13 games. The City team augured disaster at 3 p.m. David Oldfield, David White, Clive Allen upfront, McNab and Bishop midfield. Colin Hendry, the Scot, the signing from Blackburn Rovers at

£700,000, playing his debut, and short of match practice. The side is unbalanced and febrile in key areas.

Fecund Forest fruitful, a late blossom in November – a cornucopia of midfield talent in Steve Hodge, a dark-haired smoothie like a professional snooker player, Nigel Clough a silent assassin, Garry Parker a charger. Gary Crosby, a non-leaguer with Grantham two years ago, was lightning-quick down the right flank, now here he was down the left haring for goal – brought low – penalty. Nigel Clough struck the kick heartily. One–nil down, and only 14 minutes had passed. Forest played with disdain, almost distaste at City's pallid show; they revelled in the huge gaps in midfield, naive defending at the back. Hendry's face, a normal bright pink under a mass of blond hair, was puce with wasted effort. City simply overrun. Crosby's change of pace undid City again on 20 minutes, Lee Chapman dummied the cross, Nigel Clough crisply drove the ball past Dibble, the hapless City keeper. Frustration set in like compensation sets in when Mancunians trip over flagstones. Hinchcliffe was booked, disputed the referee's finding a little too forcibly and was sent off. Brian Rice completed the debacle with the third goal, almost on the final whistle.

City's 26,000 faithful now in deep shock. They demand, if not skill, 100 per cent effort. Bishop and McNab are clever ballplayers – in a gifted team they would shine. Clive Allen has lost the muse, David Oldfield never had it. David White, possessed of stallion speed, plays under a blanket of self-doubt and inferiority – psychiatrist's couch for him, maybe. Ian Brightwell stayed on the bench. Surely, with his Olympic pedigree (his dad is Robbie, erstwhile British Olympic captain, his mum is Anne Packer, erstwhile gold and silver Olympic medallist) his sheer pace and enthusiasm would have disturbed Forest's cool aplomb.

Is it the fond farewell for Frizzell and Machin before it is farewell with tears, yet again, from the top flight for City?

Forest, meanwhile, left the disaster scene at precisely five minutes past five with nary a smile, nor a word. Mr Clough, I presume, will take his evening stroll on the waters of the Trent.

Manchester City: Andy Dibble, Gary Fleming, Andy Hinchcliffe, Colin Hendry, Steve Redmond, David White, David Oldfield, Clive Allen, Neil McNab, Brian Gayle, Ian Bishop. Substitute: Ian Brightwell.

Nottingham Forest: Steve Sutton, Brian Laws, Stuart Pearce, Des Walker, Terry Wilson, Steve Hodge, Gary Crosby, Garry Parker, Nigel Clough, Lee Chapman, Brian Rice.

SHEFFIELD WEDNESDAY 2 – CRYSTAL PALACE 2

Barclays Football League, Division One, 25 November 1989

Having approached this fixture in an earlier life, I approached Sheffield Wednesday versus Crystal Palace with as much relish as sharing an omelette with Edwina Currie. But lo! Wright, Bright and McGoldrick, like a firm of City solicitors, had solicited a goal. Brilliant goal conceived by Ian Wright, whose pace astonished the strolling Brigadier Madden, and a pedestrian Nigel Worthington. Bright on to McGoldrick, a pause for Andy Gray to thunder up from midfield, Gray's daisycutter. One–nil to Palace. On the hour big Jeff Hopkins, the Palace number five, headed them to a two–nil half-time lead.

Big Ron Atkinson was beside himself, apoplectic with rage. An ill wind had ruffled his bouffant, hairsprayed coiffeur; Palace had ruffled and rumbled his tactics. Palace a yard quicker, slippery upfront, in control of midfield. Nigel Martyn, their keeper, a frozen bystander. He is Britain's first £1 million goalkeeper, signed from Bristol Rovers two weeks back. His first club was St Blazey – if only Wednesday would blazey away today – if only to chip the ice off his mitts. Wednesday's first half was a disaster. The front men lonely as a cloud. At the back Worthington like a dromedary in the Derby, Madden simply ambling, like a retired brigadier in search of a pink gin – all pomp and no circumstance.

'C'mon, lads, wek oop,' came the cry.

Needs must when devil drives. Big Ron threw big Steve Whitton into the fray. A raw-boned hunk, he cut the mustard, as the Yanks say – a battling, surging, boring run at Palace – a humdinger of a shot. Two–one. Palace panicked, lost their cool and poise. Gray, Hopkins and Wright booked for acts of rashness. Ian Wright is a mobile incendiary bomb; he relishes the battle, he is looking to explode, confrontation is second nature to him, he has an attitude problem the size of Selhurst Park. It could impair his career – a shame, as he is an intuitive, natural player, stimulating to watch in full flight, with the attributes to merit an England place. He lost the plot. Sheridan assumed the mantle of authority; as Palace blew hot, Sheridan blew cool. He operates like a surgeon, deftly incising with his scalpel; he calculates his passes and executes them with panache. The last gasp of the match – Sheridan felled in the box – penalty! Martyn must have looked as large as the north face of the Eiger to David Hirst. Hirst ran like a Centurion tank to zoom the ball past Martyn. Big Ron smiled his expansive smile. Palace still have not won here since 1924.

Postscript: The Wednesday substitute was one Master Shakespeare. He did not feature today, but at full time he whispered in Big Ron's ear:

Thy favours are like the wind

That kisseth everything it meets.

Sheffield Wednesday: Kevin Pressman, Nigel Pearson, Phil King, Carlton Palmer, Peter Shirtliff, Lawrie Madden, Dave Bennett, John Sheridan, David Hirst, Dalian Atkinson, Nigel Worthington. Substitutes: Steve Whitton, Craig Shakespeare.

Crystal Palace: Nigel Martyn, John Pemberton, Mark Dennis, Andy Gray, Jeff Hopkins, Philip Barber, Eddie McGoldrick, Geoff Thomas, Mark Bright, Ian Wright, Alan Pardew. Substitutes: John Salako, Gary O'Reilly.

MANCHESTER UNITED 1 – CRYSTAL PALACE 2

Barclays Football League, Division One, 9 December 1989

The Shrine is stilled, foundations rocked by the verbal battering at the annual general shoutin'. The supplicants stunned by Palace's first away win. Alex Ferguson, once swathed in onyx, gold and rubies, now has the albatross. He dropped Mark Hughes and packed the side with youth. On 15 minutes Alex was a winner – Russell Beardsmore, with a thrilling, diving header near the post, gave United the lead.

And United upped the tempo, flowing down on Palace's back five. Danny Wallace playing strike force with McClair looking like a pygmy in the long grass of the Palace defence. But on the flanks Sharpe and Martin winged over cross after cross. Enter Nigel Martyn, Palace's keeper, a Cornishman with frying-pan hands. Two saves, from Beardsmore and McClair, were breathtaking. He kept Palace alive.

Suddenly the Palace corpse twitched. Mark Bright, unmarked, headed a typical goal from the Wright/Bright portfolio. These two the most potent strike force in Division One. Time, 43 minutes.

Now on the hour Bright again; foozling in the winner as the United defence looked on. Hughes immediately appeared, but Sparky was short-circuited. Palace had grown in stature. Martyn was immovable.

Poor Alex. As Will said: 'It is the bright day that brings forth the adder, and that craves wary walking.'

Manchester United: Jim Leighton, Russell Beardsmore, Lee Martin, Steve Bruce, Mike Phelan, Gary Pallister, Bryan Robson, Paul Ince, Brian McClair, Danny Wallace, Lee Sharpe. Substitutes: Clayton Blackmore, Mark Hughes.

Crystal Palace: Nigel Martyn, John Pemberton, Mark Dennis, Andy Gray, Jeff Hopkins, Gary O'Reilly, Andy Thorn, Geoff Thomas, Mark Bright, Ian Wright, Alan Pardew.

LIVERPOOL 1 – CHARLTON ATHLETIC 0
Barclays Football League, Division One, 30 December 1989

Chairman Mr Smith became Sir John. John Barnes played in fetching black tights and matching gloves. Frankly, they were the only pretty things at the Colosseum on a chilling winter's afternoon. Mr Dalglish, always his own man, dropped McMahon and Beardsley, where they shivered on the substitutes' bench until drummed into late action. Ray Houghton was mysteriously absent. And so Liverpool's midfield of Whelan, Molby, Staunton and Nicol strove to re-establish the Anfield basics of sweat, one touch to feet, and speed of thought. Alas, it looked, and was, hard work. The ball often gifted to Charlton, the final ball a nightmare. Like herding elephants up Mount Everest. Charlton were confident, skilful but shot-shy. The jewel, John Barnes, smote the goal on 17 minutes, a sweet half-volley from Staunton's cross. But the audience cold, silent, reflective, critical, never bolstered this strange insipid Liverpool performance.

At one stage on the tannoy an Orwellian voice declared: 'Police, execute Operation Anfield.'

A disgruntled fan exclaimed: 'Execute the team!'

At last, too late, Mr Dalglish unleashed McMahon and Beardsley. Rush had his penalty saved by Bolder. Charlton, with Peake and MacKenzie outstanding, were chagrined. An orchestra played 'Auld Lang Syne', the crowd drifted away to 1990 and better days.

Liverpool: Bruce Grobbelaar, Glenn Hysen, Barry Venison, Steve Nicol, Ronnie Whelan, Alan Hansen, Gary Ablett, Steve Staunton, Ian Rush, John Barnes, Jan Molby. Substitutes: Peter Beardsley, Steve McMahon.

Charlton Athletic: Bob Bolder, John Humphrey, Mark Reid, Andy Peake, Joe McLaughlin, Colin Pates, Robert Lee, Paul Williams, Steve MacKenzie, Colin Walsh, Michael Bennett. Substitutes: Carl Leaburn, Paul Mortimer.

ROCHDALE 1 – WHITLEY BAY 0
The FA Challenge Cup – Round Three, 6 January 1990

A glorious day for your scribe at tiny Spotland, all corrugated iron and rustic stands; astride the tannoy in the minuscule press box, a large old Reptonian gent sitting on my lap. Hot pies, steaming tea, broad smiles, even broader Lancashire vowels, and a highly vocal 1,500 Whitley Bayers, sardined on the terraces. Grass-roots football, nostalgia for bygone days when the game was brimming with bonhomie.

Rochdale were always prepared to play football of a standard that would astonish the cynics. Little one-twos; ball into space, eager to display skills before the enthusiastic crowd.

Whitley Bay opened with a speedy spell centred round Kenny Wharton and the ball upfield for Kevin Todd, their risen-from-the-sickbed star. He found the Pennine air to his liking – I have never heard or seen such a vocal footballer since Alan Ball. The game ebbed and flowed with passion. But on the hour Steve Johnson, Rochdale's brick outhouse number eight, let fly from the edge of the penalty area. The ball whistled in the net, at the foot of the far post. Rochdale turned up the wick. Whitley Bay held. Their number five, Andy Gowens, took a bludgeon in the groin and never flinched. Praise to fine referee Mr West. On a note of light relief, in a tiny room I shared a half-time stall with him. A version of taking the waters – or giving. Another notable first at memorable Rochdale.

Rochdale: Keith Welch, Wayne Goodison, William Burns, Tony Brown, David Cole, Peter Ward, Micky Holmes, Steve Johnson, Jason Dawson, S O'Shaughnessy, Jimmy Graham. Substitutes: Steve Elliot, Jonathon Hill.

Whitley Bay: Tony Harrison, Mark Liddle, Warren Teasdale, Peter Robinson, Andy Gowens, Kenny Wharton, Paul Walker, Tony Dawson, Laurie Pearson, Kevin Todd, Billy Johnson. Substitutes: Chris Scott, Garry Haire.

LIVERPOOL 2 – LUTON TOWN 2
Barclays Football League, Division One, 13 January 1990

Thirty-five thousand rolled up in glee to the Colosseum to see a reprise of the Swansea wipeout. Luton with a defensive, tentative reputation; demoralized, a new manager at the helm of a doomed ship. They left in amazement and relief at two–two.

The match opened with majestic football from Liverpool. Bewildering, rippling moves to feet at speed, inspired running off the ball. Breacker, the Luton fullback, cleared off the line. A Barnes shot hit Harvey's face and felled the poor chap. Wilson off the line. At last the goal, John Barnes's speciality. A flighted free kick that bent yards as it whistled past the Luton goalkeeper, Chamberlain. Luton apace were playing dainty football midfield. Dreyer was magnificent at centre back, Harford a man mountain in the air. Splendid stuff. First half of quality, Grobbelaar a spectator.

The second half was dying like the woodman's fire when Harford suddenly raked the embers. Yet again he won the ball in the air. This time Kingsley Black was on it, his wicked left-foot shot beat Grobbelaar, by now half-frozen. Time, 71 minutes. Before we could draw breath, young Nogan tore down the left. The cross was turned in by Kingsley Black. The Kop was stunned. Could Liverpool come back from one–two? John Barnes's reply was a floated cross on 76 minutes. Steve Nicol met it on the forehead meet. Two–two. A rip-roaring finish, but Liverpool will regret their casual, arrogant approach to that crucial second half.

Liverpool: Bruce Grobbelaar, Glenn Hysen, Barry Venison, Steve Nicol, Ronnie Whelan, Alan Hansen, Peter Beardsley, Steve Staunton, Ian Rush, John Barnes, Steve McMahon. Substitutes: David Burrows, Jan Molby.

Luton Town: Alec Chamberlain, Tim Breacker, Richard Harvey, Mick Kennedy, Mal Donaghy, John Dreyer, Danny Wilson, Kurt Nogan, Mick Harford, David Preece, Kingsley Black. Substitutes: Iain Dowie, Julian James.

MANCHESTER CITY 1 – ARSENAL 1

Barclays Football League, Division One, 10 March 1990

Two imponderables at 3 p.m.

First, could Arsenal, who won the championship last season with the last kick of that incredible game at Anfield, Michael Thomas flying through the Liverpool defence to score and win two–nil, win today? Their away form is abysmal – nine games lost. Their home form is the league's best – unbeaten in 13 games. Trailing Liverpool by seven points, they have to beat City.

Secondly, could Andy Dibble repeat his clowning of last week when, bewitched, he lost his marbles, allowing Crosby of Forest to head the ball out of his hands and gift Forest a victory?

The Theatre of Base Comedy braced itself. Various music-hall acts have been played here – is it to be sit comedy or sit tragedy? City, peering down the abyss, ditched the sweeper playing Harper at orthodox right back. Peter Reid, all stooping gait and bandy legs, was father figure in midfield. Paul Lake was his sideman with craft and guile. Gary Megson flung himself at anything mobile, like a fairground busker.

The Arsenal settled down to trench warfare, Michael Thomas, Kevin

Richardson and 'Rocky' Rocastle, steel-helmeted, all knees and elbows. 'Twas raw stuff, not for the purist. Colin Hendry was Rob Roy. One day I expect him to wield a couple of claymores and sport a sporran. If he has not shed blood, he has not played. Lee Dixon, a local yokel, a free transfer at Chester a few years ago, relished it. Winterburn, once anonymous at Oxford, played as a rapier. The foil to Bould and Adams, those pillars of Highbury marble sustaining the Arsenal's defence.

Stalemate until 25 minutes. A rare City goal (in 15 matches only 11 scored). The glorious twelfth a product of Paul Lake. A classic early ball down the right to Megson, Megson's hoof goalward. David White hit one of his celebrated right-foot howitzers.

Just after half-time, Brian Marwood equalized – a blazing volley – a net-ripper. We had a dashing finale, both teams on the charge, chances came and went. A draw that neither side desired. George Graham, a double winner as a player with Arsenal in 1971, a double winner as manager last season, is troubled. Alan Smith and Kevin Campbell are firing on six cylinders, not eight. The turbocharger is untwitched. All is not well. And City – only Charlton Athletic and Millwall keep them off the bottom.

The imponderable is now ponderable. Arsenal will not win the championship. Andy Dibble did not commit howlers. He observed the Green Cross Code: look right, then left, then right again to avoid flashy opposition crosses. Howard Kendall, City's manager, still has a few strands of hair on his pate. He will have lost a few more on this acid afternoon.

Manchester City: Andy Dibble, Alan Harper, Andy Hinchcliffe, Peter Reid, Colin Hendry, Steve Redmond, David White, Mark Ward, Adrian Heath, Gary Megson, Paul Lake. Substitutes: Clive Allen, Ian Brightwell.

Arsenal: John Lukic, Lee Dixon, Nigel Winterburn, Michael Thomas, Steve Bould, Tony Adams, David Rocastle, Kevin Richardson, Alan Smith, Kevin Campbell, Brian Marwood. Substitutes: Martin Hayes, David O'Leary.

LIVERPOOL 3 – SOUTHAMPTON 2
Barclays Football League, Division One, 31 March 1990
The Colosseum in blazing sun. Mutterings about Liverpool's lack of motivation – tantamount to blasphemy. Thirty-seven thousand shoehorned in.

Southampton opened with skill at speed, Le Tissier sauntering around the opposition with a saucy, arrogant flair, Rod Wallace a pocket-sized dynamo, and the old warhorse Jimmy Case on his old stomping ground a little Napoleon, the master of midfield. But on 15 minutes from a Houghton free kick, John Barnes rose unmarked and headed Liverpool into the lead. Thirty-five minutes a Jimmy Case free kick – Paul Rideout on the far post a definitive header. One apiece. Three minutes of the second half. Rod Wallace off the blocks, past Venison and Hansen, inside to, yes – James Case. A blockbusting, rasping, howitzer shot – incredible velocity. Brucie never twitched. Liverpool two–one down, the Kop in torment. Were the motivation mutterings well founded? The answer from Mr Dalglish. The Israeli player Ronnie Rosenthal replaced England hero McMahon. Gillespie on for Venison. Liverpool were fired up. Like a Panzer charge they rolled on Southampton. Barnes hit the bar. The crowd bayed, screamed, roared. Seventy-five minutes Flowers, the Southampton keeper, under pressure, punched out Osman and Moore, his defenders panicked – own goal to Osman. Southampton bounce back, histrionics. But then Hansen broke out a fine run – inside to Rush – a vintage right shot. Three–two. The Colosseum erupted. Standing ovation. Liverpool back right on line for the silver.

Liverpool: Bruce Grobbelaar, Glenn Hysen, Barry Venison, Steve Stauton, Ronnie Whelan, Alan Hansen, Peter Beardsley, Ray Houghton, Ian Rush, John Barnes, Steve McMahon. Substitutes: Ronny Rosenthal, Gary Gillespie.

Southampton: Tim Flowers, Jason Dodd, Andy Cook, Micky Adams, Kevin Moore, Russell Osman, Rodney Wallace, Jimmy Case, Paul Rideout, Barry Horne, Matthew Le Tissier. Substitutes: Alexei Cherednik, Glenn Cockerill.

SHEFFIELD WEDNESDAY 0 – SOUTHAMPTON 1
Barclays Football League, Division One, 7 April 1990
Alexei Cherednik, late of the Soviet Union, played number two for Southampton. Sheffield felt like home as a bitter wind blew straight from the Russian steppes. It numbed the mind, froze the blood, reduced the pedal extremities to lumps of ice. This shapeless match stumbled from farce to error, to its disastrous final conclusion for Wednesday. It was as long as *Anna Karenina.* We *knew* she was doomed to die, but for Tolstoy's sake let it be quick. Woefully, really, as Southampton were so inventive last week at Anfield. There was no spring in the air, no spring in the step. Le Tissier in a velvet fog of ineptitude, Rod Wallace like a small urchin on a beach hurling himself at white-tipped rollers. Wednesday's uncompromising defence rolled him over – all long legs and fearsome tackles. Jimmy Case, though, was a 12-bore hotshot, a little Napoleon peppering opponents with tackles to fell an ox. Two of these felled Trevor Francis and reduced him to mere mortality. Barry Horne, too, was magnificent. So much of Horne's play is unnoticed, but he flits into space, gives the intelligent pass, and is deadly in the tackle.

The goal came in 65 minutes. Rod Wallace cut inside Lawrie Madden; Madden plays like a strolling benevolent brigadier inspecting troops on Horse Guards Parade. He was offended by Wallace's impetuosity; before he could recover composure and adjust his medals, Wallace was gone. A quick square pass to Glenn Cockerill unmarked. Cockerill wallops the ball at some speed past Turner. The frozen masses on the terraces chipped ice from chapped lips and gave voice. Dalian Atkinson flew at Southampton like a wild condor. John Sheridan, the knock-kneed artist, tried close passing skills, but blue-and-white striped shirts failed to respond. Carlton Palmer played like a Hilton hotel. Carton Palmer Towers – but little ace David Hirst, the complete enigma, was elsewhere – injured again? Le Tissier and Wallace retired from boredom.

The match sank into wind-blown apathy. A match worth the phrase, 'Note this before my notes. There's not a note of mine worth the noting.'

Sheffield Wednesday: Chris Turner, Roland Nilsson, Lawrie Madden, Carlton Palmer, Peter Shirtliff, Nigel Pearson, Trevor Francis, John Sheridan, David Hirst, Dalian Atkinson, Steve Whitton. Substitutes: Dave Bennett, Stuart McCall.

Southampton: Tim Flowers, Alexei Cherednik, Micky Adams, Jimmy Case, Neil Ruddock, Russell Osman, Rodney Wallace, Glenn Cockerill, Paul Rideout, Barry Horne, Matthew Le Tissier. Substitutes: Alan Shearer, Andy Cook.

LIVERPOOL 2 – NOTTINGHAM FOREST 2
Barclays Football League, Division One, 14 April 1990

From tomorrow this Colosseum will become a shrine for the 95 who perished at Hillsborough. An eternal flame will burn close to the Shankly gates. Thus the heart shall break, yet brokenly live on. It was 14 minutes into the match before the pall was lifted. A brilliant goal, conceived in joy, performed at leisure. Hansen's through ball to Barnes. Barnes in flight – the cross met on the volley by Rosenthal again lusting down the left. His booming cross soared over the Forest defence. Rush headed back to McMahon. His rasping shot was deflected in. Two–nil. Forest downcast, subjected to humiliation as Liverpool indulged in one-touch rhythmic play. Mr Clough senior was dilatory and reluctant to return the ball when it was propelled into his dugout. But Forest, having lost six of their last seven games, salvaged pride, dredged up their basic skills, tightened up and suddenly Hodge, Clough and Jemson were up and running. Sixty-three minutes Nigel Clough's cross, Steve Hodge wriggled free of his marker – a low shot. Two–one. Seventy minutes Nigel Jemson turned fullback Tanner, literally on a tanner, Brucie was a trifle slow to react. Jemson's shot squeezed in, two–two.

Liverpool's McMahon drove forward to inspire Liverpool. Barnes's header smote the bar. Barnes's goal-bound shot, cleared by Pearce. Rush hit a howitzer – a goal? No – Pearce again off the line. Forest were euphoric, their pride and reputation enhanced. Liverpool hearts broken, live on. Forest it was, you remember, who were Liverpool's opponents on that fateful day at Hillsborough.

Liverpool: Bruce Grobbelaar, Glenn Hysen, David Burrows, Steve Staunton, Ronnie Whelan, Alan Hansen, Nicky Tanner, Ronny Rosenthal, Ian Rush, John Barnes, Steve McMahon. Substitutes: Gary Ablett, Jan Molby.

Nottingham Forest: Mark Crossley, Brian Laws, Stuart Pearce, Des Walker, Steve Chettle, Steve Hodge, Franz Carr, Terry Wilson, Nigel Clough, Nigel Jemson, Garry Parker. Substitutes: Tommy Gaynor, David Currie.

LEEDS UNITED 2 – LEICESTER FOSSE 1
Barclays Football League, Division Two, 28 April 1990

The final whistle blew, the final match of the season. Leeds are promoted. The crowd flooded on to the pitch in a tidal wave. The players disappeared under a welter of relief. No more Brighton and Hove, Goldstone, Dean Park, the Manor Ground, Boundary Park, Valley Parade and other locations in the sticks. It is hello, Old Trafford, Anfield, Highbury. Howard Wilkinson, a potent philosopher, has been at Yelland Road 18 months. A basically shy Yorkshire man, his husbandry and wisdom have revitalized Leeds. Huge crowds, one home defeat all season, three days ago to Barnsley. That stung him, Yorkshire derby, Barnsley fighting relegation.

Thirty-five thousand here today. Leeds fought like bantam cocks. They overwhelmed the Fosse; a young feller called Martin Hodge, in the Fosse goal, had a golden day. Magnificent, like Joan of Arc amid the bonfire. Explosive start; 14 minutes Mel Sterland lit the torch, a stampede down the right; Mel on the charge is awesome, he is a strapping lad. We all expected the cross. He went for gold. He blasted the ball in, I swear, through a gap the size of a key-hole. The crowd's din was bedlam.

My notes read: Davison shot – Hodge smothers: Davison shoots wide; Vinnie Jones inspired ball to Davison – Hodge fantastic save: Strachan how-itzer – Hodge tips over the bar. Davison through on goal – Hodge defies death at Davison's feet.

On the hour Davison was unwillingly led from the fray, stunned with dis-belief as if struck with a humane killer in the abattoir. Varadi took his place. The referee, Mr Allison, like the Lone Ranger engulfed in a forest fire, tried to extinguish the flames, lecturing Fosse and Leeds firebrands. In vain, like putting out the Great Fire of London with a holed bucket.

Then on 62 minutes Oldfield, the Fosse substitute, crossed from the left, three Fosse players dummied over the ball – McAllister volleyed the equalizer. Another firecracker. McAllister's intuitive play was incredible. The more the battle raged, the cooler he became. Leeds must sign him now!

The din roared on. It was impossible to think – what could Leeds achieve? Varadi struck a post. Hodge impenetrable. Enter Gordon Strachan, the pocket battleship, oozing class honed at Aberdeen and Old Trafford. Eighty-four min-utes a fantastic volley. All over as celebrations began.

I sat in my little seat in front of the directors' box. The audience, wild, ecstatic, overjoyed, trampled me to the ground. The Leeds players reappeared in my arena. *They* trampled me to the ground. Most of my notes were snaffled by a fan. The Yorkist peelers rescued me – eventually. They lost their helmets, appropriated by the madding crowd. Howard Wilkinson simply looked on, bemused by this flood tide of emotion. Behind him, even the well-heeled cart-wheeled. Fur coats, Rolls-Royces, fine jewels have returned to Yelland Road.

Leeds United: Mervyn Day, Mel Sterland, Jim Beglin, Vinnie Jones, Chris Fairclough, John McClelland, Gordon Strachan, Chris Kamara, Lee Chapman, Imre Varadi, Gary Speed.

Leicester Fosse: Martin Hodge, Ali Mauchlen, Alan Paris, Paul Ramsey, Steve Walsh, Tony James, Paul Reid, Marc North, David Kelly, Gary McAllister. Tommy Wright.

IN PRAISE OF BOB PAISLEY
The Greatest Football Manager of All Time.

In 1977 Liverpool were poised for a unique treble: League Championship, FA Cup, European Cup. Liverpool lost to Manchester United in the FA Cup. Won the Championship. But, four days after the Wembley debacle, had to play Borussia Moenchengladbach in Rome.

I persuaded the BBC to film the massive exodus to the Eternal City, 40,000 trekking to the event of their lives. By jet in style. By motorcar and motorcoach. By thumbing lifts. Travelling steerage. By passenger and goods train, sleeping rough without food or drink. The glory of Rome spurred them on. Dreams and the light imaginings of men, of all that faith creates and love desires. Rome, the Eternal City. The cradle of civilization. This was not simply a football match; it was a distillation of people's lives crystallized into 90 minutes.

Rome was a sea of red and white. Thousands invaded the Vatican. Played football in St Peter's Square, asked the Pope for spare tickets. They occupied bars and trattorias. Swarmed the streets with cacophony and wit. They even pimped for the ladies of easy virtue who throng the Via Veneto. Always with low-key style. No rioting. No vandalizing. No head-breaking. I was proud to be with them.

My second camera team was to film in the Olympic Stadium. I required passes to gain access. The day before the match, Peter Robinson, that truly magnificent administrator, and I loaded a taxi with 40 pieces of silver and set off for the headquarters of the Italian FA.

'Gifts,' said Peter, 'will always sweeten labour.'

On the Via Veneto we stopped on a red traffic light. On instinct, I peered through the rear window to observe a light lorry bearing down at great speed. It tore into the rear of our taxi, crumpling the boot and the driver's temper. He leapt out – *'Basta, basta! Multo cattivo!'* His temper evaporated, as from the back of the lorry jumped forty carabinieri, armed to the teeth, and threatening instant access to heaven for us all.

'Tell 'em you were reversing and apologize, for God's sake,' I implored. He acquiesced, acquired a jemmy, opened the boot, transferred the silver to another cab, and we were off and away.

Inside the building the gifts were distributed. The passes smilingly issued. Just then, Gigi Peronace, 'Mr Big', strolled in, the head of Italy's football Mafia. Black hair greased back, bespoke suit, Gucci shoes, mohair coat swung casually over his shoulders. He viewed the passes and ripped them to shreds.

'Only Italian cameras inside the stadium!' he said in Italian. He was adamant. We withdrew, abashed – but undaunted. Peter, that smashing bloke, was stunned. I was poleaxed. I had committed the BBC to vast expenditure for nothing.

Back at the ranch, our hotel, Bob Paisley drew up the master plan.

'Disguise yourselves as players. Hop on the team coach. The rest is up to you.'

Joe Fagan carried the camera inside a team bag. Ronnie Moran and Tom Saunders carried the lighting equipment, Phil Thompson and John Toshack assorted paraphernalia. Police escorts, lights flashing, sirens screaming, hot-foot it to the stadium. Straight through the portals unchallenged. Up the marble staircase into the Michelangelo marble of dressing-room one. Hastily, Terry Wheeler, the film director, and the crew were hidden in the treatment room to escape the marauding Italian FA officials. Suddenly they spotted me, smelling a rat; I was apprehended.

'Take them for a walk,' advised Bob. So off I trotted around the perimeter hyping the red-and-white hordes basking in the blazing Roman sunshine. Lions and gladiators, the giant Colosseum, 2,000 years of history encircled this panoply of colour.

On my return to the dressing-room, nerves had gripped the players. Kevin Keegan sporting two black eyes – a gift from Jimmy Case on hearing the Hamburg news, led the charge to the loo. Alas, the loo was in the treatment room and, folks, there was no water in there. The piles of excreta were Vesuvius high, and there was no escape for my camera boys.

'Handkerchiefs over faces, lads – face up to the faeces'. The stench was asphyxiating, but my valiant lads withstood it. It was Britain versus Italy. Anzio all over again. This was the bridgehead, lavatorial version.

Came the kick-off, I had nowhere to sit!

'File out with the team,' suggested Bob. 'Sit on the subs' bench.' Cool, matter-of-fact, still smiling – phlegmatic Bob Paisley, on the eve of his finest hour. No histrionics, arm-waving, cigar-chewing, gum-munching, heavy sweating, foul-mouthed behaviour synonymous with some football management. Bob could have been a bank manager on his way to the Toxteth branch.

Imagine the scene. All the players drummed their boots on the marble floor. A battle cry. The drumming rose to a crescendo. The atmosphere charged like a storm over the Himalayas. Two great teams. England versus Germany. Clemence, Neal, Jones, Hughes, Smith, Case, Kennedy, Callaghan, McDermott, Keegan, Heighway, Toshack, Thompson and co. and, bringing up the rear of this great football team, Hall, carrying the dressing-room key – I was last to leave.

Two yards from the most gripping, exciting, dramatic match I have ever seen, clad in my Liverpool tracksuit. Keegan played out of his shirt. As Bertie Vogts was up that shirt most of the time, butting, punching, reaping and binding, Keegan's performance was heroic. Crazy Horse was at the Battle of Little Big Horn. Tommy Smith was Mafioso. Case layered in sweat. Heighway leaping down the left with that high-stepping impala gait, threaded through a pass, McDermott in full cry from midfield hit a super goal.

For Borussia, Simonsen stopped my heart with skill at speed. Steilike was Rommel, the total general, Simonsen and Vogts simply epic. We were one up at half-time. I dashed to the dressing-room. I had lost my voice in the sheer tumult. The cameras turned as the team trooped in. Nerves jangled, limbs twanged. The players, with the loos running like Venetian sewers, simply peed on the marble floor, in the shower, anywhere to relieve tension. Bob moved among them – quiet words here, a pat on the back there. Ronnie Moran like the staff nurse ministering to his charges. Joe Fagan smoking through his third pack of the match. The bell for second half. Suddenly, the players began stamping their boots. The cavalry on the charge, the drumbeat of Balaclava, the battle ground in the blazing sun. A mass of hysterical red and white, a crucible of noise. I locked the door behind me and filed out with the team.

Borussia equalized. Steilike was hurt and rolled over the line of our dugout. A torrent of pure Scouse, anti-German invective so terrified him that he rolled back on the pitch. Tension gripped me in a paralysis like a child's Christmas Eve, a thousand of them encapsulated in one. Tommy Smith smote the goal of the century. Phil Neale's penalty. Uproar. Joy such as I have never seen. Voiceless, I hared back to the dressing-room. My crew, with handkerchiefs over their faces, enquired about the score.

'Three–one to us,' I croaked. 'Stand by to roll. Lights, action, scene 32, take one.'

But trudging towards us were the Germans. Tearfully led by Vogts, shirts in their hands. They congratulated us. In faltering German, I tried to explain that we were not club officials but the BBC. They still parted with their shirts and disappeared within the marble bowels. Crazy Horse on the jig led the joy, prancing, kissing, holding the European Cup aloft. The camera rolled and made history. The first time a European Cup winners' dressing-room filmed.

As the junket reached its zenith, Peronace entered – mohair coat still draped over the shoulders, Italian style. His mouth, prepared to utter congratulations, dropped open. He could not believe the scene. We were here, arc lights illuminating his beloved territory, working in defiance of his sole authority. We had beaten his system. For us there was no such thing as 'impossible'. He shrugged his shoulders, gave me a withering stare, and stalked away.

As the stadium emptied, the supporters wending from the dazzling amphitheatre of the Eternal City through Europe back home would carry the moments of that match through their lives. Liverpool had left their mark: *venite, vidite, vicite* – they came, they saw, they conquered.

The players departed, leaving Bob Paisley, Tom Saunders, Ronnie Moran, Joe Fagan and Roy Evans in the stench-laden yet elegant marble edifice of dressing-room one. 'Evans the coach', the young backroom boy schooled for management, cast me a look that said, 'Do you appreciate exactly what you've had today?' There we were, sitting on the team skip, sipping warm Coca-Cola. Anticlimax hung in the air. I humbly, voicelessly, thanked Bob Paisley, and his 'boot room' boys. Bob smiled enigmatically.

'It's the second time I've been to Rome and beaten the Italians. The first was driving a tank in the Second World War.' Laughter pealed around the marble hall. Men of quality, that on this, their proudest day, they had shown such patience and kindness to me and my team. No wonder I hold them in such esteem and affection. The film was a mega-success and now lies in the archives. A mighty effort.

Oh, I forget. I locked the door of dressing-room one at the Olympic Stadium, leaving behind golden memories and mountains of excreta. I still have the key. It is a treasured possession.

WÜRDEN SIE MIR BITTE MEINE WARMFLASCHE AUFFÜLLEN?
(Would you fill my hot-water bottle?)

Strange fits of passion I have known and I will dare to tell. Teams of yore. Players of such panache. 'O! For a Muse of fire, that would ascend the brightest heaven of invention; a kingdom for a stage, princes to act and monarchs to behold the swelling scene.'

For bizarre, off-the-wall fanatics, a literary flourish… I dream of the greatest teams in an imagined tournament. Four gods of management, Matt Busby, Bob Paisley, Don Revie and Alf Ramsey, prognosticate. I shall pontificate.

LIVERPOOL 1984 VERSUS AC MILAN 1989

Liverpool: Bruce Grobbelaar, Phil Neal, Ray Kennedy, Mark Lawrenson, Ronnie Whelan, Alan Hansen, Kenny Dalglish, Sammy Lee, Ian Rush, Maurice Johnson, Graham Souness.

AC Milan: Galli, Tassotti, Alessandro Costacurta, Franco Baresi, Paolo Maldini, Franck Rijkaard, Colombo, Carlo Ancelotti, Ruud Gullit, Roberto Donadoni, Marco Van Basten.

BOB PAISLEY I would say that my Liverpool side of 1977 were mentally better than the 1984 side. Crazy Horse the inspiration, Heighway the ace. But then the 1984 team still had many of the same qualities. AC Milan learnt much of what they did from Liverpool and Forest. They wouldn't let you settle on the ball; a real test of Liverpool's passing. Once you lost it to them you'd have to go man to man very quickly.

DON REVIE Rush's movement upfront would trouble them. Dalglish obviously is a genius.

MATT BUSBY It's an absolutely fascinating game. I don't think Liverpool would be in awe of Milan. Souness is the finest midfield player in Europe. Rush can materialize anywhere. Dalglish is world class.

ALF RAMSEY Milan go to Anfield first. I think they'd be happy with a draw. The Dutch trio, Rijkaard, Gullit, Van Basten, will play the game at control pace. Liverpool's weakness is lack of quality flank players – Lee lacks class. And will Grobbelaar be the clown or the fine keeper I know him to be?

Great managers' forecast:

First Leg: Liverpool 1 – AC Milan 1 (Rush, Rijkaard)

Second Leg: AC Milan 2 – Liverpool 1 (Van Basten 2; Dalglish)

170

LIVERPOOL VERSUS AC MILAN (FIRST LEG)

The Colosseum was a crucible of emotion on this balmy April evening. The gods themselves, the talismen of the beautiful game, the names you breathe in your dreams. Tonight was the exposition of dreams. Souness arrogant, peacock proud, flamboyant, jousted with Donadoni, the itinerant Gypsy. Whelan's fluent inventive running a contrast with Gullit's change of pace and game plan. Milan so tight at the back – Baresi the terminator.

Suddenly, Dalglish peeled off Maldini as a striking black mamba. Rush lurking vehemently. A quick 10-yard pass. Rush in his stride struck a typical Rush goal. Time, 38 minutes. The second half was all Milan. They powered forward, Van Basten totally majestic. Eighty-two minutes Hansen, wrong-footed, brought down Van Basten outside the box. Rijkaard's free kick turned like a Shane Warne leg break. Grobbelaar, mystified, retrieved the ball from his net. Genius at work. One apiece. The stage is set for San Siro.

AC MILAN VERSUS LIVERPOOL (SECOND LEG)

The Milanese fog enveloped the San Siro. The flares lit by the excited fans burnt like an ancient religious festival. Smoke, fog billowed. 'Twas surreal – bedlam and erupting volcano.

Tension crackled like a forest fire. Liverpool had to score an early goal and they did. Twenty minutes into the match, Souness barrelled into the Milan penalty area, Dalglish corralled by defenders. A quick one–two, Dalglish past Costacurta and Baresi, a left-foot shot of blinding ferocity. One up. The crowd now in torment. Would Milan buckle or respond? Milan poured forward, their control awesome. Their running, as free as Scottish Highlands air. Breathtaking and beautiful.

Thirty-eight minutes Van Basten took Gullit's 50-yard pass on his left foot and volleyed with his right – goal of the season? The sting and the muse deserted Liverpool. Chasing shadows, they fell further behind on 70 minutes. A Van Basten special. Worming through on the left past Neal, through Lawrenson like a wraith in the mist. A thundering left-foot drive. The match won. Unforgettable.

The Milanese *tifosi* lit flares and torches. They stood as both teams took a lap of honour. Applause for Liverpool – they had stretched Milan and brought forth football of magnificence – from another planet.

BAYERN MUNICH 1974 VERSUS AJAX 1973 (SEMI-FINAL)

Bayern Munich: Maier, Hansen, Breitner, Schwarzenbeck, Beckenbauer, Roth, Tortensson, Zobel, Müller, Hoeness, Kapplemann.
Ajax: Stuy, Suurbier, Hulshoff, Blankenburg, Krol, Neeskens, Haan, G. Muhren, Cruyff, Keizer, Rep.
MATT BUSBY Absolutely fascinating. It's a real clash of styles here. Bayern compact, powerful and solid, Ajax refining total football with their fantastic technique. It's German efficiency versus Dutch flair.

171

DON REVIE Ajax were at their peak, because they were about to lose Cruyff and the team was breaking up. Both teams in effect became the country's national sides as well.

BOB PAISLEY Both countries still approach the game in the same way now. The Dutch went on to reach the World Cup Final against Germany, and they also won the European Championship. Most of the Bayern side won the World Cup in 1974 in Germany. The game is about quality players. Cruyff, Neeskens and Krol have the keys to unlock Bayern.

ALF RAMSEY Obviously, you have to get past Beckenbauer; stretch them and use the ball quickly. No one likes to defend against pace. Discipline is the key, like my 1966 England. Gerd Müller will score. Look at his record: 68 goals in 64 internationals. He'll put the Germans ahead; the Dutch would defeat them in Holland. That would set up my perfect final if Liverpool aren't in it!

Great managers' forecast:
First Leg: Bayern Munich 2 – Ajax 2 (Müller 2; Neeskens, Cruyff)
Second Leg: Ajax 1 – Bayern Munich 0 (Rep)

BAYERN MUNICH VERSUS AJAX (FIRST LEG)

There is something intimidating, nay daunting, about Munich. The city is architecturally beautiful. The Bavarians are lederhosen cheerful! But the Olympic Stadium has overtones of the Third Reich. Flags fly, the Germans are noisy. Full of anthems. Arrogance is in the air. The match never reached the heights. It did on the terraces. I've never experienced such volcanic fervour. Bayern pragmatic and drilled like a Panzer corps; Beckenbauer, the Kaiser, dictating the flow. By half-time, Bayern were two up. Gerd Müller two identical goals. Buffalo charges and two howitzer shots.

The second half saw the Dutch emerge. Breitner, exhausted by constant runs down the left, was himself run ragged by Keizer. His two flighted crosses led to goals, the first a glancing header from Neeskens, the second a volley from Cruyff. Two–two.

Now for Amsterdam.

AJAX VERSUS BAYERN MUNICH (SECOND LEG)

Amsterdam is *en fête*. The bars are bulging, the streets alive with buskers. Jazz bands play. Everything is orange. The Dutch, all clogs and tulip field tenders, have never matched the German industrial machine. There is no love lost betwixt the nations. Tonight Dutch flair will overcome. And so it came to pass. Cruyff destroyed Bayern. The Kaiser was thought a mere mortal. Schwarzenbeck, normally the north face of the Eiger, was reduced to the size of a hillock (yes, hillock). I glory in style, and Cruyff crystallized it in amber. From ambling gait to panther speed in the twinkling of an eye. He ghosted round defenders, peeled off them as Mosimann would peel an orange. Rep flailed like a windmill. Neeskens' pace exposed the immobility in Bayern's ranks. Neeskens could find Cruyff even if they were on different planets.

But the match was Cruyff's. In life there can be nothing but style. A Carl Lewis electric sprint, Nureyev's power and control, a Brian Lara century, Senna's awesome belief and style, an Oscar Wilde aphorism, a Churchill speech, a Cliff Morgan try. They are beacons lit to enliven our dull lives. They are the gods.

The goal was almost an adjunct to the game. Scored by that mobile tornado Johnny Rep. A horizontal diving header from a pass by – guess who? – Cruyff. Ajax win the tie three–two.

And now the finale.

THE WEMBLEY FINAL: AC MILAN 1989 VERSUS AJAX 1973

AC Milan: Galli, Tassotti, Costacurta, Baresi, Maldini, Rijkaard, Colombo, Ancelotti, Gullit, Donadoni, Van Basten.

Ajax: Stuy, Suurbier, Hulshoff, Blankenburg, Krol, Neeskens, Haan, G. Muhren, Rep, Cruyff, Keizer.

ALF RAMSEY I was ahead of my time with 'wingless wonders'. Ajax were ahead of their time. You could rotate players in any position, and their perfect technique would enable them to blend. Liverpool, Forest and Villa took their passing ideas, added the English approach of strength and organization.

DON REVIE Milan, like my Leeds team, had been functional and effective, then they added Dutch flair. They took which I could not, four-four-two, and played it properly, allowed everyone to express themselves in it.

BOB PAISLEY Milan do not have a weakness. Costacurta, Baresi, Maldini combine strength and flair. Van Basten and Gullit will win it for Milan.

MATT BUSBY Ajax remind me of my 1948 side. Delaney, Mitten, Rowley, Pearson – such flair and style. I confess though that Ajax have taken the game beyond our conception of football. In my day players were specialists. A winger, a centre forward, a fullback, a centre half, a creative wing half. It was job description. These players of Ajax and Milan can play anywhere. Just marvellous.

THE FINAL: AC MILAN 1989 VERSUS AJAX 1973

The world desired it. Wembley got it. The world is here. A sea of orange, and red and black. It is a world flag day. Banners of all nations; shirts of every hue and allegiance worn with pride on this glorious May day. Anticipation ran through me with a thousand-volt charge. The nape hairs stood on end at this momentous sight; a sea, a wall of faces, all here to pay homage to the beautiful game. Almost before we were seated, Milan were ahead. Ajax surged forward seeking the early goal. Milan hit them on the break. Maldini, the giraffe of Series A, loped down the left, whipped in the cross. Van Basten's glancing header near post. Time, two minutes. Cacophony from the multitude. Delirium set in. The Dutch band muted. Ten minutes later Van Basten struck again. Baresi the provider. Built like a gladiator, legs like a Roman centurion, Horatio on the bridge. Donadoni and Gullit swarmed round Baresi as he made his charge. A flurry of passes at bewildering speed. Baresi thumped the cross, Van Basten at the far post whipped the ball past a bemused Ajax keeper. Two–nil.

Could Cruyff raise the standard? He was inscrutable. No emotion, no histrionics. He began to probe the Milan defence. He sensed the doubt in the Milanese. Go for the jugular? The third goal? Or sit back and defend the lead? This is the genius of Cruyff. His goal just before half-time was worth preserving in amber. His acceleration powered him past Costacurta and Maldini; he turned Rijkaard into a pillar of salt and scored a fantastic goal. The football majestic, a cornucopia of wonderful, exciting moves, rippling skills, extemporization of breathtaking beauty. Of Tchaikovsky, Beethoven, Bach and Bernstein. Symphonic, rhapsodic.

Two–one to Milan at half-time.

The first-half pace was blistering. The Wembley turf was lush. The sun blazed down. Would it be sheer physical exhaustion or nerves? Which team would buckle? Questions were answered just after the break. As the Milan defence marshalled to corral Cruyff, Haan, the unsung workhorse, ran like a hungry leopard on the prey to a long ball from Krol. He half-hit the shot, and the ball trickled over the line as Galli, the Milan keeper, groped like a drunk after his car keys.

Two apiece and 20 minutes to play, 20 minutes of the purest football ever seen. Gone the discipline, the pragmatic Italian stance. Enter the flair of Gullit, Van Basten and Rijkaard. All-out attack. The most marvellous exposition of total football since the Real Madrid of Puskas and Di Stefano.

Wembley must have resembled the Sahara to Ajax. Milan explored the vast spaces that opened. Rijkaard was inspired. Playing behind the front two, his passes were like a surgeon's scalpel, incising the soft underbelly of the Ajax defence. Five minutes from time, yet another pass found Gullit 25 yards from goal. Gullit, with no back lift whatsoever, smote the unstoppable drive.

Three–two. All over. Tears from Ajax. Exultation from Milan. The dream final.

The beautiful game lives. Let action ever be directed to some definite object and be perfect in its way.

Stuart O'Hall for *Sports Report* on Celestial Fathers FM.

TOMMY DOCHERTY

The Doc is schismatic. He has two personalities. Neither knows what t' other thinks or does. He is a classic Gemini – Castor and Pollux, the heavenly twins. Or, Caster and Bollocks!

His golden era was with Manchester United. Knowing of my leaning towards Manchester City, which goes back to snotty noses and Wellingtons, Frank Swift and Peter Doherty, he would take fiendish delight in throwing me into his dressing-room before a match.

The atmosphere was alight. Gordon Hill's cockney humour; Stuart Pearson's hamstrings in a hot pickle, Martin Budan's sly wit. It was like a junior common room – the faces were of boys – pink and laughing. No nerves, no team talk, no furrowed brow.

On the park they played with freedom. One Saturday yet again he threw me into his dressing-room at Coventry. Same humour, everyone sent up my yeti boots and the wireless: 'Get back in yer cage.' They clobbered Coventry four–nil.

With all this in mind, a few of us were disturbed when he was sacked by United. He could have had a clandestine affair with Mary Brown, but he told the truth. The naive side of the Doc. Out of football he is artless and unworldly.

So when Derby County came off the top of their world with Dave McKay, the same friends of the Doc began to lay plans to get him to the Baseball Ground.

Dead-of-night meetings with Sam Longson, the chairman of Derby, a collector of teapots and large sums of money. A most delightful man, honest, rugged, with County's interests paramount. Hushed tones in the snug of the George and Dragon Inn at Charlesworth. The whole village was electric with rumour. The Doc, me, Sam and a well-known MP and Minister of the Crown. Like a surreptitious conclave in the Pentagon. Doc got the job. Little did we know, but a rival faction had persuaded Brian Clough to return to Derby. The Doc won. We awaited glory.

Subsequently, he arrived at Derby; arms aloft; the Gorbals twinkle and barking wit. Alas, his mind, and inclinations, were at Old Trafford. Abrasive as ever, he dismissed Archie Gemmill and Colin Todd, Kevin Hector and the old guard. He bought Gordon Hill and other boyos from Ireland and elsewhere. They did not add up to a team. Doc lost the plot. Backstage rumours flew, tempers blew. Derby sank in a morass of scandal and debt. George Hardy lost his shirt, Sam Longson lost heart and pride – and money – and a few of us licked our wounded pride and dignity. The Doc does not have pride; battered by shock waves from Chelsea to Rotherham, he blinks like a prizefighter and stumbles to his next contest. He lost a court case that finished his football career.

But one day he did give his word. Drove miles through ice and snow to play a charity five-a-side. What a man! Then, two weeks ago, he was contracted to a fund-raising dinner for young boys in Cheshire. He did not show. Joe Mercer subbed yet again.

Doc's dichotomy – he is still a pal, though, and my oh my does he need them.

His Chelsea side of Hollins, Venables, Bridges and co. was one of the finest young sides in living memory. Doc was a great loss to management – they do not breed mavericks like that any more.

SEASON 1986/87: AND NOW I HAVE SENT A CUNNING MAN, ENDUED WITH UNDERSTANDING, SKILFUL, TO WORK IN GOLD AND SILVER

EVERTON 0 – ARSENAL 1
Today Football League, Division One, 4 October 1986
I stumbled across George Graham, the Arsenal manager, before the match: browsing among faded photographs of yesteryear, Everton teams, whimsically musing on the sheer quality gazing at him. George is a sincere, upright, sympathetic fellow. He is rebuilding, he has time and demands commitment. Certainly, his Arsenal team gave him sweat and resilience as Everton dominated the match. His centre back Adams, the infant prodigy, found Graeme Sharp in elusive form, but Sharp was prodigal with the chances, and Arsenal punished him and his side. On 23 minutes with the mystery goal. They have Watson at Everton but Sherlock Holmes sleuthed it. Steve Williams, taking a corner on the left, gave notice to all that the kick was near post. As the ball swerved in the wind a posse of players rushed to meet it. They missed. Mimms, the Everton goalkeeper, rushed across the goal line where Sheedy was keeping guard on the post. To their chagrin, nay horror, the ball eluded both, although Mimms's boot may have touched the ball over the line. The goal fired up Everton. Trevor Steven was inspired even by his marathon-man watermark. The youngster Neil Adams, Kevin Langley, Paul Wilkinson played School of Science football. Lukic in goal rose to the occasion. A safe pair of hands, a little luck and wild shooting, plus the referee's decision going against, aborted their skills. But when one considers that Reid, Bracewell, Southall, Heath, Van Den Hauwe plus four others are out, Howard Kendall can still smile.
Everton: Bobby Mimms, Derek Mountfield, Paul Power, Kevin Ratcliffe, Dave Watson, Kevin Langley, Trevor Steven, Neil Adams, Graeme Sharp, Paul Wilkinson, Kevin Sheedy. Substitute: Warren Aspinall.
Arsenal: John Lukic, Viv Anderson, Kenny Sansom, Steve Williams, David O'Leary, Tony Adams, David Rocastle, Paul Davis, Niall Quinn, Ian Allinson, Perry Groves. Substitute: Gus Caesar.

LIVERPOOL 4 – OXFORD UNITED 0
Today Football League, Division One, 18 October 1986
Arriverderci. Ciao. Va bene. Che cora significo questo? (Goodbye. Ta-ta. That's all right. What does this mean?) It means that Signor Ian Rush is Juventus-bound, off down the Yellow Brick Road to Turin seeking loads of lire. Rush is one of the greats. Only Jupiter knows why he is going. He is a Liverpool player. His scouse is incomprehensible to outsiders, his environs are here at Anfield. The Stadio delle'Alpi will be like Alcatraz. I give him one season and a return ticket. Player/manager Kenny Dalglish hopefully has a replacement – it could be John Aldridge, that scoring phenomenon playing for Oxford today at the Colosseum. Liverpool need a handsome victory today as, unbelievably,

Norwich City top the division, losing but one game in ten. Forest are second, then Spurs and West Ham.

Liverpool duly walloped Oxford. Rush scored two hallmark goals, his first on the half-hour. Steve Nicol's neat chip on to Ian's head – not often Rush heads a goal. It was his 15th of the season, the 200th in a short career. To think, I saw his debut and wondered if he would ever make top class. His second goal, one minute from time, made nonsense of my early judgement. Kenny Dalglish's quicksilver through ball – Rush appearing as if from outer space, simply ghosting from nowhere to strike, like an angry viper, Liverpool's fourth goal. The other goals came from Kenny Dalglish on 35 minutes – a flashing move down the left and a typical Dalglish flourish: Jan Molby's classic penalty kick, high and wide to Parks, the Oxford keeper's left, on 52 minutes. Dreyer, Oxford's massive number six, did protest too much after he handled the ball for that penalty. Mr Courtney, the courteous referee, doth report him. Liverpool, judged by their own standards, were disappointing. I know that oftentimes I am a pedagogue, but Lawrenson looked unhappy at left back, Steve Nicol even unhappier wide on the right. Gillespie played central defence with Hansen, but does not have the turn of speed to combat Hansen's weakness when exposed to the pinging ball in the box and attackers getting goalside of him. Some of the build-up was exciting, the final ball disappointing. We anticipated a ruthless annihilation of Oxford, especially as Billy Whitehurst, their combustible centre forward, retired hurt after 25 minutes. Aldridge was thus Oxford's sole strike force – he was potent, often embarrassing Hansen. Aldridge, I am convinced, is Anfield-bound.

Midfield, Ronnie Whelan was a sorcerer, a subtle will-o'-the-wisp, but McMahon and Molby do not dovetail into that classic Liverpool pattern. They are short of a genuine wide player – would John Barnes or Pat Nevin fill the bill? Great sides at Anfield always had a wide player, namely Peter Thompson and Steve Heighway. Maybe Mr Dalglish, who more and more resembles Robert Redford, will take heed.

Meanwhile, Signor Rush: *Tante grazie e pasta Inglese?*

Liverpool: Bruce Grobbelaar, Steve Nicol, Jim Beglin, Mark Lawrenson, Ronnie Whelan, Alan Hansen, Kenny Dalglish, Jan Molby, Ian Rush, Gary Gillespie, Steve McMahon. Substitute: John Wark.

Oxford United: Tony Parks, David Langan, Neil Slatter, Les Philips, Gary Briggs, John Dreyer, Ray Houghton, John Aldridge, David Leworthy, Trevor Hebberd , John Trewick. Substitute: Billy Whitehurst.

MANCHESTER CITY 1 – EVERTON 3

Today Football League, Division One, 29 November 1986

A moment of high chagrin one hour into the match. The score one apiece. Paul Power, playing number six for Everton, former City skipper, raised his left boot, hit a hopeful shot towards the City goal. Like the sorcerer's apprentice the ball evaded Perry Suckling's dive, and lodged wickedly in the corner of the

City net. Power looked like a Rent-a-Gun trusty who had shot himself in the foot. He almost apologized for cardinal sin. He retired shortly after to the dressing-room. He is a lawyer, a self-confessed lover of City. He will now sue himself for breach of promise. I believe he only scored twice in 14 seasons at Maine Road.

Everton's euphoria began in bright sun on six minutes. Mountfield thumped a wide ball to Adams. Adams's cross was swept in by Adrian Heath. Nil–two. City's cherubic youths were in shock, overrun in midfield, desperate in defence. Slowly they emerged from a white-hot chrysalis, and Paul Moulden ran to a White pass, leant over the ball à la Steve Davis on the cue, and shot, low and hard, past Southall. His seventh goal in six games. One–two.

Came the Paul Power debacle, City's demise, and suddenly Everton's experience gained sway. Sheedy was finding space in the hurly-burly. Trevor Steven was on incisive runs, Sharp winning the hard-headed duel with McCarthy. Five minutes from time, Wilkinson and Heath found no one barring their way, exchanged passes like lovers, Heath whacked the goal. Everton on course for the championship. City for a Wembley appearance in the Full Members', Freight Rover, Gola, Alliance, Multipart Trophy or whatever it is.

Manchester City: Perry Suckling, John Gidman, Clive Wilson, Kenny Clements, Mick McCarthy, Tony Grealish, David White, Neil McNab, Paul Moulden, Graham Baker, Paul Simpson. Substitute: Imre Varadi.

Everton: Neville Southall, Alan Harper, Neil Pointon, Kevin Ratcliffe, Derek Mountfield, Paul Power, Trevor Steven, Adrian Heath, Graeme Sharp, Neil Adams, Kevin Sheedy. Substitute: Paul Wilkinson.

EVERTON 4 – NORWICH CITY 0

Today Football League, Division One, 6 December 1986

Nonagenarian Sir John Moores, swathed in the biggest Everton scarf ever knitted, left this fine, ambient match wreathed in smiles. He has the connoisseur's palate for quality football, sportsmanship and memorable goals. We had a cornucopia this afternoon. A horn of fulsome plenty. The banquet opened quietly. Norwich were dainty servers of the first-time ball. Their sweeper swept up the unconsidered trifles.

But on 18 minutes the hors d'oeuvre from Paul Power. He normally stands on his right foot and plays with his left. Suddenly, via Heath and Sharp, the ball arrived on his wrong foot. He swung it, the ball hurtled past Gunn in the Norwich goal with a deafening report. Twenty-eight minutes the entrée. Gunn, left stranded by gross negligence, headed the ball outside his area. Sheedy's shot was handled. A penalty. Gunn orated in high dudgeon, the referee booked him. Trevor Steven hit the classic penalty low, hard and fast to Gunn's left.

The second half was leavened bread after the sating feast. Norwich stayed to football principles, and Ken Brown can be proud of the applause wrung from his discerning audience at Goodison. Came then the dessert. With 13 minutes to play, fullback Neil Pointon came on the surge, and with his wrong foot, his right, blasted number three.

But with 30 seconds to go, the Stilton with vintage port. A sublime goal. Kevin Sheedy scooped the ball over the Norwich defence, Adrian Heath in his stride struck the goal to savour and remember. Keats would have adored it all – a draught of pure vintage from the deep delvéd earth of the School of Science.

Everton: Neville Southall, Alan Harper, Neil Pointon, Kevin Ratcliffe, Derek Mountfield, Paul Power, Trevor Steven, Adrian Heath, Graeme Sharp, Neil Adams, Kevin Sheedy.

Norwich City: Bryan Gunn, Ian Culverhouse, Mark Seagraves, Steve Bruce, Ian Crook, Ian Butterworth, Ruel Fox, Kevin Drinkell, Wayne Biggins, Trevor Putney, Dale Gordon.

MANCHESTER CITY 3 – WEST HAM UNITED 1

Today Football League, Division One, 13 December 1986

Jimmy Frizzell is manager at the Theatre of Base Comedy. If City win, it is *Frizzell*; when they lose it's *Frizzle*, to rhyme with sizzle. Frizzell is sizzling in the relegation pan. Bottom of the league, played eighteen, won three, lost nine. We have seen it all before – it has generated the farcical humour that permeates Moss Side, Manchester 14. The programme advertises the appearance at the Social Club of the north's top comedian – one Ricky Livid – we are all comedians here, and we are all LIVID.

The Mancunian rain fell like a soft grey safety curtain at the Theatre. Rain that gives us fresh complexions, open minds, stunted growth, bronchitis, pneumonia, anthrax, brucellosis, alopecia, flat feet and ingrowing toenails. Our maxim is to look misfortune in the eye and repeat, ''Tis a kind of happiness to know exactly how far one ought to be unhappy'. The Frizzell drizzle turned fierce, monsoon raged. City were inspired, opted for brash, bold, brazen attack. As the pitch glistened, the ball came off like an ice-rink puck, City played fine, one-touch football, the length and breadth of Stanley Gibson's excellent pitch. Eighteen minutes David White toe-poked City into the lead from Simpson's corner. Varadi hit the bar. Parkes, in West Ham's goal, flung his huge frame around as if on a trampoline.

Alas, City's failing is lack of concentration. One minute into the second half Alvin Martin, West Ham's centre half, lurched up-field and in the twink of an eye equalized. West Ham began to lay their classic carpet football. Alan Devonshire oozed poise, Paul Ince snapped into tackles, Tony Cottee buzzed and beavered like an army of ants, Mark Ward, the Dandini of Upton Park, was wizard. Glorious entertainment. The match ball was donated by one Ronald Stratton, purveyor of grandiose horseless carriages to the nobility. West Ham were Rolls-Royces, City Ford Escorts. But this is the Theatre of Base Comedy – no plot runs its course. City's Ford Escorts became Ferraris. Down each flank, Simpson and White rampaged like Ferrari's prancing horse, turbocharger at full chat, accelerating from nought to 30 in two seconds, leaving West Ham trailing in exhaust smoke. Fifty-seven minutes Simpson off down his left wing, Gale and Potts in his wake, a low cross into the flying boots – Imre Varadi's brave diving header. Two–one. Five minutes from time, Simpson, revelling in the tumult, the driving rain, the passion, the excitement, raced for the by line, a perfect touch, a mere touch of the ball to Varadi, Varadi's screaming shot to finish three–one.

A superb match of high quality. West Ham riding high will play worse and win. For City it is a sizzle in the pan, not a banger – more a toad-in-the-hole. *Manchester City:* Perry Suckling, John Gidman, Clive Wilson, Kenny Clements, Mick McCarthy, Tony Grealish, David White, Neil McNab, Imre Varadi, Paul Moulden, Paul Simpson. Substitute: Steve Redmond.

West Ham United: Phil Parkes, Steve Potts, George Parris, Tony Gale, Alvin Martin, Alan Devonshire, Mark Ward, Frank McAvennie, Paul Ince, Tony Cottee, Neil Orr. Substitute: Alan Dickens.

MANCHESTER CITY 1 – SHEFFIELD WEDNESDAY 0

Today Football League, Division One, 26 December 1986

Thirty-nine thousand here and frisson in the chill air before the match. Two sides of complete contrast, City committed to attack with two wingers, Wednesday a baffling amalgam of science and bulldoze. It began as a civilized First Division affair and finished as Wythenshawe Comprehensive School versus Attercliffe Grammar. To the first half. Shelton, Megson and Jonsson ran midfield for Wednesday. Shelton excelled, brilliant reader of the game; fast in the tackle, silk with skills. Little McNab, City's sole midfield, was like a tiny tot in the January sales rush. But City scored the vital goal. Free kick on the edge of the 'D', Gidman dummied; Paul Simpson curled the kick past the diving Hodge.

The second half, we mused, could be the Alamo. It was. Shelton retired on the hour; Wednesday cast science to the wind and gave the ball some real wellie. Jonsson assumed the Shelton role and everything was boomed to Chapman's head. Wednesday hit Suckling's bar twice. Higher went the ball, higher the crowd's excitement. It was fever, pantomime, St Trinian's stuff. Clements, in the absence of McCarthy, was so airborne he could claim a para-trooper's badge. Gidman was shed of 10 years, diving into tackles, hacking off the line. City's boys were growing up by the minute. Suckling made a despair-ing save, as Megson was clear; still on his knees he reflexed another fantastic save. Blue shirts embraced him and showered him with so many kisses I swear mistletoe hung from the bar. The whistle blew amid cacophony. To both sides, thanks for the vintage excitement. Nowt wrong with the game here – now!

Manchester City: Perry Suckling, John Gidman, Clive Wilson, Kenny Clements, Peter Reid, Steve Redmond, David White, Neil McNab, Imre Varadi, Paul Moulden, Paul Simpson. Substitute: Ian Brightwell.

Sheffield Wednesday: Martin Hodge, Chris Morris, Nigel Worthington, Paul

Hart, Lawrie Madden, Glynn Snodin, Siggi Jonsson, Gary Megson, Lee Chapman, Carl Shutt, Gary Shelton. Substitute: David Hirst.

MANCHESTER UNITED 0 – NORWICH 1

Today Football League, Division One, 27 December 1986
A Light in the North – Seven Years with Aberdeen – the title of Alex Ferguson's autobiography. How he accumulated the nous to succeed and lay low the Rangers/Celtic domination of *Ecosse*. A rough, tough, sharpened-elbows player with Queens Park, St Johnstone, Dunfermline, Rangers, Falkirk and Ayr United. He was a feared opponent. A gentleman who rivets ships on the Clyde, with a background in Govan, is not one to bandy words or blows with – a 16-stone stevedore from the Bronx is a softer touch. His management style is abrasive and confrontational, almost ruthless. He is now charged with restoring the glory to the Shrine and winning the Holy Grail – the League Championship.

Gone is flash Ron, the gold jewellery, the Pol Roger champagne, the cigars and the bantering bonhomie. It is a boot camp regime. R.S.M. Ferguson rules. Jankers, doghouse, confined to barracks, time on the hill, a sojourn in the glasshouse await those unfortunates who dare cross him. A man with a mission. Will he write another autobiography? *Another Light in the North – Eight Years with Manchester United.* It will be lively reading. His tenure at the Shrine has been but a few weeks. In that time United have lost at Oxford, Wimbledon, Norwich and Southampton. They lie eighth from bottom. Even Luton Town, Watford, Norwich, Wimbledon and Southampton are above them. The supplicants are restless. Ten thousand supplicants, disciples, apostles and agnostics returned to the Shrine today to pay homage to the heroes of Anfield yesterday (they won). Forty-four thousand six hundred and ten gave heart and voice to a first half of oohs and aahs. Bryan Robson, Captain Marvel, playing centre back, still contrived two headers and a shot on goal. Strachan's boomer was tipped over the bar by Gunn. The Norwich keeper. 'Ooh, aah, Strachers – you be havin' ye old black spot,' said Bryan Gunn. Long John Silver Ferguson applied his non-silver tongue to his team – they responded as if 'Fiery Jack' was in their jockstraps. Olsen impishly. Sivebaek stylish and composed, Whiteside, as always, the mobile roadroller. The team looked tight, good shape, good heart. Nil–nil at half-time. Norwich were organized, tempering skill with caution. A little ambition from Crook, Gordon and Rosario, nothing to suggest a win.

In every match there is a turning point. The apocalypse came five minutes into the second half. Bryan Robson stretched to a tackle, fearless and feckless as ever, collapsed in a writhing heap, a scenario all too familiar at the Shrine. Jim McGregor, the physiotherapist, rushed on – Captain Marvel hobbled off – yes, the hamstring again.

'Fortune is not satisfied with injuring a man only once.' Inspiration gone, doubts return. Stapleton, that player's player, the fearsome striker, dropped to centre back. O'Brien played midfield. United became mortal and vulnerable. Norwich are a sweet team, well-coached, organized like a Royal Marines platoon, no hedonists or gargantuans in their midst, and they blossomed. Ian Crook, their number seven, revealed the Puskas touch, rolling the ball under his right boot, then taking off with his left, at speed. A slick ground pass to Culverhouse, his fullback, Culverhouse's chip near post – Kevin Drinkell headed unopposed past a stranded Walsh, the United keeper. Norwich thus began the grand assault, broad sweeping strokes on the canvas full of fire and imagination. Biggins shot full of meat, Walsh made the save of the season. One–nil to Norwich, and they jumped for joy at the whistle.

Christmas is ruined at the Shrine. Mr Ferguson, having carved his turkey, will wield the cleaver on his team. Davenport, such a success at Forest, is lost among the Big Oaks here. Too fitful, too frail. Peter Barnes is not a Ferguson player – lacks focus. McGrath, a tower at centre back, has dodgy knees. Kevin Moran is injury-prone – a one-man accident looking for somewhere to happen. Sivebaek and Duxberry at fullback, super-smooth going forward, lack snap, crackle and pop in retreat. Mr Ferguson is misanthropic – to be a friend of the human race is not in my line.

Manchester United: Gary Walsh, Jan Sivebaek, Colin Gibson, Norman Whiteside, Billy Earton, Mike Duxberry, Bryan Robson, Gordon Strachan, Frank Stapleton, Peter Davenport, Jesper Olsen. Substitute: Liam O'Brien.

Norwich City: Bryan Gunn, Ian Culverhouse, Tony Spearing, Steve Bruce, Mike Phelan, Ian Butterworth, Ian Crook, Kevin Drinkell, Wayne Biggins, Robert Rosario, Dale Gordon. Substitute: Trevor Putney.

EVERTON 2 – SHEFFIELD WEDNESDAY 0

Today Football League, Division One, 17 January 1987

> *We learn wisdom from failure much more than success. We discover what will do by finding out what will not do.*

Transported back to New Year's Eve 1983. Desolation at Goodison. I wrote then, 'A chilling east wind blew the Christmas goodwill through the echoing rafters as 13,000, the lowest gate of the season, huddled in critical apprehension.' Everton have scored one goal in December.

The game was stale and barren. Coventry played long ball and offside. Misplaced passes, grotesque shooting, tension flooding the terraces and the players. The match was goalless, without passion, and dreary. Boos, jeers and catcalls. The crisis of 1983 was real. Was Howard Kendall about to board the Everton taxi, the Mafiosi ride to anonymity?

What ensued is almost fictional. The celebrated suicidal back pass of Brock at Oxford that turned a flood tide of failure into glorious success. Inspirational signing of players. The establishing of pure style along with success. The glitter of the silver of the boardroom table. The return of the faithful. The end of gloom and despond, and above all the silencing of Golden Era nostalgia.

The fans remember with joy Ball, Harvey and Kendall, but the talk today is euphoric about the current side of Sharp and Heath, no longer Lineker. Of Ratcliffe and Watson – another two inspired signings. Of Neville, the Bury binman, now the world's finest goalkeeper. Of Kevin, lock-picking left boot. Of Paul Power's metamorphosis from ugly duckling to white swan.

The pitch at Goodison was perfection, the under-soil temperature several degrees higher than the frozen faithful numbering 33,000, stamping feet and clapping chapped hands in the bitter chill.

Howard Kendall received a gallon of amber nectar to celebrate six wins on the trot. A small damsel with blue shirt and blue, slim, matching limbs was the Everton mascot. Everton were quickly in overdrive, Sheedy bringing a save from Hodge's hardly warmed-up palms in the first minute.

On 15 minutes, Power's shot was handled by Megson. Trevor Steven took the classic penalty. Low, hard, fast to Hodge's left. Hodge guessed the direction, got a hand to the ball, but it hit the back stanchion as Hodge stamped his feet in disgust. Wednesday had disputed the penalty – the linesman, though, was adamant.

Thirty minutes Sheedy's free kick – headed by Megson almost on to Dave Watson's mighty frame. Dave nonchalantly headed the bouncing ball over the advancing Hodge. Two–nil.

Everton were on song. Sheedy, under the gaze of that mighty wing half Joe Mercer, was pure delight. Little sly passes; chips; booming long balls; a vast repertoire of time-old skills. Steven was in flight. Heath will-o'-the-wisp. Sharp a yard quicker than Madden – who isn't? But Heath was unlucky, and profligate with the chances. Half-time, two–nil.

We awaited the second half. Wednesday's aerial bombardment never materialized. The match declined into a scramble; Chamberlain, the substitute, was on. Snodin was second-half substitute for Dave Watson. He played centre midfield. He is very fast; slick passes – a nose for the game. It is his debut. The midfield has power and style.

Snodin, Sheedy and Steven could become as famed as Ball, Kendall and Harvey – a classic blend of the busy and the beautiful. Everton are second in the league behind the Arsenal. They have the highest gate of the season: 48,247. Mr Kendall – you alchemist – the championship is yours.

Everton: Neville Southall, Gary Stevens, Neil Pointon, Kevin Ratcliffe, Dave Watson, Paul Power, Trevor Steven, Adrian Heath, Graeme Sharp, Alan Harper, Kevin Sheedy. Substitute: Ian Snodin.

Sheffield Wednesday: Martin Hodge, Chris Morris, Nigel Worthington, Mark Smith, Lawrie Madden, Glynn Snodin, Siggi Jonsson, Gary Megson, Lee Chapman, Carl Bradshaw, Gary Shelton. Substitute: Mark Chamberlain.

LIVERPOOL 2 – NEWCASTLE UNITED 0

Today Football League, Division One, 27 January 1987

Liverpool's casualty ward of walking wounded and bedridden is critical. Beglin and McDonald – fractured limbs. Nicol, McMahon and Mr Dalglish carrying chronic strains. Thus, today Lawrenson played unorthodox number three, Venison number two, Wark, Molby and Whelan midfield. The style that flowed as from nature last season was forced. Molby looked as is he had led a Viking invasion and could not pillage or even find the enemy. Wark is well adrift, never found his touch, saw two booming shots travel wide, and is clearly not a happy footballer. But at the back Gillespie is in brilliant form, and Lawrenson embarking on those exciting surging runs at least drew adrenalin. The first half, apart from three hefty shots from Wark, Walsh and Rush, was insipid. But on 54 minutes Johnston on the right took a rapid throw-in to Molby, Molby thumped far post, McDonald jumped and missed, Paul Walsh's first goal in 15 games. Liverpool upped the pace as of yore. Roeder and Jackson were competitive at centre backs for Newcastle. Grobbelaar made two crucial saves. But Ian Rush, with his twenty-seventh goal of the season, drove Newcastle to mere distraction. 'Of all ills that men endure – the cheap and universal cure.'

Rush took the ball cleanly as Gillespie headed down Whelan's lob. A goal of venom that rips hearts from brave men. And Newcastle were brave in defeat. At the whistle, Beardsley stayed on the pitch, obviously overwhelmed by the Geordies, several thousand strong who had Blaydon Raced vociferously throughout a frankly inspiring match.

Liverpool: Bruce Grobbelaar, Gary Gillespie, Barry Venison, Mark Lawrenson, Ronnie Whelan, Alan Hansen, Paul Walsh, Craig Johnston, Ian Rush, Jan Molby, John Wark. Substitute: Alan Irvine.

Newcastle United: Martin Thomas, Alan Davies, Ken Wharton, David McCreery, Peter Jackson, Glenn Roeder, Neil McDonald, Andy Thomas, Paul Goddard, Peter Beardsley, Darren Jackson. Substitute: Tony Nesbit.

LIVERPOOL 3 – LEICESTER FOSSE 3

Today Football League, Division One, 14 February 1987

"Tis St Valentines's Day. Lovers entwined on banks of sweet musk. 'There's rosemary, that's for remembrance; pray, love, remember; and there is pansies – that's for thoughts.' Liverpool today were schizoid. Fosse unwilling lovers; a match of non-remembrance unworthy of cerebral thought. Liverpool were divorced from their principles.

Sometime a little skill, a modicum of commitment, but a defence that exposed itself like a strumpet in Montmartre. A cataclysmic finish to a barren heretofore. How did Leicester put three past Grobbelaar? Why were Leicester not dispatched to the knacker's yard?

Let me chart the goals. Walsh and Rush had clouted the bar and post before Walsh, taking Rush's wall pass, put Liverpool one up. Time, 30 minutes. Five minutes later Craig Johnston headed into his own goal. One–one. Forty minutes Ian Rush took Molby's pass and bundled a goal. Half-time, two–one.

The second half was four minutes old when Johnston's rather soft centre was neatly nicked in for a goal by Ian Rush. Three–one. Leicester now were reeling as Liverpool heaved and sweated through a greasy spell and poured on the Leicester goal. Hectic scenes ensued but from a large clearance Alan Smith loped away for a goal suiting his price tag. Three–two.

Two minutes from time, Paul Walsh centred far post. Ian Rush headed down – lovely goal. Surely Leicester Fosse were down? The battle of the bantams between Wilson and Johnston ended in a fall and two submissions for Johnston. We laughed a lot. Alan Smith wiped the smiles away, stealing in for his second goal and Leicester's third. No St Valentine's Day Massacre and Leicester Fosse steal the bouquets, hearts and minds.

Liverpool: Bruce Grobbelaar, Gary Gillespie, Barry Venison, Mark Lawrenson, Ronnie Whelan, Alan Hansen, Paul Walsh, Craig Johnston, Ian Rush, Jan Molby, Steve McMahon. Substitute: Kenny Dalglish.

Leicester Fosse: Ian Andrews, Simon Morgan, Mark Venus, John O'Neill, Steve Walsh, Gary McAllister, Ali Mauchlen, Mitch D'Avray, Alan Smith, Paul Ramsey, Ian Wilson. Substitute: Phil Horner.

LEEDS UNITED 2 – QUEENS PARK RANGERS 1
The FA Cup – Fifth Round, 21 February 1987

Billy Bremner's Rubicon today. He crosses the river of no return. In 49 BC the mighty Caesar crossed the Rubicon, the river that divided old Italy from Gaul. Once crossed, he could never retrace his steps – civil war was declared. No civil war at Yelland Road yet, but civil unrest, civil disobedience.

Among the fur coats and Rolls-Royces that thronged like old times, a large hooligan fringe element defied law and order, a taint of the times we endure. For five minutes in the second half they taunted and fought the police. Helmets tumbled, fists flew, the mob ebbed and flowed. Yelland Road was a bear pit, a cockpit of incessant din. Miscreants were hauled off to the cells, uneasy peace set in. Leeds are marooned in Division Two. Even Millwall, Oldham, Portsmouth, Plymouth Argyle and Stoke City are above them. QPR are safe midway in the First Division. Jim Smith, the Bald Eagle, the manager, has built a team around honest sweat and the work ethic. Billy's Rubicon.

Leeds, roared on by 31,000, sprang to, attacked, nothing to lose but pride and Bremner's job. Fifteen minutes a long ball played far post to John Pearson, their beanpole centre forward. He headed back across goal, Ian Baird rose above a mass of hooped shirts to head past David Seaman, the QPR keeper. Seaman, a Yorkshire lad, never made the first team here at Leeds. In 1982 he went to Peterborough, on to Birmingham and thence QPR. He is in the England squad – how Leeds could use his talents now. Andy Ritchie, that titchy, itchy, Ritchie, should have scored – Seaman denied him. QPR hustled out of their sophisticated carpet soccer, rolled up their sleeves for a blow, wind and cataract Yorkshire battle. Sixty-four minutes under severe QPR pressure, in a packed goal-mouth, David Rennie put through his own goal for the QPR equalizer.

This was the iron test for Bremner's young side. QPR have seasoned players like Fenwick, Robbie James, Martin Allen, Clive Walker, Sammy Lee; they have seen it, been there, kept the T-shirt. Bremner's team gave all like a pack of wild dogs. Contested every yard of ground, tackling like starving lions, closing down space. Young John Sheridan, slight and knock-kneed, sprayed passes like John Giles of yore: he ran the show. QPR, vulnerable at the back, reeled under pressure. Near misses, Seaman's huge height in the thick, a rollicking Cup tie. Eighty-five minutes a Leeds corner near post; Pearson once again back-headed across goal. Brendan Ormsby flung his all-in wrestler frame through the ruck to head bullet-style at the far post. The exuberant mob flooded the pitch – chaired off the players. The fur coats retired to the Dom Pérignon, the hoi polloi to the greasy spoon. A quaint mix again at Leeds – there is real money here. All fans, rich and impoverished, ask: 'Did Bremner cross the Rubicon?'

Leeds United: Mervyn Day, Neil Aspin, Micky Adams, David Rennie, Jack Ashurst, Brendan Ormsby, John Stiles, John Sheridan, John Pearson, Ian Baird, Andy Ritchie.

Queens Park Rangers: David Seaman, Warren Neil, Robbie James, Clive Walker, Gary Chivers, Terry Fenwick, Martin Allen, Mike Fillery, Gary Bannister, John Byrne, Wayne Fereday. Substitute: M. Lee, McGuire.

LIVERPOOL 1 – SOUTHAMPTON 0

Today Football League, Division One, 28 February 1987

John Aldridge, on his first full game for Liverpool, repaid the first instalment of the £750,000 invested in him by the club. The high-water mark in a low-water match of shifting defence, ill-tempered skirmish, niggly tackling and negated skill. The goal was retribution for a ghastly foul on Irvine by Cockerill, Southampton's motorman.

Jan Molby shaped as if to thunder a shot from the resultant free kick. But with a little shimmy he floated the ball wide and left of the massed blue shirts. Aldridge, lurking with intent, rose high and headed with enormous power past Shilton.

I suppose we expected too much of Liverpool. Aldridge playing alongside Ian Rush. Nigel Spackman on his full debut. Gillespie, the Liverpool centre back, hobbled off early in the match. Irvine replaced him. Liverpool with three strikers and Whelan at left back. Players made runs, the ball went t' other way. Players bumped into each other in patternless endeavour. I expected Deborah Kerr to materialize and croon, 'Getting to know you – getting to know all about you'.

Southampton, apace fielding reserves with anonymous names, had seen Lawrence, their centre forward, spoon a chance over Grobbelaar's bar, then bring a brilliant save from that worthy Brucie. Townsend, the fire-eating Southampton number four, smote the bar. Southampton funnelled back fast restricted space and boredom set in, enlivened by titch Danny Wallace, a cross between Che Guevara and Blackbeard the pirate! He was eventually booked. He smiled. There were not many of those about today – smiles, that is!

Liverpool: Bruce Grobbelaar, Gary Gillespie, Barry Venison, Mark Lawrenson, Ronnie Whelan, Alan Hansen, Nigel Spackman, Craig Johnston, Ian Rush, Jan Molby, John Aldridge. Substitute: Alan Irvine.

Southampton: Peter Shilton, Gerry Forrest, Steve Baker, Andy Townsend, Mark Wright, Kevin Bond, Matthew Le Tissier, Glenn Cockerill, George Lawrence, Gordon Hobson, Danny Wallace. Substitute: N.F. Gittens.

MANCHESTER UNITED 2 – MANCHESTER CITY 0

Today Football League, Division One, 7 March 1987

Manchester United are the champions, of Manchester. Both managers had to hype the match frenetically to attract 48,000 fans and dispel 'end-of-season' apathy. Mr Ferguson by scouring Europe eyeing up Mark Hughes, who is distinctly '*non viva España*' nowadays. Mr Frizzell playing for the Bank of Scotland overdraft, costing £1,000 a day in interest charges, floating stories of signing international talent, anybody from Paul Walsh to Robert Redford and Joan Collins.

So, chilled with expectation, the faithful supplicants arrived at the Shrine. United's to glory, City to pray!

As the snowflakes fell, whirling in the icy wind, and as the non-committed froze to their seats, United generated a hot rhythm that threatened to overwhelm City. Bryan Robson and Gordon Strachan were a mile high in class, Robson, the 'all-action man', back to his inspirational best. Behind them McGrath and Gibson were arrogant, almost contemptuous of City's puny attack. City were in desperation, flying into tackles, chasing the ball – and rampant red shirts. Half-time, no score. City goalkeeper with stinging palms. Bailey, his opposite number, blue and numb with cold.

On the hour, Strachan floated the ball to City's goal area. Suckling, magnificent all afternoon, keeping his side alive, found the ball eluding him. McGrath and Robson were in fast. The ball ricocheted into the goal from Reid's lunging legs. Goal to Robson, or own goal Reid.

No doubt about the second goal four minutes from time. Davenport, the substitute, a square pass, swept into goal by Robson. Several personal *tête-à-têtes*. Octopus Whiteside, whose elbows are from the Hammer House of Horrors, versus McCarthy and Clements. Both the latter were booked for clattering fouls on Norman. Norman thus wins on points. Alas, Division Two and a distraught bank manager await impoverished Manchester City.

Manchester United: Gary Bailey, Jan Sivebaek, Colin Gibson, Norman Whiteside, Paul McGrath, Kevin Moran, Bryan Robson, Mike Duxbury, Liam O'Brien, Terry Gibson, Gordon Strachan. Substitute: Peter Davenport.

Manchester City: Perry Suckling, Peter Reid, Clive Wilson, Kenny Clements, Mick McCarthy, Ian Brightwell, Graham Baker, Neil McNab, Imre Varadi, Paul Moulden, Paul Simpson. Substitute: Steve Redmond.

EVERTON 3 – SOUTHAMPTON 0
Today Football League, Division One, 14 March 1987

Everton's winless run of misery is over. Mark Wright, the Southampton centre back, did not fire the starting pistol; he shot himself and Peter Shilton with an astonishing 12th-minute own goal. He tried to head clear Adrian Heath's volley. The ball flew like Concorde between Shilton and his near post. I swear a mere twelve inches of space. Shilton shook his head as a Parliamentary hack at *Question Time*. Two minutes later Paul Power took Heath's little tip and ran, and smote Everton's second. Mr Shilton by now had, as they say up here, a little 'cob' on. His display subsequently was inspired, brave and sometimes beyond belief. Adrian Heath, shooting into an empty net, will ask: 'How, and from where, did Shilton materialize?' Half-time, two–nil. On 55 minutes even Shilton was defeated. Trevor Steven's raking cross – the massive frame of Dave Watson rucking through – a final horizontal launch at the ball; bullet header, number three.

Southampton, despite a flurry of elbows, tackles and combat, never showed, Everton firing on all 12 cylinders at least for a few laps. Watson at last dominant. Snodin or Mr Snodin, as they say in Fazakerley, now sure of touch and position – he is looking class. Van Den Hauwe back in his positive style after injury. Wayne Clarke on his debut was subtle in the air with his deflections; his control was economic, his laying off augurs well for the School of Science. Sheedy's return will prime the V12 to peak power. But as this is the year of the big bang, figures are paramount, profit the motive. Twenty-six thousand, five hundred and sixty-four were here. Ninety-three Southampton followers on the terraces, 86 sitting in the stand. Guarded by 27 bobbies. I counted them – that is what you call insider trading.

Everton: Neville Southall, Gary Stevens, Pat Van Den Hauwe, Kevin Ratcliffe, Dave Watson, Peter Reid, Trevor Steven, Adrian Heath, Wayne Clarke, Ian Snodin, Paul Power. Substitute: Alan Harper.

Southampton: Peter Shilton, Gerry Forrest, Steve Baker, Jimmy Case, Mark Wright, Kevin Bond, Matthew Le Tissier, Glenn Cockerill, George Lawrence, Gordon Hobson, Andy Townsend. Substitute: Gary Bull.

MANCHESTER CITY 0 – NEWCASTLE UNITED 0
Today Football League, Division One, 21 March 1987

Division Two beckons both sides like the grim reaper bottom of Division One. At 2.30 p.m. this afternoon, Mr Swales, the beleaguered chairman of City, known to close associates as P.J., to the hoi polloi less politely, led me to a secret room. On a table lay a computer silently tabulating bodies through turnstiles, a middle graphic totalled up. Seven thousand were in at 2.35 p.m. We knelt before it in supplication, P.J. earnestly, your reporter ambivalently. I did not wish to be present at City's interment. The game of football, adored by romantics, died though. The match was riddled by fear; performed at high speed, elbows, nudges, block tackles, misplaced passes – a hectic catalogue of base relegation struggle. The first half was suffocating. Paul Stewart, City's £200,000 centre forward, was neat with lay-off; looked strong on the ground; weak in the air where Roeder picked him off. Thomas, in Newcastle's goal, was the busier of the two goalkeepers. One flying save from McCarthy's head was memorable. At the other end, Suckling was athletic, Cunningham, the Newcastle number nine, profligate. Varadi hashed the chance of the match. There were delicacies on view, there is always something to savour. Today it was Clive Wilson's rhythm and class for City, and Stephenson's bandy legs beating a Terry McDermott tune. Peter Beardsley also delighted. But it is back to the computer, a large gin and tonic, P.J., and the vespers to keep City in the hallowed division.

Manchester City: Perry Suckling, John Gidman, Clive Wilson, Kenny Clements, Mick McCarthy, Tony Grealish, David White, Neil McNab, Imre Varadi, Paul Stewart, Steve Redmond. Substitute: Paul Simpson.

Newcastle United: Martin Thomas, Neil McDonald, Ken Wharton, David McCreery, Peter Jackson, Glenn Roeder, Paul Stephenson, Paul Goddard, Tony Cunningham, Peter Beardsley, Andy Anderson. Substitute: Darren Jackson.

MANCHESTER UNITED 2 – NOTTINGHAM FOREST 0
Today Football League, Division One, 28 March 1987

Once upon a music-hall time, there was a famous duo – Nervo and Knox. I ponder if Alex and his sidekick, Archie Knox, achieve fame on that plane. Certainly 'Nervo' Ferguson will have twanged a nerve end or two afore then. Today he shuffled the pack of high-priced stars, ex-stars and stargazers. Eight positional changes to bring style to satisfy the 39,000 parishioners. They opened with a rampage. Woods, his number 11 prodigy, smote a drive that Walker, in contortion, hoofed off the line. But then, on 13 minutes, Frank Stapleton, not really wanted on voyage, jumped high to a cross, headed down to McGrath's bootlace. McGrath half-volleyed past Sutton.

Thirty-five minutes. Norman the war-man Whiteside was felled as an oak tree in a gale. Chris Fairclough, the Forest number five, jumped on the prone Norman, and the referee dismissed Mr Fairclough. Forest, with 10 men, were swamped with United's ideas and new-found aggression. Robson's left foot began the moves. Moses, that mobile reaper and binder, tackled everything above grass that moved. O'Brien and Woods abetted with skills. Forty-six minutes a sweet cross-field move involving Stapleton and O'Brien. Robson on the far post swung his left boot. Two–nil.

The second half was wind-blown and forgettable. Forest, without Carr, lacked width and missed Walsh. They played three strikers, including Paul Wilkinson, but Walsh in United's goal was in deep-freeze throughout. Mr Clough has pause for thought, as Forest fly tonight to the sun in Malta. By the way, were not Nervo and Knox part of the Crazy Gang? Who were the others? Flanaghan and Allen and Monsewer Eddie Gray!

Manchester United: Gary Walsh, Jan Sivebaek, Colin Gibson, Liam O'Brien,

Paul McGrath, Mike Duxbury, Bryan Robson, Remi Moses, Frank Stapleton, Norman Whiteside, Wood 'Pecker'. Substitute: Arthur Albiston.
Nottingham Forest: Steve Sutton, Gary Fleming, Stuart Pearce, Des Walker, Chris Fairclough, Ian Bowyer, Brett Williams, Johnny Metgod, Nigel Clough, Gary Birtles, Gary Mills. Substitute: 'Bravo' Fortes.

LIVERPOOL 3 – NOTTINGHAM FOREST 0
Today Football League, Division One, 18 April 1987
The dichotomy of Dalglish is the story here. Mr Dalglish the manager, whose enigmatic style bemuses most critics. Kenny Dalglish the player. An ageing maestro whose legs are going, but the brain is still computerized; brilliant and light years in thought above the dross. Today he selected an orthodox side. Rush and Walsh upfront. Himself behind them. Ablett, a beanpole youngster, at number three. Thirty-seven thousand fans backed them with vocal support, and the result is great joy at Anfield. Dalglish began the scoring. Lovely sweeping move with Johnston in firecracker mood, and Rush involved. Dalglish, on the edge of the box, cocked his right boot, and a Dalglish special zoomed past Sutton.

Forest apace had points to prove. Metgod was intelligently probing, Clough was subtle in distribution. Franz Carr was a delight on the right. Revelling in his innate shills, beating Ablett, his marker, at will. An old-fashioned winger in top form. But Liverpool were determined and fought hard. Venison was composed; Walsh ran like a weasel on a rabbit, McMahon the motorman, a better player than he is with Molby. Dalglish himself, like all great players in the twilight zone, was in turn magnificent and abysmal. But groans were dispelled on 52 minutes. Dalglish a defence-splitting pass to the new boy Ablett. A fast low centre and Whelan volleyed the second. Confidence came on the flood. Sixty-eight minutes Rush set up number three. Fighting off a challenge, a bobbled ball across goal. Ablett blasted his first goal for the club. Forest left to an ovation, they smote the bar and post three times. Mr Dalglish was smiling. Will his legs recover for Monday?

Dalglish is/was a great. His body swerve and balance equal to Peter Doherty, Raich Carter, Alex Young, George Best, even the iron Pele. His goals something to cherish. Exhuberant, sometimes flash, always clinical. A fantastic brain. Vision like a night-fighter pilot or a bombardier. Dalglishes are rare animals.
Liverpool: Bruce Grobbelaar, Gary Gillespie, Barry Venison, Gary Ablett, Ronnie Whelan, Alan Hansen, Kenny Dalglish, Craig Johnston, Ian Rush, Paul Walsh, Steve McMahon. Substitute: John Aldridge.
Nottingham Forest: Steve Sutton, Gary Fleming, Stuart Pearce, Des Walker, Colin Foster, Ian Bowyer, Franz Carr, Johnny Metgod, Nigel Clough, Paul Wilkinson, Brian Rice. Substitute: Gary Mills.

EVERTON 3 – NEWCASTLE UNITED 0
Today Football League, Division One, 20 April 1987
The School of Science is a pressure cooker in the boiling sun. Five thousand

Geordies in high spirits to blow the lid off. Forty-three thousand, five hundred and seventy-six in all – dismayed by the fact that Everton's engine room was defunct. Reid and Sheedy out with injury. A day for men in the blue shirts. What an unforgettable day for Wayne Clarke. A hat trick for him to crown a display that had the Goodison faithful hoarse, frenetic, in paroxysms of unrestrained joy. But Everton had to graft and sweat; apply and concentrate for their lives. Ian Snodin assumed from the start the total responsibility for the absence of stars. He, Alan Harper, Trevor Steven and Paul Power covered length and width at Goodison. Newcastle, on a confidence high, tried to match the football pedigree. Gascoigne was ebullient; too much so and was booked. Snodin cleared off his line. Thomas in Newcastle's goal pulled off incredible saves.

Half-time, no goals. But at last, nerves were raw and pressure rising – deadlock broken. Paul Power's left foot produced a floating cross to the far post. Wayne Clarke rose high, his header hit the post but the ball was in the net. Some brilliant football flowed from Steven, Stevens, Heath and Snodin. Nine minutes from time, Harper's inspired through ball to Heath; Heath's little ball juggle a pass square to Wayne Clarke – Clarke hesitated for an age – then the shot: two–nil. That pause was like a reprise – a dream. Then, in the dying seconds, Heath's fast cross from the right. Wayne Clarke's header. Pandemonium. McDonald sent off. The crowd delirious with joy at the news from Old Trafford and at the 24-carat show at the School of Science.

I monitored young Gascoigne, about whom incredible deeds are forecast. He is talented, looks for and finds space. His touch is delicate, almost fey, but incisive. He dribbles in the old-fashioned way, taking an almost childish delight in embarrassing the opposition. He has unique style, wasted on inferior players around him. Either Newcastle enlist talent or Gascoigne will move on. He obviously has a weight problem. He is porky – too many Mars bars or Newcastle Browns!

Everton: Neville Southall, Gary Stevens, Neil Pointon, Kevin Ratcliffe, Dave Watson, Alan Harper, Trevor Steven, Adrian Heath, Wayne Clarke, Ian Snodin, Paul Power. Substitute: Ian Marshall.

Newcastle United: Martin Thomas, Neil McDonald, Ken Wharton, Darren Jackson, Glenn Roeder, Paul Stephenson, Paul Gascoigne, Paul Goddard, Martin Thomas, Brian Tinnion, Peter Jackson. Substitute: Ian Stewart.

ROBB WILTON, BARNEY COLEHAN

Robb Wilton, a post-war comedian of wit drier than Krug champagne. Barney Colehan, the great impresario, the maestro, the great BBC producer.

FOOTBALL DIRECTOR: RECORDED 26 OCTOBER 1952

The day I became director of our football club, the Rambling Wanderers, my missus said to me: 'What do you have to do as a football director?'

Well, for the life of me I couldn't think, so I said: 'You're supposed to sit in the directors' box and watch the match, and at half-time you have to nip in the boardroom in case they have any booze, and when the team is playing away you're supposed to go with them.'

She said: 'Well, I can't see there's a lot of brain work attached to that.'

I said: 'Perhaps you can't, but there's a lot of responsibilities, tons of responsibilities. I can't think of any at the moment, but you have to have your wits about you.'

Look at our team, the Rambling Wanderers, only a small team, but they're triers, been trying to win a match ever since they started. I've sat in the directors' box, match after match, through rain, hail, snow and sleet, year in, year out, all on my own. The other director, Tom Atkinson, used to sit with me, but he got so ashamed of our team he always sits in the visitors' box now, pretending he belongs to the other side.

But our team's too old, that's what's the matter. Our centre forward, Alec Moorhouse, he's 57, another 10 years and he'll be finished altogether as a player. Then there's the goalkeeper, Jack Rogers. He never seems to be trying to stop 'em, let two through one match. Of course, he's not well. He's got lumbago. That's all through him stooping down so much picking the ball up out of the back of the net.

The nearest we've ever been to winning a match was five years ago, when we only lost seven–nil, then we seemed to go all to pieces.

But our spectators are a miserable lot. The lads get no encouragement from them at all. A few weeks ago at one match, the names they called our players, and the language they used; if there had been a policeman about I could have had the three of them arrested. We used to always have a policeman on duty at every match years ago, but he got fed up and we never see him now.

And our other director, Tom Atkinson, he gets so despondent, says he wants to see our team win one match before he dies. He's not well either. I asked him the other day, I said: 'What's the matter with you, Tom? What's the trouble?'

He said: 'I've got a bad back.'

So I told him, I said: 'There's no need to worry about that. Our team's got two.' But it's no good grumbling about the team, they're all good lads, not at football, but they're all good lads, they're only a reserve team. We haven't got a first; the second is bad enough.

Our manager, Tom Shaw… well, Tom's one of the best fellows in the world, but he's no idea of football. He's got no control over them, he's too soft-hearted. If it's a very cold day he tells them to keep their overcoats on. Now every time it rains, I wouldn't be a bit surprised to see them all turn out with umbrellas.

But there was one match we played a bad game; oh our side played a shocking game. We never looked like scoring; I don't think we could have scored if the other side hadn't turned up. Our outside right, he's got no brains at all, and he's a very touchy sort of fellow. Just because I shouted to him, 'Get

Bob Paisley, the greatest manager in history.
I dedicate my offering to him, and wax long about him
and his wonderful teams.

Above left: The immortals – Joe Mercer, Stanley Matthews, Jackie Mudie, Stan Mortenson. Joe, my best pal in football. The '53 Wembley Trio. The great Stanley I praise in an essay. Jackie Mudie – that tiny inside forward; so little-mentioned, but a class, clever, inventive player; disadvantaged by heavyweight ball and bog pitches. He never received the praise he deserved. Stan Mortenson – my blood brother; fiery, dynamic, archetypal centre forward of the old Dixie Dean/ Tommy Lawton/Ted Drake school of dashers, shooters and headers.

Below left: What would these be worth in today's barmy currency? Gary Lineker, pre-Walker's Crisps – a super centre forward; with more aggression, he could have been in the top ten of all time. Peter Reid, with real hair. First name on my team sheet. What a player!

Top: Bobby Charlton joined me on a launch of the Over Fifties' Fitness Club. Bob, benign as ever, let it all hang out – I breathed in!

Right: Arthur Ellis – 'Ay! Stuart! Two and two mek five!' I devote a chapter to this great referee and gentleman.

Above: The inimitable George Best. One of three footballers, icons, legends, whose genius will live forever. Best, Pelé, Matthews. George would help me every Christmas to entertain 2,000 underprivileged children on stage in Manchester. It was always a riot; the children wild with excitement. *Regardez* the mini Christmas beauties. Behind me is Beverley Dunn – a gorgeous airhead who married Omar Sharif. On George's immediate right: Jennifer Lowe, a milkmaid from Warrington. Beverley and Jenny were score girls on *Knockout*. Far left is Yvonne Ormes, Miss UK, Europe and the World. She never realised she was Venus de Milo. She preferred Crewe.

Right: Happy days at BBC Manchester. An Armstrong Siddeley Star Sapphire folding bicycle and a snappy salute from Harry, my beloved commisionaire. Note the crease in Harry's immaculate trousers. The BBC – a league of gentlemen in those days. Officer corps and other ranks in harmony, sharing respect and love of the job. The hair was all mine, or mane.

Left: BBC days at Manchester. The studio: a shoebox above the District Bank. No VT in those days – only film which broke regularly. I treasured those breakdowns – it gave me a chance to be human. Mr Birt curtailed all that, giving you real hard news.

Below: *A Question of Sport*. Not very sporting. I was the first question master on this show. Somebody up there did not take a shine – I was shunted off to *It's A Knockout*.

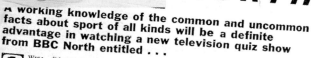

ABOUT THE NORTH

A working knowledge of the common and uncommon facts about sport of all kinds will be a definite advantage in watching a new television quiz show from BBC North entitled . . .

A Question of SPORT

1 **MON** **6.15** WELL, did you know who won the world's face-slapping championship? Or who were the batsmen at the other end with Len Hutton when he made his record-breaking score of 364 in a Test Match? Or who was the first man to be beaten by Rocky Marciano—when he won the world heavyweight championship title?

This sort of question may never have kept you unduly awake at night. But a working knowledge of the common and the uncommon facts about sport will be a definite advantage in watching BBC North's quiz-show, *A Question of Sport*.

'Essentially,' says producer Nick Hunter, 'the quiz will be visual. It is not the kind of thing that you can enjoy without the picture. What we have tried to do is to present each question in television terms.'

The programme will be introduced by Stuart Hall, a familiar face in Northern living rooms as the breezy anchorman of the Manchester edition of *Look North*. And Stuart would seem to be an appropriate sporting choice, because sport plays a vital role in his life.

He made his debut as a broadcaster as a contributor to *Sport Spotlight*. He has covered virtually every kind of sport in the course of his career. As a teenager he could run 100 yards in ten seconds. He played soccer as an amateur for Crystal Palace. And he has roared round Oulton Park and Silverstone in an Elva-Climax and an Austin Healey.

'My only claim to fame as a racing driver,' says Stuart wryly, 'is that I never won a race. I only ever came second.'

In *A Question of Sport* Stuart Hall will find himself in some top-class sporting company. Captaining one team will be Fred Trueman; captaining the other will be Cliff Morgan. Making up Fred's team will be Mary Rand and Henry Cooper, and kicking for goal with Cliff will be Roger Taylor and Bobby Moore.

'The important thing about the show,' says Nick Hunter, 'is that it is not a statistical exercise. In other words, we're not really interested in asking someone how many goals someone won the Cup with in 1922.

'Sports fans, after all, remember incidents, not statistics—great deeds which remain in the mind for years afterwards. And we shall be showing them film clips of many of these memorable incidents in sport—and inviting them to pit their wits against the stars.'

The ability to identify great occasions will be only one aspect of *A Question of Sport*. There will also be a historical section; another where the hobbies of famous sporting personalities are described, and competitors are invited to identify them; one in which they are challenged about unusual world records; and an oddball section where film of some of the most unusual 'sporting' events ever seen will be featured.

The programme will be introduced by Stuart Hall, the breezy anchorman of the Manchester edition of *Look North*

Mary Rand   Henry Cooper

FRED TRUEMAN'S TEAM

Roger Taylor   Bobby Moore

CLIFF MORGAN'S TEAM

Above: Hi there, folks – it's Tim. He's British; he's wholesome; he's terrific – can he pull out the big one?

Above left: From *This is Your Life* – Frannie Lee (centre) and Bumbles Summerbee. Iconoclastic Frannie's memorable moments are described in full. Bumbles was – still is – a bubbling eccentric. I treasure them both.

Left: From *This is Your Life*. On the set with Sgt Major Moran (centre) and Caesar Souness. Magic moments I shared with them, recounted within these pages.

Above: Real motor racing – you don't give a toss when it's someone else's machinery. More dodgems than Fangio; keep the tin basher happy. Hall leads Close, Lilford, Davina Galica through Old Hall – how apt.

Right: VLG 359 – where is she now? My first race on the opening day of Mallory Park. A pretty hot Austin Healey BN1 supported by the factory. I finished fourth. Observe the background. My pal in practice came off through the fence and put the steering wheel through his chest. (He recovered; the motor car didn't.)

Right: The aftermath of an epic motor race at Oulton Park. Lord Lilford (right) explains how Hall and Brian Close (left) fought like tigers over 15 laps. I beat Closie, who is totally fearless, with the crowd on its feet. I discovered later that he had the faster car and the heavy money at 25–1 was on him. His fondness for a wager is legendary!

rid of it,' he kicked the darned ball clean over the top of the stand right outside the ground, and we haven't seen it since, and it wasn't ours.

We play away our first match, playing the Rose and Crown on their ground. They don't close till three, so we can't kick off till half-past. They beat us 14–0 last season. Of course, there were two or three of them stone-cold sober. When we played them on our ground, it was a very different story: they only beat us 9–0.

But our defence is the weak part. I know where the trouble is, it's the defence. You can't blame forwards, they never yet got near enough to know if they could have scored if they had.

Then we've got Charlie Evans on the gate taking the money. What a headache that is. He's all right if they come in one at a time, every five minutes, but if there's a bit of a rush, like three or four all at once, he gets in a hell of a tangle. And when we put the prices up to 3d and 4d, that seemed to confuse him altogether. We took eleven and four pence at one match; of course, it was a cup tie, but he was eight and nine pence short on that. I wouldn't have cared, only we'd had a spot of bother over that game before it started. Their directors told ours, me and Tom, that before they turned up they wanted a guarantee of the gate money; they wanted 75 per cent. So we had to have a special directors' meeting, me and Tom, and Tom said: 'What is it they want?'

I told him, I said: 'They want 75 per cent of the gate money or we look like having no match.'

He said: 'They want what?'

I said: 'Seventy-five per cent.'

He said: 'Well, let 'em have it. We shall never take it.'

There was a bit of trouble at one match. A great big burly fellow, about six feet four, he wasn't half making a disturbance, shouting out and calling players for everything. He'd had a few. I went over to him and told him he'd have to leave the ground if he didn't keep quiet. As a matter of fact I went further than that. I said: 'Any more of that language and you'll be thrown out.'

He squared up to me and said: 'Oh, and who's going to throw me out?'

I said: 'I… can't just think at the moment.'

Anyhow, he said: 'What right have you to tell me I'll be thrown off the ground?'

I said: 'I'm the director.'

He said: 'And what reason have you for telling me I'll be thrown out?'

I said: 'Now that you ask me, and if you really want to know, you're drunk.'

He said: 'I'm drunk?'

I said: 'Definitely.'

He said: 'Do you think I'd be here if I was sober?'

I took the missus to see a match, the first game of football she'd ever seen, but it turned out a shocking day: poured with rain, the ground an absolute quagmire. We were sitting together on the stand, when all of a sudden our left back – oh, a big awkward lad, red-headed lad – took one lunging kick at the wet ball and hit the missus slap-bang right in the face. A damned good job we'd just changed seats.

And another time I remember – oh, great scot, look at the time. I've forgotten all about our directors' meeting, and they close at ten. Ta-ta, see you later.

SEASON 1985/86: 'I HAVE NEITHER WIT, NOR WORDS, NOR WORTH, ACTION, UTTERANCE OR POWER OF SPEECH TO STIR MEN'S BLOOD. I SPEAK ONLY RIGHT ON. I TELL YOU THAT WHICH YOU YOURSELVES DO KNOW.'

MANCHESTER CITY 1 – EVERTON 1
Canon Football League, Division One, October 1985

John Keats, an avid football fan, once wrote at this time of year, 'Season of mists and mellow fruitfulness, close bosom friend of the maturing City bank manager.' Poor City, submerged under a £4.6 million debt costing £1,000 per day in interest charges alone, have desperation writ large upon them. The first half deepened the gloom and frowns in the home directors' box. Everton playing intuitive, suave football at leisure, the touch passing, the hallmark of the trade, a joy to behold. Yet an aggressive City brought three acrobatic, incredible saves from young Mimms in the Everton goal for his first match. One a lunging header from McCarthy left that Yorkshire worthy simply open-mouthed. Then on 35 minutes a goal of quality. Gary Stevens cross, Gary Lineker's headed lay-off to Adrian Heath, who lashed the ball – through the ruck and past a helpless Nixon.

The City dressing-room at half-time must have been debtors' retreat, with Billy McNeil flourishing the bank balance. He is City's manager – not the bank's! Remember now thy Creator in the days of thy youth while the evil days come not.

Whatever, City tore into Everton with Goliath endeavour. Four minutes into the second half, Paul Simpson half-volleyed the equalizer courtesy of McNab's sleight of foot, and Gordon Davies's centre. Simpson, a young left winger, recalled to the side, had an immediate adrenalin transfusion. He disturbed Steven's cool with fluent running and drew two more astonishing saves from Mimms. Ratcliffe was booked for a foul and did not approve at all. Van Den Hauwe was fortunate to stay on the park for a grisly professional foul. All muck and nettles from City, laid back, or knocked back if you were Everton's well-mauled strikers. Twenty-eight thousand, though, enjoyed it and chipped a few grand off that £4.6 million overdraft.

EVERTON 2 – OXFORD UNITED 0
Canon Football League, Division One, October 1985

A little melodrama. Here is the scenario. The match was gently expiring at sunlit Goodison, Everton leading by a Graeme Sharp goal shuffled in just before half-time. Twenty-four thousand had seen this beefy abrasive Oxford side tame the champions, albeit Stevens had smote the bar, with Lineker striking a post. Steve Hardwick, the Oxford goalie, the hero with four amazing saves. There had been two bookings: Gary Briggs, the colossus in the Oxford number five jersey, and Paul Bracewell of Everton.

Then, one minute from time, an extraordinary chain of events, culminating in a denouement of drama and pure farce. An Oxford attack. Ian Marshall of Everton, John Aldridge of Oxford, jousting for the ball in the penalty area. Marshall clearly did not just put both hands on the ball; he almost made off with it.

Did he fall or was he pushed, you ask?

The incident happened under referee Tyson's whistle. Like a vicar refusing cream buns at the choirboys' party, Mr Tyson shunned the penalty claim. The ball was punted up-field by Bracewell, who thus beat his man and scored with a looping right-foot drive.

At which point hero Hardwick raced from his goal to the referee like a hound on the fox. Grasping Mr Tyson warmly by the throat, he propounded a voluble, rather physical protest. Alas, our hero was booked. Thirty seconds later Mr Tyson blew time. Mr Hardwick screamed off the pitch in high dudgeon, aimed a fearful blow at a bucket of water which showered all and sundry. Oxford boss Maurice Evans livid, full of GBH, ran to the referee, but a large police superintendent with scrambled eggs on his cap restrained Maurice and ushered him, plus by now a small delegation of Oxfordites and a posse of big bobbies, off the arena. Peace of a relative sort descended. Quite an afternoon.

EVERTON 6 – ARSENAL 1
Canon Football League, Division One, 9 November 1985
And their Father gave them great gifts of silver, and of gold, and of precious things, with fenced cities in Judah. He slew a man of Arsenal, a man of great stature, six cubits and a span high, and in the Arsenal hand a spear like a weaver's beam.

Exhilarated Everton fans gave the team and the match a rapturous standing ovation. Wreathed in smiles they exhort me to dip into the superlative and poetic. If the palate was jaded then this meeting was a mega-tonic – tantalizing – titillating, then replete.

Football by Einstein out of Slip Anchor and Barry McGuigan. The crystallization of the quintessential British game. Moves of rippling beauty. High intelligence on and off the ball. Individual skills. Superb goals, and a dash of the physical.

The Arsenal appraised Everton's gossamer back four. Young Pointon playing his debut at number three. Gary Stevens out of position. Alan Harper, the reserve, at number two. And Arsenal attacked. The match was open – *there to be won*. What a challenge. Everton took it. Trevor Steven's beautiful punt up-field began it, Sharp's glancing header put Lineker in possession. He streaked through the Arsenal defence, drew Lukic and his ground shot was a diamond. 'A Tommy Lawton goal', someone breathed. Lineker sniffed out number two on 39 minutes as Lukic fumbled a save.

Charlie Nicholas's impudent goal just into the second half simply lifted Everton Everest high. Four minutes later Adrian Heath jabbed in number three. Trevor Steven thumped a penalty high to Lukic's left, and Arsenal chins were lower than their knees.

Then 10 minutes from time Paul Bracewell, the inspiration of the afternoon, advanced; could have played the wall pass, did not; lofted a 40-yard pass to Stevens, his centre, and Adrian Heath blasted the fifth. Pure rapture. Graeme Sharp juggled and foozled number six in the dying minutes with a little jig of joy and a theatrical bow! And young Neil Pointon, last Tuesday quaffing ale as Scunthorpe cipher, today thrust into battle, had an incredible debut. Superb left foot, crisp tackler, clean header – a worthy member of the School of Science, last to depart the fray, that ovation a lifetime's memory.

Everton: Neville Southall, Alan Harper, Neil Pointon, Kevin Ratcliffe, Gary Stevens, Adrian Heath, Trevor Steven, Gary 'David' Lineker, Graeme Sharp, Paul Bracewell, Kevin Sheedy. Substitute: Kevin Richardson.

Philistines: John 'Goliath' Lukic, Viv 'Ishbi-benob' Anderson, Kenny 'Saph' Sansom. Other Gittites: Paul Davis, David O'Leary, Tommy Caton, Steve Williams, Ian Allinson, Charlie Nicholas, Tony Woodcock, Graham Rix. Substitute: Goliath's fourth brother who shall remain nameless.

SHEFFIELD WEDNESDAY 2 – SOUTHAMPTON 1

Canon Football League, Division One, 23 November 1985

Dark clouds glower and brood atop the grey Pennines. They obscure the pylons and the little houses surrounding Hillsborough. The chilling damp is the atmosphere of *Room at the Top* and *Hindle Wakes*.

It breeds the football of flat vowels and no frills. To the Sloane Ranger it is a culture shock. To the Peak Ranger it makes the blood course.

Sheffield Wednesday are the Panzer corps. Highly disciplined, they strike with deadly speed and venom, and the skill factor is Rommel high. They boom the ball forward, the tiny Snodin and Marwood race like light infantry down the flanks, Blair and Shelton weave a little magic midfield and Lee Chapman beanpoles the headers. Gary Thompson endures hard luck.

A biting wind from the eastern steppes blown down the pitch. On 18 minutes Mel Sterland, the firebrand, high-stepping Wednesday fullback, whacked a fine through ball to Andy Blair. Blair without hesitation chipped the ball square into space just inside the Southampton penalty area. Lee Chapman had computed the move – racing sweetly, he met the ball first bounce and half-volleyed past Shilton. The goal unleashed the Panzer attack. Wednesday rolled over Southampton. Shilton's Southampton literally hanging on by their fingertips. Exhilarating stuff, tribal and traditional to render you smiling happy.

Half-time, one–nil. The Yorkshire crowd, never the ones to emote, rose to Shilton, a master craftsman whose dedicated skills and sheer bravery kept his team in the battle. But Southampton have storm troopers too. David Armstrong and Jimmy Case relished the blood and thunder, rattling the sabre, blockbuster in the tackle. Glenn Cockerill, ex-Sheffield United, had survived the first-half whirlwind of ceaseless attack, and began to reveal some cultured football. Mark Wright, the Southampton and England centre back, was a rock, a true international.

But Wednesday summoned the reserves of strength. On 71 minutes Mel Sterland battered down the right wing, flung over a booming cross – little Sherwood flung his frame into the battle path for a glancing header of pure beauty. Shilton ruefully applauded.

Ten minutes later, Mark Wright headed a goal for Southampton from a corner kick that Hodge, the Wednesday goalkeeper, could only parry. Came the final stampede and, as Stygian dark descended, the referee's final whistle.

The players rushed to congratulate opposite numbers.

MANCHESTER UNITED 1 – WATFORD 1

Canon Football League, Division One, 30 November 1985

Forty-two thousand, one hundred and eighty-one rolled up at Old Trafford on a dank day. At half-time a certain Stella Cartwright was plucked from the Stretford End and anointed the one-millionth spectator this season to pass through the turnstiles. The event was greeted by deafening apathy – scarcely a cheer. Fickle disaffection has set in – a result of a grim November and a first half of stuttering, confidence-drained football, barely credible when compared with the brilliant September/October.

Watford played four up – Blissett and West leaping upfront, Sterling and Barnes on the flanks. Talbot, the skipper, abrasive, physical, voluble, set the charges for the rest to fire. Barnes ran riot, the ball araldited to his boots. He wandered left to right, leaving Gidman, and Gibson, playing his high-priced debut, puce with embarrassment.

So after the half-time non-event, United had points to prove. Olsen wove a little magic, Strachan hit the sprint, Gidman drove forward. Moran retired hurt on the hour. Alan Brazil trotted on, to low groans from the disenchanted. Five minutes later Brazil was the hero. He lurked far post as Strachan lofted in a corner. As the ball ricocheted out, Brazil bicycled, nicked the goal.

With the pressure lifted, United powered forward, but Hughes is a fitful shadow of himself, and Stapleton is labouring. Watford withstood the assault. Once again, John Barnes, with fluent ease, teased Gidman, fled down the left, chipped in the cross, and Colin West headed the goal. 'Twas one minute from time. Bryan Robson, United need you – now.

Manchester United: Gary Bailey, John Gidman, Colin Gibson, Norman

Whiteside, Kevin Moran, Graeme Hogg, Paul McGrath, Mark Hughes, Gordon Strachan, Frank Stapleton, Jesper Olsen. Substitute: Alan Brazil.

Watford: Tony Coton, David Bardsley, Wilf Rostron, Brian Talbot, Steve Terry, Lee Sinnott, Worrall Sterling, Luther Blissett, Colin West, Kenny Jackett, John Barnes. Substitute: Neil Smillie.

LIVERPOOL 3 – ASTON VILLA 0
Canon Football League, Division One, 7 December 1985

Kenny Dalglish, king of footballers, is beginning to emerge as a fearless, innovative manager playing chess with his team selection and outflanking the opposition. He has replaced the ageing Neal and Kennedy, loyal servants both, but arthritic with experience, with Nicol and Beglin. Nicol, with his borstal haircut, is square-rigged for battle, Beglin is lean and fleet of foot – a thoroughbred. Lawrenson a clever, mean, street fighter, and Hansen, the introvert, complete his back four.

Steel and style, both for acquiring yet more boardroom silver.

But Dalglish has more variations than Elgar. Today he played MacDonald, the misfit bought from Leicester by predecessor Joe Fagan, in midfield. Played Sammy Lee wide on the right and Craig Johnston equally wide down the left – almost the orthodox left winger – only Johnston is a right-footed player. The result of all the machinations – freedom on the park, relaxed confidence on the ball, sweeping moves of ecstasy, and that air of leisure that is the bosom friend of quality.

Jan Molby, the Great Dane, has skill in abundance, a beautiful touch on the ball, a fine tactical brain. After 90 seconds, Liverpool gained a free kick on the edge of the penalty area. Six Villa players lined up in the wall. Molby sauntered up and caressed the ball in a beautiful parabola over and round the bemused Villa team for a goal worthy of Platini. But Villa got off the canvas. Manager Graham Turner is doing a massive revamp of the team. Paul Elliot, bought from Luton for £400,000, was engulfed for the first 10 minutes, began to live with the pace – albeit looking a very expensive chunk of footballer at the price.

Mark Walters ran with intuitive ease down the left flank, occasioning Nicol some moments of blank despair.

Steve Hodge, a mobile little man, took the challenge midfield. Andy Gray, that crag of a vintage centre forward, thrust his battered head into the fray, and Grobbelaar was leaping, jumping and fisting. Half-time, one–nil.

But Liverpool in the second half was pure joy.

MacDonald had his finest game to date. Always free in space, doing the simple ploy – control and first touch. Craig Johnston was a whirlwind – but how do his colleagues read his play? Walsh was incisive and flashy, Molby the orchestrator.

Ian Rush, one-time devourer of goals, is now so anxious after a barren three games that he snatches at everything. His long legs extend like a builder's ladder, but he whacked one chance against the bar, missed three gaping goals that normally he wallops in his sleep, and suffered a nightmare. But on 68 minutes Jan Molby's silky pass to feet. Paul Walsh sidestepped former team-mate Elliot and zapped a perfect striker's goal, his 13th of the season. This young man, so unsure of his place in the side some weeks ago, sealed the match. Eighty-one minutes he smacked a ball into space behind the Villa's disarrayed back four. Craig Johnston was in like a stoat on a rabbit, an oblique shot across Spinks – and Villa were tonked.

Liverpool: Bruce Grobbelaar, Steve Nicol, James Beglin, Mark Lawrenson, Sammy Lee, Alan Hansen, Paul Walsh, Craig Johnston, Ian Rush, Jan Molby, Kevin MacDonald. Substitute: Ronnie Whelan.

Aston Villa: Nigel Spinks, Jim Williams, Tony Dorigo, Dean Glover, Paul Elliot, Darren Bradley, Tony Daley, Simon Stainrod, Andy Gray, Steve Hodge, Mark Walters. Substitute: Gary Shaw.

MANCHESTER CITY 1 – LIVERPOOL 0
Canon Football League, Division One, 26 December 1985

City fans, buoyantly joyful, believe in Santa Claus; I should imagine Liverpool's footballers will rewrap their presents and jump on them. In the most one-sided first half I have seen for years, Liverpool rolled over City. Their football was arrogant possession. McMahon, MacDonald, Whelan and Johnston played to feet in the strong wind. Steve Nicol overlapped down the right almost at will. Beglin also advanced with menace, and City were simply chasing fruitlessly. Johnston, especially, tantalized Paul Power, and City's fickle fans left their players in no doubt as to their lack of class compared with Liverpool.

But City it was, against all the run of play, who took the lead. Gordon Davies's shot on the hour was parried by Grobbelaar, Clive Wilson running in far post shot into the empty net. Liverpool then became anxious and frustrated. Nixon saved brilliantly from MacDonald. McMahon hit the bar. Dalglish's superb weighted ball saw Johnston balloon over the bar. The ghastly realization dawned that Liverpool's class was going to lose out. Celtic fires were stoked. Beglin and McNab wrestled under the referee's nose. McMahon was spoiling for a scuffle or two. But City held on. I believe the film *The Great Escape* was on the telly this afternoon – the Maine Road version was even more incredible.

Manchester City: Eric Nixon, Nicky Reid, Paul Power, Kenny Clements, Mick McCarthy, David Phillips, Jim Melrose, Andy May, Gordon Davies, Neil McNab, Clive Wilson. Substitute: Paul Simpson.

Liverpool: Bruce Grobbelaar, Steve Nicol, Jim Beglin, Mark Lawrenson, Ronnie Whelan, Alan Hansen, Paul Walsh, Craig Johnston, Ian Rush, Kevin MacDonald, Steve McMahon. Substitute: Kenny Dalglish.

EVERTON 3 – SHEFFIELD WEDNESDAY 2
Canon Football League, Division One, 28 December 1985

Thanks to Goodison under-soil heating, 41,000, including umpteen thousand

Wednesday fans, revelled in this typically English winter football joust. Rumbustious, rollicking football of no quarter expected or gifted. Tackles of such power that thwacks could be heard and ouched at the back of the stand.

Wednesday had a patched-up back four and several other second-choice players, but whatever the selection Wednesday's Panzer corps rolls on – Field Marshal Wilkinson directing from the dugout.

The opening play was a trifle lax and tepid, Wednesday's players getting to know each other, Everton assisting by giving away the ball as 'tis the season of charity. But, Gary Stevens, Everton and England number two, declared his intent on 19 minutes. From 35 yards he smote a shot of terrific power, bending past Hodge's clawing fingers. Gary put hands on his hips in insouciance. Follow that! Mighty goal. Gary Lineker did six minutes later, easing into his graceful stride past the Wednesday markers for a fine goal.

But Wednesday have a well of Yorkist spirit and passion. Garry Thompson, a fearsome sight with his socks rolled down over legs like a Roman centurion's, won ball after ball in the air. A perfect header beat Southall. Six minutes in the second half, Gary Stevens punting the ball into his own goal. Wednesday were on a hype. Mark Chamberlain revealed touches of class. But after hectic moments in both goal-mouths, Kevin Sheedy's perfect cross was headed in by Gary Lineker, lovely diagonal header of perfect class. Twenty-first goal five minutes from time.

Lineker follows in the fine tradition of School of Science centre forwards. Dixie Dean and Tommy Lawton were spectacular headers of the ball and at real pace. He does not relish the physical – would rather be slippery and cunning.

He exemplifies my dad's favourite adage: 'If you catch a weasel asleep – piss in its ear'.

Everton: Neville Southall, Gary Stevens, Neil Pointon, Kevin Ratcliffe, Pat Van Den Hauwe, Adrian Heath, Trevor Steven, Gary Lineker, Graeme Sharp, Paul Bracewell, Kevin Sheedy. Substitute: Alan Harper.

Sheffield Wednesday: Martin Hodge, Peter Shirtliff, Nigel Worthington, Lawrie Madden, Chris Morris, Mark Smith, Brian Marwood, Andy Blair, Garry Thompson, Gary Megson, Mark Chamberlain. Substitute: Tony Gregory.

EVERTON 4 – QUEENS PARK RANGERS 3
Canon Football League, Division One, 11 January 1986

Test of character for Everton's walking wounded on the pitch, and for wounded pride in the stands, as QPR strolled to a two-goal lead after 25 minutes. The first goal was a lovely Gary Bannister strike on 12 minutes. Neat, precise, build-up, Warren Neil catching the eye with impudent skill. John Byrne a remould of the fallible Rodney Marsh. And Byrne's ferocious left-foot howitzer on 25 minutes left Mr Southall incredulous at the sheer power. Jim Smith's team looked compact, skilled and steely. A little too much steel conceded a penalty one minute from half-time. Graeme Sharp scored.

And so to an amazing second half. Sheedy, who had hit a post with a free kick, retired. Paul Wilkinson replaced him, wide on the left. He relished the battle, gave QPR a fresh poser. He interchanged passes with Sharp. Sharp sped down the left, boomed in the cross – Lineker scooped the ball in the net. Two–two, and his 22nd goal of the season. One minute later, Gary Stevens crossed from the right, Paul Wilkinson's deflected angled header put Everton in front. QPR lost composure. Everton's use of both flanks and crossing has been a major factor in this magnificent run of theirs, and on 67 minutes the plot again unfurled, Graeme Sharp tucking away a neat goal, to the rapturous delight of his fans. But as the match expired Fereday and Bannister wove a little magic. Bannister headed a clever goal.

In the New Year Honours List Everton rate MBE.

'My bloody efforts,' as Cyril Smith says.

Everton: Neville Southall, Gary Stevens, Neil Pointon, Kevin Ratcliffe, Pat Van Den Hauwe, Adrian Heath, Alan Harper, Gary Lineker, Graeme Sharp, Kevin Richardson, Kevin Sheedy. Substitute: Paul Wilkinson.

Queens Park Rangers: Paul Barron, Alan McDonald, Ian Dawes, Warren Neil, Steve Wicks, Terry Fenwick, Michael Robinson, Martin Allen, Gary Bannister, John Byrne, Wayne Fereday. Substitute: Robbie James.

MANCHESTER CITY 2 – QUEENS PARK RANGERS 0
Canon Football League, Division One, February 1986
I write this in bad odour – literally!

Snowflakes fell gently from Moss Side's azure-grey industrial pollution. But Stanley Gibson, the groundsman with a visage like burnt cork, grinned and pronounced his heated pitch perfect for football. Alas, much of the fare smacked of 'end of term'. End of term in early February, the price of no European soccer – what is a game without a prize?

City began with a fortunate goal. On nine minutes, Mark Lillis, foraging right for Reid's through ball, looked yards offside. No linesman's flag, no referee's whistle, so he punted over a centre which Paul Simpson obligingly rattled past an astounded Hucker in the QPR goal to give City the lead. Subsequently, instead of heeding the lesson QPR persisted with this mad offside trap. Without Steve Wicks to orchestrate it, the QPR penalty area was like a chicken run with fox amok. Hucker lived dangerously, as City could have amassed a healthy goals bag.

Just before half-time, Gordon Davies, running swiftly again on to a Reid pass, struck a lovely striker's goal. Reid was dissecting the left-side weakness of QPR with exploratory probes. The second half was a mix of artisan and pantomime. I enjoyed Mark Lillis, the City centre forward, a large, red-headed, flailing lad, a bit like a stevedore in a *corps de ballet.* But occasionally he revealed Astaire footwork that took one's breath away. He either tilts at windmills or lies horizontal, beating the turf. But, in truth, this match was somewhat tainted by an insanitary tom cat.

He micturated over the six telephone directories that serve as my seat in the press box here at Maine Road. The stench of stale cattery put me in solitary. As I was wearing my granny's mangy old mink coat, there were dubious stares and downright rancid comments. Next time here, I will bring a bag of mothballs – if I can capture the moths.

SHEFFIELD UNITED 3 – BRIGHTON AND HOVE ALBION 0
Canon Football League, Division One, 1 February 1986

The ultimate sacrifice for your humble reporter is to leave the warm bosom of my Wilmslow shack and my frugal meal of plovers' eggs, larks' tongues in aspic, dromedary steaks washed down with 1979 Chambertin, and cross the icy, desolate, bitter, unforgiving wasteland of the snow-covered Snake Pass on the Pennine Tundra. I observed a solitary blue tit nibbling half a coconut. Beside the storm-tossed waters of the reservoir, a herd of yak searched for fodder. Until, at last, on the grey horizon, the concrete finger of Bramall Lane, the Taj Mahal of Yorkshire.

I clambered from my Snow-Cat, clad in yeti boots and mangy fur, to ascend 120 steps to my eyrie, buffeted by gales and Yorkist vowels. Diminutive players cavorted on a tacky pitch, spread thin the 7,000 frozen faithful.

We endured an excruciating first half, noting some neat but inconclusive Brighton play, and Peter Withe – the Big Daddy of football – putting himself about somewhat. Hail to thee, Withe spirit. Little bird thou art, never wert on eagle's wings; this day inspired a barnstorming Sheffield onslaught in the second half. Colin Morris took a penalty on 55 minutes. Digweed saved the power shot, but Morris himself lashed in the rebound. Keith Edwards, with a classic header from a deep cross, scored the second goal. Peter Withe sealed a meritorious win with a mighty shot from a corner kick. Brighton came on riposte, Danny Wilson casting off the South Coast effete, lathering himself with Yorkshire sweat. The eccentric Burridge in Sheffield's goal denied them. Yorkshire spirit had triumphed. A drop of spirit from further north will revive me as the ice is chipped from the ball boys.

Sheffield United: John Burridge, Paul Smith, Brian Smith, Steve Foley, Paul Stancliffe, Ken McNaught, Colin Morris, Keith Edwards, Peter Withe, Ray Lewington, Mel Eves. Substitute: Jeff Eckhard.

Brighton and Hove Albion: Perry Digweed, Chris Hutchings, Graham Pearce, Danny Wilson, Eric Young, Gary O'Reilly, Dean Saunders, Steve Penney, Mick Ferguson, Terry Connor, Dennis Mortimer. Substitute: Steve Gatting.

MANCHESTER UNITED 3 – WEST BROMWICH ALBION 0
Canon Football League, Division One, 22 February 1986

If I was the installer of United's under-soil heating I would by now have emigrated or guillotined mesel'. Half the pitch was thawed in the equatorial Manchester sun; the other half was sand over frost, like the Sahara on top of an ice floe.

United had circumspect appraisal of it. Perfidious Albion tested its resilience by crudely felling myriad United bodies to see whether they would bounce. The net result – United's brilliant ballplayers Strachan, Hughes and Olsen had to pick up their heels to avoid the flailing boot, the niggling trip and various assorted mantraps. 'Twas akin to watching tentative young virgins running the gauntlet of a lusting rugby pack. Mr Tyson, the referee, was benignly lax, but just as we waited for a United player to be devoured by voracious Albion came retribution. A penalty as Colin Gibson was chopped. Jesper approached the ball like a *Come Dancing* foxtrotter. A little jink, a touch of sway – and wallop! The ball zoomed past Naylor's left ear as his body dived right. Naylor scratched his head at the Olsen stroll. Forty-two minutes a reprise foul on Colin Gibson in the penalty area. Jesper again on the saunter, a replica kick – two–nil – and with a shambles of a team in front of him, pondered on the wisdom of selecting Stuart Naylor for his debut at Old Trafford. Sixty-nine minutes Jesper Olsen again. From the ruck the ball rolled to him; instinctively, he aimed a mighty left-foot swipe. Three–nil. Once again, United's class carried them throughout, despite the midfield engine room missing vital components in Whiteside, Moses and Robson.

Mr Saunders, Albion's new manager, sacked his midfield before the match. Methinks he will rue the day.

Manchester United: Chris Turner, John Gidman, Arthur Albiston, Clayton Blackmore, Paul McGrath, Kevin Moran, Gordon Strachan, Colin Gibson, Mark Hughes, Frank Stapleton, Jesper Olsen. Substitute: Terry Gibson.

West Bromwich Albion: Stuart Naylor, Jimmy Nicholl, Derek Statham, Mick Forsyth, Carlton Palmer, Martyn Bennett, Gary Robson, Steve MacKenzie, George Reilly, Robbie Denison, Garth Crooks. Substitute: Imre Varadi.

MANCHESTER CITY 0 – OXFORD UNITED 3

Canon Football League, Division One, 1 March 1986

'*Non sum qualis eram,*' (I am not what once I was) uttered Maurice Evans, who once knocked on the door of Christ Church to establish his credentials. Maurice inherited the manager's job at the Manor Ground after Jim Smith, the Bald Eagle, walked out last summer. Robert Maxwell owns the club: 'Utter one diatribe and I'll sue.' Maxwell the mogul, the monster, who bought the club three years ago and has altercations with everybody, from hostile media to the tea lady. Oxford entered the league only because Accrington Stanley went bust in 1962. Since then Oxford created a record, winning the Third and Second Division Championships in successive seasons. They were promoted to the First Division last season with Birmingham and Manchester City. *O tempora! O mores!* (Alas for the times and the manners!) Oxford do not belong in this exalted company. Like Carlisle, Luton Town, Northampton Town and Millwall, they are one-season wonders. They will never grace the First Division again. They are a mixed bag of low-cost transfers from high-flying clubs with two class acts – Ray Houghton (£150,000 from Fulham) and John Aldridge (£70,000 from Newport). Aldridge blasted 34 goals last season, and in this team at the foot of the table he has scored 13 times. Aldridge is hot – *notandum*. Well, Oxford is the centre of learning – is it not?

City, meanwhile, are mightily miffed. They did not want to play Oxford today but cavort instead against Chelsea in the Members' Cup. Whether this is a phallic joust or a toy-town tournament like the Freight Rover Trophy I shall leave to your fertile imagination. Gross indignity is that Oxford drubbed City and rubbed City's noses in the Maine Road dustbowl, buffeted by severe Pennine gales. City opened with a ripple of rhapsodic football. Neil McNab can play pretty but niggly football. Mark Lillis, the centre forward, was on the charge, Paul Simpson scampers down the left. The gale nullifies their efforts. Fourteen minutes later, Slatter, the Oxford fullback, launched a hopeful punt anywhere, the capricious gale whisked it to the feet of Aldridge: he drew Nixon from goal and neatly flicked a typical striker's goal. I imagine Aldridge in a good team. He would be superb. He has the nose, a sniffer in the Alan Clarke mode. He is not elegant, more a Toxteth ruffian in appearance and manner, but surely he will not be at Oxford for long.

As the gale roared, so did Peter Rhoades–Brown – there's an Oxfordian high-class name for you. Rhoades-Brown browned the City right back, Nicky Reid, a simple low cross – Jeremy Charles, son of Mel, tucked the ball past Nixon for a half-time lead of two–nil.

Surely City must play up and under in the second half? Surely Baker, McNab and Phillips compete robustly? Billy McNeil, the City manager, danced a fandango. This mighty Celtic centre half, this macho-macho competitor, the motivator of team-mates. Surely, Billy, thou must stir City's loins? The loins were laid low by Rhoades-Brown – a sinuous dribble swaying past the City defence sculpted from marble – a clip into space – Aldridge floated in on gossamer wings and steered the ball into the goal. Three–nil, Aldridge's fifteenth goal of the season.

City were distraught. Less than 20,000 present on the day. The ides of March foretell financial ruin. Once again, City need a golden fleece. Oxford apace will return to the nether regions, never to return. Their fans sense it. On one terrace I counted four lonely souls guarded by eight bobbies on foot, and one atop a huge horse. The mountie disappeared at half-time not to return – will the City faithful follow suit?

Manchester City: Eric Nixon, Nicky Reid, Paul Power, Kenny Clements, Nigel Johnson, David Phillips, Mark Lillis, Graham Baker, Gordon Davies, Neil McNab, Paul Simpson. Substitute: Andy May.

Oxford United: Alan Judge, Neil Slatter, John Trewick, Les Philips, Gary Briggs, Malcolm Shotton, Ray Houghton, John Aldridge, Jeremy Charles, Trevor Hebbard, Peter Rhoades-Brown. Substitute: David Langan.

LIVERPOOL 4 – QUEENS PARK RANGERS 1
Canon Football League, Division One, 8 March 1986

There is an old popular song, 'What a difference Dalglish makes, 24 little hours'. In this case it is 72 little hours. The player/manager reinstated himself after midweek Milk Cup shambles, losing three–two in the semi-final to, irony of ironies, today's opponents, QPR. Clarity and stability have returned. Recent tactics have deflated the Colosseum populace and mystified the players. Gillespie and Johnston are dropped. Dalglish plays himself, and John Wark, that swarthy bosun of a striker, struts the quarterdeck, bullying the crew as they round the Horn in a force-ten south-wester. Lawrenson is back where he desires – Alan Hansen minder in central defence. The team is under full sail for attack. This is a revenge game. The pulse quickens, the blood courses, it is horripilation time, hubris at the Colosseum, followed by its nemesis.

QPR care not a fig for pride, reputation, gladiatorial Rome or the gods. They took the lead before we could draw breath. Rosenoir and Robinson (the black rose and the water buffalo) looked offside, played on. Rosenoir neatly clipped Robinson's pass over Grobbelaar. Eccentric Brucie, that star-crossed goalkeeper, that idiosyncratic vaudeville artist straight from Barnum and Bailey's circus, was disgusted. He kicked a post. The tempo became *allegro*. Steve McMahon, the Graeme Souness elect, gripped the game. He has the style, the ebullience, the bravura to achieve Souness's exalted position. Twenty-four minutes a flurry of one-twos. An incisive shot. One–one.

Thirty minutes Hansen's forward gallop, like a trotting horse harnessed to a hansom cab, a long punt to Wark, a knockdown to Dalglish, a shrug of the shoulders from Dalglish drew QPR defenders like moths to a flame. Dalglish unleashed Ian Rush. Rush's shot was clinical. Two–one. Dalglish's intuitive brilliance at last allowed less gifted team members to express talent or lack of it. Dalglish a fine-cut diamond in a coal seam.

Forty-five minutes Dalglish's mesmerizing dribble past Wicks and Fenwick, that dip of the shoulder, electrifying pace into space; a floated ball over an incredulous QPR defence. John Wark whipped the ball past Barron: three–one.

The second half was a walkover. Johnston came on for Wark, who hobbled off to an ovation. Master mariner Wark, who would lash himself to the wheel, storm raging, waves foaming, engulfing his ship. Maybe one day he will play in oilskins complete with RNLI sou'wester. Liverpool began to showboat. Fluent moves rippled through QPR as if knives shredded tatty gauze. Dalglish, McMahon, Molby overwhelmed hapless QPR, Steve Wicks excepted.

Seventy-five minutes Beglin's deep cross from the left – McMahon's header – simplicity. Four–one. Liverpool are back, lying third behind Everton and Manchester United – in contention, pride restored, 35,000 thousand happy.

This week's away 'Supportawatch' revealed 22 chilled QPR fans huddled in a stand with 17 recumbent bobbies, de-helmeted, holding a relaxed surveillance. Literally, low-profile policing, methinks.

Liverpool: Bruce Grobbelaar, Sammy Lee, Jim Beglin, Mark Lawrenson, Ronnie Whelan, Alan Hansen, Kenny Dalglish, John Wark, Ian Rush, Jan Molby, Steve McMahon. Substitute: Craig Johnston.

Queens Park Rangers: Paul Barron, Alan McDonald, Ian Dawes, Warren Neil, Steve Wicks, Terry Fenwick, Mike Fillery, Martin Allen, Mike Robinson, Leroy Rosenoir, Wayne Fereday. Substitute: David Kerslake.

MANCHESTER UNITED 4 – LEICESTER FOSSE 0
Canon Football League, Division One, 26 April 1986

The pews will empty, the candles will be snuffed, the vestry dusted, the choir stall decontaminated, the shutters will come down on the Shrine, this vast cathedral for this, the last match of the season. Thirty-nine thousand in the congregation, many with shattered hopes and fractured faith. Either Liverpool or Everton will be champions. Both have 79 points. United have 72. Finishing third means failure. They won their first eight games, but March and April have been fallow. Two home defeats in April at the hands of Chelsea and Sheffield Wednesday have finished the season. United are more than a football club. They are merchant bank, a rampant commercial enterprise, a monolith, a testament to mammon. For Ronald Atkinson it is a savage case of winning, or lose the vestments and the golden trappings.

At 4.45 p.m. the disciples and the Philistines were *happy* with a four–nil victory. The cognoscenti were plainly *unhappy* with the quality and the style – there are calls for Cardinal Atkinson to be exiled. The goals flattered. Eighteen minutes Peter Davenport chipped from the right, Frank Stapleton headed in. The rest came late. Fosse were marshalled by Osman and O'Neill. Behind them, Andrews was superb, as Fosse goalkeepers are always. They rendered Mark Hughes, as the third striker, totally obsolete, Whiteside and Stapleton being sufficient. Both subs entered the fray after half-time. Lynex for Fosse hit a post, which could have changed the nature of the game. Olsen for United began to excite with his consummate but fragile skills. As Fosse closed down the left to combat the marauding Olsen, space appeared in the middle. Mark Hughes ran to a sweet Blackmore pass and smote his farewell goal eight minutes from time. Two minutes later, Blackmore volleyed number three. Peter Davenport thumped a penalty just before time – his first for the club.

The Stretford End revelled in the late romp. Hardened oldies frowned, and then vowed their allegiance to the cause. Supplicants at the Shrine have numbered 1,198,278 – the offertory swollen by their groats and farthings. It is now 19 years since the Shrine last husbanded the Holy Grail – the championship. The quest has broken McGuinness, O'Farrell, Docherty, Sexton. The question, not the quest, that is: how long will Big Ron be patron saint?

Manchester United: Chris Turner, John Gidman, Arthur Albiston, Norman Whiteside, Paul McGrath, Billy Garton, Mike Duxbury, Peter Davenport, Mark Hughes, Frank Stapleton, Clayton Blackmore. Substitute: Jesper Olsen.

Leicester Fosse: Ian Andrews, Simon Morgan, Bobby Smith, Gary McAllister, Russell Osman, John O'Neill, Paul Ramsey, Tony Sealy, Lawrie Cunningham, Ali Mauchlen, Ian Banks. Substitute: Steve Lynex.

FOOTBALL GEOGRAPHIC

THE SHRINE

Old Trafford. Supplicants well-heeled. Wraths of Munich whisper from the rafters. Hard to detect amid the rustle of money. 'Golden Balls' Edwards high priest. 'Roy the Good' composes matins and dogma. 'Doggerels of war'.

THE COLOSSEUM

Anfield. Christians (usually Chelsea) devoured by lions in red shirts.

'Virgil' P. Robinson, not for the faint-hearted. 'Caesar Pious', Pontius Houllier. 'Senator Vox Populi', Prelate Philipus Thompson. 'Senator Voce', Centurion, Sam Lee. 'Legionary', Ron Yeats.

THE SCHOOL OF SCIENCE

Goodison Park. The Golden Vision (Alex Young) still strolls and struts his sublime stuff. The beautiful game is cherished here. Visiting professor, Walter Smith OBE. Bill Kenwright's latest production. Will it run or be a turkey?

MAUSOLEUM

Ewood Park. Graveyard of abandoned dreams. A garden of remembrance of tangled Rosenbourgs. Uncle Jack was sheared (see Palazzio).

THE PALAZZIO

St James's Park. Sir John's Palace. He shears the wool from people's backs. Stuffs the opposition livestock breeders. 'Brown alers' trysting spot. Not recommended for quaffing sarsaparilla.

THE THEATRE OF BASE COMEDY

Maine Road, Moss Side, Manchester 14. The Royle comedy series now starring for a limited run. End-of-the-pier stuff. Sense of humour essential for the audience. They know the plot. Relished the gags for 25 years. Wear a banana when visiting. Bone up on 'Blue Moon'.

THE GROUCHO

Stamford Bridge's rest-home for foreign footballers past their sell-by dates. Fancy, bordello-style away strip best worn with M&S carpet slippers embroidered KB. If you are not castigated in his programme notes, you are nobody.

AWESOME PARK

Riverside Stadium, Middlesbrough. Spendthrift, spindthift Robbo doing a Barings Bank job. Centre of north-east surgery – grafting the beautiful game to total pragmatism.

YELL AND BE HEARD

Yelland Road, Leeds. Vociferous, tetchy, cockpit of yell. Centre of elocution for

Yorkists. Visiting Professor O'Leary lectures word use. Never use one when you can use six.

STADIUM OF LIGHT
Des res of Gayleford Reid, the Mississippi gambler. Never let the left hand know what the right's doing. A haven of peace washed by the blue wavelets of the North Sea. Students of heritage welcome.

THE SHAY
I must go down the Shay again, the lonely Shay and the sky. Home to Halifax. Have you seen the Halifax share price? The sky has fallen in.
> And all I have is a lovely mien
> And no football to guide me by.

(Apologies to J. Masefield, ex-Accrington Stanley and Grimsby Town.)

THE MERMAID
White Hart Lane. All Shakespeare's plays enacted here. Gory tragedies. Pounds of flesh. Macabre assassinations. Treachery, gore, jealousy, blood-letting, traditional fare. Alan Sugar stars as Macbeth, Shylock, Richard II, Cassius, Othello and Portia.
> *Famous final line:* 'Exit – pursued by a bear.'

'Tumbrils for George' now in the charts.

VICTORIA PALACE
Selhurst Park, Caverns of the Crazy Gang.
> They are all here. Nervo and Knox. Flanaghan and Allen, Monsewer Eddie Gray. Head-banging rap, rollicking rock. The original party poopers. Favourite venue the Colosseum. They never read the plot. Tear up the script and terrorize the red shirts.

'HEY, UPTON PARK'
Hey up, it is the Hammers. All those burst balloons and bubbles. I am forever blowing and losing. Hammers' fans need replaceable wigs; they are always tearing their hair out. Heirs to the beautiful game crown. Steel-capped boots a wondrous Christmas present. Harry please note.

GRACELANDS
On the Trent. Elvis Clough still haunts. Can still be seen walking on the Trent after midnight. 'Put a bung in' does not refer to lavatories.
> S. Pearce of yesteryear starred as Norman in Hitchcock's remake of *Psycho*.
> David Platt once could plait sawdust. His head on a David Platter anticipated.
> Those thunder thighs in shorts, ye know.

THE HIGHFIELD BOWL
Downtown, down-market, ersatz, kitsch, imitation Hollywood Bowl. Resident compere was Big Ron, Ron's rendition of 'New York, New York' the big hit. Dolly Parton, Elvis, Francis Albert, James Dean – all the stars past and present used to genuflect at Big Ron's size 14.

Now off the gold standard, Big Ron induces flash floods. 'Down the Channel', 'In the Hole', 'Deep Throat', 'Up Your Tunnel' – all have passed into popular parlance. But will Ron Godiva ever ride bareback?

A HAND IN THE BIRD IS WORTH TWO IN THE BUSH
QPR. Up for the lark. Rodney Marsh, Stan Bowles, Jack the lad. Play it again, Sam. Pop culture club. Striving, aspirational, the Bush prepares for Rugby League. Those striped jerseys already qualify them.

PRIDE AND PREJUDICE PARK
Derby County. The Rams without horns. Bald Eagles rule. Old Buffaloes should. Much preferred the Baseball Ground. This apology for a stadium in antediluvian Victorian-dank darkness. I once complained that the illumination in my commentary box was a naked 40-watt bulb. In quick response, management, abreast of high technology, replaced it with a 60-watt bulb.

THE SHED (ALAS, REPLACED BY THE REEBOK)
Burnden Park, Bolton. A no-smoking area straight from the Chelsea flower show, 1912. Still secured by 'Knarled Gnomes' in flat hats.

Once upon a New Year's Day, snowbound, icebound on the Lancashire steppes, I was apprehended in full flow by such a gentleman.

'Move your bloody car,' he expostulated. My car, a Jensen Interceptor, pride and joy Hupmobile, was the only car on the car park. Removing the microphone from my nonstop gabbling gob, I muttered: 'I'm on the air addressing the multitude.'

'Bugger that,' he bellowed. 'Move your bloody car.'

A frisson developed. A hiatus. I threw him the keys.

'Sod off to Cleethorpes.'

THE MARBLE HALLS
Highbury. Old Etonians meet the hoi polloi. Marble edifice and larks' tongues in aspic for me – hot dogs and Bovril for you, mate.

'The Arsenal', not simply 'Arsenal'. Aristos in Oasis. A cult theatre. Those red strips and white sleeves inspire sharp intake of breath. George devalued the currency just as the world began to love him. Just keep intoning 'The Arsenal'. It grows on you. Bit like poison ivy with Spurs' fans.

GAY MEADOW
The Earl of Shrewsbury turns in his grave. The gay blade of his day. He and I

invented football using severed heads or pigs' bladders. Apoplectic whiskers tremble and quiver at the appropriation.

THE GLOSSARY

A Is for Arsene – the Jacques Tati of the beautiful game. Tenant of the Marble Halls. Is it Clochemerle (famous French farce about a public pissoir) or Tunes of Glory?

B Is for Bestial. Vincent Jones, ex-hod carrier, ex-Wimbledon axeman, some time star of celluloid.

C Is for Cantona, provider of proverbs for the masses. 'When the sardine follows the trawler it expects to be thrown a seagull.'

D Is for David Pleat. Talks a fine game. Pleatism is for convoluted phrases with enigmatic meaning.

E Is for Egg on face, viz Uncle Jack Walker. Fleeced by Shearer. Hoodwinked by Hodgson. Kidded by Kiddo. Walkerism is being hoofed at the Ewood.

F FU2. Chairman's vote of confidence. Fanny Adams or Sweet FA. A rapid, tangled web of sophistry. Mystic Meg myopia. Refer Glenn Hoddle.

G Is for Gazza. Nothing is here for tears. Soothe the savage breast with a Newcastle Brown or a Mars bar. Drifting lonely as a cloud.

H Is for Hall. Gay blade of Wilmslow. Nicknamed the San Wilmslow Fault. Underachieving is an achievement. Raised mediocrity to a fine art. He was nearly somebody.

I Is for 'Indiana Jones (Vincent) and the Last Crusade' for Wimbledon. Grab the opposition by the lunchbox, crunch the gonads.

J Is for Joe Mercer. One of the greats. A believer in God-given talent, had the faith in players to express it. Now, alas, one of the heavenly selection committee, Cliff Britton, Dixie Dean and Tommy Lawton stars of his team.

K Is for Kinkladze. Twinkle, twinkle, twirl, tantalize, titillate, titivate, tintinnabulate. Terpsichorean. A form of Georgian dance. 'Now take your partner for a Kinkladze.'

L Is for Lineker. Gretel to Hansen's Hansel. From the Brothers Grimm. A fairy story. Verb, 'to Lineker' – to spin a bland blandness.

M Is for Mark, as in Hughes. Sparky needing a jump-start. Red cards, yellow cards. Verb, 'to Sparky' – do not stop the show; simply slow it down.

N Is for Nutter. The head-butters' union. See Wise, D., Walsh, S., Beckham, D., Keane, R. Motto: 'You can't make an omelette without breaking eggs.' Transcribed: 'You can't win a match without scrambling brains.' See G for Gazza.

O Is for Opidum, Odious, Opiate, as in Olympics. A vanished ideal, a pumpkin for politicians. Newspeak for nationalism.

P Is for Plonker. Those who can, do. Those who cannot, teach. Those who cannot, never will do but imagine they can. Make your own choice.

Q Is for Quest. The golden fleece. Mission: impossible. The tonsils of Andy Gray. The libido of Clare Short. The hide of Jack Straw. The hymen of Vanessa Feltz. Luca's championship aspirations. Eileen as Southampton's ball boy.

R Is for Ruud Rasta. Speaks English like a Polynesian polyglot. The only TV pundit to require subtitles. TV pundits have to be Scottish. It approximates to English, appeals to primates. Ruud is to English what rude is to gesture.

S Is for Sugar. Sugar the pill. Proffer the poisoned chalice. Verb, 'to Sugar' – to suffer in silence and sue.

T Is for Terry. As in Venables, shenabels, jezebels. Verb, 'to Terry' – to tarry with the facts, eschew your ethics, screw your sensibilities, mollify your mates. Declare black is white and believe it. Terry a thing of beauty and joy for ever.

U Is for Uncle Jack Walker. All that glisters is not gold. The bull that could not get out of a tight jersey. Verb, 'to Walker' – to walk out before you are pushed.

V Is for Victory. Victory in England is not winning but being placed, or coming a valiant second. National heroes are non-winners.

Bruno, Cooper, Henman, Rusedski, Wright, Coulthard, Black. Mansell is *never* mentioned – the real winner.

It is the principle, lads and ladettes.

The English do everything on principle.

They fight on patriotic principles.

Rob you on business principles.

Enslave you on imperial principles.

Come second on the principle of sportsmanship.

W Is for Wednesday, as in Sheffield. Wednesday's child is full of woe; Danny

Wilson had far to go. Fine man, articulate, inventive player – shame about the management. I have been fond of Wednesday since the Harry Catterick/Eric Taylor days. Eric's dictum: 'It's better to travel safely than to arrive.' Danny took heed.

X Is for cross in anger, bile, vitriol, altercation, dispute, confrontation, war. Joe Kinnear was cross when after a Wimbledon defeat he gave me the briefest interview ever. 'Fuck off,' he said tacitly. I did.

Y Yallop, as in Frank. Rhymes with wallop, trollop. To Yallop is to score the winner, blast a century: a winning smash at tennis, a goal at Wembley, breast the tape first in the 100 metres. Then pull the shirt over your head and Yallop.

Z Is for Zimbabwe. The thorn in the paw of the English Lion. For gaffes in the line of duty. As in Brucie, the Zimbabwean Grobbelaar. Brucie the entertainer, an outrage looking for somewhere to happen.

Verb: 'to Brucie' – to let something slip through your fingers. 'If golde ruste, what shall irone do?'

EPILOGUE
'A pile of shit in a silk stocking.' (Napoleon, on Talleyrand)
'I wonder what he meant by that?' (Louis-Philippe)

PART TWO:
A PRODIGAL LIFE

A PRODIGAL LIFE REVISITED

My headmaster, Gauleiter Lord, instructed: 'Everything matters, but nothing matters terribly', and '*De gustibus non est disputandum*' (there is no disputing taste).

Thus, I embarked on the prodigal, maverick life: look on the bright side, ignore the dark, leave skeletons in cupboards, take nothing seriously.

As we are all grains of sand awaiting the sieve, shall we enjoy life, savour and cherish it, or worry ourselves out of it consumed by anxiety, low self-esteem and feelings of inadequacy? My own salve:

Time, with the ceaseless stroke of his wings,
Brushed off the bloom of their soul.

I collect clocks. Their ticking, chiming, booming bells and gongs remind me of mortality. I tend them, centuries of history, and ponder – what went before?

So I present a series of essays, the ramblings of an incoherent mind, an inchoate life. I have lived, not existed. We either laugh or weep.

AN IDYLL

I am a workaholic. Capricorn, the mountain goat, forever scrambling from shifting shale to barren outcrop. Progress is slow and arduous. I have to suppress guilt if I take too much leisure.

Swinging a golf club at the weekend seems somewhat decadent. Three weeks of holiday would deepen the guilt. I can never envisage retirement. I like my work; the family resent it as they say I love work. But the guilt was born in pre-war Hyde. Holidays then meant work in the bakehouse.

I remember only fragments of those far-off days; the kaleidoscope of my memory will not give a clear picture. At 151 Mottram Road, Hyde, bread-baking and muffins were more important than the holiday. By 1936 the family Hall had accumulated enough wealth to buy another shop. If anything, the living accommodation was even worse than 151 Mottram Road. The outside lavatory for ever freezing in the Pennine winds. Sandstoning the floor and whitewashing the walls were undertaken by the youngest baking apprentice. It was a long, hard road from donkey stoning to royal icing a four-tiered wedding cake. I hated that loo. It was situated at the end of a long, narrow bakehouse. Stone floors, white-stoned walls with decades of whitewash caked solid.

There were four or five girls working with Dad. He sang and danced. 'Begin the Beguine' was his favourite. I chuckled when Julio Iglesias gave it an injection of Spanish fly – and took it to number one.

Wine was sold over the counter, as our new shop, 52 Station Road, had a wine licence. Shortly after we took residence, Mother became a Christian Scientist. The great carboys of wine were emptied, the licence revoked. We employed a bevy of baking girls. Mary Hunt, tall, auburn hair, long legs, truculent and short-tempered. I loved it when she and Dad exchanged furies. He was a short-fuse chap too. Winnie Critchlow. I used to draw Winnie in art lessons. She was the archetypal Pennine lass, as if attached to the hills and rocks like a limpet.

Marion Wadsworth, also in the shop, played the piano for everybody; in church, old folks' tea parties, and upstairs in the bedroom.

Finally, Florrie Nuttall. The Bo Derek of Hadfield. What a tease; flighty, chirpy. My, she was good-looking, and she knew it. She tantalized the boys. She emitted more sparks than the Flying Scotsman. Living among the girls was fun. I have loved the ladies ever since. But! I had to pass them all to get to the loo. It was, and still is, the most embarrassing journey I ever took. No wonder I suffered from constipation. How can a chap complete his metabolic cycle knowing that those lasses were counting the minutes spent on that accursed throne? In those years I cannot remember one of the staff leaving. They were a proud, happy lot. The family exchequer geared to capitalism: Mum and Dad chained themselves to the workbench with the girls.

In that period I remember only one holiday. My brother Keith, always a frail lad, fell ill with pneumonia. Keith needed sun. By car to Bournemouth. September 1939. I remember little of Bournemouth – it was where you went when you had a bob or two. So 'Spot the Hyde locals' was the craze.

'There's Joe Bennett, our garage man – Donald Ross the butcher.' Stanley Wilkinson – addicted to Danish blue cheese and as a consequence was flatulent – told dubious stories and fell out with his wife Bessie, whose favourite retort was, 'Kiss my arse, Stanley'. When you are ten, adults using language like that seems very daring. Ooh, and the hotel! Good one, though. Potted palms, chintz curtains, two eggs for breakfast, Typhoo tea – or, as it was known in Hadfield, 'a quarten of Typhoon tea'. But despite the sea and sun, something was amiss. One Friday Dad heard that Britain was blacked out – war with Germany was imminent. It was 6 p.m. Dad ordered us to pack at once. He was on a short fuse. Mother pleaded: 'Stuart and Keith are hungry.' No, insisted Dad. War kills. Into the black Austin 12 BG 3140. Why is it that I can remember that registration from 1939, yet if the police stop me to enquire my present one I just cannot remember? But I remember that journey from Bournemouth. Darkness fell on Britain with the lights gone out. No street or shop lights. Windows blacked out. Mother pleads the children are hungry. Dad in a white-hot temper stops at a café in Cheltenham. The waitress in a panic about the war. Poached eggs on toast that took an hour to serve. Back to the Austin. Dad looking for signposts by the light of a flickering match. So we guttered through England at snail's pace – almost in convoy, as holidaymakers returned home with hearts heavy with fear and sadness. Mother was flat and cheerless. Dad still bad-tempered. A crisis always did reduce him to rage. He was a brave, brash man who could master a crisis – but to do it in a rage. I still do not understand. We crept up Station Road, Hadfield, in the darkest hours before dawn. What was war, I wondered? Whatever it was, it ruined my holiday. On Sunday, the wireless announced, along with the Ovaltinies and Master OK, the saucy boy, that Britain was at war with Nazi Germany.

A NOT-SO-GREAT WAR

> *'My friend, you would not tell with such high zest*
> *To children ardent for some desperate glory*
> *The old lie: Dulce et decorum est*
> *Pro patria mori.'*

How the character of Hall changeth. The acid in my stomach has been neutralized by age. My bile is less bitter. My head, once so often awhirl with gross uncharitable thought for my fellow man, now cools to a temperature which allows charity, humour and kindness to burgeon. I am a changed fellow and you all know it. It is the mellowness of the autumn's life.

The recollection. To collect anything implies at least a love of what is collected. When you collect memories even pinchbeck can be gold. So to my Mrs Jackson, my first teacher in pre-war Leigh Street School. In those days my life was lived as a very puny animal born to James Stuart and Mary Hall, living happily in the baker's shop at Hyde.

My father has been dead for 38 years. In each of those years I have searched deeply for emotional ties in the days of my youth. We are so fearful of asking those penetrating questions lest the answers disturb us. It is like gazing down a bottomless well, dark, dark – beckoning – explore it to find – explore it – find its depth. No, it is not safe! So to pre-war Hyde and a little soul search. In those days, life for big Stuart, my dad, and his wife, Mary, was anything but idyllic. His father was a watchmaker and jeweller of Portland Place, Stalybridge, his mother a bonny lass from a village near Barnsley – Cawthorne. His father was superintendent of Stalybridge at the turn of the century.

My father ran away to war in 1915, a 16-year-old boy, to join the 22nd Foot, the Cheshire Regiment. He fought on the Somme, was wounded twice and returned twice to the front. His stories of the Great War were graphic. Of Ypres, of Hill 10 and Armentières, and Lone Tree Ridge. Ten thousand tommies advanced on the German machine-guns. In three hours of slaughter they suffered 8,226 casualties. The Germans suffered more. Kitchener wants you for carnage. Ten million die for 'King and Country'. Dad was three years in the trenches. Mud up to the armpits; disease and filth, of rats gnawing both the dead and the living. The general advance of 20 yards – another 1,000 men cut down by the German guns; and the subsequent 20-yard retreat.

He emerged from his war an embattled, bemused, cynical young man who would never taste discipline again. He hurled his war medals into the fire in disgust. He was meant to take a career in metals. He would not apply himself. He began to drift, kept by his sister Beatrice. While he was at the front, his father died. Before the war ended, his mother had also died. The years after the war were never discussed. (He was then 19.) But he used to talk about the Menin Gate in Flanders.

Three years ago, I went to Flanders for the first time. In Ypres is the Menin Gate, a marble arch on the edge of the town square under which a road leads to France. I saw on this gate thousands of names of the fallen. I went closer. Leading from the gate is another wall. Enormous, marble: and on it, thousands and thousands of names. There embossed; carved in the stone, the men of the 22nd Foot who gave their lives for this, the most useless of wars. Suddenly the burden of that war fell on my shoulders. I felt the hot tears brimming and gently coming down my embarrassed cheeks. And my mind a mix of heavy sadness, jingoistic pride, and resentment of the politicians, industrialists and vested interests who began, and still begin, wars.

At eight o'clock, the Belgians honour the British dead. The buglers, with an escort, march to the gate. All traffic is stilled, all pedestrians stand silent.

The Last Post is sounded; and it reverberates through the silent throng; wafting gently into the wraiths of the 22nd Foot, ciphers of the war to end wars. Respect and dignity, and not a football yobbo in sight to scream an obscenity and shatter the solitude and peace that the Belgians bestow on Ypres every day at 8 p.m. And this, 64 years after the Armistice. My father often spoke of Passchendaele. A sea of mud, barbed wire, trenches full of water, blackened, gnarled, leafless trees where no birds sang.

One autumn morning, the sun high, I drove to Passchendaele. The little white road through neat farmhouses, the corn bending gold in the wind. Not a sound. The sky blue as blue, no jumbo jets hanging in it, or vapour trails to Never-Never. And then, like a mirage above the dancing wheatfields, the great memorial of the dead. Like a Hollywood set of Tara; white and dominating, the marble shrine, and the endless crosses – the husbands, sons, sweethearts lost forever. Maybe football yobbos should see Passchendaele. Or should they? Would they understand? I digress because in my little family history the discipline of this disgusting, indecent, shameful and horrific war became the indiscipline of the survivor, one James Stuart Hall. He never totally rehabilitated to the peace. He eventually became a baker and confectioner of 151 Mottram Road, Hyde.

Across the road lived a volatile red-headed girl who shopped for the family bread – a certain Barbara Betts, now Baroness Castle.

My father hated the trade, but the Depression meant hardship, the means test, humiliation and poverty, not the poverty of today, which is simply choosing between a new colour TV or a holiday abroad, but rags and begging, clogs and outside lavatories. Nightfall, then grubbing in the garbage. I remember when Dad had disappeared into the bowels of the Bank Field pub: the queues of the local needy outside our back door. Each received a bag of stale buns, pies, tarts and loaves doled out by my mother. She was a Hennessey from County Waterford, where the staple diet was potatoes and poverty. The 'stales', of course, were not 'stales' at all. They were fresh, sometimes even baked for those poor folk. Mother thought Dad did not know as he sank his pint of mild and cheerfully broke some loudmouth's jaw with his frying-pan fist. Dad knew, all right, but as she rose at 5 a.m. with him it was her conscience and merchandize. So among the walnut loaves, kegs of white fat, hundredweights of flour, crates of eggs and, 'Hello Mrs Smith. Your usual white, two brown, three custards and a cream sandwich', I grew up. Once I came across a batch of walnut loaves hot and delicious from the oven – the tops decorated with fragrant browned almonds. On impulse, I decided to decorate them. I took a pencil and prodded a hole in each one. They all promptly subsided, as I had allowed the hot gases held within to escape. I avoided Dad's rage under Mother's apron. It always seemed the safest place.

Sundays were bliss days. Dad owned a black fabric-bodied Riley Nine saloon. Rileys were fast and furious little cars: this one was driven until the engine glowed red and the gear stick laser-beamed. Blackpool was the favourite hike. The favourite smell of those pre-1939 days was stale beer and sawdust. I can smell both of them now, but always in the heat of a summer's day. And do not tell me it is nostalgic. It is not. It was hot; melting tar on cobbled streets and knotted hankies; trousers rolled up, and skirts tucked into bloomers. Was it happiness, or was it hardship? You tell me.

JESUS WANTS ME FOR A RAINBOW

My mixed bag of religions. Am I a Catholic, an Anglican or a Christian Scientist? I have been immersed in all three tubs and doctrines.

In the beginning, God created the heaven and the earth.
And God said, Let there be light: and there was light.
And God called the dry land Earth; and the gathering together of the
waters called he Seas: and God saw that it was good.

Chapter one of Genesis as the translators of the Bible described it for the most High and Mighty Prince, James, King of Great Britain, France and Ireland, in 1611. They had collated centuries of writings in Hebrew, Aramaic and Greek and produced with a single cover the world's best seller.

In the book of Psalms, lyrical poetry; in Kings, astonishing prose; in Mark, an almost modern newspaper. The Bible has been translated into over a thousand different languages.

But as it is the cornerstone of Christianity, the fundamental question is: do you believe it? Did God in one single stroke create heaven and earth, the planets, stars, oceans, and if he did – how did he do it?

Asking rhetorical questions, are we? Well, here is another. Why are we here born on earth? Who put us here? What are we supposed to do while we are here? Who decides when we should leave the earth? And where do we head for when we depart? Children are always asking these questions. Adults seldom do – lest the answers terrify. Mind-probing is not a healthy pastime. I always regard it as stepping on a carousel that is revolving at catastrophic speeds. Before I can imbibe a couple of answers to a couple of searching questions – I am hustled off again. Millions of neutrons, spinning in the head of subterranean juices wrought from the madhouse: the beatings and flutterings of the insane who have thought too much and severed the mind.

It requires an act of supreme bravery to ask if God exists. Most adults are faintly guilty and suppress doubt. Most churchgoers never ask. Atheists seldom give evidence. Agnostics never could tell 'Stork' from butter anyway.

Where is my stance? First, I must relate the history.

When my father died in 1974, my mother relied on me, her eldest son, to pick up the fragments of her shattered life. Grief is personal. Unless it has been experienced, it cannot be understood. It is the awful loneliness; the void of feeling; the bitter cold of the body, even on the hottest day – and the nagging hunger, that desperate grey pain in the pit of the stomach, as if the whole person were drowning in fathoms of dark grey cold seas.

When from time to time letter-writers ask why I am so cheerful in disposition, I long to tell them that after the first three years of marriage our eldest son Nicholas died as I was taking him to Pendlebury Children's Hospital.

And how painful the rehabilitation. And how we restored ourselves to what we were before. I do not think true happiness can ever be achieved without prior suffering. We never appreciate the sunrise until it sets. But to my mother.

One morning I arrived at her house. She was in tears. Unlike her, because she had led a life where emotions were hidden. In trade, her belief that the customer was always right – and the last thing the customer wanted was your problems. He or she was about to impart his or her own – in full Technicolor and at enormous length. She collapsed on my shoulder.

'I have a burden,' she said. 'A secret that I kept to myself.' There were many secrets of the Hall family known to myself – none that would shock her now. I have a cupboard of rattling skeletons. Back to Mama.

'When you were a week old you were baptized a Roman Catholic. Only Grandmother Hennessy, the high priest and I were present. Your father never knew. One week later you were baptized with the Hall family present into the Church of England.'

I collapsed, not with anguish but in gales of laughter. To think that the Hall skeleton lay in the Roman Catholic cupboard.

I have twice been to the Vatican. My rosary beads could have been blessed. An audience with the Pope. I never knew!

On the religious road, I attended a Church of England school – St Andrew's in Hadfield, where we spent hours over prayers and catechisms, hours that should have been spent in Latin, French and German.

What a fatuous waste of time, ask any prep-school boy. Schooled in subjects to prepare for the academic life. Not in prayers and prayers and more prayers. If we wonder why Eton, Harrow and Oxbridge rule, then look to our village schools and compare them with the battery education for the public school. So Church of England at Hadfield. So there I am – a conformist. C of E – a good little lad.

Well, something happened to me. Not atheism. No. In the intervening years 'twixt Hyde and Hadfield came – Christian Science! Oh, no, not Christian Science! Oh yes! Because it was necessary.

In the list of family tragedies was the death of my sister Patricia. So young that I do not even remember her. Nothing at all. But a child's death sears the parents, if not engulfs them. My mother saw no solace in the Catholic Church. Turned to Christian Science. A religion founded in Massachusetts, USA, by Mary Baker Eddy in 1875. Her manual was this: *Science and Health with Key to the Scriptures.*

In the preface she says: 'Ignorance of God is no longer the stepping stone to faith.' She proceeds to interpret the Bible to liberate her followers. My mother was one. In crisis there are two options: cry, 'Woe is me, bury the head and die,' or fight the affliction or oppression.

Having lost a daughter, came there a diphtheria plague in the 1930s. My brother was seriously ill. The disease killed many children, nearly killed him, and during the days of fever Mother turned to Christian Science, especially page 261. 'The effect of mortal mind on health and happiness is seen in this: if one turns away from the body with such absorbed interest as to forget it, the body experiences no pain. We should forget our bodies in remembering God and the human race.' Keith recovered. Subsequently mown down by a lorry – he was virtually dead for seven days. But as he lay dying, his injuries so dire, Christian Science was invoked.

The sheer weight of positive prayer must have shifted the needle of life and death into the life sector. Keith survived, went up to Oxford and now leads the academic life.

As he grew up, we travelled from Hyde to Manchester, to Peter Street, to the Fourth Church of Christ Scientist. The treat was to travel by tram through Denton, Reddish, Gorton, Ardwick and Piccadilly. It took an hour, but it was thrilling to sit behind the driver swinging that shiny brass handle through the speeds. I still believe in the tram – slightly more than I believe in God.

I attended Sunday School, and sat through discussions about life, truth and love. Tobacco and alcohol were banned. Sex was never discussed. There seemed an air of pseudo-holiness pervading. And, frankly, nobody quite knew where it began and where it finished. Suspended like *Last Year in Marienbad*, that weird movie of ethereal character.

My brother contracted pneumonia, again a killer in those days. My father applied steaming hot poultices to his red, raw chest. Mother applied the poultice of Christian Science.

At 18 I left Sunday School for the Big Church. I was understanding the concept that 'Life is Spirit. Matter, which is the life form, is ephemeral'.

And Mrs Eddy sees Genesis as life, truth and love unfolding as spiritual ideas with no supposition of error. In other words, your life improves in relation to the amount of God you allow to enter it.

It is a pattern of goodness; never condemn goodness, it is so easy to be cynical and nihilistic. And Christian Science is an everyday religion.

A quarterly is issued with suggested reading from the Bible, science and health. These are read in the morning to prepare the readers for the day.

It is a great solace for believers. But I never wanted to be *that good*. Like all boys, a pint of ale from the wood, watching the creamy head subside and cling to the pot, was a delight. I fancied myself with a Sherlock Holmes pipe, and the girls were irresistible. Goodness would have to wait for my dotage. Yet I listened at testimony meetings to the minor miracles that had been achieved. Of broken limbs mended. Of fevers cured. Pestilence ended. And one dramatic testimony from the commander of a submarine depth-charged to the bottom of the sea. The pressure springing leaks and gas filtering from split batteries. He implored his crew to join him in prayer. Suddenly, the submarine raised itself to the surface. During that experience, the young lieutenant's hair had changed from brown to white. Nobody could fail to be impressed, in fact *inspired* by these people just standing there and speaking the truth. But I did not want to be *that good*.

It is no use dabbling with a religion – either embrace it or leave it.

So I left. My brother left. My Mother stays. She does the lesson daily. I am proud of her. But she never smoked or touched alcohol. And searches for purity and sanctity.

I confess that when I was crushed beneath a lorry I prayed. And prayed hard. It is no joke having three tons of lorry parked on your groin. When Nicholas, our eldest son, died we prayed again. It did seem futile, but when Danny was born he appeared a replica of Nicholas. Coincidence, the power of prayer, or what? Please do not sneer. Doubt, discuss, disagree, yes – but do not deride.

So Christian Science has left me with a touch of guilt. But guilt is with everyone. It is conscience that makes most of us good most of the time. To live in a society where the strong help the weak and the rich give to the poor. There is much good around; nowadays it tends to be hidden, but it is there.

Future generations will be able to tap it. Hypocrisy and double standards are moving out of orbit, and I can foresee us returning to the Church. We shall have to think of churches as theatres, centres for the community where we go to enjoy ourselves. Bible Bingo with the Sacrament? One-armed bandits in the vestry? A rock and pop choir? A punk vicar with red, white and blue hair? If Queen played Manchester or Liverpool Cathedral there would be one hell of a congregation. Maybe goodness could rub off. Whatever the future – today we should open our minds. Close the Sunday supplement – the trench of middle-class society; turn off the telly and ask yourselves – is a little more goodness a bad thing?

Common sense still has a place in our sometimes ninny society. In my case, discipline did not cure irresponsibility but tempered it. Another lesson to illustrate. Early Hyde days. Dad the reluctant baker. Mother a willing slave. The one employee – Dora – like Dora Bryan. She was a surrogate mother.

Breakfast, a boiled egg, eaten perched on a baker's bench with dozens of piles of virgin dough being pounded into dozens of calories of daily bread – and off to school as soon as the school would allow. But at school I was a danger to society. I led a marauding gang. We placed sleepers on railway lines, and stood on them awaiting the locomotives to steam through Godley Junction at speed on their way to Dinting, Sheffield, London and beyond. At the last moment, jump out of the way. A miracle that we were not killed or a train derailed. One day a rail official called with an outraged parent. A gutless little nasty had informed. The chicken-hearted, lily-livered pansy had ratted on me!

Dad administered a stern warning. The following day I led my gang to the railway; I returned, smiling triumphant, with my dog, a black retriever. We were both black. He naturally; me from the escapade. Dad took from the wall his razor strop. It was my first beating. He took me to the small bedroom, removed my trousers and underpants and in silence beat me and beat me and beat me.

My mother was screaming hysterically, throwing herself at the door. My father was impassive. He knew that argument and logic had failed. I never went near the railway again.

If we spare the rod, do we spoil the child? Corporal punishment is one of those emotive topics that the English clutch to their hypocritical breasts. We allow our sons to be murdered by IRA scum in Northern Ireland. We are pusil-lanimous in opposing power blocks – anti-hunting, animal rights, anti-smok-ing, anti-motorist. Big issues terrify us, so we shelter in the safety of 'Shall we whack our children?' STOP (The Society of Teachers Opposed to Physical Punishment) proudly announced that Strathclyde, the largest education authority in Britain, voted to ban the cane in all schools. Thirty of the local authorities in England and Wales have banned the cane. STOP say that in Greece, Italy, Iceland and Luxembourg, corporal punishment has never been allowed. It was outlawed in Germany and Switzerland in 1970. Denmark and Spain in the 1960s, Portugal and Sweden in the 1950s, Romania in the 1940s.

If we cannot make one rule for all, leave the decision to the head of school. Assess the child and administer justice. There is no such thing as justice; muscle is the reality.

And let justice be seen in adult society. How – and by whom?

I do not believe that everybody is born equal: I do believe that everybody is born with equal opportunity. And I look around my friends. Dr Strangelove, the mad dentist, came from a backstreet in Preston. Dr Dave from a Liverpool slum. Bernard Ganley from a fruit stall in Leigh. Fred Pye from a rag-and-bone cart. Andrew Marsden, mini-tycoon, from a coalface back-to-back. Ron Stratton from Farrago to Ferrari. Not a silver spoon in sight. Plenty of brains, a dash of luck, a lake full of sweat, and a mountain of ambition.

There is a lot wrong in our society, but there is a darned lot *right* – if you want it that way.

IT'S A MAN'S LIFE IN THE ARMY. BUT WHAT IF YOU'RE A WIMP?

Crewe Station at 3 a.m. Dank. Grimy with 300 years of industrial pollution. Wisps of steam drifting into the autumn chill. Platforms full of National Servicemen forever serving 'King and Country' and catching up with neither. Catching up with 'Change at Crewe' was for most of us the distillation of post-war effort. 1950 was a bleak year. Most of our sixth form were conscripted, blackguarded, nay dragooned into the 'mob'. Pitchforked from warm suburbia, mother's milk and cornflakes, roast beef and relatives on Sunday, into the living hell of Aldershot.

Mind you, I had been forewarned. At the army recruiting office sat a war-weary officer. His eyes like pink gins. His leathery face heavily-lined, like a relief map of Cologne, dewlaps like a spaniel. He asked me for a choice of regiment. My father served in the 22nd Foot – the Cheshires. My grandfather with the Lancashire Fusiliers. Six VCs before breakfast. The Dardanelles running red with Lancashire blood. The Turks on the heights raining death on the luckless attempting the futile assault. Another of Churchill's calamitous mistakes. Armed with this meritorious soldiery I volunteered, not for the cavalry, the infantry, not even the education corps, but for the Catering Corps. Prefixed not royal – even the 'service corps' had 'royal', but simply 'the Catering Corps'.

Even the badge was an upturned chamber pot with a flame attached. Major Disgruntled, still enveloped in the charms of Cairo or 'up the Djellaba' – he certainly was not mentally in Manchester – reacted as if struck by a Polaris.

'For Christ's sake, why?' Calmly I told him that the family business was catering and motorcars and, if I was to spend two of my valuable years in uniform, then at least I was not toting a gun over Salisbury Plain fighting imaginary Huns who were busy winning the peace in the Saar anyway. He winced, shrugged his shoulders, signed the inevitable form in quadruplicate, and resumed his dream of vamping Mata Hari – the celebrated, exquisitely beautiful spy, who, rumour has it – was a feller!

So to Aldershot. The back of a khaki Bedford. The chat was school chat. The sports field – *Victor Ludorum*, the triumphs in bed and out. Never the failures. 'Memories distilled of all their coarseness, and what remains is precious gold.' Memories, sadly, rudely shattered by parade-ground coarseness, never the same again.

I was off-loaded into a bare Nissen hut. My head was shaved. I was issued with a uniform to fit Geoff Capes, boots that I swear were soled with lead, and was assaulted by a constant high-pitched scream emanating from the gaping cavern just below the nose of an ogre – the camp corporal. 'Camp' he lived up to. Within two days he seduced 'Amber', a rather squat, big-bottomed boy, a ballet dancer (so he claimed) from South Kensington. Amber had deep brown eyes like an Arab mare. His chestnut hair had been spared the barbarous barber. He really was quite divine.

To our unconcealed joy, Amber was a male whore from Battersea. The camp corporal received severe clap – Amber received a passionate discharge (from the army).

The eternal smell over Aldershot that ghastly autumn was of wood smoke and dead leaves. The smell of death. It pervaded the nostrils, clothes and mind. It almost augured death itself. In those first few days in the army I met the dregs of the earth. The Catering Corps had sent its earth-delving JCB to Glasgow and scooped from the bowels of Glasgow 'the Gorbals gang'. They swiped my uniform, walking-out clothes, money, even my morale. They beat up two young gents fresh from Cambridge. They threatened with bayonet and Sten gun. They terrorized. Borstal could not tame them, neither could the army. Do not even ask me if there is such an animal as the hardened criminal. I lived among them. My brother Keith, his mind extended liberally by 10 years at Oxford, labels me reactionary. My answer to him is – track down Hargan and his gang. If by now, dear reader, you are wondering how it all finished, let me inform you that even the army filtered the dregs. I was popped into a War Office Selection Board after four weeks, and hence lived a nomadic, placid life, dwelling in sleazy bars and copious khaki knickers. The ATS, now the Women's Royal Army Corps, were the real education corps of life.

In those far-off days, my dearest friend was a madcap called 'Ginger' Marlowe. A former sergeant in the Guards, he took a commission in the Catering Corps. While he rampaged in Aldershot, I was steadfastly at work poisoning 2,000 ex-Desert Rats in Wales. They were under canvas. I was overseeing the cleaning of cooking equipment unused since the war, covered in creosote – paint, brown, cans for the use of or suchlike. My patent method of removal was to burn it off, with disastrous results. The food prepared in tins, billies, dixies did what Hitler failed to do – lay 'em low. Another blot on the Hall family escutcheon. Twenty-five years on, after exchanging Christmas cards each of those years, the BBC made *It's a Knockout* in Aldershot. I wrote to 'Ginger', now a colonel. I well remember rushing into the officers' mess, embracing him and recalling the days of 'Ginger'. He blushed to the roots of his fading mop. His cockney accent hidden under the most tortured vowel sounds of Eton and Harrow. Before his flock of subalterns he whispered:

'Please forget Ginger – call me Humphrey.'

Humphrey! I corpsed. The army had beaten him too.

Looking back, very few of my friends benefited from National Service.

Most took it like a dose of castor oil. Some found it a charade, all bull and whitewashing coal for some VIP. Some regarded it as fun, a sort of academic half-time in the game of life.

I talk of National Service because it is again seriously being paraded as the palliative for our social downfall. That somehow those mindless morons who follow English football, breaking foreign heads and our patriotic hearts, would mend their ways on the parade grounds of Aldershot. Substitute the dugouts of Derry for the battlefields of Berne and Brussels. Would swapping bovver boots and half-bricks for khaki and Armalite rifle cure the hooligan of the English malaise? Would they return after two years to fit into our social jigsaw? Certainly in Europe, boys still are conscripted into their armies, but then in Europe social disciplines are still upheld. One can still walk the streets of Vienna or Berlin, Berne or Brussels without fear. Leave the car unlocked, even the house. No, I believe National Service should begin where discipline begins – in the home. Pride begins in the family entity and is promulgated in the schools, then in the job. To ask a third party to shoulder responsibility is abnegation of ours. Our generation, history may stigmatize as the one that failed. Your views, dear reader, are welcome.

WHEN IN ROME, DO AS THE ROMANS DO, BUT NOT TOO OFTEN!
What is the saying about great oaks from little acorns grow?

It is amazing the way things develop out of the most uncompromising beginnings. I can remember how, in June 1940, Churchill, with France down on its knees, under the German occupation, offered them common nationality with us, the British. From that one remark grew an obsession with Europe which ultimately led, I suppose, to the Common Market, which I am tempted to call *Sans Frontières, sans Jeux*.

What a vexed issue, the Common Market. When we went in it was as a second-rate power. Dwindling raw materials, truncated industry. Our authority and reputation simply an imperial echo. Today we have oil, cars, coal – billions' worth – if we do not waste it.

Those poor Europeans. Economics flattened by 500 per cent oil price rises – split by different economical agricultural prices. Should we have done it – more to the point, shall we get out?

If only the Channel Tunnel had been built in 1946. We could then have pronounced Noilly Prat successfully. I first discovered the Continent with a school trip. To Paris by train. High adventure with French teachers, Gladys Wanklin and a mixed staff. Gladys had high cheekbones, black swept-back hair, long legs rife with excitement upon recital of Cyrano de Bergerac. Many were the nuances of Gladys. Her face had a certain oriental inscrutability that made fifth-formers wonder deeply. She was at times distraught; on others frivolous; but she had a frisson, maybe an overdose of de Maupassant.

I was 17 and in Paris, a gay blade. I fancied the totty, but could not afford it! I stayed late at the Lido; even later at a nightly performance of Wagner's *Flying Dutchman* at the opera. I suffered my first absinthe, that 'rotter of the brain' that subsequently put me out for three days in Spain. It is amazing with what clarity the early past can be recalled.

My next foray was by 1938 Wolsley 10 open tourer with Higginstein and Zoller to Spain. The year 1953. It was traumatic. We drove down Boulevard Haussmann, Paris, a *one-way* high-speed autoway, as the rest were *coming up*. Even the gendarmerie gave up. They had never seen such a car – nicknamed 'The Shed'.

We made Spain in four days. Compare that with two-and-a-half hours in a flight nowadays.

We arrived on the Costa Brava. The exhaust had fallen off, so we stuck it in the back. We lost the spare wheel. A mudguard was discarded. Descending the cliffs in tortuous fashion we made Tamariu, a tiny fishing village of one hotel with two shops and a straw and wood bar. Our accommodation was akin to a bullock pen. Barred windows, stone floor, wrought-iron roof. The Spanish food was simple. If it did not move, eat it; if it did move, stand on it – then eat it.

First day on the white, so dry sandy beach. My first dip in the blue, blue Mediterranean. Clear, clean and warm.

I swam to a rock. Sat gazing at the steep rugged cliffs of this most beautiful part of the world. Four hours later my back was bright red. Slowly it blistered. Señorita Rosa, the daughter of the house, bathed me constantly in warm olive oil. Nobody had told me of the appalling heat of a July sun.

As I could not bathe or swim, I helped in the hotel. I quickly understood that her father had died three months ago. She and her mother ran the hotel with the barman. Naturally, I helped with the chores; cooking, cleaning, washing-up.

It was obvious that being virtually fisherfolk they could not run a hotel. Bear in mind that the British still had not discovered Spain in those halcyon days. The package tour had not been invented.

Only Thomas Cook with their faintly imperial manners were conducting any sort of tour and were they not the 'Far East people' anyway? Suddenly out of the blue, Rosa asked if the three of us, Pete Higg, Zoller and me, would buy the hotel and the beach. The price £25,000.

We held a meeting. Pete Higg owned a laundry, a dry-cleaning factory, a wastepaper business and a few bits and bobs. Zoller was an industrial chemist, a rebel, who at school insisted that, as he was above organized games by dint of his lofty mind, he would dress for them in dancing pumps, suspenders, dinner jacket and bow tie. But he was impecunious. And me. Could I unlock the family treasury? But the whole venture was a Pandora's box of mixed ills and blessings, brought from heaven but with hope trapped inside.

What if Franco decided to nationalize all foreign-owned properties? What if some insurgents decided the British were not welcome? What if nobody came to the hotel? How would we transport holidaymakers here? It is too far in distance, and far too crude for your average traveller. So we reluctantly said no.

Five years later I returned, blasting through France in an ice-blue, factory-tuned Austin Healey. My mate Rock had a twin model, so we rocketed along emitting blood and thunder; burnt rubber, showered with speeding tickets like confetti at a society wedding. To Tamariu, the scene of balmy, dreamy days. The beach was a postage stamp. It had been invaded by six parking-block-sized hotels. Nightclubs, bars. Teashops flogging English tea and buns. It was a nightmare. Blackpool on bank holiday Monday. The Hotel Jano, Rosa's concoction of driftwood and wrought iron, was a hideous white monster. Over a jug of sangria she told me that a developer from Barcelona had bought the whole lot for half a million pounds. Then sold out for £55 million. It was sold out to the package tours. If only we had had the vision five years earlier. To realize that air travel in the jet age would reduce a thousand miles to the length of the M1.

From that moment, as I drooped back over the Pyrenees, I resolved to remove the scales from my eyes. Abandon the blinkers, and think, 'What does happen over the pond?' I was determined to drink strange concoctions in dubious dives, to eat dishes with unpronounceable names in the great cause of 'finding out'. The 'chef's speciality'. Often a hugely rewarding experience. Sometimes like Tripes à la môde de Caen – stewed tripe as tough as a baked wellie in brown Windsor soup.

I have had the vapours in Venice, palpitations in Paris, retchings in Rome, the runs in Romania, fevers in Florence. But I am a committed European. I am game for anything. In Bordeaux I was inveigled into a dawn party on the top floor of a garret. As I stepped on to the balcony to observe the dawn over the city tenements, I glimpsed something grey and shiny from a window across. The host, a Rabelaisian, rather tatty pseudo-artist cried: 'Duck!' I flung myself to the floor as a shot rang out from a 12-bore. His neighbour, a nutter, did not like dawn parties. I left for a 6 a.m. stroll through the famous closed market of Bordeaux.

A vast floodlit arena where day and night merge. Couples in evening dress mingled casually with early-rising housewives, clucking and scuttling like frightened hens; around them the traders with their cries. It was like a scene from an opera, so unreal that I had to keep looking and peering to see whether the Paul Ricard really made me hallucinate.

I staggered to the bar. What did I want? Breakfast, lunch, supper or champagne? An experience and a half. What I have learnt is that between each nation there is a great divide. Making television together is difficult. The Italians just did not like the Dutch. The Belgians did not trust the Germans. The Germans did not trust anybody, but they thought the BBC were the best. The French thought the Belgians doltish. The Belgians were inclined to agree, and so pinched the French language and their customs too. The Swiss resented the fact that all the countries thought Swiss cooking rotten; that all countries thought the Swiss were solid, stolid, humourless, money grabbers forever in lederhosen donging cowbells, yodelling up the Eiger in a sing-along bastardized German language. The Dutch loathed Italian food and ate Chinese whenever they could. The Italians loathed Dutch food, kicked their cheeses and ate Chinese food. Which is good news for all Chinese cooks.

But the *entente cordiale* is not so cordial. Everybody lampoons the English.

They cannot understand the dialects. And after 15 years of Eddie Waring, who can raise an eyebrow?

Our licensing laws baffle them, like our Sunday trading. They arrive here amazed and leave shaking their heads. Why tax pleasure they ask? A Frenchman regards his Gauloises and vin as day-to-day necessities. No government dare tax them as punitively as we do. No, a gulf the size of the Channel separates us. I still cannot think in kilometres. I know it is roughly half a mile. And litres – I always calculate twenty litres as roughly four gallons. And grammes. Again, 250 grammes about half a pound and so on. I still think in gallons, pints, pounds, ounces, miles and yards and feet. Rods, poles, perches and furlongs. Until we abolish the daft laws, I will not even attempt to don my beret, take up the palette and sing *'Frère Jacques'*.

But now I embrace and kiss my friends. It does embarrass them so. But the physical contact reassures me. I stretch out my hand and kiss on both cheeks. Never the lips! Both cheeks. Try it if you will and give your mates a hug. Far better than a nod or a wink.

A TOUCH OF THE PARANORMAL

In 1962 I went to Ibiza with my wife Hazel. It was enchanting, sophisticated, the watering hole of international celebrities. There were few hotels, the package-tour industry was not as yet fully charged. Our hotel was the Cala Gracio, family-managed, simple, homely and packed with French, German and British honeymooners. It was a holiday to file away in the 'Happy Times' folder.

Several years later I returned, with Hazel plus the siblings, Francesca and Danny. I tried, in vain, to book the Cala Gracio. It had gone under the bulldozer. Gigantic package-tour hotels had sprouted like army barracks. We stayed in one. The first breakfast was a disaster. Hordes of folk invaded the self-service buffet. Plates piled high with cornflakes, muesli, muffins, eggs, bacon, salami, sausage, cheese, ham. We were left gaping as this wild stampede continued. We were left with nothing to eat. Gripping the maître d' warmly by the throat, I demanded sustenance.

'Be early next time,' was his advice. As a wild Irishman, I have a short fuse when confronted by morons and imbeciles. He was dumped on the floor. The Germans quailed: the Third World War imminent. I sought and found management. Was assured all would be well. As my dad would say: 'Catch the next tram home.' I was all for up-sticks and away. Hazel prevailed, and we stayed.

The children put abed, we toyed with a little sangria in San Antonio

Square. I confess that after rampaging round Europe with *It's a Knockout*, living on the fat of the land, roistering with equally mad but civilized fellow spirits, being pampered in five-star hotels, this was the absolute pits. Reduced to life as a simple punter, blown like chaff in the wind. I felt like a sweet wrapper blown down a miserable, lonely tube platform.

The bars around the square were packed with trippers. Merriment and gaiety everywhere. I was morose; I came to Spain in 1953. The real Spain of quaint backward villages that had never seen an Englishman. Medieval plumbing from the days of the Inquisition. Quaint little brass bands playing plaintive music as the villagers held hands and performed intricate steps. Days of the corrida in Barcelona when Dominquin, that most aristocratic of matadors, caped a bull to a standstill. The bull on that blistering hot Sunday was part of the ballet. The crowd rose as one with each pass, choreographed to perfection. Dominquin arched his back as a conquistador of the sixteenth century, motionless as the bull awaited the coup de grâce. The plot of the corrida demands that the bull die. The sword was delivered with surgical precision. The President signalled. One ear was cut off. Dominquin, with his back to us, threw it to his paramour. From 20 yards it hit her. Blood poured down her Hollywood silk dress. Another ear – same scenario: then the tail, caught by his lover. She was ecstatic with joy. She had witnessed a perfect exposition of the matador's art. And it is an art – not a slaughter. Her beautiful face beamed. She was covered in blood, the dress ruined. Her name – Ava Gardner, the quintessential Hollywood movie queen.

All these memories flooded back as I sat in this cultural desert. I am seldom down, but I was that night. Suddenly the crowd focused on a little happening. An ice-blue Austin Healey ripped into the square, the driver wearing a matching sweater and ice-blue silk scarf trailing over his shoulder like a 1920s buckaroo. I smiled at last. 'Reminds me of my racing days.' In the 1950s I raced an ice-blue Healey, yes, with matching sweater, scarf and Herbie Johnson helmet. I had works support and was fairly quick: enough to win here and there. My trophies are now tarnished and hidden away. The guy buzzed the square, the twin Derrington exhausts bellowing, 'I'm macho – adore me'. We all did, but with insouciance he blasted away into the still of the night air, leaving a cloud of dust. At least he had enlivened the night. We settled back to contemplate.

Five minutes later he was back, strafing the square like a fighter pilot. Now, dear reader, I am asking you to interpret a sequence of events verging on the paranormal. He stormed up to the bar, where we sat observing him. He bounded up to me, proffered his hand and said: 'My name is Gershe from Munich.' Baffled, I offered a glass of nectar. He refused and said: 'Come to Ibiza Town.'

We abandoned our bar followed by admiring gazes. He threw me the keys. 'You know how to drive this machine – you've raced them.'

I was dumbstruck: an unknown German had been impelled to return, seek me out and befriend me, an inchoate friendship. But in the air, something unusual was about to unfold further. We parked on Ibiza's esplanade. Twinkling lights of many bars welcomed us. We tumbled into the first one, the A1 Bar, descended a graceful wrought-iron staircase. Greeting us a small Spanish lady, blonde hair in a tight bun, graceful features, slender, slight figure, immaculately dressed, subdued but very, very expensive jewellery. Working the bar a tall, handsome young Spaniard, obviously of some quality. Another slightly older, smaller man assisting. To the right of the bar was a small, carpeted alcove surrounded by a wrought-iron balustrade. There were five people sitting there. They motioned us to join them. They introduced themselves. One, a Spanish lady of some 40 summers, was leader of the pack. She was a lawyer, her family Ibiza landowners. She had just closed a hotel because she could not stand the package tourists. She accused them of raping, plundering, despoiling this beautiful island of her birth. She had simply boarded the place up and left it. Another visitor was an American guy – late fifties – directed B movies and was moving on. He had silver hair and could, being tall, twirl one leg around the other when sitting down. I wish I could do that – it reminds me of a pedigree cat on the preen. Another was a musician from Madrid – a conductor of an orchestra; with him a businessman, also from Madrid. The fifth member was a tall woman with long flowing black hair, aquiline nose, attractive, not beautiful – Ibiza gentility. The conversation flowed with the champagne cocktails. It was lively:

'Was Franco the despot who held Spain in a nineteenth-century time warp?'

'Would Spain evolve into a Pan-European industrial power?'

'Would the American influence exert itself here as it has throughout the civilized world: imposing its commercialism, outright monetarism, pop culture, Big Mac, "live-for-today" ideals that have eroded centuries of individual European culture that used to be treasured?'

I find it stimulating, educational and a trifle unnerving when foreigners dissemble Britain. It is difficult to analyse one's own country from the inside. Foreigners take an objective view, and sometimes it hurts. These were pre-Thatcher days of the three-day working week, the dead lying unburied, Red Robbo and the British Leyland malaise, wildcat strikes, trade union limitless power. Britain in the early 1970s was the sick man of Europe. After a couple of hours we left to trawl the other bars, the German – Gershe, Hazel and me. None of them compared to the A1, so we returned. Down the staircase into the well. Nothing had changed or moved. The same five people sat in the alcove.

'We were waiting for you. We knew you'd come back.' This was now surreal, like *Last Year in Marienbad*. Was this preordained? Were we obeying a force greater than our understanding? The bar's owner introduced herself. An aristocrat, an escapee from the rigid corset of Catholic conformity which is old Spain. So the A1 Bar was something special. We returned every night to the same scene.

You know, I am acquainted with people here in Wilmslow, Cheshire, who claim *never* to have known happiness despite all the trappings of wealth, their lives clouded with anxiety, frustration, worry and depression. Happiness is a state of mind, nothing else.

So the holiday drew to a close. Gershe's skin, burned by the sun, peeled off in sheets. 'It's my winter skin' – he never used sun creams or oil – he just peeled like a ripe banana.

We said farewells to all, by now our bosom friends, at the A1.

Gershe said goodbye, never to meet again, never to write, not even a Christmas card. It was an episode in life, he explained with German pragmatism.

The story, already surreal, now takes a further twist. Ten years on, I journeyed again to Ibiza to construct a travelogue for television. With some haste I rushed to the A1 Bar. It was not there. I put myself about, made dozens of enquiries. Not only was it not there, they said; it never existed. Nobody on the island had even heard of it. My nape hairs bristled. I shivered, despite the heat of a Balearic summer. Ghosts invaded me. It was supernatural. It confounds me to this day. I am a fond and foolish man – I fear I am not in perfect mind.

IS LIFE A BOWL OF CHERRIES, OR ANOTHER BOWL?

Life is a serious business – or is it? The ultimate rhetorical question! Or, is it that life is so daft that we have to layer it with seriousness to make it work at all?

Harbingers of doom forecast the end in the middle of the 1960s from interglobal nuclear war. Now that idea is trashed, the same pundits intone that the icecaps are melting, the ozone layer holed, the world is a greenhouse, acid rain will destroy the environment, pollution from the motorcar will eventually poison us all.

But only this month a report has revealed that the greatest danger – methane gas – is posed by cows breaking wind. No! Not you, dear! It is those billions of beasts, quietly ruminating and farting as they go. All those doe-eyed, ever-so-lovely meat on the hoof, with their dangling fetching udders – they are poisoning you... and you know it not. Mind you, as I write these words, and observe the bubbles gently rising in the bath, the end product, literally, of three pints of Greenalls Best Bitter, I recall the autumn of 1868. The *Dodge City Bugle* of that year forewarned of the pollution of the world's atmosphere not from buffalo wind but from those heroes of the Wild West themselves... the cowpunchers. When you think of it – mountains and mountains of pork and beans washed down with two fingers of 'Red Eye'. And then all that bumping about on those dreadful saddles, every jolt a break of wind. Oh, my word! No wonder those gigantic herds of cattle stampeded. They couldn't bear the stench!

No, gentle, dear reader, life is totally absurd. Ignore the pundits, the economists, the politicians, the media figures – unleash the corset and laugh at yourself. A yuppie friend, tall, dark, gruesome, married a rather fey, slender, nubile young damsel of rich parentage. They took off for Phuket – where else? – for the honeymoon. On the first night abed, as the lobster and champagne fought with the digestive system, the libido rose. 'Darling,' she whispered softly, 'I must swiftly to the lav.'

I must explain at this juncture that the upper classes never refer to a water closet in vulgar lower-class terms as 'the loo', 'the toilet', 'the can', 'the john', 'the ladies' or 'the gents'. No, it is 'the lav'. Just bear that in mind and nothing else!

Meanwhile, back in the marital bed, in her diaphanous silk chemise, she lifted herself from recumbent, slowly over his prostrate, trembling torso. Alas, the lobster and champagne made their presence distinctly and flatulently audible. Roger smiled, a patronizing, loving smile, patted her upper-class, small, rounded bottom and quoth: 'Whose little bot-bot uttered that gentle whisper like a fluttering of a moth's wings before the dying embers of the woodman's fire?' She returned his loving smile, completed the metabolic cycle, and returned flushed (twice).

I shall draw a discreet veil over the rude, base, animal contortions which followed. Suffice to say, demands were made on his manhood that even non-stop immersions in *Health and Efficiency* in the days of his youth had not prepared him for. He took a right old tousling. If in the *Kama Sutra* there are 95 methods for coitus, she had ten more.

'Wonderful for you – how was it for me?' she breathed.

I put it all down to upper-class breeding. All that riding to hounds, firing off fowling pieces at everything that moves, a Mellors in every herbaceous border, a Jeeves in every boudoir.

After wrestling for five hours with this mobile reaper and binder, this Rambo of the Shires, he lay inert.

'Darling,' she whispered, 'I'll have to visit the lav.' Exactly as before she essayed over his body. Again she emitted the bubble and squeak.

'Go on,' he snarled. 'Stink the place down.' Ah well, the course of true love! But what a revelation of human nature.

The theatre of the absurd. Since schooldays, I've exploited my own sense of humour – at my own expense, may I add. My headmaster was really to blame. As head boy 'twas my task to ring the school bell for morning assembly at precisely 8.55 a.m. That scrofulous, shuffling tide of bleary-eyed, dirty-necked, socks-around-ankles, spotted, reluctant, truculent, recalcitrant non-humanity, awaiting the daily intake of forced feeding daily bread. Alas, I always arrived at 9 a.m. My headmaster would be leaning laconically on the bell.

'My only adage,' breathed he in mock remonstration, 'is "Everything matters, but nothing matters terribly".'

Mind you, I stretched that dictum to breaking point. On a school trip to Paris, I detached myself from the crocodile filing in and out of the Louvre, Napoleon's tomb, Versailles, Fontainebleu and the incessant tourism rounds for a solo round of Montmartre. Women with skirts held high, silk stockings, suspenders, bright red lipstick, rouged cheeks and the price in Braille tattooed on their naughty bits. I was caught red-handed in the small hours in Place Pigalle. Dimly, through the smoke haze, I observed the grim visage of 'Wof', the physics master, gimlet gaze, as I dabbled in the fleshpots. My carafe of *vin* turned instantly to vinegar. The 17-year-old Salome 'pon his knee became Edwina Currie and was, in a word, dumped. The newly-lit cigarette an instant dimp. The pimp became a wimp. I didn't resist arrest. Confined to hotel for the day and night. Do you know where the staff retired to for a fact-finding, educational, instructional tour the following night? Yes! To my naughty little Bar Escapade. Rough justice, isn't it?

The head was, as always, forbearing. After all, he has seen me lying under a dustbin cart's wheels, when I crashed into it on my motorbike. Caught me on the playing fields, not playing cricket, with the head girl. Pardoned me for setting fire to the chemistry laboratory on VE Night. Fully understood me vamping the English mistress, a Carmen in her youth, a Wagnerian figure in maturity. As Falstaff in his eighties observed, 'Young men must live'.

So you see, dear reader, the seeds of youth sown. Life is a potty or a bidet really. Here to be enjoyed. That is why I enjoy life. Somewhere, sometime, there is a laugh or two – or three or…!

A PEEP BEHIND THE IRON CURTAIN
19 March 1985

I have unfolded my misadventures while motorcycling to school. If you remember, I was pinned beneath a refuse lorry, which reversed off my crushed limbs, leaving me with a dented ego in more ways than libido can dream up. I subsequently recovered. The motorcycle was sold. But to this day I still ride hairy two-wheeled beasts. As my dear friend Beryl Reid used to say: 'When you have 60 horsepower between your thighs, *everything* lights up.'

Since those traumatic early years I have owned around 400 motorcars and been totally in love with many of them. My favourite was a 1955 Austin Healey 100 much modified by Healeys. Ice-blue, it was aesthetically the most beautiful sports car ever designed, along with the E-type Jaguar. I raced and rallied her for two years. She was temperamental, loved to be petted, never forgave a mistake. On wet roads her behaviour was Parisian courtesan on the love couch: all over the shop and never in the same place twice.

My divorce from my Healey was painful. VLG 359, where are you now? I still have love pangs. Since the leaving, I have owned Jaguars, Astons, Bristols, MGs, Lotus, Bentleys, Rolls-Royces, Frazer Nash, Morgan. For the life of me I cannot recall a single registration number of any of them.

Currently the stable includes two Rolls-Royces, one an immaculate Silver Shadow cosseted all its life by a doting chauffeur, the other a 'Donington' two-seater, originally a 1948 Rolls Bentley saloon, re-engineered by a perfectionist in 1978 into a sports motorcar. The suspensions and gearbox are strictly vintage. The chassis would support a Chieftain tank. The upholstery is

Crimson Conelly hide. It is white, a block long, and stimulating to the pilot. The conversion cost was like the national debt. No more were laid down. It is an amazing motorcar, but do not ask me its registration number – I cannot remember it. It is a cherished car, but not really loved.

So, dear reader, how important is your car? Cherished member of the family or working tool? Does it possess character and personality, or is it merely a lump of computerized mechanics without a soul? Does your car impart real pleasure or leave you ambivalent, purring with delight or cringeing at its plastic, modern conformity?

Once there was snobbery in motorcars. A man's social position dictated by his choice of vehicle. In a socialist world etiquette has eroded. The roads are congested with anonymous pillboxes and anonymous drivers. Fortunately, nothing to compare with Eastern Europe yet, where every vehicle is a Lada or Moskvitch in pale grey or dark blue.

I will never forget the sadness of my first crossing of Checkpoint Charlie into East Berlin. Eight of us jauntily embarked on a motorcoach from West Berlin. Joyously singing, smoking huge pipes of toxic tobacco. West Berlin with its garish modern glass and vitrolite buildings – a monument to capitalism. The shops bright and bulging with merchandise, the streets packed with Mercedes. Wealth in abundance.

At Checkpoint Charlie, we evacuated our plush coach on to another – stark, cold, unwelcoming. Our buxom West German departed. On to the East German coach came a woman dressed in heavy Cossack grey. Grey hair, grey boots, grey complexion. Her face devoid of make-up, her eyes sunk deep in a careworn visage. She demanded our passports. Now, my passport once upon a yesteryear was incarcerated in a bagful of duty-free booze somewhere in the Alps. A careless porter threw it into my room along with my good self. The bottles broke and the contents gave my passport a permanent gin mark – all the signs of a watermark – but neat alcohol. The East German regarded my passport. In glee, I said: 'Neat gin.'

She snorted and snarled: 'Decadent capitalist.'

The trip from henceforth was a disaster. I have always wanted to see the Unter den Linden. As a student of *Mein Kampf*, I have always been fascinated by Hitler's rise to absolute power and his domination of Europe. His use of the spoken word to inspire legions to follow him. His huge rallies with uniforms and badges, flags and anthems to unite the German race into a fearful fighting force that changed the face of the world. His subsequent insanity and demise are well tabulated, but the Unter den Linden was synonymous with his ascendance. But that famous street was desolate. War ruins, huge blocks of drab apartments, shops that sold only books and propaganda, no smiling faces, just grey cheerlessness. Empty of traffic save for Lada and Moskvitch cars in blue or grey.

On the back seat of that ersatz motorcoach, I decided to light my pipe. Clouds of 'amphora' rose like a geyser. The plump American lit a cheroot and we beamed beatifically.

Suddenly the coach braked to a halt. We were ordered out peremptorily...

'Hell,' I thought. 'Over the hedge is a train bound for Siberia, and we're on it.' Fears were stilled by the Cossack guide who ordered us not on to the train but up a hill, where we were commanded to view the tomb of the unknown Soviet soldier. Dutifully, still smoking, we went our way, passing several groups of school children on a similar mission. I am very fond of children, as 12 years of *It's a Knockout* might indicate.

The children were blond, blue-eyed, neat of dress and comportment. They filed past without a word, no jokes, balloons, catapults, leapfrogs – just orderliness. I tried clowning, pulling faces, a little conversation. Nothing – no reaction; simply stony stares. I began to feel desolate. Where was simple happiness? The air was fresh, a watery sun was peeping through. In despair, I galloped down the hill with a senior British Airways executive.

We ran into a café-bar at the foot of the hill. At several deal tables sat workmen, grey and unsmiling. I ordered coffee and cognac. Then, like a hurricane, in rushed our Cossack guide. Grabbing my lapel, she propelled me through the door. We were not allowed to drink in that bar. Shamefaced and thoroughly downhearted, we piled back on the bus to the only specified hotel for western visitors. The currency in that hotel was the West German mark. At last we boarded the bus for Checkpoint Charlie and freedom. At that awful doom-laden place, barriers were raised and lowered, militia mutterings seemed endless. The Cossack guide departed, smileless and wordless.

Back on the West German bus we raised three cheers for democracy, the cheers tempered by the sober pondering: why do we, this side of the Iron Curtain, so abuse our privileges? Football riots, muggings of our old folk, vandalism, graffiti and mountains of filthy litter. Is there a middle ground where rigid discipline can marry freedom? But to return to the motorcar – prosaic, sanitized tin box or erotic delight?

Where I dwell, in Cheshire's leafy lanes, German cars hold sway. A multitude of Mercedes, a plethora of Porsches, a vortex of VWs, an ambush of Audis, battalions of BMWs. The Germans have, with great subtlety, structured society per choice of car. Herr Doctor is Merc. Herr Accountant is BMW. Herr Playboy is Porsche. Herr Banker is Audi. Herr Up and Coming is VW GTI.

I acknowledge that German cars are brilliantly engineered, long-lasting and have instant resale value. But do they induce wolf whistles from small boys? Meanwhile, I shall don my Biggles kit and warm up the Donington.

NOW FOR THE NEWS

Some locations are well away from beaten tracks and English newspapers. Recently, I was in Yugoslavia, and the headlines were disturbing. Let me be clear. The more I travel, the more I love to return home. California sounded fun, as the commercial says. I went; but after three weeks I returned home satisfied that I had discussed working there – even to the extent of meeting studio heads in Hollywood – but I preferred my native heath. We have, in the north-west, the ingredients to sustain one in reasonable financial and social health. We may cough a lot, but it only hurts when we smile. So abroad, we like to keep in touch. Not any more.

On location, I bought a copy of the *Daily Telegraph*. I am by nature of good humour; seldom, unless by idiocy or ill health, put down. The *Telegraph* put me down.

I think it was the shock of reading awful news. At home there is a ceaseless bombardment of it. And, you know, shock wave after shock wave induces a built-in resistance to bad news. At home we scan the print, watch the box, hear the bulletins. We absorb what we want and, brutalized by headlines, look at the horoscope, sports news or the great placebo – what's on telly tonight? I rejoice for old Hollywood movies. I have seen *Casablanca* at least 20 times – I still weep for Bogart.

There is no escape from the welter of journalists feeding the hammerhead sharks on the body of bad news. But away from it in a remote outpost in Yugoslavia the news sears like napalm.

'PC crippled by a bullet, then kicked in face.' (When I was a lad the uniform was inviolate. PC Sam Simonite ruled Glossop with a big voice and fists like gammon legs.) 'A surgeon's wife, her African toy boy murdered in a car park.' 'Secret navy tests killing off whales.' 'IRA hospital killers used girl as shield.' 'Fare dodger hurls clippie off bus. Spinal injuries, broken hip and leg.' 'Armed police storm hotel.' 'Peace process collapses.'

To sport. England's dismal prospects. Worse still the Sports Minister reneging the responsibility for hooligans' behaviour abroad. The British have sunk low. I am ashamed – it reflects on us all, and the government must act.

At the BBC, a young reporter rushed back to the TV studios having reported a house fire. 'How was the film?' asked the laconic news editor.

'Spoilt,' she said with the earnest freshness of a Girl Guide at her first camp. 'They'd got the bodies out before I arrived.'

I feel a sense of outrage if stories like that are true. If she was that unaffected by disaster, then how empty must be her mind? I long to say, life is not like this. Evil deeds are wrought by individuals, not communities. In my life the goodies will win. John Wayne will enter stage right, on a giant horse, and slay the baddies. The cynics classify me as naive. But 40 years have made me ambivalent and pragmatic. One man can terrorize a community. The Yorkshire Ripper virtually brought the county to a standstill for five years. Imagine what ten of him could accomplish. Then one hundred. Ian Brady, Myra Hindley and Harold Shipman have made Hyde, my birthplace, the world centre for serial killing. The evil caucus is still small. We outnumber them thousands to one. When a government comes along to put us all on the wartime footing, that makes us act as one, and believe in the future. We shall win. With a *divided* society, we shall shrink further back into our individual shells.

I WANDERED LONELY...

Only report what ostensibly you want to hear. Years ago I had a salutary lesson. I had just begun to present *Look North*. I have a style that irritates many people. One night at 6.20 p.m. I had finished the programme. The telephone rang. I picked it up. A woman said: 'Is that Stuart Hall?'

'Yes.'

'I hate you,' she said.

'Why?' I asked.

'Because you smile.'

'But I like to smile.'

'I don't,' she snarled, and thumped her receiver down.

The following night, the same scene. Having got over the shock of being hated – I have never hated anyone in my life, so it was a shock – I was patient. I explained that my way of telly was informal. To relax in the studio, we have jokes on and off camera. That to have an ambience like no other studio we have that northern humour.

She then said: 'I live alone – crippled with arthritis and confined to a wheelchair – I resent your happiness. Goodbye.' And she replaced the receiver with a click.

The following night the telephone rang again. Oh, no! I couldn't stand another wigging. I thought of asking a secretary to stand in the breach but changed my mind. It was Mrs X. The message was brief: 'You know, I'm quite beginning to like you.'

Suffusing relief, I have never forgotten the incident. It made me even more conscious that I am privileged to enter your homes, maybe touch your lives. Television is still for human beings and not technology. On *Look North* as I sit at the *Star Wars* desk in the *Empire Fights Back* set I wonder if at the touch of a button I can make it ascend to the Milky Way.

Neutrons, mutrons, butrons bonk – self-destruct. Remote: synthesized tunes and voices. Give me a chair, a camera, a cameraman I know, make it simple. Or do you want the computer to succeed us? Computers cannot create images that are not already in the brain of man. Remembering always, of course, that 'man' embraces woman. What a smashing idea! I am glad God thought of it. But so stereotyped are we that we tend to mythologize places as well as people. Let me tell you a story that both proves and disproves it.

The myth is that the north-west coast is just a longer Blackpool. Rock with letters all the way through, sandwiches gritty to the bite, brown ale going down and coming up, deckchairs, transistors, the Tower, the garish Golden Mile, cockles, mussels, oysters, whelks, the crash of trams, the clip-clop of landaus, the scream of voices and the never-ending tug of the wind.

Nothing could be further from the truth. Long stretches are like that, but not as many as you would think. Forget the concrete reach from Lytham up to Fleetwood. Forget the anaesthetic miles of Morecambe. Forget all Southport's rich, Edwardian charm.

Look for the lonely. And it can be found. I know, because I found it one day years ago, and never have forgotten. It still has dream-like overtones, like the magic, fairy casements of one of Barrie's plays.

I was driving north along the A6, our only highway then, specially designed, it often seemed, to be a traffic jam. But this was in the summer, it was the middle of the week. I was heading for Lancaster. It was 10 o'clock and lovely. The weather was delicious, and I will not allow a different word. A few miles south of the long drop down to the valley of the Lune, I saw a signpost on the left. It said Glasson Dock. On an impulse I swung the wheel and followed the road round. Round as it happened the southern shore of Morecambe Bay. A place I had never been to. A place I had never seen. A place I had never imagined could possibly exist and least of all in busy Lancashire. I pulled on to the quayside of a dock designed for little ships, or perhaps as a setting for a film about the sea. To the north, a shimmering blue, was a hazy lump I recognized as the hills of southern Lakeland. Too far away, too soft and indeterminate for any mountain to be named, but welcoming; and the perfect backcloth for all the silver acres of shining Morecambe Bay, all the golden acres of glistening sand. Above, a sky as blue as porcelain, and not a whisper of a wind. Only the cry of the gulls, the footprints of oystercatchers and the grey white flash of wheeling common terns.

I sat on a bollard on the old stone quay and slowly soaked it in. No boat on all the water, no soul there to be seen. And no sound to be heard, except for that mysterious, barely audible rustle of the sea, and the gentle slap of shrouds against a mast.

The loneliness began to work on me. Was I the only man that day alive? I wandered back along the quay, past chandlers' stores, provision shops and a pub whose doors were sandblasted and tight closed. Still no one to be seen. I wandered over that little sea-centred settlement and could have been the only man on earth. I looked down into tiny yachts, bobbing on the slowly rising tide. All were empty. I knew that this was magic, that I was in the middle of a highly personal dream. Was it really here? Was I really here, I had to ask myself?

Time must have a stop one day. Why now? On that day, Glasson was as quiet as the grave. And that felt like the right word. For though I was alive, there was no other life. Even my watch, I am sure, stopped ticking.

I sat on a bollard, looked at the sparkling water and the shining, clear-blue sky. I listened to the bird cries and smelt the air, in which I could have sworn I smelt not just the salt, but the smell of the bracken on the bay – encircling hills.

I lost all track of time as I sat there, and had no notion of how long it was. But then things clicked. Time started up again. I heard voices of two men who came from nowhere. I noticed smoke curling up from the chimney of the pub. A Customs man came ambling along. The quayside filled with people. Where had everybody been?

The spell was broken. Glasson was alive again. I got into my car and drove away, still thinking of it all. And 25 years on, I have never since gone back. Dreams are precious things, especially ones like that. And I do not want it broken.

REFLECTION IN TIME

We got to the garden gate. A little girl came struggling up the hill.

'Hello.' She was really talking to the dog.

'Hello,' I replied. 'Been to school?'

She sighed and said: 'Yes.'

Worried by her sigh, I asked her: 'What have you learnt today?'

She thought for a moment. 'We've learnt inverted commas,' she said, and went her way, leaving me perplexed. As I walked the dog, I kept thinking about what she had said. Two other dog-walkers thought I was dotty, because from time to time I burst out laughing. It cannot have been anything my dog said: she wasn't in the mood for conversation.

But the longer I walked, the more it dawned on me that there was something in what the little girl had said.

When I first started learning English formally, yonks ago, it used to be divided into English Language and English Literature. It did not strike me as daft at the time, but it does now. You can write English Literature – not that much of what I write is that – but you cannot write English Literature without using English Language.

Yet in my day – maybe still – they were strictly separated. The thinking presumably was that as long as you could write a nice 'Thank You' letter if you had been to a party, it did not matter a damn if you had never read a word of Shakespeare, Dickens, the Authorized Version of the Bible, Jane Austen, Milton (whom we always used to call 'Mouthwash' at school), Alexander Pope, John Dryden, John Bunyan, the three Williams – Hazlitt, Cobbett and Blake – Jonathan Swift, Daniel Defoe, Samuel Johnson (or rather James Boswell, without whose marvellous biography the crusty old doctor would probably not be much read any more) – or any of the rest of that enormous body of writers who have made English Literature the greatest in the world. You have only got to put it like that to see how silly the idea is. In my day – they used to teach us history and geography separately. It seemed natural to me then. But how stupid! So much of history depends on geography. Why do you think, say, the famous British battles of the past were fought where they were? Obviously because of the lie of the land.

If there is only one route through the mountains or across the marshes, then two opposing armies will meet on that route and fight there. Geography determining history.

They are interconnected, interwoven, interlocked. It goes even further back. Geology, the science of rocks, shows how things that happened hundreds, maybe thousands, millions of years ago, have created the geography surrounding us today. And if geology influences geography, and geography influences history, and history influences the way we live today, then what happened maybe a thousand million years ago is affecting our way of life today.

Take our industries after the Second World War; coal, cotton, engineering, shipping.

About 250 million years ago, the north-west was a vast mangrove swamp, the delta of a gigantic river running down from somewhere near where Norway is today. Over the years, the decades, the centuries, the millennia, trees grew, fell, rotted and bedded down into layers of peat-like material. They were covered with delta deposits, and the land slowly sank, and the process was repeated many times. Those beds of organic material gradually became seams of coal. Gigantic earth movements ultimately brought them within our present-day reach. Lancashire had become a coalfield.

Something else. Those same earth movements which raised the coal seams to within our reach also raised the Pennines, on whose flanks the coalfields lie. Those Pennine hills cause the wet, westerly winds to rise as they cross them. As they rise, they drop their rain. Which is why the north-west has weather and not a climate, and why cotton flourished here. Breakages in the fragile cotton threads being spun and woven were far less frequent than in other parts of the country, because Lancashire is p***ing wet!

So our coal and cotton industries were almost a direct result of what happened 250 million years ago.

Our deeply indented coastline – particularly the wide and deep Mersey Channel, the Ribble Estuary, and Morecambe Bay, and the deep-water access to the iron ore deposits around Barrow-in-Furness – all those are the result of geology influencing geography. And that meant that the history of this area was influenced, in those industries of iron and steel, engineering and shipping, by what happened all those millions of years ago.

So why am I telling you all this? Not to give you the sort of geography lesson I never had at school – or you, I daresay. No. I think there is a wider moral to be drawn. It is this. That life is not divided up into compartments. 'No man is an island, entire of itself.' John Donne said that more than 300 years ago, but I think we still have not really realized it yet. All life is unified, all one interrelated happening. And we, too, are therefore interrelated. Every man is a piece of the continent, a part of the main. Whether you think of it as another way of saying we are all one in the sight of God, or in the sight of men, does not matter to me. It is the one-ness that matters. The unity is all.

A POLITICAL WAVERER

Politically I am one of the great wedge, maybe 70 per cent of the electorate lodged firmly in the middle of the road.

We want government seen but not heard. The right to work, without being bowed down by taxes. A mixed economy. Private enterprise working alongside nationalized giants – neither looking over the shoulder to see what the other is getting. The politics of greed have tainted industrial relations since the war, the faults lying both with weak management and irresponsible unions. We want the right to buy our homes, educate our children to our own dictates and pockets. We want fair rewards for those who deserve them.

We are a cocktail of Gaitskell Socialism and Macmillan Toryism, with a dash of the Jo Grimond. You could say to the cocktail shaker, to crib from James Bond, two fingers of rye. In our case it's two fingers of wry at the extreme left and the extreme right. We have no voice because we are slow to militancy, preferring reason to the flying picket, words before petrol bombs.

As a result we are paranoiac, bullied and distrustful of our leaders. I am inclined therefore in elections to look for the person, rather than the party, to be the recipient of my cross – as you may be aware. I look for quality and guts. Principles and social conscience. Independence of mind, and not the lick-spittling of lesser backbenchers. In the north-west we are all served. I will not catalogue, but we have fighters who more than earn their money. Men and women of intelligence who, unlike some, could leave the Commons for a better salary. They serve their community rather than shovel their perks on their fires of non-ambition. Some will never achieve high office, but that does not concern me. It is what he or she does with my vote for me, mine and my community.

A LETTER FROM DORIS

Down the years I have cherished many letters, none more than this. It came from Doris Jackson.

> *Dear Stuart, I wonder if you remember me. I was your first teacher at Leigh Street Infant School, Hyde. I can remember you offering to sing in our class. 'There came to my window, one morning in spring, a sweet little robin, he came to sing.' You liked entertaining then, and would only be about four years old.*

The whole of Leigh Street was in love with her. The sweetest, kindest, most beautiful woman in the world. Innately loving. Slim and tall, blonde curls arambling, blue eyes tender and caring – totally unsuited to a little prat like me, poised on the knife-edge of juvenile delinquency. 'Memories distilled of all their coarseness – and what remains is precious gold.' I shall wallow in the iridescent glow of Doris Jackson. Here is the picture she had of me – baker's boy and Doris – aged four. It is an 'Aah', isn't it? I am here as someone to be loved. My whole demeanour is, 'I'm sweet and clean, hair pomaded ready to be loved by everybody'.

Do recalcitrant schoolboys occasionally dress up to impress? – not little girls, because they are like little boys. The nature ramble really does mean picking bluebells and buttercups; nettle rash on bare knees; frogs, toads and newts in Bankswood. Although we did have a competition between rival frog marchers, each equipped with a straw to blow up the backside of our own frog, to make it win the race of the Hyde frogs.

But Mrs Jackson.

For her I would produce my work. It was the work of an artist. Do you know why? Because she would inspire creativity. Creativity is within some men and women because, not as convention says 'It is placed by God', but because they desire recognition. Recognition! Means affection. Means love. Love me for what I have done for you. Mrs Jackson. Kiss my cheek – I have done it for you – not to show or prove how clever I am, but to ask you to show me that you, you exquisite human being, can love a little horror like Stuart Hall. I will work until I have won you – then what? Can the teacher and the child progress? My sympathies are with you, the teacher. How far involved in that life are you? Fledglings to adults – a miasma of thought. Mother, Father, confidante – a shaper of personality.

The responsibility is like Vesuvius, gently rumbling, occasionally groaning; aching; despairing; retching; and erupting. To quell, or to overwhelm the fledglings. But my childhood needed, I am afraid, all the moods of the volcano. Doris Jackson never knew – or did she? English convention demands naivety, or scandal. The Victorians laid down the pattern of non-emotional relationship between teacher and child, and even to this day we still conform.

But to Doris. Despite my work, my play was decidedly torrid. My play was divorced from Doris, home and love. I was naughty. I defied authority and, much as I loved Doris, naughtiness was a way of life. I was barred from other boys' houses.

'A bad influence; criminal tendencies; puny and nasty.'

The dichotomy of the personality began at that tender age – it is still with me and maybe still troubles me even today. Do I still present myself – on television and wireless – to say, do you love me?

YOU ARE OLD, FATHER HALL

Why do I look into the future? Time races along and years now seem short. Shakespeare chilled me in youth with:-

All the world's a stage,
And all the men and women merely players:
They have their exits and their entrances;
And one man in his time plays many parts,
His acts being seven ages.

At first the infant,
Mewling and puking in the nurse's arms,
And then the whining schoolboy, with his satchel,
And shining morning face, creeping like snail
Unwillingly to school...

Then a soldier,
Full of strange oaths, and bearded like the pard,
Jealous in honour, sudden and quick in quarrel,
Seeking the bubble reputation
Even in the cannon's mouth. And then the justice,
In fair round belly with good capon lined...

The sixth age shifts
Into the lean and slippered pantaloon,
With spectacles on nose and pouch on side,
His youthful hose well saved a world too wide
For his shrunk shank...

Last scene of all,
That ends this strange, eventful history,
In second childishness, and mere oblivion,
Sans eyes, sans teeth, sans taste, sans everything.'

'Men of age object too much, consult too long, adventure too little, repent too soon.' True or false?

I have developed an interest in astrology. Some years ago I took part in a programme with several other guests, including Denis Healey, Geoff Boycott, Harvey Smith, Marti Caine and so on. We all had to submit one week prior to the programme our exact date and time of birth, a sample of our handwriting and a handprint.

Three experts analysed each before the programme. Then on the programme the analyst had to discuss the personality, past, present and future. Traits, qualities, defects, relationships. He had to guess the identity of the personality. The results were a revelation to each of us. So accurate that it was tantamount to being undressed in public. The astrologer Bryan Lee drew up this chart, which is a mirror of my life.

I was born on Christmas Day at midnight plus two. So his calculations say I am Capricorn sun-type with Libra ascending. What does that mean? On the chart, Libra rises aspected by Mars in the first house. Conclusion:
• A pretty powerful personality – a 'can of instant friendship'. Sometimes people react to it negatively because they do not believe it is sincere.
• Out-and-out drive, the urge to take action.
• A nose for whiffing and enjoying danger.
• Sheer energy and impulsiveness.
• Supporters will back you.
• Others will regard you as pushy and arrogant.
• The strange aspect here is that the superior image of the 'larger than life' is a core because the man does not feel too sure of himself. He could even be shy.
• Mars is a powerful sexual symbol which needs to be aired.

• You talk, natter and debate. Yet you are impatient with people stating opposite views.

• The sun ascendant puts you above the crowd.

Mr Lee is right. That is the present. Here is with the past.

Guilt and fear are present in childhood. Warring parents upset the delicate male/female balance that exists within you. The structure of your chart indicates the need for love. It triggers the need to be popular, important, envied, but loved. Despite that, you will never recognize your significance and have a strange sense of inadequacy. You will make terrific attempts to find yourself, to catch a glimpse of yourself and your own value in the eyes of others. To see yourself and your actions mirrored in the eyes and reactions of an audience. It is the challenge to find inner centre away from the ego. There is a great need for family and a secure career. The aspect of the sun brings a dichotomy of interests. One content to have fun whenever, wherever it can. The other – serious, initiate, gets things done. You have a mental bridge between past and present, allowing easy communications with young and old. You are open, a seeker of truth, and steadfastly loyal to fault. You have intuitive understanding of people. You have a drive, a life force that inspires others, but you get your feelings and logic mixed up, react emotionally and fail to make the correct intellectual appraisal. You are frank and delve into knowledge like a ferret. Diplomacy and tact will only come with increasing age. A large number of people trust you. You will eventually work exclusively with them – to show them the fine things of life. You are vulnerable to women, especially warm, genuine, out-flowing Leos. The fourth house sun and Cancer mid-heaven bring an urge to nurture and collect. When you were six years old, you were bright and intelligent. In 1951 you had not fulfilled that promise. In 1959, despite terrible emotional family problems, you changed professions. In 1974 you were successful.

From October 1980 to Christmas 1988 mature inner change will redefine your basic outlook on life. Two sides of you will meet in conflict – one side will gamble in business, the other will need you to stay put. Early in 1985 you will blow a fuse.

All that Mr Lee put down here, all of it terrifyingly correct.

Is it any wonder I feel a need to create a children's museum? I have a vision of somewhere that will accommodate crowds of 40,000 to 50,000 each weekend. Bars, restaurants, shops, areas for tuition and learning areas for enquiring. Children must make noise. They must ask questions, receive answers. It would be staffed by experts; under their aegis, teenagers without jobs. Craft shops would be in a complex, creating merchandise sold by jobless teenagers. I intend to persevere. It is what I want to do with my life. It is part of the great jigsaw. Where do we all fit? We are here for a purpose; it is predestined.

It is a need to be loved. It is not a weakness, I am sure. His analysis of the ups and downs is a revelation. And I now know why my father had such a terrible temper when all about him was apeace. He was Scorpio – the sting in the tail. Diane Simpson, the graphologist, was equally succinct and accurate.

Obviously, I do not govern my life by astrology or graphology. They are a guide – so do not scoff or spurn. There are millions like me.

'You are old, Father William,' the young man said,
'And your hair has become very white;
And yet you incessantly stand on your head –
Do you think, at your age, it is right?'
'In my youth,' Father William replied to his son,
'I feared it might injure the brain.
But now that I'm perfectly sure I have none,
Why, I do it again and again.'

TO EVERY THING THERE IS A SEASON AND A TIME FOR EVERY PURPOSE...

Are you going to move house? Have you seen the domicile of your dreams? Has your spouse convinced you that you have been sitting in that chair in front of the same television, in the same sitting room, kitchen or lavatory or wherever you view, in the same street, avenue, or road for just too long?

Are you listening to her? Well, are you? DO NOT! I will tell you a cautionary tale of two houses and a cataclysm that castrated my finances, my future and put me in a straitjacket of no escape. The term 'financial corset' has taken a new meaning. For a lifetime I have lived in the Pennines. It shows in my present rustic dress, my liking for woad, the hammertoes from wearing clogs, even in bed. It is revealed by the segs on mi palms and broken fingernails!

I once helicoptered to the fingernail clinic. 'Never again,' said the snotty manicurist. 'They are North country fingernails with dirt underneath.' My long johns and Wolsey vest, my winceyette nightie – changed once a fortnit, mind. My love of black tripe, chitterlings, chunks, pig's dick and wezzell, savoury ducks, cowheel pie and raw sausage. In Glossop, we ate our sausage raw – health inspectors turned puce, but my guts are still intact and if you can withstand the Bull's Head bitter for a lifetime, then raw sausage holds no fears.

My love for the Pennines shows in my love for Vera, the post girl, who grew to a lady but was never late with letters. For Don Jones – a rough-yed, right half with the local team, who took the local newspaper shop, and his wife, who was once courted at the Victoria Hall hop dance by a hard-swearing able seaman, now turned respectable vicar.

It is reflected in scores of trophies for Old Boys' League Championships, county caps, little silver tankards for bantam kicking or sheep strangling. A lifetime of battling against the elements. The inhumanity of a Pennine winter. Blizzards, snow drifts, hurricane winds from the Atlantic meeting tornadoes from Siberia. Here in Glossop, East met West, weather wise. It bred a comradeship of of a true community in true Glossopians. The folklore is handed from family to family. Our football team trainer was Jack Gruff. As Jack's only qualification was that of stretcher-bearer in the last rough-up with the foe, Jack added the suffix RAMC (Royal Army Medical Corps) after his name.

Needless to say, his treatments were exceedingly efficacious. He could cure anything from polio to piles, diphtheria to dyspepsia, acne to angina. What he could not do with a bucket of hot water and comfrey leaves would leave your average orthopaedic surgeon apoplectic. His healing fingers would weave spells over torn, bleeding muscles and restore them to Mr Universe proportions. Fractures and tissues would mend at the torrent of medical jargon that forever issued from Jack's epiglottis. He was the man for every Glossop season. But he was idiosyncratic. His diagnoses were all his own.

Once he examined a leg mangled by some hairy full-back from Wigan.

'Ah, ah,' he mused, 'a little traptation on't bone.' A bucket of comfrey for a start.

On another occasion a young lady requested an 'audience' with him – he disliked the word 'consultation'; smacked too much of the charlatans of medics in far-off Manchester. Two words to them and they would take it off. It was never quite clear what 'it' was. So the young lady – a highly-strung, string-bag of nerves – quivered jelly-wise before Jack, and after a bucket of comfrey, left. As I sat nursing a broken wrist with my right foot in a bucket of comfrey, I asked about the lady's condition. Do you know, 'She's feasible to jumpity,' he said. It said it all. A bucket of comfrey for a thousand Valium.

I was addicted to Jack like the whole of Glossop. Once I visited again, ravaged by some savage – I was a rather dandy, clever, creative wing half in my time. Ron Greenwood describes me as a 'fanny merchant' and liked my style, but it meant being butchered on the ball. So I visited. Jack was disturbed. 'I'm worried, very worried,' he said. 'Do you know you've got the promes?' He cured them, whatever they were, with – you've guessed it – a bucket of comfrey. Grandma Bennett had her diabetes immersed in comfrey; Aunt Lissie, the Queen of the Co-op, had a mystery affliction – comfrey cured it. In short, Jack is a legend.

Like my wife's great-uncle. His favourite actors – Bingo Crossley and Al Johnson; his favourite film *Whisky Gallory*. Nobody knew his name. He was wild. A farmer who rode his milk float down Station Road, Hadfield, like a mad horseman of the Apocalypse. He would stand in the float, whip poised; the great horse flecked with foam for the charge down the street. He wore a black suit, the trousers polished to a fine sheen from years of 'sat sitting'. His boots had 10 years of swill decorating them. He wore a white shirt with a brass collar stud, but no collar. His lips were like motor car inner tubes. He was to all in Hadfield, 'Nigger Bennett'. It was an affectionate term in those days; it was innocent. He was never known to speak. We observed in awe the mad charge... until one day when my mate Oz – lucky Oz – had his milk delivered by Hazel's uncle. Suddenly Oz observed that the mountain to the west of Glossop, known as the Nab, had marks on it. The marks were those of a plough. Some incredibly foolish optimist was 'digging for victory' on the Nab.

'Mr Bennett,' said Oz, who had never spoken to Mr Bennett, ever, 'They're ploughing the Nab.'

'Aye,' said Mr Bennett, 'but nowt'll grow there – it's te neer Moon.' And he jumped into the float, leaving us forever to ponder what man of marvel was he.

But there came the time to leave beloved Glossop. As Ecclesiastes says: 'To every thing there is a season, and a time to every purpose…' There were many reasons. My little Georgian house had been invaded by clocks. Danny, my son, was off to law school, my daughter Francesca away to London as a drama student. 'Don't put your daughter on the stage, Mr Hall.' Who can stop them, I ask? And I needed to be near Manchester Airport, so we searched for a house at the bottom end of runway two. In a moment, the anguish, the heart-searching, not to say heart arrest that the search entailed. Suffice to say the uprooting was painful – not terminal – but nearly.

So to the house at the bottom of runway two. Away from the rustic Pennines. I was in glib, glossy brochure land. I hate house-hunting. Home is – damn it – where the heart is. But where to lodge the heart? I was helped in the search by friendly estate agents who assured me that prices of £150,000 were commonplace in Cheshire. That half the neighbourhood was on sale convinced me that the occupants were well aware that somebody, somewhere, wanted paying for past aberrations.

My wife, Hazel, fell for a house that was a mix of early oast with bourgeois Algarve. It was upside down; live upstairs, sleep down. In principle, it is fine. The kitchen is raised and through the large French windows the garden stretches to the pines and cypresses, the golden beech hedge that, noble and tall, protects us from the westerlies that sweep down Alderley Edge.

We arranged a purchase on the spot. Our friendly estate agent took his commission. And so did everybody else. A surveyor to survey. Ah, yes, desirable. The garage leaks. 'Can I come back to you,' I said to the friendly surveyor, 'for redress if your survey is wrong?'

'Certainly not,' he said. And one cannot. If he blows the job, you have no redress. So why have a survey?

Then to the lawyer job. Oh! Oh! Oh! Search fees, unsearch fees, fees for this, stamp duty. Already stretched thinly, the finances begin to look like a sausage skin about to burst. The bank arranges a bridging loan of £80,000. Do not worry, says the friendly estate agent – your lovely Georgian house will sell for £70,000 and your problems are over.

Next week MIR or bank rate is jacked up by three per cent. My loan now carried 16 per cent. I begin the move. Pickfords arrive with crates, boxes, cases, piles of cardboard. Effects of a lifetime need to be packed.

Have you tried squeezing your marriage dinner service into a packing case, wrapping a painting in rags so that it will not fracture? Have you tried packing a clock? And I had 200. It is like dismembering a 2,000-year-old mummy, 200 times. It drove us all to madness.

Is it worth the upheaval, the sheer impossibility of trying without succeeding? To carry on working as if life were a bowl of cornflakes. The cornflakes were buried under a pile of old clothes, under the recorder, under that old dinghy – remember the fun we had in 1974? Remember the snapshots spilling from old boxes like coffee beans from a split bag? Remember the coffee beans spilling everywhere as I split the blasted bag? It was turmoil.

Pickfords came. The miracle happened. We had decorated the oast house, meanwhile. The furniture fitted. The carpets were recut and the move was complete.

Then the local farmer set fire to his stubble and incinerated my garden. Beech hedge, cypresses and pine suffered his scorched-earth policy. If it moves, burn it.

Welcome to Wilmslow! Goodbye, Glossop! Now winter was here.

The friendly estate agent A who sold the property now joined forces with the friendly Glossop estate agent B to sell my Glossop house.

My bank asked estate agent A for a valuation on the Wilmslow house. They would not unless I prepaid £135. This on top of the commission for selling it in the first place. Friends – this is rip-off time.

The bank press for a mortgage to assist me with the crippling interest charges.

The Glossop property, valued at £70,000, descends to £65,000, £60,000. I suddenly changed to estate agent C, who suggests a deal. Estate agent B in Glossop submits his account. Several purchasers have seen and not bid. I pay his bill. He has tried on a difficult market.

But then estate agent A submits his. I think he must have invented the charges. Now I know I should have been an estate agent. No liabilities, no comebacks; just take the money.

Eventually, estate agent C sold the Glossop property at a price at least £15,000 less than one could build the property new. So much for Mrs Thatcher and her property-owning society. So much for crippling interest rates that have bled us white. So much for the army of parasites who live on the unsuspecting simpletons like you and me.

And, of course, the government dips into your slender resources. Stamp duty! If ever there was a rip-off it is stamp duty. Each year hundred of thousands of pounds paid into the government kitty simply because people change their homes. It is iniquitous!

And we do not finish there. Estate agents, surveyors and all the other people involved. If there is no comeback when professional services rendered turn out to be unprofessional, then what happened to responsibility?

Yes, it is the Hall mad plan! Need for something to be done.

I can go to a car showroom tomorrow, pay £40,000 for a third-hand Rolls-Royce and be secure in my purchase. Why? Because reason has prevailed. The dealer gives a guarantee, the logbook shows ownership, the banks provide the money.

Why not a house? Why all the mumbo-jumbo of surveyor, estate agent, building society, search fees, stamp duty and pay through the snout?

A house could have a logbook. It is lodged with the council in which area it is built. A copy is issued to the owner. When the house is sold, the estate agent has a surveyor compile a report, a report that is binding, like a car guarantee.

My garage in Wilmslow is like the Niagara Falls. I have no redress on the estate agent who did not declare a leaking garage in his blurb. Or faulty drains either. So along comes a buyer. He reads the report and arranges his finance. A central clearing house conveys the property. A simple task of comparing the logbook with the original in the local offices.

A similar task is accomplished for nothing in the car world by telexing Hire Purchase Information. They have recorded all details of finance on any car. The charge for the service is minimal. The government of the day fix the per-centage on the mortgage. The pain is removed; the mystery resolved. What is more, as one or two builders have shown, houses can be traded as part exchanges either below or above the value of the property desired. It is common sense, it is anti-parasite and what is more it will happen if Stuart Hall Estate Agents/Solicitors/Surveyors etc… have their way.

Now I can see all my professional friends leaping to the phone or at least penning earnest letters in vitriol.

But to the estate agent I say: 'Surely house-trading will become simpler. You will still be needed to advertise the property on the market, and you will still get your commission.'

To the banker. Nine per cent will suffice.

To the lawyer. You can still levy a fee for rubber-stamping the logbook.

But if it cuts down time and time is money, is it too simple?

OH TO BE A PAGAN NOW THAT WILMSLOW'S HERE!

What makes a snob? Is it wealth, position in society, breeding or lack of breeding, education or lack of education? I'm asking rhetorical questions because, on the face of it, large dollops of socialism since the war have eroded the snob persona, yet, deep down, because of 'one for all and all for one', snobbery is more firmly entrenched than ever. Nowadays it is subtler and piquantly perverse.

Yesteryear the spanking new Rolls-Royce, polished like a jewel, was parked prominently in the drive, a four-square symbol of ultimate success. Chauffeur-driven and cosseted, the owner an aristocrat, merchant banker or industrial baron. Not a scrap-metal dealer or pop star in sight. In those days pop stars were yclept 'musical comedy artistes'; songwriters were composers; groups were bands with leaders. They were patronized by top society. Harry Roy. Geraldo. Ambrose. Carroll Gibbons. Hutch. Top society threw the parties. The bands played; champagne from milady's slipper; high jinks in the foun-tain; kedgeree for breakfast and then on to the following night's shindig. The

Dorchester, the Ritz, the Savoy, Quaglino's and Claridge's were the stomping grounds of the elite – a carefully selected and structured society that one could not join; one either belonged to or simply did not. Oscar Wilde, in *A Woman of No Importance*, described it thus:

GERALD: 'I suppose society is wonderfully delightful.'

LORD ILLINGWORTH: 'To be in it is merely a bore. But to be out of it simply a tragedy.'

Another acerbic wit, George Bernard Shaw, said, 'I assure you that if you will only take the trouble to do, and say, the perfectly correct thing, you can do what you like.'

Try telling that to a luckless BBC cricket commentator, a famous one at that, who committed an apocryphal boo-boo at Lord's. Summing up an over from Michael Holding, he said, 'the bowler's Holding, the batsman's Willey'.

But to return to snobbery – the maze of U and non-U, naff and non-naff. Where once it was deemed superior to be sent down from Oxford than gain a first at Nottingham. Where to inherit a thousand acres in Norfolk was preferable to a woollen mill in Bradford, and aristos and trade never mixed. In my work as radio and television observer I have become a 'sounding brass or tinkling cymbal', looking, enquiring, nosy-parkering into people's lives through both ends of the telescope. I have supped and dined with royalty and shared morning coffee with the corporation dustcart lads in the cab of their garbage wagon, to the bemused incredulity of two army generals. I was strolling down Lancaster's High Street with the 'brass hats', deep in conversation on the opening of a military museum. Suddenly along came the lads. 'Ey-up, it's our Stuart,' they cried, leapt from the cart, shook me warmly by the hand, and led me to their driver's cabin. Hot, sweet coffee (I cannot take sugar, but I did this day), much hearty laughter and banter and away they went. The generals were aghast. There I sat in the slightly less than salubrious surroundings of the garbage, in dove-grey suit now smudged with much darker grey, obviously happy. What did I have in common with them? they enquired. I told them that I was a classless person and that I had been awarded the supreme accolade – the prefix 'our'. To be called 'our Stuart' means to be embraced by one's fellow men, to be involved in their lives, hopes and fears. I was both humble and eternally grateful. You see, I cannot stand snobs.

Many years ago, I met a little old woman on a railway station platform. It was in the days of first and third class. As the train drew into the station, she grasped my arm and asked me to put her in her compartment. She was clutching a third-class ticket. Why, I enquired, did she not travel first?

'Oh no, first is not for the likes of me. I am a third-class person.'

This little cameo depressed me, and has stayed with me for 30-odd years. It began a chain of thought that recurs in my mind, that sets me pondering, yet I never arrive at a solution. Were people happier in those days when the toffs owned the best car in the world, and the biggest houses? When travel was for them, and not for us? When great chunks of the world were coloured red?

When the working lad donned khaki, shouldered his rifle and spilt his blood for King and Country? Life then was a time warp. Structured in a council school, for a council house, for a factory job. A holiday on Wakes Week at Blackpool. I remember as a small boy the smell of summer in Blackpool. Stale mild and bitter beer and sawdust. The Golden Mile, the aroma of rock on a thousand stalls. Freak shows, peepshows, Pablos and Petrulengo. In the crystal ball, the future would always be stale beer, darts and dominoes. But the smiles on the faces were real, the laughter genuine, the pleasure lasting. Those two weeks were earned by sheer graft; the determination to enjoy them heightened the pleasure.

My simple grandparents adored Blackpool. They were Irish and had fled with the potato famine. Grandpa used to regale me with his Great War stories. He was proud to have fought for his two square yards of the Somme while thousands perished over their two square yards. Filth, mud, rats gnawing the dead. Bare trees, no birds singing, only the scream of the howitzers, and the death rattle of machine-guns.

Miles and Annie Hennessey were happy with society. A small house in Droylsden. Albert Street alive with neighbourly gossip. Chintz curtains washed by hand. The doorstep donkey stoned. A few chickens on the plot, and the pub. The folk had time for the children, the sick and the old. Hospitals were for dying in. 'Carter's Little Liver Pills', 'Fennings Fever Cure', 'Bile Beans' and 'Angers Emulsion' cured everything. 'The doctor' was a pillar of society, wore gold-rimmed spectacles, carried a Gladstone bag, slung his stethoscope around his neck like a scarf, and cured most pestilence and pain with a kaolin poultice.

The corner shop was Mecca. Sterilized milk, boiled mutton or tongue, OK sauce and a newfangled product called 'a sliced loaf'. The baker baked fresh bread and pork pies. The butcher made real sausages and savoury ducks himself, and dispensed hot pork with gravy plus his own line of banter. The hairdresser cut round a basin for fourpence and incessantly gossiped the news. The grocer patted butter with wooden pallets, offered real cheese on his knife and wore a white apron over his shoes, dragging in the sawdust covering his bare wooden floor. Was it all so uncomplicated? Or have the sands of time obscured vision and truth?

What I do observe is that the 30 years of advance into high technology has fragmented society. We all want and give so little. The planner bunged people into high-rise flats and soulless housing estates. The shops, so personal and pleasing, have been swallowed into vast supermarkets. Have you ever observed the supermarket shopper? Grim-faced, silent, intent on gobbling up the shelves and beating a retreat.

Parents are too busy to bother with their children. Old folks are left to wither, and we gather the durables. The car, the fridge, deep freeze, television set plus recorder, and plan the foreign holiday. The acquisitive society. And from it has bred, like weeds in a field, the snob.

He brags about his work, his golf, the mountains of jewellery festooning his wife. The cruise, when not only did he dine with the captain, but ensured that his fellow travellers never had a dull moment. He knows the best eating-houses. Is on Christian-name terms with the *maître d'*, whom he calls 'head waiter'! Snaps his fingers at the staff and bellows, 'Waiter!' every other minute. My son Danny, who recently obtained his law degree, has worked his vacations as a commis waiter in a well-known Cheshire hostelry. He needed, he said, a little independence, a working knowledge of good food and wine and a deeper insight into people.

He will confirm that the snob is not only alive and well, but also proliferating. The status symbols are assessed and acquired. An 18-carat gold watch and massive bracelet. A Dupont lighter. A very expensive motorcar constantly the topic of conversation. The house, the pool, the servants (in reality the 'daily' and her husband, the 'handyman'). The expensive public school. The villa abroad, the biggest in the complex. And above all the utter contempt for anyone beneath him. Vulgar, ostentatious, without wit or charm. The product of the new society. Whatever happened to the gentleman?

Obviously you, the reader, cannot identify with that picture – but I will wager you know somebody who does.

A DOG CALLED ROVER
19 October 1999. I had a visitation to my Cheshire two-up, two-down domicile from Messrs J. Clarkson and A.A. Gill. They both admired my outside lavatory, which is 45 feet by 20 feet and nine feet deep. Visitors sorely afflicted by modern living have been known to throw themselves in it hoping for a cure. It is the Wilmslow equivalent of the Ganges. They both demurred, muttering about sacred rights and weighted bricks round necks.

Mr Gill, never having been so far north, was amazed at us wearing woad and hobnail boots, eating locusts, beating wives, human burning, open fires, wild elk, taxis, huge tits and a Porsche for each foot.

I excused myself, and with a jawbone of an ass slew a wandering dromedary in the back garden. A herd of yak, grazing for fodder, drew my attention – but I was not in the mood for yak gonads. I diced the dromedary and repaired to my favourite hostelry, the Edge. The diced elk risotto is a speciality. I dined sumptuously. Mr Gill was rather contemptuous of the fare, and subsequently castigated Cheshirites as '*jus*' people. Short on taste, long on money, Mr Clarkson devoured his leg of brontosaurus as the Prodigal Son devoured harlots.

Mr Clarkson, motormouth and petrol-head, knows nothing of life unless it is fuel-injected, does 500mph and makes a fashion statement. He was at Repton with my son. He was agog at my orange Interceptor III, and my Blydenstein Bomb, a droop snoot Firenza. The latter would cream your jeans, went like excreta off a shovel, but had a German gearbox that needed the strength of Garth to shift.

You could always tell a Blydenstein driver. They had left wrists the size of the Matterhorn. It gave rise to rather smutty remarks from the envious about one's sexual predilections.

Mr Clarkson left Repton amid gossip about drinking sessions and toying with tartlets. Gobbets of tittle-tattle imply that bike sheds were involved. 'Tis now on the ether, as is Mr Clarkson. Well, he is on something.

Fast forward to our *repas* at the Edge. I like a good roister with a dash of the vulgar. Not just a kick over the traces, but a high jump with triple salchow. Clarkson and I drooled over the claret. A.A. simply drank water.

A.A. is a fascinating chap. Dark, brooding, handsome, with chocolate eyes. He has an Egyptian look about him. I imagine him astride a camel, a swarm of Tueregs around him, swaging yet another itinerant white damsel to join his thousand concubines in his desert palace. His looks entice. Even the diapason would swell. Imagine him in a surplice. Me with my surplus, in the beatific choir.

The evening ended. A.A. had to drive Clarkson's Cadillac. A.A. is the worst driver in the world. The Cadillac was the size of the QEII. You do not drive it: you dock it. A.A. promptly reversed into a parked BMW. Being a gent, he rushed back into the hostelry to administer sorrow and, more succinctly, his name and address. The owner, not knowing his A.A. from A.A. Adam, wanted to punch out his lights. Reason prevailed – we were safe.

I tell this salutary tale because it gives penetrating insight into these two. A.A. did not blanche when I decanted Daddies sauce on my *saumon fumé au blinis a la russe*. Clarkson thought it a breach of the peace.

What is apparent, though, is that both hate people and court controversy. So naturally they are both 'journos'. A.A. is a darting rapier, Clarkson the elephantine bludgeon. Jeremy is a nice lad, but his head is up his arse. Consequently, when breaking wind, or hot air, it exudes orally. I recommend a silk handkerchief to dispel the odours.

Now to the cars. Mine is a three-car stable. The third is a Rover 75. Clarkson, on perceiving it, dissolved into base mirth. 'Why don't you put a thatch on it?' 'Is that your age, 75?' 'Couldn't you afford a Jaguar?' 'They lower those into open graves.' Explanations to Clarkson are useless. He forbears logic.

Logic is the Rover 75. It is a great motorcar. Its looks are feline, not bland. The roadholding is superb, air-conditioning the best in class. The two-litre V6 works like a turbine. Nothing doing under 3,000 rpm but then it whirls into action until breathless at 8,000 rpm. It has to be whistled through its five gears to get the response. It bristles with brilliant design features that would bore you at this stage. It is a workhorse. It needs hard use. I know most people think I am dead. I am not. I tear about the country with my own *It's a Knockout* – a huge travelling circus. I broadcast around the world, and I am very, very busy.

Last week I was in London, Southampton, Leeds and Liverpool. Have you tried commuting in a Ferrari or a Boxster? I have, and reduced myself to a quivering jelly. White-faced, stressed out of my bollocks, world-weary to the point of tears.

The Rover 75 sailed through thousands of miles at ease with itself. An eater up of boring miles at some *vitesse*. I emerged from these tortuous, mind-bending journeys without pain or anxiety. On the Southampton journey 'twas the usual M6 Friday gridlock. All the way from the M42 to the Sandbach Junction 16 on the M6. Horrendous stop, start, stop, start, a yard at a time. Five-and-a half hours of bloody torture. Plus road works. In Germany I once observed a posse of drivers literally stoning workmen during daylight hours. Since then German road works are completed at night. Please, Johnny Two Jags, follow the master race!

From Sandbach the road to Wilmslow is a switchback. Long straights, tight corners, tricky sweeping curves, hump-back bridges. A road for men, not boys. I gave the Rover some wellie. A real tonking. Heel and toe changes – hit the rhythm, feel the power – let the FWD work its todger off. Down through the box for the Withington Corner. Get the hammer down. The road dark and empty. My time to home, the best I have achieved in 20 years. I have owned the best machines around. Raced Frazer Nash's big Healeys and Lotus. I think I know a thing or two, having owned over 400 motorcars.

I tell you this 75 is a fine car. Forget fashion statements, posing, effete joshing in the Clarkson mode. Drivers today want a reliable beast that will not deflate faster than Clarkson's erection. Will be worth 50 per cent of its value three years hence. That will not cost a mortgage to service. That is comfortable for its passengers. Rewarding to drive. That receives an appreciative nod from fellow travellers. Sound as a bell and British-built. We do not need young women emitting screams and throwing soiled panties at the car. We do not need Tara Farmer-Plonkington to bathe it in Krug. We want value for money. The 75 delivers it. Take my word – I drive it.

A DRAUGHT FROM THE DEEP-DELVED EARTH

Are you a wine snob? Sniff the cork, swill the liquid round the glass, inhale the bouquet, wrinkle your nostrils, or smile the knowing smile?

My friends are. They serve Lafite-Rothschild and Montrachets like I serve Babycham. Monster wines that crash the brain, dull the palate and kill conversation. If it is old and expensive, then produce it. The more expensive, the more impressive!

As I write, I am toying with a glass of Orvieto, the classic wine of Umbria; dry, crisp, full of wit and elegance – and cheap. One of the great delights I had was the privilege to work in Italy. Wherever you travel in that fascinating country, you discover that it's not really a country but hundreds of different countries rolled into one.

Each region has its different cuisine, customs and wine. Each region its own pride – even its own language. It is often said that the Milanese refer to the people of the deep south as Africans. In turn, the folk in the south – Calabria, Puglia, Basilicata – refer to the Milanese as Germans.

I tool it all with a pinch of spaghetti and learned to love the Italian life. Mind you, I left the operatic tenor bit, and goosing the gals to them, leaving the wine to me! I absorbed their wines as a sponge. Lovely velvety Barolo. Frascati so fresh and *pétillant* that music could be distilled from the bubbles. Verdicchio in that absurd green bottle – but the aroma! The superb Brolio Chianti Classico – more body than Marilyn Monroe, more iron than Margaret Thatcher! More velvet and soporific than a Geoffrey Howe speech – and just as somnambulant. And from the Fruili, that region north of Venice, the classic Pinot Grigio – as dry as a Garbo kiss!

Why are Italian wines so oft neglected, even spurned? Why are we so rooted in our tastes – conditioned by price and label?

In France, the French imbibe anything. In the Loire, they will drink their Sancerre. In the Dordogne, it is claret – simple claret, not big growths. In the south, they will swill the wines heady and soft, nurtured in the Mediterranean sun. In Macon, a Fleurie, Pommard or Volnay. They have a catholic, carefree attitude to their wine. If it is good, drink it – to hell with the label.

I have absorbed the Italian and French attitude. Wherever I go in the world, I drink the wine of that country. I know it's trick or treat. I have had superb moments tasting the unknown, and quite frankly almost succumbed to the poison in some bottles.

I remember tossing back a full Yugoslavian red in the Gypsy quarter of Belgrade. The 'Skadalia' music was joyful, the girls pirouetting in full skirts. The laughter raised the ceiling. I awoke two days later with scrambled brains and all my hair cut off. Apparently, according to messmates, I had staggered into a barber, ordered a haircut, and never realized he was the local sheepshearer. Even my children did not recognize me when I lurched off a train in Salerno a week later. They thought I was a German POW.

I had a little comeuppance, too, in Switzerland. They are also proud of their fine, dry, tangy white wines. But at a special retreat in the Jura Mountains, Gennaro – the Swiss referee of *It's a Knockout* – invited me to sample a red. 'Twas called Dôle. Deep, rich and heady. Now the Swiss sip their wine. A moderate race interested in money, discipline, the evaporating pound in your pocket and the quality of your watch. God help you if it is Japanese. They are not given, unlike us, to excesses. Well, I quaffed, and quaffed, and quaffed again. A miniature Oliver Reed, I was!

I awoke in my bunk in the pine chalet wearing a dress. Well, it was not a dress – it was a tent, if not a marquee! And it was soaking wet. I took breakfast at suppertime. Sheepishly I enquired how yet another tragedy had befallen me. Amid enormous mirth, my fellow guest told me I had been 'Dôled'. Even worse, several other foreign guests equally stoned… one of them, a Belgian presenter called Paule Herreman. A lady weighing in at 29 stones. A veritable Sophie Tucker, a man mountain, a mass of quivering chins; a chest like the north face of the Eiger. A quivering mass of molecules and jelly. We had decided to take a swim. And, to do it with decorum, swapped clothes! My pants had a split bigger than the Labour Party's. My jacket fitted an elephant. So beware of Dôle, folks!

Another 'beware of' is Brian Cash, one-time factotum of the world-famous Belfry – the jewel of the De Vere crown. Cashie is one of the greatest hoteliers in the universe. A memory like Leslie Welsh; the wit of Noël Coward; the swing and lilt of John Wayne; the looks of an angel; plus a bottomless thirst for bubbly. Last year, at the De Vere conference, we imbibed a little at supper, a vast quantity after it and – after two hours, yes, two hours' fitful sleep – another bottle for breakfast. Even Stuart Reid (chairman of De Vere), the Sydney Greenstreet of the trade, was seen to stagger and observe that he must have had one too many because at 4 a.m. he saw two guys beating up the Belfry on a turbocharged golf trolley, shouting rather risqué songs into the night air. Cashie and I reassured big Stu that it was pure hallucination as only Cashie had the keys to the golf trolleys!

Which champagne induced the Jackie Stewart mood? 'Twas Madame Bollinger's NV, a cool quaff to be swallowed at any time of day. If pressed I will take Taittinger, Pol Roger and Canard Duchesne. The snag with the last is that you need a cavalry sabre to swipe off the neck of the bottle and cork. Apparently, in 19th-century Paris brave hussars returning from battle just did not have the patience to thumb off the corks. Ladies were champing at the bit. So out with the sabre, and on with the motley.

So the world of wine: a territory so vast that it is virtually unnavigable without a guide. The first principle is – select a wine merchant with quality tastes and prices that reflect that quality.

Cheshire vintners have that in-depth knowledge that guarantees to satisfy the most discriminating nose, palate and pocket. Go to it – there is a genie like Peter Clark in every bottle! 'Clarkie', me and naughty French wine – but that is another story!

THE HOLIDAY

Whoopee – it is holiday time. Yes, as the timbers crash through your *Mon Repos*, the hurricanes whip the tiles off your roof, the taxman's avalanche hits the wallet, school fees are due, the mortgage feeling like the QEII anchor – God damn it, let's take a holiday.

It is a fact that the businessman suffers more stress taking the wife and children abroad than he does wheeling and dealing. All his overseas travel is arranged by a loving secretary. He travels Club Class. Cosseted by stewardesses. Fawned on by ground staff. Filet mignon and Château Margaux at 40,000 feet. Met at point of arrival. Shuffle through Customs. The job's a good 'un.

And then the annual holiday. All those travel arrangements by Economy, or charter flight. Queuing – inching forward with enough luggage for a year.

And that 'Oh dear, you bucket and spade punters' look on a distinctly superior stewardess. Mislaid passports, the harrowing drive to the airport, the sweating, groaning, grumbling, recalcitrant passengers. And the holiday flat. Hot, airless, grubby, greasy, badly plumbed, peeling paint, cockroaches like crocodiles, mosquitoes like vultures, filthy beach, red flags on it, polluted sea, weeping children, ill-tempered mama. We have all endured it. Pretending sleep under a copy of the *Financial Times* three days old. Roll on the journey home, or a rest-home of an office.

I have rambled around the world, especially Europe, as I combined work with holidays. And yes, I took Hazel and my two children, Danny and Francesca. Danny is now a lawyer, Francesca an actress. They are grown up. They no longer take the family holiday.

This year I consulted my wife on destination. 1989 was a bad year for me. Two cars stolen, one vandalized. A nasty burglary at home with all my priceless watches stolen. We wanted to get away. We chose Young Island, off St Vincent. It was an inspired choice from Caribbean Connection, based in Chester. Barbados I find cosmetically commercial. Trinidad and Jamaica non-relaxing. So, off on an adventure.

Board the Barbados flight in Manchester. British Airways staff, as always, courteous, brilliantly efficient, never effusive, ever smiling. Halfway through the flight my old chum, Paul Daniels, whistled up the aisle. Produced a pack of cards from a white rabbit and mystified me for an hour. I am sure he was born with a pack in his tiny mitt.

Arrive Barbados. Overnight at the Grand Hotel. Rise at eight. Check in for the Liat flight to St Vincent. The airport, normally a hive, is deserted. We board the small aircraft. The Caribbean below, that translucent, deep blue under the morning sun. Arrive St Vincent. Met by Mr Adams, a tall, distinguished, rather portly taxi-driver.

'Dis island is peace, Stuart. De folks have food and water aplenty. Your holiday the best of yoh life.' Ten minutes we are at the jetty. Two hundred yards offshore, Young Island. Aboard the *African Queen* phut-phutting, my wife and I laughed as we have not for years. This is paradise. Thirty-five acres of tropical island rising like a dream, a mirage, from the clearest sea you will ever view. The *African Queen* docks. A large, very large 'Young Island Special' thrust into the hand by a tall boy in Robinson Crusoe pants. One quaff of this amazing concoction and the holiday was in orbit.

We meandered to our cottage, 150 feet up through the lush vegetation. *The Thirty-Nine Steps*. Palm trees gently nodded in the cool trade wind. Lush vegetation whispered at us. Hibiscus in 30 brightly hued colours trumpeted 'Forget the world'. Oleander, bougainvillea, frangipani – the national flower of St Vincent, 'Exora'. All smiled, lit up the spirits and laid a gentle fragrance on this mini tropical forest.

Up the steps and at the crest was number 30, our cottage. A beautiful lounge in Caribbean style. A large bedroom with warm terracotta tiles. The shower virtually outside. The French windows wide open – on to the verandah with a sweeping view. What a vista – beyond the azure sea the fabled Grenadines. Thirty-two islands awaiting the explorer. Mustique, Bequia, Palm Island, Tobago Cays. This is the real Caribbean, friendly – real friendliness – nothing forced or feigned – genuine happiness.

We ambled to the beach, white sand stretching to the reef, boats rocking at anchor to the lush green backdrop of St Vincent. 'Twas time for dinner. We had packed three suitcases of sophisticated, elegant 'meeting royalty' clobber. They were never worn. 'It had cast its magic spell.' We were interwoven in its tapestry. Time stood still. Dinner was angelic.

First, Violet, a plump lady with winning ways, and a 500-kilowatt smile, welcomed us. Then her staff – exquisite young St Vincentians introduced themselves. Louise, rather shy; Bernadette, vivaciously coquettish; Anna, tall, winsome and beautiful; Hazel (the waitress), jolly, carefree and happy. The food matched the welcome.

A mosaic of international cuisine, and native West Indian. Washed down with a million (or so it seemed) rum punches. I refuse to imbibe imported wines, when the wine of the Caribbean is so rich and potent. I will not dwell on the evening meals, only to say that every night was a fresh experience to savour, to store away and reflect on with joy.

Breakfast was a totally different experience. Taken at little tables amid the palms. Violet welcomes. Stuart sits and gorges on eggs, bacon, sausage, West Indian specialities, two hot pancakes, maple syrup and cream and a thousand litres of scalding coffee.

'Where's yoh Hazel?' they cry.

'Doesn't take breakfast,' sigh I.

'Den we'll take it.' Incredible service.

On day two we boarded Young Island's yacht, *Wind Song*, a 44-footer. Simeon, our captain, sailed. The crew, me, Hazel, two Yorkshire gentlemen with spouses and two existentialist Germans, who boarded at the last second. To Mustique – the fabled island of Princess Margaret. I took the helm, as Simeon hoisted more sail. Three hours later the tiny harbour of Mustique and Basil's Bar – in reality a wooden jetty, wooden bar, wooden tables.

We snorkelled on the reefs and adjourned for lunch. In reality a rave-up. A thousand rum punches. A lobster like a Rugby League's forward's thighs, and a ribald song or two. Even the bill was a song! Back on the *Hispaniola* we were all Captain Bligh, Fletcher Christian or Captain Ahab – until a squall blew up. The Yorkists were Methodists so – would you believe? – the Caribbean rocked and rolled to 'Those in Peril on the Sea'.

When we rounded the point in high wind and drenching (but warm) rain, Young Island resounded to the strains of 'Onward, Christian Soldiers'. Here followed a quick sojourn in Lord Harry's Bar on Young Island, Harry being a witty St Vincentian with the whitest teeth since Farrah Fawcett-Majors. I am sure he brushes with salt and hydrogen peroxide. Electric personality. It became obvious during our balmy, yes, and sometimes barmy holiday that the owner of Young Island, Vidal Browne, had put this magical jigsaw together with enormous care.

He is a giant of a man in stature, black-bearded like some fearsome pirate of yore. Big voice, strong nature – in touch with all 60 guests. He decided that this island would have the alchemist's blend of natural rustic, exotic flora, traditional Caribbean, with a dash of international cuisine.

There is a tennis court atop the island. I took two racquets and the latest gear. I played once. I preferred the 20-yard sea dash to the Coconut Bar – a little shack offshore, where Lord Harry mixed flying bombs and served them in coconut shells. The swim back was hilarious.

We blended into this carefree life with ease. Fellow guests also fell under the magic spell. No newspapers, no television, no radio, no telephones. The dying art of conversation was revived. The frantic pace of life, the stress, the anxiety, all ebbed away from the brain cells. Simple peace reigned. Time to spare. Time to dwell on the basic reasons for being on the planet. Alas, 'twas time to leave. Two weeks in a time warp.

I dished out England football jerseys and shorts to the staff. They were overjoyed and wore them with pride. Would our supporters in Italy emulate, I wistfully wondered?

Regrets all round from Vidal and his marvellous staff. Not staff really – but friends. Temporary regrets, as we all know that we are returning, again and again – and again.

The *African Queen* chugged gently away from the jetty and across the azure bay under a full morning sun. Back to rising mortgages, a record deficit, balance of payments, industrial strife, a huge tax demand, storms, gales, hurricanes, television, famine, wars, elections, politicians. Do birds only sing on Young Island? Vidal Browne, are you listening?

PS I did not forget to deposit the key for cottage number 30. I never had one. There are no locked doors in paradise!

IN A HOLE – TRY A SEMINOLE

Florida, 1993. There is a right way to do it and there is Hallie's way. A salutary tale of burnt fingers, world traveller howlers and near disaster.

Miami Airport was hot and sweaty. People everywhere. Hispanic, Japanese, Filipinos – cross-section of the world. Hailed a passing Buick estate car driven by a Second World War veteran.

'Hell – Naples – it's 100 miles. Two hours' drive.'

We were bushwhacked. As we negotiated Miami's four-lane highway, my heart dropped as the meter ticked away. Me, the seasoned travel professional, hoodwinked, shanghaied, literally. The drive was endless. Miles of nothing. No road signs, cafés, rest stops, garages, nothing. Despair set in as the meter clocked $200.

Naples in sight. It is now 1 a.m. Long manicured boulevards. Driver suddenly pips horn to stop an elegant lady in foreign car. She tells us Holiday Inn is north. We arrive. Do deal with ex-army at $175. Chastened, we check in with half-Mexican night boy clerk. Hungry, shattered, ask for food – none. Lug bags to room 210. They now weigh two tons. Room is cramped, small, musty. A large pizza arrives, from Mickey's. We devour it like starving peasants. Sleep falls like a sledgehammer.

Ten a.m. In the debris of suitcases, creased clothes, toothpaste, creams *et al*, try to take stock. It is *le plus grand* cockup.

Breakfast is a shambles. Mario's restaurant is franchised by the poky Holiday Inn, the staff non-existent. They are running out of food – even jelly and butter.

Hazel has her fruit – me, the two eggs once over lightly with streaky bacon. We sit on the bare concrete around the tiny frozen pool. The Holiday Inn is in middle-of-nowhere Naples, opposite an exquisite golf course – but we do not play golf!

By now, I am a jelly bag. My nerve has gone. Gallons of coffee precipitating anxiety. Out of control. What a balls-up. South-west Florida is full. All America is here for President's Day, St Valentine's Day, high season. For me it is high treason. To embark on this holiday without even measuring the odds or shaping the game plan.

Sink or swim. I ring the Chamber of Commerce. Speak to Susan. She says go to the Old Market. Take a beer and supper. See her 10 a.m.

Friday. Tin City by taxi. Old wharves and boardwalks turmoil into kitsch boutiques, cafés, fudge factories, glassware, knick-knackery, like San Francisco's Giradelli Square. Old history, nostalgia.

Naples is so manicured and laidback, long, white, wide boulevards that bring calm to tortured soul. Elegant buildings carefully created to suit the Naples character. An aura of wealth pervades. A sprinkling of Mercedes, Porsches, Cadillacs, the odd Rolls. No graffiti, no litter – not even a cigarette butt despoils. This is the cleanest, tidiest city I have seen. Obvious pride is reflected here. Even the motorcars float at ease, gently gathering momentum – suspended animation. Speed, noise, fiercely gunning the gas totally contrary to the spirit of Naples. To transgress would be akin to breaking wind in the Savoy Grill!

As a child in the 1940s I remember the same pride in English towns. Now in Britain that is a theme park, surrounded by riots, awash with graffiti, buried in an avalanche of litter, an army of unemployed tramping its soiled streets; I long for Naples. Trendy demographic ecologists would call Naples characterless, overly manicured, even soulless. Praise the Naples city fathers. They have blueprinted the blueprint.

But to the business. At the Chamber, Susie is summoned. A pert, attractive 'on-the-ball long skirt', flat shoes. She is an asset to Naples. Information at fingertip. An oasis for the ignorant. Three hours of phone calls, and no room at the inn for the Halls. Florida is full – totally full. The world is here for golf – President's Day, Valentine's Day. *Mein Gott.* Even Susie's perpetual ebullience and self-control is waning – waxing to despair.

At last – gold. Port of the Islands on highway 41. Relief. Back at the Holiday Inn, we stay on one more night. Hire a Ford Taunus built by Germans in Atlanta, Georgia. A cruise machine. Lunch was euphoric at the Naples Beach Hotel. Lovely open restaurant – breeze blowing from the beach. Open smiles – happiness. Golden honey.

Nine-thirty a.m. Friday: depart Naples down the 41 to Port of the Islands. Cruise at 55 mph on the cruise control. Thirty minutes, here we are. Pink-walled, red-tiled, colonnaded, surrounded by palm trees – the main building.

To the right of our block is a blue lagoon, motorboats in dock. The lagoon leads to a canal, 10 miles long to the Gulf itself. A large sign says, 'Do not feed or tease the alligators'. Ahem! Let's go find them.

We meet the chef, Frank Shaw, from Ashton-under-Lyne. In the dining room, he seats himself with us to mark our card. The seafood starter, all fresh scallops, scampi, frogs' legs and alligator tail, in batter, deep-fried. Delicious. I waltz round his kitchen. All heat – ready for action. His staff, Haitian, so laid-back they are asleep. A few gins after a lie by the pool. To sound sleep.

Down the 41 to a sign 'Wildlife Check Station – One Mile', and here a dozen pick-up trucks, and those wild beasts the airboats. Five-litre Cadillac engine turning a wooden aircraft propeller. No silencer. Deafening noise but thrills galore.

One pick-up truck had five people arranged in and around like some Hillbilly film. Check shirts, jeans, moustaches.

Equipped with a sweater apiece, we roared off over the shallow water into the wilderness, up the half-dried bed of a river to a pond, the biggest pond you will see – about a mile across. The water shallow and brown – brackish with thousands of years of peat. The mangrove swamps. The trees bending and twisting to tortuous shapes by water, lack of water, typhoon, tempest and hurricane.

At last, in a dark pond in the mangrove, some young alligators. But today we will not spot Big Al, the 12-footer.

A breeze springs up – soon a cool wind. We are freezing at the front of the Wright Brothers' contraption. At last, we are perished, base camp. An amazing nature tour. Lovely homely guys. Real experience to cherish.

Saturday, breakfast in the Garden Court Restaurant. Eggs and streaky bacon for me with rye toast. Fresh fruit for Hazel.

Ten a.m. We are taken on a Cessna 172 flight over the islands. What a panorama! Ten thousand islands of cypress, mangrove, pine – 100 miles in length, 50 miles wide. A miracle of ecology. The sky azure blue, cloudless, gentle warm wind. Life is now splendid.

Lunch at a chickee hut in the grounds of the hotel on the water. A chickee hut is a straw hut, originally leaves bound together to make walls and roof, of the Seminole Indians, a tribe that migrated to Florida 200 years ago. The war between the Seminoles and the white man is another bloody saga just coming to light.

Sunday. Brunch. A layout of food that would embellish any top hotel. Rare rib of beef. A monster boiled ham so moist. Chickens. Linguine. Fish galore. Salmon, smoked salmon. Salads by the mile. A plethora of desserts. Two hundred clients clamber over it. Hazel and I sit it out waiting. At the table, I am helping myself to delicious shrimp chowder. Five folk are beside me.

'What's that?' they enquire.

'Nectar,' said I.

'Oh, my Gawd, let's have it.' And I delivered five bowls of creamy bisque.

The Americans here are so open and friendly. It is middle-class America, older, staider, yes, but – they will talk and discuss. They love the talk. We chat to everybody about everything. Clinton is distrusted. It's solid Republican at Port of the Islands. Hell – life is so hectic I have lost a day. I think after lunch we drove down to the old Indian settlement of Chokoloskee.

As the Everglades are seven million acres, we have little chance on this tour but to sample the culture, and merely sniff the atmosphere. So off to the island linked to 41 and 29. A causeway links Chokoloskee to the mainland.

We aim for Smallwood's store, where in the last century Ted Smallwood ran a trading post for whites and Indians. He spoke the Seminole language. He bought alligator skins, deer hides, buckskin, fresh venison, wild turkeys, carved canoes at between 25 cents and a dollar apiece. He sold the Indians sewing machines, needles and thread, sugar, flour and liquid.

The store is on stilts, testimony to the violent hurricanes that swept, still sweep, Florida. The last, Andrew, devastated the 10,000 islands. Smallwood describes how winds of 140 mph swept away buildings, destroyed millions of trees, killed thousands of rare birds.

Hammocks, the little islands where the Seminoles lived, were covered in water. Livestock drowned, and life was lawless. E.J. Watson was the villain. Takin' up with Belle Starr, he apparently killed her in some quarrel, came to Chokoloskee, which had never heard of police or law. He killed another 80 folk, so legend hath it. But mob law got him – buried him in Rabbits Key. A Sheriff Tippins ventured down to arraign the suspects. There were too many – they turned 'em all loose to clear up the hurricane debris.

Smallwood had one hundred dead chickens floating under the store. Fish lay a foot deep on the shore.

In 1915 another violent episode with a bad actor called Rice. Bank robber who wanted Smallwood to store a cache in a handkerchief. Smallwood refused. More shootings. One robber, Tucker, was drowned. Brought to Smallwood in a skiff.

Hurricanes and violence – frontier land. In 1921, 1924, 1926, 1935, 1938 and 1944, hurricanes just blew in and they accepted them. One quote: 'Blowed down some houses – blowed Frank Hamilton's house down and tore it up completely.'

On the jetty of Smallwood's store lay a brand-new 24-foot boat. A couple were mooring it. Frank and Georgia. She slight and slim, he a big Virginian.

The following day we arranged a four-hour trip around the islands. It was now 6 p.m. The sun was setting over the bay. A huge red orb with a ribbon of crimson lying across the water, blue/pink cirrus clouds racing across the dark blue sky. On the other side of the road, the lake surface was glassy calm, with a pink hue. Quiet, peaceful, a glorious breath of life as it should be.

The following day we drove back to the trading post. There, the grand-daughter of old Smallwood showed us the store. Old tins and jars, from beans to snakebite cures, pots and pans of a hundred years ago. The floors of board, the walls and ceilings of old timber too. Tarnished brass scales, mahogany rocking chairs. And seated on his favourite chair, Ted Smallwood in wax – huge man, rimless specs, drooping grey moustache. Indian artefacts in cases – hack and tack of yesteryear.

On the boat out to the islands. Frank, Virginia drawl, reformed banker, now informed guide. A plethora of grey pelicans diving for fish. Squadrons of white pelicans on sandbars like a splendid army. Alas, on our approach, a flap of white wings with black feathers on the tip – and they were away. So grace-ful in flight – so goofy on the ground in walk. Bald eagles, egrets, the white-plumed ibis shyly flitting from mangrove to mangrove, herons blue and grey, cormorants diving as deep as 80 feet for fish. Underneath the boat, thousands of grey fish and mullets, here and there bubbles rising as an alligator slowly subsides at our presence.

On the boat, afternoon tea with four American guests. A large, very large gentleman who confesses to five homes in the US. A former vice-president of General Motors, lean, bespectacled, dry wit. And their wives, as all Americans, dress down, exactly opposite to the British; it is difficult to ascertain who's who in the US pecking order. It is not accent, it is not clothes, it is not upfront brag – it just is 'feel the wallet, size up the assets'.

After four hours in the islands and on the Gulf of Mexico, it is chilly – so back to base at $60 apiece. Frank's trip is not cheap, but essential to under-stand, if but slightly, the sheer majesty of the Everglades.

Back at Port of the Islands. It is Frank, the chef; I glide in the kitchen. Must try his seafood fettucine. A dish of heaven. Poached lobster, crab, scallops, shrimps. The fettucine boiled and immersed in a creamy light parmigiano sauce with chives, white wine and chicken stock. An angelic dish washed down with a gallon of Sauvignon. I am pigging out on Frank's delicious offerings.

Frank brings out the old photographs of the Caledonian Pipe band. Suddenly a plumpish, dark-haired gentleman, in baggy shorts, materializes. He lives in a large house on the lagoon. He has a set of pipes he cannot play. He will have them dispatched from Oregon or Michigan. Discussion about the chanter.

'Dip 'em in whisky,' says Frank in old Ashtonian.

Off to Marco Island and the Radisson Beach Resort. Marco is virtually man-made, reclaimed from the marshes. Canals traverse it. Down the beach an array of high-rise hotels. All America is here. A battalion of children, hundreds of adults. Americans *en masse* can be daunting. Bluebeard's Café Bar by the pool was heaving, all tomato ketchup, fancy dressing on salads, cartons of food, cartons of coke. All packaged, for ready consumption. It is a culture shock to European eyes and tastes.

Once acclimatized, it is all a great laugh. I had a grouper sandwich, Hazel a shrimp salad – or was it chicken? Whatever, they smothered it all in some sauce, and we ate it.

Relax on the beach until sundown.

2.24 p.m. The Trolley Tour of Marco. A miniature Cooks Tour of enormous houses in varied styles from Old Florida to baroque cathedral edifices. Most on the canals and rivers, bays and cays. Again Naples, scaled down, but elegant and civilized.

Dinner at the Pineapple Restaurant in the Radisson. Cool décor in green, laid back, Florida-style. Food excellent, wide choice of fresh fish, gargantuan steaks and a nice arrangement on the plate. Relaxing atmosphere with views from the large windows of the gardens and Gulf.

Friday. Met Harry and Audrey from Connecticut. The four of us played tennis. Hazel retired, and Mike – sales director of Radisson – made up the four. Suddenly Harry knocked the ball back to me. Going backwards at speed, I tripped head over heels. Knuckles, knees, shoulder, and masses of blood everywhere. Vaguely through my right eye I saw my torn-off eyebrow dripping blood. A lump of raw flesh. Oh my God! God dammit! Into the lobby, a large gent rushed for towel and ice pack. Audrey did likewise. The blood oozed out. Into Mike's car – down to the Urgent Care Center. A very large nurse admitted me. I lay on a bed for three hours talking with another patient – a millionaire – who bashed his head on his yacht. Eventually, a doctor appeared and stitched this bloke's head. I looked to my right to observe this great red gash in the yachtsman's forehead, saline solution and blood flowing. I felt sick. Then my turn.

'I'll give you a shot of lignocaine,' said the doctor. My face was covered with a cloth – blood-letting time.

Now, the last occasion I had lignocaine my heart stopped – total heart block. I felt my heart beating fast. I was hyperventilating. It required excessive self-control to prevent another near tragedy. I am so indisciplined that my iconoclastic brain would instruct my heart to stop, or go irrationally unstable. I know I have this capacity to loose my brain and let it run free, wild, uncontrollable. It is a madness that springs from the Irish, I am sure. I do not want to die yet – I do not really care if I do. I regard life, my life, really as a charade. I do not know why I am on the planet. Who brought me here, or who, or what, will transport me away.

Eight stitches later. Four hours later and $270 worse off, I am acquitted. My eye is like a mandrill's arse. The Americans make light.

'How's the other guy?'

'Oh, my! That's beautiful, really beautiful.'

I thank God for the NHS. Back home, where stitches are the land of the free – laugh – they have you in sutures. Later I dine heartily. Hazel is in shock, thinking I am about to snuff it.

Saturday. The eye is several shades of blue/black. Hazel, having been lectured as to the severity of a head wound at the hospital – no food, no alcohol, awaken him every two hours during the night to make sure he is alive – is tired. We lie on the beach. The beach is pure white – it is made of shells – millions of seashells crunched up. The surf rolls in. It is cold, 68°F, but blue and clean. A daiquiri, a piña colada and lunch is taken in Bluebeard's Café, a boardwalk beach bar, American-style. A little doze. Now on to the lagoon for the fishermen's return and the pelican feast. Dozens fighting for the filleted fish remains. Suddenly from the depth a nose, crenulated body, a swishing knobbly tail. An alligator of green eyes. A prehistoric monster. Its little fat legs with claws beating the water. Primeval, threatening. A fisherman (against the rules) threw a fish. Mighty jaws gaped – thrash of water, floating like a dark brownish green log again.

So, down to Stan's hoedown at Greenlands. A small island on the highway to Marco. A milling mass of polyglots dancing to a band. Hot sun, broad smiles, and the broadest folk I have ever seen. All sizes from oversize to gross magnitude. They did not give a toot. They hopped, squeaked, sang, consumed their beers and fancy drinks with total lack of inhibition. We simply gaped as they did their own thing oblivious of any watching world. It was a joy to see folk happy – where is depression, where are the dark clouds, where is the bad news? There is none at Stan's.

In the turmoil, Stan entered the stage, left. He sang the 'Fish Song', a complete and witty send-up of the tourist who must know the generic name of fish and whence it came.

Here, in an arena bounded by a clapperboard bar, restaurant, a boardwalk to a neat little harbour and a chickee hut was America. Dumpling ladies in gross gold and pink outfits, gents in ill-fitting shorts with overhanging paunches, matrons in tight jeans. Stan held 'em all. Grey-bearded, tanned as a cowhide, small blue eyes, a great marketer. A composer of songs and ballads, a man of Florida, a son of the pioneers, a veteran, a hillbilly but, my gosh, when he got the whole mob to sing 'God Bless America' I could have thrown my stetson into the hot air.

Monday. Last two days before cold, grey England. Repressive, downhill, a third-class nation masquerading as a world power. What a farce. Nothing, but nothing, appears on USA TV or in newspapers about Britain. It is a banana country, led by apes.

Our recovery will be led by businessmen and a dedicated workforce. When will Major realize that we begin with an industrial base? – not service industries.

But here on Marco Island life is idyllic. Judy from the Chamber of Commerce is perfection. She recommends Hideaway Beach, a pink-and-white village with a golf course in its grounds. I could not believe my eyes at white-attired Americans playing croquet. Their immaculate white beach was deserted. Again the ambience was 1950s Britain.

Back to the Radisson for a country and western night, all 'yee-hah' fancy cowboy dancin', and the Marco Chamber of Commerce entourage. Judy and the crew were delightful. Young, progressive, positive, bright-eyed, bushy-tailed and so helpful. I cannot thank them and Susan Kairalla from the Naples Chamber enough for opening the book on south-west Florida. An experience I recommend to any jaded palate.

YUGOSLAVIA

It is April in England. When proud pied April, dressed in all his trim, hath put a spirit of youth in everything. I have just shaved a visage like a bilious brontosaurus, wiped a bronto sore-arse, inspected a tongue like rat's fur, cleaned teeth like decayed rotting roof rafters, gazing from eyes purging thick yellow amber and plum tree gum. My wit is weak, my hams are gone. Youth's muse has deserted me. I sit in my kitchen, browsing a newspaper over the bacon.

Snowflakes like dinnerplates floating leisurely past the patio window and going splat on the verandah. The Victorian garden furniture, white and elegant, lies under a silent veil of snow. The quiet is disturbed by two grey squirrels fighting a pitched battle with an angry magpie. It is a daily confrontation over possession of the conifers; its ferocity intrigues me. They snap, scream and bite each other in turn. Neither side ever wins. The crows, jays and starlings watch and wait. The chaffinches, bluetits, blackbirds, kingfishers and solitary cock pheasant take cover. Like me, they ponder the vagaries of the animal world. Two plump rabbits, for ever puzzled, sit in wonderment. The nocturnal fox, as big as an Alsatian, will have them for supper. It is war out there. Could not the squirrels and the magpie allot themselves a territory apiece, and live harmoniously? Will the tiny birds, which give so much pleasure, be allowed a life? The answer is – no. The animal kingdom is no different from our own human existence; the bullies always win, the weak are destroyed. Which is why I present to you a couple of essays on Yugoslavia, the first a family holiday of unbounding joy, the second a revisit as the country was torn apart by civil war.

VILLA DUBROVNIK

I began the diary at 6.15 p.m., Sunday 15 July, on the verandah of my room in the Villa Dubrovnik.

The hotel is a half-a-mile from the city, 60 bedrooms, built like a cake rising from the rocks, lapped by the clear blue sea. The bottom tiers are bars, restaurants, lounges, the upper ones the rooms, furnished in style, light and cool.

I sipped an Istra bitter, that is Campari, but made in Yugoslavia and half the price. Ice tinkling in glass. Gazing at Dubrovnik, a unique city. Little cobbled streets lead off squares paved with marble. There are whiffs of ancient Rome in the colonnades and friezes, all beautifully restored, graffiti- and litter-free. The streets are lit by antique 'gas lights' and thronged with folk chattering, talking, ambling, strolling, relaxed yet stimulated. Festival time. A little Berlioz in the castle, romantic music on the clear night sky. Little alleyways of pizzerias, bars, cafés. Colour and light, like a set from Aida. I reflect on the last 24 hours. *Mein Gott.* Our journey began at Ringway or, as Gill Thompson, the airport director prefers, Manchester International Airport. It is, with the exception of Schiphol, the finest airport in Europe. The staff have a private-enterprise air about them. Facilities are excellent and to hand. Flying holds no terrors in a predominantly homely atmosphere.

I remember one snowbound winter morning, with flights delayed and cancelled, arriving in the Executive Lounge. It was crammed with travellers, a vast array of dirty crockery – the staff en route fighting through snowdrifts. Gill Thompson arrived. I suggested that we don the staff pinnies – that is, overalls, in Prestbury – and wash up the dishes. It was a huge joke, going well until two frosty ladies demanded fresh coffee. With a wink, we provided tea and coffee for one and all. 'Twas like the taproom at the Dog and Frozen Leper. Gone the cares of missed connections, the frenzy of business; it was simply good to be alive, with a freezing blizzard sweeping in from the east. All save the two ladies. They grumbled constantly that the service was wretched, the noise level much too high, and the stewards (Gill and myself) far too friendly. We should know our place. Ladies apart, can you imagine London's airport director mashing tea and sympathy?

So back to my holiday. Coffee, then shuttle to Heathrow, Terminal Two, on Sunday afternoon, the cesspit of humanity, throwing up its flotsam of human debris. Queues of travellers of all nationalities trying to check in. Desks undermanned, destinations jumbled together. In my queue, labelled first-class, were excited, frustrated, sweating folk bound for Copenhagen, Malmö, Algeria, Trieste, Zagreb, Faro. The conveyor belt broke, and it appeared that the whole stinking mess had ground to disaster.

My flight closed abruptly. I scrambled to the front of the angry mob, where a perspiring, long-serving chap with gunmetal hair and hangdog face checked me in. That two-ringer was Horatio on the bridge. He apologized profusely, adding ruefully: 'If you exec guys sat here and spent the weekend with me, it would blow your balls off.'

Sprinting to the gate, we piled on to our flight, 2.15 p.m. It was awful. Surly cabin staff, reluctant service, inedible food, wine on ration, and it was freezing cold. How an airline can employ such appalling folk mystifies me. In an age of intense competition for your backside on an aircraft seat, the cabin staff are

266

the first line. They are ambassadors, the welcomers, the cosseters, the vital link. But we survived – optimism gets its own reward.

But why Yugoslavia? Well, for the past four years I have made TV programmes there and found that, like most Eastern Europeans, they have innate pride that hides behind dark features: dark hair, dark eyes, impassive faces. Once the façade crumbles, there is laughter and gaiety – a love of food and drink, a zest for living. But most of my experiences were in the north: Belgrade, Zagreb, Pula, Portoroz. The hotels there were large and impersonal, the service *laissez-faire*, huge groups of people acting as one. So I opted for the Dalmatian Coast. Two hundred and fifty kilometres of coast, from Split to Cavtat. And as Yugoslavia has a thousand idyllic islands: chuck in one or two for starters.

The family Hall is, I am pleased to say, off-beat. For first-time readers, my wife Hazel is a blue-eyed, petite blonde. She embodies all the vivacity and eccentricities that only Aquarians possess. When I tell you that I am a Capricorn, littered under Saturn, aspected by Mercury, delivered on Christmas Day, then the sparks fly, not merely upward, but everywhere. My son Danny is 21, a law graduate. My daughter Francesca is an actress of 23 summers. We are a potty family, forever sending up one or the other. We have laughed our way through life, and love has naturally followed. A sense of humour is the most essential thread in the tapestry of life. I yclept myself 'Daddikins' and the children 'Kiddywinkies'. They call me 'Big Stu' and their mama 'Little Haze'. We still take family holidays. They surmise that wherever I go there will be excitement, adventure and gross indiscipline – and they are correct in their judgement.

So here we are, mid-afternoon, pitchforked into the heat of a Dalmatian afternoon. Baking heat and little wind. Into the hire car, but first find the route out of the airport. After two fast laps of the nearby oil terminal, to the howling derision of non-drivers, I salvage pride and orientation and blast north to the city of Dubrovnik.

Our hotel, Villa Dubrovnik, was located down several flights of steps sheltered from the sun by overhanging palm, pine and almond trees. At reception, genuine smiles of welcome. Large, comfortable rooms overlooking the shimmering, crystal-clear blue sea. We dined in the hotel restaurant on grilled grouper, that ugly fish with snarling mouth – but divine on the taste buds. Replete, we repaired to the city half a mile away.

My knowledge of wine, especially European, is both extensive and catholic. Put simply, I will imbibe, nay swill, whatever is put before me. I have learnt that in every nook and cranny in *every* village that nurtures the vine, they tread and bottle nectar that they keep. What they do not want, they export, adorned with fancy labels, coats of arms, ambiguous appellations, and delude us into snobbery and false appreciation of their wines.

So in the enchanting squares of Dubrovnik we began the adventure into Yugoslav wines. Beyond the vale of Lutomer Riesling lay many delights. Posip is a pale dry white wine of some character and strength, Mostar a little heavier on the palate and the head. And the local wine, served in a litre bottle or carafe, is known as Dejelho. At 200 dinar (£1) a litre, it is marvellous value. We sat chatting, relaxed and happy, watching that nocturnal parade that is so European, folks meeting, embracing, laughing. Life became, as it should be, quite simple. Industrial disputes ebbed away on the tide of the simple life.

And so to the following day of swimming, skin-diving, eating and drinking. Day two by old motorboat to the island of Lokrum. The sea was choppy, the wind brisk, but the ancient craft chugged slowly into the harbour. We alighted, and, faced with four rocky paths, chose the one we thought led to the beach. Alas and alack, it meandered, albeit pleasantly, to – the public loo! So another route, this one to the nude beach. There, sprawled in various poses, large and small willies, dropped boobs, varicose veins, enormous bottoms. The long the short and the tall. Hazel took fright, Danny took pictures, Francesca tut-tutted, I was all for dropping my trunks and joining 'em. The family all repaired to some razor-sharp rocks and impaled ourselves on them like slaves at a crucifixion.

At last, lunch in a castle. Castles proliferate in Yugoslavia. The food simple: a mixed grill of pork, lamb, delicious smoked sausage, a salad, two litres of, yes, Bejelho, Turkish coffee. Price for four – £8. Now, are you warming to Yugoslavia?

After dinner that evening, back to the city. Hereabouts a small mistake. Stu, hearing symphonic strains from ancient walled castle, dives in followed by family. The fort is of warm stone, the concert hall a vaulted chamber. On stage the Zagreb Symphony Orchestra, a contralto singing Mahler. Now, if one likes Mahler one enthuses. Danny takes a wobbler and departs. Hazel did likewise, returned, and departed again in a huff. Francesca and I hidden behind a pillar, move swiftly to the front and impudently sit beside the conductor's wife. The violins gave off Slavonic passion, the cellos, dark in intensity, bending forward like willows in a breeze. Outside, Hazel and Danny were contrite – two litres of, yes, Bejelho softened the grizzled old visage, and we laughed a lot.

The next day, following an itinerant New Yorker's advice, we journeyed a few miles down the grandiloquent Adriatic coast up, down and through mountains to a small village called Frada and a famous restaurant, Konavaski Dvori. It is an old water-mill, the river flowing by over three waterfalls, gurgling noisily. A stream runs straight past the simple oak dining tables as it rotates two ancient wooden mills. Wheat is milled and made into the most delicious bread I have tasted. Baked in copper tins, immersed in red-hot charcoal for an hour, and served from the tin to the table. The baker, a large jolly man, already into the local wine, laughed constantly. The waitresses, in blue flowing dresses and little white lace hats, were from the village.

Now I have a theory – a proven one at that. When I am enjoying myself I like everybody to join in. It is the old Redcoat, Butlin's, chara-ride to Blackpool syndrome. I really am Chesterton's 'Militant Rambler'. So grabbing the startled proprietor by the hand, I dived into the kitchen to meet the staff. I invited them to wine. Their dark eyes flashed. Who was this mad foreigner? I told them that once upon a glorious time I presented that crazy frolic *It's a Knockout*. They know it as *Igra Bez Graniza*. Their ruddy faces beamed. The smiles were broad, and foreign barriers were downed. The meal was superb. Dalmatian ham and local cheese, trout from the river, gutted, doused in lemon juice, olive oil and dill, charcoal-grilled; mountains of hot bread and local wine; followed then by chunks of lamb from the rotating carcass on the spit. Laughter and song. The bill – £20. In the West End of London it would have cost £200. The mistral or bora was blowing hard. But umpteen Slibovitz later we could appreciate the beauty of Cavtat. Nightcap is Cavtat.

Three little harbours, elegant houses clinging to cliffs. Charming little streets. Room to move, to breathe the atmosphere. No crime, no muggings, no litter, no graffiti, no English tea and Ramsbottom fruitcake. Just like Spain used to be 30 years ago before the package tour raped it.

Another day of soaking up the sun and interesting cosmopolitan chat. Australians, Italians, Americans, French, all stay at the hotel. Their views on us, our lifestyle, politics included, are fascinating. Here I have not time to dwell, the issues are too complex.

We revelled in the splendour of old Dubrovnik, ate like kings on a pauper's budget, and after a week set off for the islands.

First stage north by car to Split by the A2, the Adriatic route. After 20 laps of the new town, we were off. The sun burning, the road narrow and single highway. I shall be older, wiser and sweatier by the time we reach Split. My hire car is a small Opel and it is laden to the gunnels. The road sweeps through tortuous bends, up through pines to the volcanic mountains, down past little villages clinging to them, back to the clearest blue sea with ships leaving white wakes. Hundreds of tiny islands lush with trees that some giant hand seemed to have scattered like confetti millions of years ago.

After five hours of wheel-heaving, the lunch stop. A rustic village, two or three whitewashed taverns, rustic little tumbledown houses – tranquillity. In a tiny voice – no English spoken or even heard – I order a kebab of veal, pork and sweetbreads. Danny has likewise. Daughter Francesca, an actress ever mindful of her figure, furiously counting the calories, tries to order fruit. The poor waitress smilingly nods and brings her a plate of chips. The first lesson in Serbo-Croat! The bill for that repast was £5 for four – including the statutory litre of Bejelho.

On to the harbour of Split. We are now hot and tired. We book on a ferry to Hvar; it departs in five hours. We decide to eat. Clamber aboard a swish ship moored in the harbour. First course arrives without even sighting a menu – consternation – hell, it was a private party. Bowing low, muttering an excuse that I was a fact-finding small-arms producer from Bremen, we retired. When faced with my comeuppance, I always feign German citizenship. Simply utter the phase: '*Man gibt sein Gepäck zu Aufebewahrung.*' Officials melt before it, doors hitherto closed will open, mouths drop open. It means: 'One puts one's luggage in the cloakroom.'

Helpless with laughter, we have delicious grilled octopus on the neighbouring ship, litres of Bejelho and off to catch the ferry. My car was third in the queue. But in our absence another queue had formed, and another. The ferries are pipsqueak, taking 30 cars. I was last on, the last ship of the night. It was like Dunkirk. Apart, that is, for an Italian in an ancient Fiat. After frenzied bumping and boring, arm twiddling and histrionics, he squeezed aboard. The audience applauded, bar a po-faced fellow Italian whose pristine Alfa Sud was badly bruised in the battle. In that four-hour voyage, we emptied the bar. Bejelho, Slibovitz and Istra bitters, strong ale, Turkish coffee. To arrive 'Bejelhoed', 'Sliboed' and 'Istrad' is a real joke. Poor Hazel had a fit of the vapours. In the family, the term is 'overtired'. We ladled ourselves off the ship and into Hvar town.

The town square at midnight was an operatic set, the buildings of white stone lit by small lamps, the pavement polished stone, the air like wine, the ambience divine. Our hotel, the Palace, is on the square, a former ducal palace of fine Venetian proportion, small colonnades, simple arches.

Breakfast was a scowling, prowling, Yugo waitress in her Minnie Mouse boots pushing a trolley like a punch-drunk Heathrow porter. Thick chicory with a coffee flavour. Pats of butter a metre thick. Ham and eggs.

Off to one of a hundred beaches. Hvar exemplifies the Yugo temperament. Rough-hewn, informal, please yourself. Take off your clothes, or bathe in a mink coat if you want. The men are enormous, seven feet tall, black of hair and visage. They smoke incessantly – whoever said smoking stunts the growth? In Hvar the beaches are volcanic rock, so once again it was the crucifixion job – prostrate on a bed of nails.

And so to dinner. I am the learned traveller, am I not? The man who can order dinner in Bangkok with the dexterity of a Thai, who can conjure a seven-course meal in the middle of the Gobi Desert.

Now Hvar is a town of alleyways, or ginnels as we say. Cool and calm, litter-free and charming. We had a recommendation for the Zultan restaurant. Two eating-houses faced each other. From the Zultan thick blue smoke poured from a barbecue. The other had an inviting stone courtyard, tables laid with white linen, fine glasses and polished cutlery. A large gentleman welcomed us effusively. His chef's apron bore nary a stain.

Feeling expansive and radiantly happy, I asked for his recommendation.

'Aah-ah,' he beamed; lobster, clams, pristaci (a cross between an oyster and a prawn), dent, crayfish, squid. He then disappeared.

Within minutes, dish one arrived, a delicious salad of fresh squid in onions with a sauce of vinegar, olive oil and herbs. And then dish two – remember I had not even viewed the menu – 'twas a salver of boiled clams and pristaci. We demolished them with salivating relish. We were full, but to my horror dish number three was concocted.

There was no way to stop it. That chef had grilled everything in sight, including his apron. A mountain of fish on a salver a yard wide. Now, on entering the establishment I had noted the fish – on a tray lay two giant lobsters so old and tired they would have drawn a state pension.

To my horror one of them lay atop our salver with a smear or two of dressing to cover the death odour it exuded. We were all so Bejelhoed that we fell on this heap of old leftovers and has-beens as if famished.

The bill arrived: 12,500 dinar, or £60. Cripplingly expensive for Yugo – dirt cheap in London. But I had only £50 in dinar with me, including battered old notes that Hazel used to pay for the loo. I escaped by wrapping the dinar around some old pound notes, uttered my German phrase and fled. I had been taken. Me, the old sage, the travel-stained wise man of the world.

Monday, and breakfast at the Palace: smoked Dalmatian ham, two fried eggs, thick black Turkish coffee, no sugar. I always eat breakfast; I abhor Continental fiddle-faddle. I must insist on rousting the bowel. Three times round the bowel and back in time for tea. My daddy used to say: 'Open bowels mean open mind.' Discharging waste in my terms has no relevance to Windscale – merely defecating scale. My obsession for 'being regular' occasions great mirth within the family. But I have never taken a laxative in my life, and although I have abused my body like a racing engine I have never resorted to drugs. Give the body the correct fuel, drive it to its limits, allow it to rest but occasionally, but, importantly, ensure that waste products are properly exhausted. A hot breakfast primes the engine for the day. Having worked for the BBC for 25 years, I have learnt that it may be the only meal to pass my lips that day.

So from the hotel to the beach. Beaches all around the harbour, but they are volcanic rock, and without a Lilo it is another bed-of-nails job. So off by car to Stari Grad. Up in the mountains, precipitous bends, the island a mass of wild lavender – the air perfumed for mile after mile. Twenty miles of arm-twirling, and we arrive. An ancient town founded by the Greeks. The harbour six kilometres long. On it white stone houses. Cool, clean, beautifully preserved. The twentieth century has bypassed this exquisite corner of the world. Hazel and I soon off to explore. The 'Kiddywinkies' strolled up the harbour for a swim in the clear blue sea. Ambling along, the mind roams free, easy to visualize the Romans, with their civilized way of life, sipping cooled wine within the arches of their houses.

In one corner stands a restaurant, The Three Palms. White, spotless linen, neat, inviting. Lunch was simple, a kebab of veal and pork, a crisp salad of tomato, cucumber and olives. A jug or two of wine. The waitress a shy economics student from the Hungarian border. Eventually, she tried her English, we laughed a lot. The proprietor joined in. We swapped trinkets and mementoes. Close by is the home of philosopher Paul Hektorovic. A little stone fort built round a fish pond teeming with enormous grey mullet. The kitchen off the passage which encircled the pond. Ancient butter churns, wine presses, stone jugs, a huge spit over the fire. Everything laid out just as the house was in 1520. The garden fragrant with oleander, the vines heavy with grapes. The 'loo' was literally a broom cupboard with a hole in the ground. Above it the inscription 'Know thyself then how can thee be proud'. Even in 1520 bowels were important. Reminds me of a dear friend, Anna. She is a district nurse, in her Derbyshire parish an army of old folk. Wearily one day she observed:

'Do you think there are bowels in heaven?'

From Stari Grad back over the mountains. Atop one, a small timber restaurant. A lamb roasting on the spit. An old man sitting on the stone wall constantly rotating the lamb and anointing it with baste. His face was the colour and texture of ready-rubbed Condor. I asked him the secret of his roasting, the lamb, golden-brown, oozing succulent juices.

'Beer, olive oil and rosemary,' he said. As we sat, old women bearing sacks of lavender, some leading mules ladened with 20 sacks, passed by. The scene was almost biblical.

To dinner at the Palace. A massive menu, excellent value. Around the harbour, alive with locals, to a small hotel. In the garden, a small chap named Churt was playing a three-manual Yamaha organ. He sat upright, arms outstretched like a Grand Prix driver, and he could play. He was an artist and demanded an audience. The Yugoslavs adored his interpretation of their folk dances. Small circles of young folk holding hands. Tricky little heel and toe steps. There is something touching about this dance. A unity, a bond, of proud people whose country is subsiding under a mountain of foreign debts. Since Tito's death fragmenting back into the six republics of fifty years ago.

Tuesday, and let's explore the islands. Yugoslavia has hundreds. The largest off the island of Hvar is St Clements. I still marvel at the crystal-clear sea. Arrive at the jetty. A stiff climb through the pine woods and on to a shingle beach marginally easier on the buttocks than volcanic rock. Hazel, like a beached whale, retires under a rock. Danny, an inveterate sprite, takes to surf-boarding. Expletives hit the air, much beating of fists – the lone yachtsman last seen disappearing with the stiff breeze in the direction of Albania. Lunch was broiled lobster, not the one which expired on my plate in Hvar. Pink, delicate, delicious. The price about £2.

Back on the boat, a frightful youth with acne is gnawing the cheek of a young Yugoslav damsel. Black streaks in her bleached hair. They chew gum nonstop. A fat redhead, with rubbly thighs, reads a book. Big, big Yugos with heavy beards. Was it a misshape boat, or, and I always ponder, how do we appear to them? I remember nuzzling up to a beautiful Nigerian girl, and she observed, somewhat tartly, that Englishmen always stank of milk, cheese and butter. Unabashed, I donned farmer's tweeds and stuck to my task!

Back ashore, and dinner once again a gastronomic experience. Back then to Churt's organ recital. Incredibly, he revealed himself as a television producer from Zagreb on a summer sabbatical. He also revealed himself a naughty womanizer, playing errant court to my daughter. Obviously, a man for all organs. But he was enchantingly wicked, and we argued passionately about women, the macho male Slav, music, wine and politics. At 2 a.m. he led Hazel and me to his beat-up Renault 4. An adventure dawned. A wild, nightmare drive, up three miles of boulder-strewn track, to the top of the mountain. In silence, we arrive at a large wrought-iron gate. A few lights twinkle within to illumine the Stygian darkness. A figure appears, unlocks the great gate, and we are inside the fort built by Napoleon in 1811.

By the light of storm lamps, a slim young man in T-shirt and jeans greets us. His head a dome, covered with wispy strands of brown hair. Rimless spectacles complete the picture of a spy. We are ushered into a courtyard and thence to a large room crammed full of instruments and a huge radio telescope. He presses a button, a motor whirs and the whole ceiling slides back to reveal the night sky and a million stars. He peers at the charts and myriad calculations. He focuses on Jupiter. I clamber up to observe. There is Jupiter, dark clouds of turbulence on the planet's face. Hazel gazes at the planets for the first time.

'Oh, la-la,' she screams with delight with the pigtailed wide-eyed innocence of one peering into those naughty 90s, end-of-pier peepshows. The astronomer smiles. He is Czech, a doctor of the science on a three-year study of one particular star.

At 4 a.m. we retired inside the fort, mystified by the heavens. The passageways were five feet high. Napoleon, being a mighty midget, had designed it thus. Down the stone steps to the kitchen, where a medium-sized man, brown visage, bald head and incipient pot belly, was preparing a custard with burnt sugar. He smiled a broad welcome, produced a bottle of house wine, and another. 'Bejelhoed' again, in Napoleon's fort, as close to heaven as I will ever be, at 5 a.m.

Churt, or Charlie as he is now named, drove slowly down the mountain. Halfway down we stopped to gather wild rosemary, still used in Yugoslavia as a cough and cold cure. Distilled into oil and either swallowed, rubbed into aching muscles, or anointing the buttocks for good luck. Eat your heart out, NHS.

Tuesday, and to Milna, a fishing village six kilometres from Hvar. Up and down an old Roman dirt road, through limestone mountains, into one of the prettiest sights I have ever seen. A small pebble cove, tiny jetty, boats bobbing in the clear blue sea, a handful of people, pure bliss. To a small restaurant. Istra bitter, a jug of cool wine. Lunch on broiled calamari in olive oil and garlic. I am not a lover of garlic. So often in Europe stale garlic is used, especially by pseuds. It taints the breath, one whiff gives bystanders a fit of the staggers, and personally it wreaks havoc on my bowel. But here, in Milna, the garlic was so fresh and like a sharp onion that I actually wolfed whole cloves of the stuff.

So I gaze at Milna, dazzling white sun. The white cliffs rising sheer. Tiny white houses, each with laden vines. The gentle sea washing white pebbles. What will this be, this beautiful Milna, when the capitalists rape it, as they inevitably will, in the years to come?

Meanwhile, 'Kiddywinkies' had befriended Doris of Belgrade. A middle-aged lady with a Michelin figure and a Mencap son. She was gregarious and effusive, wise too. She realized the importance of a smile and a kind word. Her little two-roomed house was open house, and two American youths, packs on backs, horsing around the world, were rooming with her. Barriers were down, laughter the great catalyst. Slav reserve melted. We learnt Slav dances to please them. They spoke openly of life without the Western artefacts we take for granted. The motorcar is still a luxury. Clothes in short supply. Housing expensive and difficult. But their pride in themselves is inspirational. Life in Hvar was so much a pleasure, and a stimulant.

But it was time to leave, and here is the rub. If it was impossible to get here, it is doubly impossible to leave. The ferries are so tiny; each one is oversubscribed at least three times. I needed to be on the 2.15 p.m., so I approached the chief of police. Through beads of sweat, he made a deal. I was to be awarded the seal of 'Commercially Important'. *Now you all know I am not.* Any port or post in a storm. Arrive at 2 p.m. Look for him, was the instruction. Was I anxious? I have known false promises melt like snowflakes in the sun, but I trusted him. Away around the rocks to say goodbye. Atop a rock the girls topless. Addresses exchanged, cameras clicked. A few tears as the Yugoslavs realized that we are all, very simply, human beings, regardless of culture, creed or wealth.

Thus to Vira, the departure point, six kilometres from Hvar. I sight the chief. Imperiously, he waves me to the front of the enormous queue of vehicles for the ferry. Mercedes, BMW, Porsche, Audi – all Austrian or German. Past the hordes of sweating humanity to the front, where a tiny police car eases out of the queue to ease me in. Protests are silenced by the chief and cohorts. To offer money would be a gross affront, so in my best English way I invite him and his policemen for drinkie-poosies. He waved a giant bronzed hand. The drinks were on him. All he asked was that we returned to Hvar. We will.

At last we dock in Split and drive through the evening and night back to Dubrovnik. A drive not for the nervous. Concentration at high. Little talk and little sightseeing. Eighty kilometres north of Dubrovnik, need for gastronomics. Cosy restaurant, menu in Serbo-Croat. Quick march into kitchen, where proprietor brings out a mountain of fresh fish. Grey mullet, John Dory, grouper, red mullet, mussels, calamari. A huge grill of the lot – the bill for four £15. If there is better value in Europe, please tell me.

The last leg to the Villa Dubrovnik, where we greet old friends. We sleep soundly in the royal suite – Danny with his Walkman absorbing pop music. The rest of us *au naturel*. The dreams were the dreams of a perfect holiday. I urge you to visit Yugoslavia, but please go with an open mind and you will discover that a holiday does not really have to open your wallet – at least not too wide!

THE ROAD TO VITEZ

Day one: 15 December 1992. The taxi from home failed to arrive at 0800 hours. Panic ensued. Danny drove me to the airport in pyjamas. Arrived somewhat ruffled. But caught shuttle to Heathrow.

Departed for Zagreb 1300 hours. Disaster one: fog at Zagreb. Directed to Maribor in northern Slovenia on the Austrian border. Met up with SBS marines in fighting trim. One marine captain had a neck size equal to my waist measurement. Much jollity and serious war chat. We dined heartily on Bassets liquorice allsorts and warm Slovenian beer.

Eventually departed for Split eight hours later. Arrive 0130 hours. Met by Gordon Bacon, ex-police inspector in his Y-reg Transit van – the 'Yellow Peril'. He was to be our saviour.

Arrived at the Palace Hotel, Split, run-down, threadbare, semi-painted, dingy – a refuge for refugees.

No room really at the Palace, so I shared a double bed with Peter Trollope. A notable first – I have never slept with a Trollope.

Day two: 16 December 1992. At Split airport we hired two Lada Cossack four-wheel-drive Jeeps. Relics of 1960s engineering when bits fall off, brakes are useless, roadholding a joke – space for four dwarfs. Loaded with a million TV boxes, the whole show was pure *Steptoe and Son*. But in bright sun we set off in convoy for Vitez. A Range Rover, a 16-tonner Merccdes, the 'Yellow Peril' and us.

The metalled roads gave way after some 50 kilometres to dangerous rutted, snowbound, muddy glorified cart tracks. Twisting, turning through miles of pine forest. Lurching, heaving, sliding first on packed ice, squirming through thick mud. The angles assumed by vehicles in front taking alarming proportions. One mistake spells disaster. The road is narrow, the bends acute. After this headbanging horrendous drive come to the Royal Engineers' redoubt, a small snow-covered enclave housing the lads who keep open this vital artery for supplies. One hundred and forty miles of hell.

We were greeted by shouts of: 'Here to cover the Cheshires, the glory boys, charging the enemy with their warriors – three cheers for Colonel Bob [the Cheshires' Battalion commander]. What about us, the f***ing forgotten boys in this war?'

The boys soon realize who we are. In a twinkling the gun-toting north-west boys make the tea and prepare for their TV debuts.

I have a link to camera as the convoy lurches drunkenly towards me. I cock it up. Cameraman Alan's expression summed it up. Twat-head! Second take OK. He accompanies me in the Heinz Lada-can for cockpit shots. It really is Big Thunder Mountain. Suddenly, on packed ice, I lose the pillocking Jeep. We slide gently into packed snow. I now know the Alan face – a pained, mournful picture of disdain. Twat-head two!

Darkness falls, but only after we have savoured the lakes and mountains of Bosnia. Savage beauty as the sun sets.

Now the real grind. Rutted roads, freezing mud. The flog to Vitez. The toughest drive of our lives. The Feed the Children HQ is one kilometre from the army base. Adjacent the Press Information Centre. 'Lord of the Rings' here is Captain John Ellis. He is young; slightly truculent, even abrasive. He resents our presence as intruders. His accent is feigned aristocratic, clipped Noël

Coward. His attitude patronizing. We do not like him. We repair to our own billet. A private house run by a young Slavonic lady. Tall, slender, jet-black hair, bad teeth. All Bosnians have bad teeth. Communism always neglected teeth.

We are allocated three rooms. I am pleased. Much as I adore Mr Trollope – 'tis better to kip alone.

We dine on smoked ham, a dram of scotch, and thick, black, hot, sweet Turkish coffee. At last we are to meet the CO, Colonel Bob. John Ellis has made the task almost impossible, but we travel to the base.

Oceans of thick brown clinging mud. Faint lights. Muffled shouts from the guards, and we are in the officers' mess.

Young men, all affecting guards' accents – thick and plummy. Suppose it is the militia tradition when one actually bought one's commission. Colonel Bob Stewart, the legend, is at our elbow. Tall, handsome, blond, blue-eyed – every inch the commander. This is his war. Every step of the campaign has Bob Stewart's name engraved on it. Derring-do – gung ho – a man's man. Clapping me on the shoulder, he torrents forth. How grateful that we should be here. How much it means to his boys that we should reflect their moves and attitudes. His drink is scotch. It is disappearing by the litre. Something is afoot. Frisson in the air.

To the consternation and horror of Captain Ellis, Colonel Bob confides that tomorrow he will drive though the Serb lines seeking dialogue with the Serb commander about a cease-fire at Christmas. We arrange to meet at 0800 tomorrow. We are sitting on an exclusive scoop. Colonel Bob knows he is safe. 'No, you can't come with me, and the mission is top-secret.' Wishing him God speed, we speed back to the billet.

The Lada-can parked up in the freezing night. Up the stairs to bed, and how we need sleep. *But, but*, in our bed is a stranger. No, not a stranger, really – he is a photographer from *The Times*. A greasy-haired, foxy, weaselly, wiseacre from Essex. That Essex accent takes me aback. That 'Fuck off, who are you? I am Essex superior'. I blow the fuse. How dare he enter our bedroom, remove our clothes and sleep in our bed. I am blazing, raging mad. I will evict him, murder him – but Master Trollope, built like a brick shithouse on billiard-table legs, restrains. I pick up my bags. Shout at young Slav. To the next-door house and demand admittance. I demand a bed – and get one. A cosy, large bed. A massive duvet. I am happy. I have imposed, demanded, but I am free from that Essex twonk. Then all hell let loose. Young Slav, white-faced, rushes in – followed by brother. They are angry! No! They are apologetic. It is embarrassing. Slibovitz, smoked ham, Slibovitz. More goodies. I bring out heavy chocolate. They bring two children from sleeping beds. They practise English – I practise sobriety but fail – and tomorrow at eight it is Colonel Bob.

Day three: 17 December 1992. I rise at 0700. The water glass is my shaving mug. I do not even bother to adjust my long johns and vest. I have slept in them and will continue to do so. Personal hygiene in a battle zone is not a priority.

At 0745 breakfasted heartily on home-cured raw bacon, an omelette, gallons of Turkish coffee.

The world is turning our way. Mr Trollope rushes in – the Lada-can has been stolen during the night. Spirited away by the Bosnians. By now repainted in camouflage and deployed against the Serbs. 'A platoon of vengeful Bosnians, armed to the teeth, disembowelled the savage Serbs.'

This war already has its horror stories, of beheadings, hangings, drawings, quarterings, eyes gouged, tripes left by mutilated bodies to rot in the snow. As the Lada-can is on my Amex card, I am already £4,500 in the red. Sod it. It is Granada's bit for the war effort.

To Colonel Bob. Amid his warriors he is frank. He does not comprehend. Is the war an East–West culture crisis? Is it Ottoman Empire versus Austro-Hungarian? Is it fascist Croatia versus Communist Serbia?

But he is going through the Serbian lines. He is afraid of casualties. Despite the Whitehall mandarins, he does care. His troops adore him.

We take his leave. Apace, Captain Ellis has been tartly informed that he will render all help. His white United Nations Land Rover will be deployed. He will be our right hand. Colonel Bob has spoken. Captain Ellis mellows. He is local, Manchester University, wanted to live in Wilmslow, settled for Disley. Now we are cooking on gas and not hot air.

He leads, of his own volition, a convoy to Travnik, a grim, grey town. A grey river running through it. It has been shelled and mortared constantly, bullet holes on the stuccoed walls. People silent, shuffling desolate. Destination Orphanage housing refugees. It was the old town hall. East Europe baroque, it was. Now a shambles reeking of stale urine and faeces. Long corridors, dark doors and everywhere stale piss. At last, with a platoon of Royal Engineers, we deliver food parcels to a room full of dark-haired, brown-eyed children, some babes in arms, orphans of the war. Forty thousand civilians dead, one hundred thousand missing. This, then, is the price.

I had expected mass deprivation. Starving children, begging, cajoling, gaunt features, the food and drink of TV. Conscience makes cowards and promotes conscience charity, say the cynics. Suddenly Derek pitches forward. His sound apparatus had been playing up – *was he*? His face greyish-green, eyes closed in agony.

'I've ruptured myself,' he whispered in his ripe Mancunian tones. 'It's happened before – I'll just push it back!' Now I know, as a working-class lad, deep into bowel movements like the Germans, that Derek had not completed his metabolic cycle that morning and was deeply troubled

'Don't f**k about,' said I. 'It's the finest Oscar-winning performance since Laurence Olivier in bleeding Khartoum.'

'Bollocks,' said Derek. 'I must push it back.'

Now, what and where to push mystified me. If I offer to help, placing my warm hand on his groin, would it be misinterpreted by the licentious soldiery? A new meaning to camp nurse.

Groaning gently, Derek was ladled into the Land Rover. Captain Ellis drove at speed to Vitez base. Derek, like a pea on a drum. Whether the speed was to avoid the Serbian shells or for grave concern for Derek's condition we will ponder for ever. Derek disappeared into the arms of Florence Nightingale to have his hernia thumbed back by a benevolent lieutenant-colonel. We had to repair his ruptured equipment – if you see what I mean.

Captain Ellis, by now thoroughly thawed, half-repaired the sound gear but Derek, like Lazarus, rose from the dead, soldered the cans (headphones) and played a blinder. We now began the tour of the base. First there were big butch tanks, the Warriors, bristling with guns and high-tech. The commander atop, open to the elements, steel helmet, black balaclava and those he-man goggles. A little boy's dream. A battlewagon that exceeds the motorway speed limit, demolishes a house with a salvo, clambers over a wall in a trice. Shells by the thousand, bullets by the mile – the real war looms. Chats now with the Cheshire boys. Near striplings, bewildered, puzzled, fearful. It is bitterly cold, a foreign land – it is not a man's life; it is awful.

The tour continues. Fifteen hundred men living in tents – appalling. Eight men to a tent, scruffy, unkempt and everything dark green. Here and there a family photo, a tinsel or two, a football shirt, a girl shirt. Anything to recall home. Lads from Stockport, Macclesfield, Sale, Chester, the Wirral, Birkenhead. Life really is crude and basic. Lavatories rudimentary sit-down jobs. Water scarce, hot water even scarcer.

Down in the cookhouse was master chef Roy Strainey. His office, living quarters and bedroom a seven-foot corner of a tent, hard by the stores of produce. The Royal Engineers had defied logic in building a field kitchen under canvas to feed 1,500 men. Roy was a brilliant chef. Dinner that night was choice of beef Wellington, navarin of lamb, roast pork with apple sauce and stuffing, four vegetables, roast potatoes roasted to perfection. All fresh, piping hot. Choice of six puddings. I had a slice of beef Wellington and it was rare – *haute cuisine.*

Christmas dinner is the real challenge. A thousand men sitting down for the full works, turkey and the trimmings. All the food, six months' supply, lies in the hold of a ship at Split harbour. Deep-frozen, brought up that awful road to Vitez.

Now to the gym. We are well fatigued, having had little sleep, but 40 squaddies had assembled to sing 'Silent Night'. They knew not the words. I wrote them on a blackboard. The singing was not silent night but a nightmare. I had to sing to myself, and that is strictly bath-time stuff.

By now, exhaustion had set in. We repaired to the officers' mess – two large gins with Captain Ellis. Tension easing, we relaxed as more young officers, regiment tankards overflowing with ale, unwound. A young captain of the 9th/12th opened up. I suppose cavalry officers are archetypal – longish, limp blond hair, plummy accent, languorous demeanour. Bob Stewart, they claimed, was too high-profile. 'Shoots from his mouth.'

'Dashing hero, but not fought in anger.'

'Cheshire heroes, but no Dragoons.'

It was astonishing; regimental rivalry within, the Serb guns without, and here we are discussing TV coverage. We dismiss the *badinage* as a mere trifle; after all, regimental rivalries have been going on for all of 300 or 400 years.

Back to the house. The family is waiting for me. On the first night I plied them with expensive Lindt nut chocolate; a two-pound bar had disappeared in a flash. I refused supper but settled for what was now our routine – endless cigarettes, Slibovitz and talk. I offered the bag of football badges, two sweaters, T-shirts, soap, toothpaste – anything I could lay my hands on. It was obvious that these people, the Bosnians, were really suffering. No work, factories closed. No schools, appropriated by the army. I was by now a family friend, and the whole family poured in. I was dead on my feet but mum, uncles, brothers, sisters, sons and daughters required my attention. Finally, this large, smiling, hewn-from-granite man. Grey moustache, twinkling eyes, Big Daddy. Like some Siberian bear, he enveloped me in a massive hug and said nothing, the hug said it all. More Slibboes down, more chat. The housewife's brother, an engineer, analysed the war. Milosevic, the Serb leader, a militant psychopath, intent on creating a greater Serbia. He never envisaged a hostile reaction from the West. His plan, to eliminate two million Muslims so that Bosnia Herzegovina, Montenegro, Kosovo and Serbia could be home to eight million Serbs. No – the war will not end until the Muslims and the Bosnians had extracted revenge for the mass killings, concentration camps and inhuman starvation policies. But, concluded brother, a mass of Serbs did not agree with the war. He had worked in Belgrade, like his Serbian counterparts, and there had been so much intermarriage since the Second World War. He was disconsolate, pessimistic, nihilistic. The need, he stressed, was military aid for the Bosnians and the Muslims. Our stolen Lada-can, he mused, was now part of the Bosnian war effort, and Granada TV have a notable first.

Well Slibboed, I slibboed to bed in my smelly long johns and vest. God bless Damart! It is bitterly cold; sleep does not come easy.

Day four: 18 December 1992. It is 0700 again. A tumbler of water for the teeth, and I wash my face in it. Ugh! But breakfast is marvellous. Smoked raw bacon, home-cooked ham, a sloppy omelette, Turkish coffee, thick, strong, black. Cake and biscuits. All the time attended by the family to see if I am really enjoying it all. Such a proud people. Such kindness and generosity. I am simply overwhelmed. I give Big Daddy a white hat – he received it as if it were a bar of gold. A family photo is taken, maybe to be reviewed in happier times. They are literally living off the garden for their Slibbo. Hand to mouth. Poverty staring them in the face.

I resent all the fatuous talk back home of recession and depression when 75 per cent of us have VCRs, the tills are jingling, the bellies are full. No time to muse. Gordon drives the Yellow Peril to Gorno Vacou – the last stop of the tour. Back down the rutted tracks, barging and bouncing for 40 miles. Turn right in the village and there is the camp amid the snow. Several battered vehicles are testimony to the treacherous state of the roads. The corporal in the guardroom faintly resents our mission. Tea is mashed. Suddenly he grins and quotes:

'The lads know you and you're welcome.' And so we are escorted to meet the CO, Major Alastair Rule.

Gorno is a factory site. Substantial compared with Vitez. Large working areas where once Bosnian engineers operated lathes, now occupied by beds and makeshift offices. Brian, the CSM – small, bright, ginger moustache, pipe-smoking, from Stockport, greeted us with genuine warmth. Alastair Rule appeared from a mass of maps, locating Serbian positions, which change by the hour. The Serbians are getting nearer.

'So you're Father Christmas bearing gifts for the lads,' said Alastair. 'Beware of Greeks bearing gifts, get set up in the canteen, there are 60 lads waiting to raise the roof!'

I had lugged the Santa Claus outfit for a thousand miles. I don it and enter the canteen to massive cheers. Alas, in the sack are few gifts. Badges from Manchester United and Liverpool, a few free tickets for the matches, T-shirts, a pair of my old tights and my old pink bobble hat labelled 'Hall'. I seat one or two forward types on my knee, ho-ho-hoing. There is much ribaldry, huge laughs and poignant messages for home. Another song – 'I'm Dreaming of a White Christmas'. Again, they do not know the words, but we struggle through it, and the jollity is over. Back to the morose business of war. We ate in the canteen, but it was no comparison to Vitez. A lump of lukewarm chicken, cold tinned tomatoes, tepid baked beans. The CSM choked on his pipe. By God, when he grips the cooks after our departure they will wish the Serbs would descend! Filming over, we depart Vitez.

1330 hours and the last lap to Split. Down the Mostar road, risky as the Serbian guns still look down on it – but passable with care and a prayer. Gordon, me and a Bosnian lady lead off in the Yellow Peril. The Bosnian lady is seated between the two of us, an escapee from Travnik. Her husband fled seven months ago to Croatia. She is now joining him and leaving her homeland for ever. It is all strictly illegal and we could be in trouble with the roadblocks that we face between here and the Croatian border. Behind follow Derek, Alan and Peter, the film crew, in the remaining Lada-can. Blasting down the road, blockades aplenty, we bluff our way through. We cannot afford armed guards enquiring about our passenger. The road follows the valley and the river, a strange cobalt blue. Past small villages clinging to the hills, holiday outposts of yesteryear, half-blown-up bridges, debris hanging in the river.

Eventually, we arrive on the outskirts of Mostar. Every house, on each side of the road, burnt, charred, a mass of churned debris. Blackened roofs caved in, splattered with huge mortar and bullet holes. And then Mostar itself. Nothing prepared us for this. A city shelled to smithereens, the population gone, nothing stirring. I stood amid the black remains of a café. The roof rafters burnt brown, gaping like decayed ribs. Broken glass, empty coke crates, books, files, accounts, drifting in the bitterly cold wind. Wrecked, upturned cars balancing crazily on the parapets overlooking the town. Every building smashed, wrecked. No water, no electricity, no people. A ghost town, ripe now for cholera, dysentery, typhoid and rats. The Bosnian lady was in tears. Man's inhumanity to man – and why?

After standing silently we return to the vehicles – not a word was spoken until our Yellow Peril missed a beat. Gordon announced a flat battery, alternator problems. No electrics, no lights, 80 miles to run on a wing and a prayer. We flogged on – by now the roadblocks were pure farce.

'Vehicle kaput' – and the guards wave us through. It is pitch black and Derek leads in the Lada-can to light the way.

In Podgorna, Croatia, Yellow Peril expires. I see lights in the village and descend the long road. Wearing absurd yeti boots and a green tracksuit I cut an alarming figure. Unabashed, I approach eight girls in the half-light. They are refugees from Vukovar – father missing in battle. Together we apprehend a young fellow loading a van with fish. Just beyond him the lovely little port, lights twinkling and boats gently bobbing. Dennis, as he is named, summoned his mama. I was led into a neat, warm house. A glass of home-brewed red wine, savoury squid and bread placed on the table. Wreathed in smiles, they attempted to solve the Yellow Peril problem. Make haste at once, said Dennis. Still eating, I jumped in the van and we drove down the Split road to the mechanic. Alas, he had departed at 6 p.m. But here come the cavalry. A tall, dark owner of a *pensione* materialized, procured a new battery, fixed the alternator and at 1900 hours we were again blasting down the Split road, and never even knew his name. At last the lights of Split. I never thought we would see them – so many dramas and catastrophes. 'One a day keeps Granada at bay,' was our catchphrase. We booked in, a room apiece – I am not sleeping with Mme Trollope again!

Off to the airport to inform the hire-car company that one of their vehicles is missing. Three of them have a mighty strop – they claim their Lada tin can was a mere two months old. We scoff and cry: 'Twenty-two months, more likely – for God's sake fix the price!' Seven thousand US dollars plus five days' hire. Bollocks, say I. The thing was stolen on day one. We never had time to discover how bad it really was. Deal done – back to the Palace. Hot meal, red Croatian wine. To bed at midnight.

At last, I thought, a hot bath. The water was icy. I forgo the bath and sleep yet again unwashed in my smelly, sweaty long johns and vest. God help anyone who gets downwind of me tomorrow!

I light a cigarette – suddenly I am overwhelmed by Mostar. What right have people to do this to anyone? I remember Mostar folk taking part in *It's a Knockout.* Full of folksy fun, rumbustious, happy boys and girls in costume with a strange little orchestra, and their beautiful evocative dancing. Above all, I remembered their national pride as they sang a little song called 'Yugoslavio'. I subsided in floods of uncontrollable tears sitting on the side of the bed. I shall never erase Mostar. The Serbs, I now know, would pay for this monstrosity. I fear for our boys up there in Vitez; the ultimate solution is nearly here.

Day five: 19 December 1992. The alarm sounds at 0300 hours. At 0400 we depart for the airport. Check in. Endless cups of tea. Finally goodbye to Gordon – a kind man of Geordie bluntness, straightforward and brave. Gordon Bacon saved our bacon. May he come to no harm. Likewise our boys, fledgling soldiers, old hands, seasoned NCOs, gallant officers. God speed and a safe return.

Years of working in Yugoslavia did not blind me to the fact that beneath the surface of unity lay centuries of Ottoman Empire and Austro-Hungarian feuds. Tito had bound the country, a mass of republics and religions, into a forward-thinking yet fragile member of Europe. It is horrific to dwell on the bombings, atrocities, murders, blood-letting and abject misery of the last 10 years.

It happened, and is still happening, a mere two hours by air from London. I present my essays to make you think and dwell. It could happen here.

Trust no Future, howe'er pleasant!
Let the dead Past bury its dead!
Act, – act in the living Present!
Heart within, and God o'erhead!
Amen.

BIBLIOGRAPHY

The Holy Bible (Authorised King James I 1611 Edition)
The British and Foreign Bible Society
Cambridge: The University Press

Romanticism – An Anthology
Edited by Duncan Wu
Blackwell Publishers Ltd, 1994

The Oxford Dictionary of Quotations (Fifth Edition)
Edited by Elizabeth Knowles
Oxford University Press, 1999

William Shakespeare: The Complete Works
General Editors: Stanley Wells and Gary Taylor *et al*
Clarendon Press, Oxford, 1994

INDEX